# TOURAINE

Touraine, the Garden of France, Ussé Castle

# THE PEOPLE'S FRANCE

# TOURAINE

## WITH ANJOU AND MAINE

EDITED BY

## ALAN HOUGHTON BRODRICK

LONDON
## HODDER AND STOUGHTON
LIMITED, ST. PAUL'S HOUSE, E.C.4

THE PEOPLE'S FRANCE
TOURAINE
*First Printed* 1948

PRINTED AND BOUND IN ENGLAND FOR
HODDER AND STOUGHTON LTD., LONDON, BY
HAZELL, WATSON AND VINEY LTD., AYLESBURY AND LONDON

TO
M.W. AND E.W.
IN MEMORY OF
TOURAINE DAYS

# A WORD ABOUT THIS BOOK

This, the second volume of "The People's France," is entitled *Touraine*, but, as its subheading indicates, it deals with much more of France than the modern department of the Indre-et-Loire. Also included in our survey are the ancient provinces of Anjou and Maine and some places in the Perche which, though in the modern department of the Orne, were not included in *Normandy*.

The regions covered have not the historic unity of Normandy, but they have known closely linked fortunes. They formed, for generations, some of the French dominions of our Plantagenet monarchs, and although these fascinating and interesting lands are identified less immediately, than is Normandy, with our English story, yet in *Touraine, with Anjou and Maine* we are still on ground where much seems familiar to us from these islands.

In order to cover, both effectively and conveniently, the whole of France in our "Inquest," it has been found necessary, generally speaking, to limit the contents of each volume to places situated within the borders of a group of modern "departments" or administrative divisions dating back only to the French Revolution. In some instances the modern departments will be found to follow the lines of division of the old provinces. In other cases we shall have to leave out of one book, and insert into another, some region or regions which, judged purely from the historical point of view, might appear to have good claims to be classed otherwise than as they will be arranged in "The People's France." We believe, however, that the advantage of keeping to a classification, dictated by the existing administrative units, will be found to outweigh any possible disadvantages.

As for *Normandy*, in *Touraine* we offer, not only a guide, but a picture-book with a text which, we trust, will explain and exhibit the "Garden of France," and some of the neighbouring regions, to the visitor and to the prospective visitor as well as to those who are not planning a pleasure pilgrimage to one of the most attractive parts of Europe.

Again, as in the case of the first volume in this series, no attempt has been made to refer to every hamlet and village in the four departments of the Indre-et-Loire, the Maine-et-Loire, the Mayenne and the Sarthe. Indeed, as the claims of the Loire valley and of the areas immediately to its north and south are paramount, since in this region may be found the great castles, manors, country-houses and monuments which make up the peculiar treasure of this countryside, we have had to deal rather succinctly with portions of the Mayenne and the Sarthe which, although they offer their own peculiar attractions, cannot be held to vie in general interest with the "*châteaux* country." And even in the case of Touraine and Anjou, so rich and varied is the scene that some things of real though secondary importance have had to be omitted.

*The next volume in "The People's France" will be:*

PARIS

*Other volumes in preparation are:*

BRITTANY.

PROVENCE (AND THE RIVIERA).

ÎLE-DE-FRANCE.

BURGUNDY.

PICARDY AND FLANDERS.

ALSACE (WITH LORRAINE).

POITOU (WITH SAINTONGE, AUNIS AND ANGOUMOIS).

# Introduction

THIS second volume of "The People's France" is, first and foremost, a book about what is aptly called the "Garden of France," that is to say, the lovely and favoured land lying on either side of the Loire's reaches.

The Loire is the French river *par excellence*. The Seine, it is true, is our natural highway into France, but the Seine is partly Norman, and its significance is, moreover, dwarfed by the mighty city of Paris.

The Rhône was the channel for Roman penetration into northern Gaul, but on that river's lower course we are reminded, at every turn, rather of the Mediterranean and of Italy than of the France which flowered nearer to us.

The Gironde, of the south-west, is a noble stream, but it is somehow rather provincial, and its tale soon becomes an enumeration of noble and magnificent vineyards.

But the Loire *is* France.

On the banks of the Loire, rather than upon those of the Seine, was elaborated the essential French tradition of attitude, of manners, of comportment and of expression.

No real understanding of the French people is possible without an attentive pilgrimage to the lands watered by this broad, shallow, pale, shifting river, whose ever-changing lights reflect a graceful and subtle sky.

For the full six hundred miles of its course from the shiny, micaceous rocks of the Marenc and down to the sea beyond Nantes, nearly every league of the way holds something to evoke a phase of the French story.

When the Loire, swollen to a majestic width, enters Touraine, then every village and castle, every manor and town upon the banks beckons us to linger, to listen and to admire.

But though the lower valley of the Loire is often described as the " Garden of France," it is not a garden all flowers and greenery. As a French geographer once defined this region, it is a robe of sackcloth fringed with gold. The sackcloth robe is the arid uplands separating the golden fringes of the vales. But these plateaux (e.g. the Gâtine and the Champeigne) are only severe if we compare them with the delightful valleys they enclose. Moreover, the higher ground is often covered by rich forests such as those of Amboise, Chinon or Loches.

The valley is, above all, the Valley of the Loire itself, the *Val de Loire*, the splendid bed of the great river of which Joachim du Bellay sang four centuries ago:

> " *Loyre, hausse ton chef ores*
> *Bien haut et bien haut encores,*
> *Et jette ton oeil divin*
> *Sur ce pays angevin*
> *Le plus heureux et fertile*
> *Qu'autre ou ton onde distille.*"

> (" *Now raise thy head, O Loire,*
> *High up and yet higher still,*
> *And cast thy divine eye*
> *Upon this Anjou land*
> *The happiest and most rich*
> *That thine or other wave lays down.*")

For the alluvial soil brought down and spread by the mighty stream is a rich though sandy earth of marvellous fertility. And this soil is richest in the so-called *varennes* which generations of gardeners have cultivated in the *boires* or dry arms of the great stream. Here the harvests are wonderful— wheat, beets, vegetables and fruits of all sorts. The largest of all the *varennes* (that is, our word "warren") is the Véron tongue of land jutting out between Loire and Vienne. Here in the Véron took place the classic combat of words between Gargantua and Picrochole as told by Rabelais.

x

Between the *varenne* gardens and the little fields (for land
is precious hereabouts) above the rush-beds and the shivering
willows are the poplar-plumes barring the pale blue of the
distant hills. And these hills are to the north trellised with
vines, while to the south they are delicately wooded though
here and there set with vineyards too.

## History

THE essential part of this country's history is quickly told.
From the earliest historical times the Loire was a line of
demarcation. The Roman administrators had, by the first
century of our era, divided Gaul into two main regions. To the
south of the Loire lay *Aquitania* (the first part of Gaul to be
colonised), while to the north of the river was *Celtica*, later
known as *Lugdunensis* or, as the French call it, *Lyonnaise*.
When, in the 5th century, the imperial system was breaking
up, the Loire again formed the boundary between Aquitania,
conquered by the Visigothic barbarians, and the Gallo-Roman
realm of Syagrius which, in 486, was wiped out by the victory
of Clovis at Soissons.

As we shall see at Amboise, the Loire for a time marked the
frontier between the new dominions of Clovis, the Frankish
victor, and those of Alaric II, King of the Visigoths. Even
after the unification of the Frankish kingdom and its extension
over most of the territory we now call France, the Loire remained, under the Merovingian and Carolingian monarchs, a
line of division between the provinces of Aquitania in the
south, of Neustria in the north and of Burgundy in the east.

When, at the end of the 10th century, the usurper Hugues
Capet was elected King of the Franks, the area of France
subjected to the direct rule of the kings was small indeed.
Capet and his immediate successors held sway only over their
hereditary domains—Paris, the regions around it (the *Île-de-
France*) and the country of the *Orléanais* (with the town of
Orleans), on the middle Loire.

In the 11th century the Loire lands, downstream from the *Orléanais*, were under the domination of the powerful Counts of Blois and of the equally puissant Counts of Anjou. Although, in theory, both these potentates were vassals of the king in Paris, they were, in effect, independent sovereigns.

In 1154, our Henry Plantagenet (Count of Anjou, of Maine and Touraine, and, furthermore, in right of his wife, Duke of Guyenne and Aquitaine, as well as Duke of Normandy by inheritance from his fathers) ascended the throne of England. He was sole sovereign of an immense empire stretching from the Tweed to the Pyrenees. Three-quarters of France was his. The French king was, compared with Henry, a petty princeling. For a short time, at least, it looked as though France would follow the way that Germany had gone, and be split up into an empire with a shadowy sovereign reigning, but not ruling.

However, during the reign of our wrong-headed and luckless John "Lackland," Philip Augustus, the French king, reconquered Touraine and Anjou, and the French monarchs, for so long confined to their sparse heritage around Paris, became great sovereigns once they had cleared the highway of the Loire down to the borders of Brittany's sovereign duchy.

During the later phases of the Hundred Years' War, the French Court had to leave the capital.

In the night of the 28th to the 29th May, 1418, as the Burgundian soldiery were advancing towards the royal palace of Saint-Paul, the old Breton courtier, Tanguy du Châtel, rushed into the room where the Dauphin was sleeping, wrapped the fifteen-year-old child in a robe and fled with him from Paris to Melun-sur-Seine. Nearly twenty years were to pass before King Charles VII was to see his capital again, and when he did re-enter Paris on the 12th November, 1437, he remained there only three weeks. And he died at Mehun-sur-Yèvre without having taken up permanent residence at Saint-Paul or any other dwelling in Paris.

It was by the Loire that Joan of Arc established her mission, and it was in the Loire valley that she struck the first blows marking the doom of our French Empire.

When the war was over and the invaders had been forced to leave the soil of France, the French monarchs had become accustomed to residence in the gracious land where their fortunes had turned. In the castles and pleasure-houses of Touraine the Valois kings held Court.

Louis XI (son of Joan of Arc's "fair Dauphin"), the cunning and able monarch to whom, more than to any other one man, the French owe the unity of their land, passed his youth at Loches and died in his manor of Plessis-lès-Tours. His son, Charles VIII (whose Italian campaigns introduced the Renaissance into France), was born at Amboise, and there also he died. The French Renaissance is a thing of the Loire valley.

Charles's successor, Louis XII, fixed his main residence at Blois, on the Loire. François I often resided there before, in 1528, he moved his Court to Fontainebleau. Thus, for well over a hundred years, the home of the French sovereigns, and the centre of French administration, were on the banks of the Loire.

## *Climate*

TOURAINE and Anjou are bright, light lands.

There is already something southern about them—southern and continental. We British do not feel in them as completely at home as we do in Normandy—there is no hint of the sea until you get towards the confines of Anjou and Brittany. But Anjou and Touraine are quintessentially French. We may say, indeed, that the lands of the Loire are those by which we may measure the degree of "Frenchness" of any other provinces in the country.

George Sand summed up well enough the climate of Touraine when she lauded its *climat souple et chaud, ses pluies abondantes et courtes*. And the climate of Anjou resembles that of its eastern neighbour.

## Inhabitants

BUT the two provinces breed two different sorts of men.

The *Tourangeau*, less open, perhaps a little more calculating, is not the same sort of fellow as the *Angevin*, fond of good living and wine, cheerful and forthcoming. It was no doubt a *Tourangeau* who composed the jingle:

> *Angevin*
> *Sac à vin.*

In the matter of looks the Angevins carry the day, and you may often see in Anjou a most delicate and attractive type of female beauty, a little archaic-seeming, it may be, and reminding one of the elegant sculptures of the Gothic cathedrals.

But, indeed, in the region of western France dealt with in this book, we can notice a subtle change in the people's manners as we travel south. The men of the Perche and of the northern parts of the Sarthe and Mayenne departments are not unlike Normans. As we approach the valley of the Loire (and the wine-producing regions), the countrymen tend to become more open in speech and in comportment. But we think those who explore the four departments will be of our opinion, that the men and women of Anjou are among the most pleasant and friendly of all the people of France.

## The Four Departments

THIS book deals with the whole of the ancient province of Anjou, of that of Maine, as well as most of the Perche and nearly all Touraine. We cover the four modern departments of Indre-et-Loire, Maine-et-Loire, Mayenne and Sarthe. The Indre-et-Loire contains small areas formerly included in the Orléanais, in Anjou and in the Perche. The Maine-et-Loire includes most of the southern parts of old Anjou. However, the regions of Montreuil-Bellay, Vihiers, Beaupréau and Cholet, together with the district to the west of the Ironne and the Thouet (known under the old *régime* as the *Mauges*), did not belong to the province of Anjou.

# INTRODUCTION

The Mayenne is made up, as to three-quarters of its area, of the old "Lower Maine," together with about one-quarter of Anjou. The Sarthe is composed of the eastern portion of Maine with, in addition, fragments of Anjou and the Perche.

The total population of the four departments is about one million and a half, distributed over 9,584 square miles and, indeed, rather unevenly distributed. With the exception of the towns in the north, the population tends to get denser as you approach the Loire valley. Of the four departments, however, only the Mayenne (with much the smallest population) shows any fall in numbers. In the other three, even a small rise has been noticeable at the last two censuses—an increase which is a sure sign of rural prosperity.

## *Countryside*

TAKING the four departments in this order—Sarthe, Mayenne, Indre-et-Loire and Maine-et-Loire—we can sum up their physical characteristics as follows:

The surface of the Sarthe department is, in the north, broken and even elevated (the highest peak reaching 1,115 feet), whereas, elsewhere, the relief is low and undulating. This lowland may be divided into three districts: (*a*) the cornlands to the north of the rivers Sarthe and Huisne; (*b*) the barren lands and moors—dotted here and there with pine plantations—between the line of the Huisne and the Sarthe on the one hand and the course of the Loire on the other; (*c*) the wine-growing regions to the south of the Loir.

The department is predominantly agricultural (more hemp is grown here for the area than in any other part of France), the Percheron breed of horses is famed, and the geese and chickens of the Sarthe are reputed.

The surface is not heavily wooded, although there is one large forest (Perseigne) in the north and another (Bercé) in the south, but the hedgerows are set with trees, and the general impression the traveller gets is that of a moderately prosperous countryside. Here and there are some not very important coal-workings, marble- and freestone-quarries, while there is a certain number of local industries, of which weaving is the most considerable.

In the Mayenne department, as in that of the Sarthe, the northern regions are part of the so-called "Armorican" system, that is, heights of ancient rocks forming the Norman *bocage* and extending right up into the Brittany peninsula. Most of the surface of northern Mayenne is agreeably undulating, patched with numerous forests and woods, and checkered by high hedgerows and lines of trees.

The hills of northern Mayenne peak up into the *Mont des Avaloires* (1,368 feet), that is, the highest point in all north-western France. Generally speaking, the relief of the land becomes lower as you go south towards the Loire valley. The principal stream is the Mayenne, which below the town of Mayenne is navigable.

Here and there, in the southern part of the department, the river valleys swell out into unhealthy marshes and the rainfall is heavier than in any neighbouring regions.

As in the Sarthe, the main occupation of the inhabitants is agriculture.

The Indre-et-Loire is a department lying wholly within the Loire valley system or within that of its immediate tributaries. Essentially the Indre-et-Loire is a region of dales and low hills cut through by the wide valley of the Loire. To the north of the Loire, however, is a peculiar area known as the *Gâtine,* which is a rather barren district of forests, heaths and lakes. For the rest, we have, apart from the Loire valley itself, the *Champeigne,* or hills separating the vales of Cher and Loire, the *Véron,* a tongue-shaped land between the courses of the Loire and the Vienne, the *plateau de Sainte-Maure,* a barren upland, and, finally, the *Brenne,* an area traversed by the rivers Claise and Creuse and full of marshes.

The Maine-et-Loire falls into two main regions. The line of demarcation is rather clear. It passes along the valley of the Sarthe and then south-west through Brissac to Doué-la-Fontaine. To the west of this line, the land is composed of granites, felspars and ancient rocks that are a continuation of the Brittany and Vendean systems. To the east of the line, schists, limestones and chalks prevail.

Most of the Maine-et-Loire is low (there is one eminence near Cholet rising to 689 feet), and is traversed by the broad band of the Loire and is watered by its numerous tributaries. The Anjou lands of the Loire valley are subject to floods, and although the department has one of the lowest rainfalls in all France, the prevalence of fogs, the abundance of running water and the rich soil make agriculture and stock-raising prosperous. The climate is mild and the land well wooded. Forests of huge oaks and beeches are not uncommon. The main occupation of the people is agriculture, although the slate-quarries of Trélazé and the local industries at Cholet, Saumur and Angers employ a good many workpeople.

In Touraine, Anjou and Maine there are few large towns, or if places such as Tours and Angers and Le Mans hold a considerable number of inhabitants, none of these cities conveys an impression of metropolitan bustle and importance such as, for instance, Rouen leaves upon us. Touraine and, especially, Anjou are, for France, still provinces of large estates, although there, as elsewhere, they are rapidly disappearing.

## The Wines of the Loire

HERE and there in this book we have given some notice of the wines, but the Loire vintages are not very well known outside France. They may be divided into eight classes.

(1) *Vouvray*. An excellent white wine, alcoholic strength about 11, slightly sweet, rarely dry, very delicate and agreeably perfumed. Often has a fine savour recalling somewhat that of quinces. The beautiful golden yellow colour gets darker with

age and often turns into a deep amber. The frothing or "tingling" (*pétillant*) wines of Vouvray are of lower alcoholic content (about 9·5).

The best-known vineyards are those of Reugny—Chançay—Noizay — Lussault — Husseau — Saint-Martin-le-Beau — Montlouis — Sainte-Radegonde — Rochecorbon — Parçay-Meslay—Vouvray. These vineyards extend to both banks of the Loire.

(2) *Coteaux de l'Aubance*. A white wine resembling that of the Coteaux du Layon, but less rich and less fruity.

The leading vineyards are those of Juigné—Saint-Saturnin—Saint-Melaine — Brissac — Quincé — Vauchrétien — Mozé—Murs—Denée—Soulaines. And the vines grow on both banks of the Loire.

(3) *Coteaux de Saumur*. The white wines of the Saumur region are drier, more lively and more robust than the *Coteaux du Layon* vintages. The white wines of Saumur have an alcoholic strength of about 9·5 and, although less sweet than the Layon growths, the Saumur are rarely really dry. The finest Saumur vintages are unsurpassed in the Loire region. Their delicacy, elegance, fine bouquet and unctuousness make them very great wines. The Saumur *pétillant* or naturally sparkling wines are delicate, fruity and full of bouquet. The Saumur red wines are also good (when they are made from *Cabernet* grapes), they are rather strong (and have an alcoholic content of about 10) but they are also delicate enough. The best come from the immediate neighbourhood of Saumur town. There is also a nice, fresh, appetising *rosé* or pink Saumur wine, but beware of imitations. Even in Anjou and often outside the province the so-called *rosé* sold as of Anjou or the Loire is vile stuff.

Among the best Saumur growths are those of Dampierre-sur-Loire, Souzay—Champigny—Turquant—Montsoreau—Fonte-vrault — Bizay — Brézé — Saint-Cyr-en-Bourg — Varrains — Chaintres—Distré—Bagneux—Saint-Florent-Saint-Hilaire.

(4) *Coteaux du Layon.* These Layon wines are very fruity and unctuous and at their best are unsurpassed. The most reputed vineyards are those of Rochefort-sur-Loire—Ardenay — Saint-Aubin-de-Ligné — Beaulieu — Faye-d'Anjou — Chavagnes—Martigné-Briand—Saint-Georges-sur-Loire—Concourson-sur-Loire—Les-Verchers-sur-Loire—Neuil-sur-Loire—Passavant-Layon—Tigné—Aubigné-Briand—Le Champ-Chanzeaux — Rablay — Saint-Lambert-du-Lattay — Chaudefonds —Chalonnes.

(5) *Muscadets des Coteaux de la Loire.* These are excellent white wines (of an alcoholic content of about 9·5); they must be drunk relatively young when they are clear, light, fresh and rather dry but agreeably perfumed. The *muscadets* from the south side of the Loire are rather stronger than those from the north.

(6) *Coteaux de la Loire.* These growths yield the excellent white wines of Savennières (*Coulée de Serrant*), of La-Roche-aux-Moines, and in the Coteaux de la Loire may be included the red (and white wines) of Chinon and Bourgueil and Saint-Nicolas-de-Bourgueil. The Bourgueil red wines are generous, nervous, lively and sometimes have a touch of acidity, their colour is a fine vermilion and there is a pronounced raspberry bouquet. There is also a rather elegant *rosé* Bourgueil. The Chinon red, pink and white wines are more delicate and softer than those of Bourgueil. The best Chinon reds have a faint perfume of violets. The whole countryside produces wines and every village, hamlet and farm has its own growth. Anywhere between Savigny in the Véron and L'Ile-Bouchard you may be sure of finding some good local vintage. And, across the Loire in the Bourgueil region, the vineyards extend from Saint-Patrice to Saint-Nicolas-de-Bourgueil and beyond.

(7) *Les Coteaux de Touraine.* Among these are some really excellent white wines, fruity, delicate and distinguished, some of them, indeed, recall or rival the good vintages of Vouvray. The Sancerre, Reuilly and particularly the Jasnières are out-

standing. The Jasnières is a fairly dry but rich wine of a very beautiful golden yellow colour.

(8) *Coteaux du Loir et de la Sarthe.* North and north-east from Angers and up the valley of the Sarthe and especially that of the Loir stretch many vineyards producing wines of a quality rather different from those of the Loire. Some of these vintages are quite excellent in a fresh, light way, though none of them can be classed as wines of the first rank. The Tiercé, Huillé, Briollay and Ecuillé growths are often very agreeable.

Since those who travel even in the rich lands of Touraine and Anjou will sometimes want to try other vintages than those of the country, here is a note on the best wine-years since the beginning of the First World War:

1915—Champagne and Red Burgundy.

1921—Red Burgundy, Anjou and Loire.

1923—Red Burgundy.

1928—Champagne.

1929—Claret, Red Burgundy, Jura.

1934—Claret.

1937—White Bordeaux.

1942—White Burgundy, Rhone, Loire.

1943—Claret and White Bordeaux.

1945—Wonderful year, first class everywhere in Champagne and Rhone valley.

1946—Good year, quality excellent, quantity relatively small, best in Bordeaux.

1947—Splendid year, probably the best this century.

## The Châteaux

THE crowning glory of the region is its *châteaux*. In our selection of places for this survey we found that we had to include a much higher proportion of villages and hamlets near or on the Loire's banks than in any other parts of the country. For the *châteaux* lie thick in the valleys.

# INTRODUCTION

Some of what are generally known as the "Châteaux of the Loire"—such as Blois, Cheverny, Chaumont, Valençay, Chambord or Sully—are not touched upon in this volume, for these places are not within the boundaries of our four departments. We shall notice them later on when we come to deal with the Orléanais.

But a rich harvest remains. Amboise, where Leonardo da Vinci died, Montrésor, Loches, with its memories of Agnes Sorel and of its cage-prisons, Langeais and Luynes, Azay-le-Rideau and Chenonceau, Richelieu and Chinon, Saumur and Angers, Serrant and Brissac, Montreuil-Bellay and Le Plessis-Bourré, and many, many more.

And each one of these splendid dwellings tells us something of the long and glittering story of France.

The most ancient fortresses were strongholds which have defied, it seems, the passage of time. The castles of the end of the 15th century—Langeais, Le Plessis-Bourré, Baugé, Le Lude or Amboise—are still fortresses—in appearance. The general plan is simple enough: four wings surrounding a court, a tower at each corner, and the whole surrounded by an outer wall and a moat. The defensive apparatus is still complete—drawbridge, machicolations and crenellations. But if these imposing places look like fortresses from the outside, within they are less grim, and have almost the appearance of country-houses.

In the Loire valley, two art styles are superlatively well represented. The first is the architecture of what we call (rather improperly) "feudalism" and the second is the architecture later Gothic and Renaissance.

In the earlier Middle Ages the great builders of the Loire valley were the Counts of Blois and the Counts of Anjou—Thibault the Trickster and Eudes, or Odo, of Blois and Fulk Nerra and his son Geoffrey Martel of Anjou.

Later on, when the French Court had its residence by the Loire's banks, it was the kings of France themselves who built castles and palaces, and the monarchs were imitated by great lords and great men of business.

During all the 15th century the architecture of the Loire remains essentially French or "Gothic." Little by little that architecture was, during the 16th century, transformed into what we know as the "Renaissance" style.

What we shall come to regard as the essential architectural style of Touraine is exemplified as Plessis-lès-Tours. Here we have the singularly happy combination of rose-red brick and white stone. But, probably, the novel mode had been first tried out in the wing of Blois castle, put up at the orders of Charles of Orleans by Charles de Reims, "master-mason."

We shall come across this "Touraine" style so often that there is no need to give details of it here. Our pictures and descriptions will prepare those who do not yet know Touraine, while we hope that the illustrations and the text will revive pleasing memories in those who are waiting to return to the "Garden of France."

In the short half-century from 1490 to 1540, a whole series of marvels sprang from the soil of the Loire valley. It was in 1495, 1496 and 1497 that there arrived at Amboise the Italian masons and architects summoned to his Court by King Charles VIII. These men from beyond the Alps formed, on the Loire's banks, an artistic colony which was the breeding-ground of a new art. The French Renaissance had dawned.

In 1498, Louis XII began Blois, Chenonceau was commenced in 1513, Azay-le-Rideau in 1518, Le Lude and Ussé about 1525, Villandry approximately in 1530 and Serrant some fifteen years later.

These 16th-century *châteaux*—and they are the peculiar jewels of the "*châteaux* country"—retain some of the features of Gothic architecture, but, little by little, the harsh and rude character of the fortress falls away. The defensive apparatus, once strictly utilitarian and "functional," is used as a basis for decoration.

Everything is subtly transmuted as though by the wave of a magician's wand. The moat at Azay-le-Rideau is no longer a defensive ditch, but a romantic mere, mirroring the graceful outline of the mansion. The drawbridge cannot be drawn up. The machicolations are soothed into charming ornaments.

During the reigns of Charles VIII and Louis XII, the Touraine style of red brick and white stone held its own, but after the accession of François I the brick disappears and stone reigns alone, until, at the end of the 16th century, the "Henry IV style" of brick and stone building comes to the fore and spreads its influence, not only over France, but also into neighbouring lands—notably our own.

*The Editor is greatly indebted to*

*Mlle Almayrac, to whom much of the text is due, to Mme Marey and also, among others, to MM. Barjot, Guillot and Vignon*

*for help with this book.*

*The Editor also wishes to acknowledge with thanks those of the .photographs placed at his disposal by the* Commissariat du Tourisme, *by the* S.N.C.F. *and by the* Touring-Club de France.

# PICTURES OF TOURAINE, ANJOU and MAINE

**Amboise**                                    The exquisite Chapel of St. Hubert

Le Clos-Lucé

Interior of Castle Chapel

The Town and Castle

Arcade of Castle Guard-Room

The Church of St. Denis

Leonardo da Vinci's Tomb

**AMBOISE**

## The Founding of France

AMBOISE. The year 496 was a fateful one for western Europe. On the Christmas Day Clovis, the founder of Frankish monarchy in France, was baptised, together with three thousand of his followers, by Saint Remigius at Rheims. And during the same year, Clovis met at Amboise Alaric II, eighth King of the Arian (i.e. non-Catholic Christian) Goths in Spain. Alaric's dominions included the whole of Spain—except the north-western corner—as well as Aquitaine and the greater part of Provence in France. Alaric was a man of peaceful disposition—he had inherited his vast domains—and Clovis was not a man of peaceful disposition—he had conquered his vast domains.

The interview at Ambatia or Amboise, like so many interviews between Heads of States before and after, just allowed the aggressive party to gain time. In 507 Clovis joined battle with the Gothic host at the *Campus Vogladensis* somewhere near Poitiers. The Franks were victorious and poor Alaric was slain, it is said by Clovis's own hand.

Clovis had found in his newly professed Catholic Christianity a pretext for crushing the Arian "heretics" of Spain and also of annexing all their possessions up to the Pyrenees. Clovis was master of France. The Frankish kingdom was established, and the history of France, as distinguished from the history of Gaul, may be said to have begun.

## *Ambatia*

THE Gallo-Roman town of Ambatia (Amboise) was flourishing in the 4th century, when the famous Saint Martin (he of the St. Martin's summer, of the Martinmas, and of the legend of the cloak he divided with the beggar) overthrew the great pyramidal temple of the town.

In Clovis's time there was already a fortress on the hill overlooking the Loire, where the little Amasse stream falls into the larger river. Louis *le Bègue* (or Louis II of France, surnamed "the Stutterer," who lived from 846 to 879), during his weak and ineffectual rule of eighteen months, granted (or was forced to admit) the lordship of Amboise to the Counts of Anjou, and one of these, Hugues, united the fiefs of the castle and of the town into one. For at Amboise, as in most important points of early medieval France, the settlement did not form one sole lordship. In the 11th century, for instance, there were four distinct lordships adjoining and making up the city of Amboise. At one time, in the ten hundreds, there held sway here, first a certain Sulpice, who caused to be built so high a tower that from its top men could see as far as Tours; then came one Foucois "de Thorigné" with his stronghold on a hill called after him *La Motte-Foucois*; the third lord was Louis *de Meung-sur-Loire*, who was keeper of the Count's palace (at a time when "counts" were not men holding a fief or a title, but were viceroys or representatives of the sovereign, and viceroys always attempting to make themselves independent feudal lords), and this palace was called in true Roman tradition the "Domicile." In addition to these three there was another strong castle in that part of the town known as the *Châteauneuf*. So grew up the towns of northern France. Then, with the increase of the great local magnates' influence and the gradual lessening and weakening of the royal power and prestige, came about a movement of consolidation, whereby the smaller tyrants were eliminated and the mighty Counts ruled their domains as autonomous monarchs.

To the Counts of Anjou as Lords of Amboise succeeded the Counts of Berry, in the days when all France was parcelled out among great barons, who were little local sovereigns.

## *Royal Amboise*

AMBOISE is a pale town on the left bank of the Loire and above the houses on the high pedestal of rock stretches the darker mass of the great castle. Amboise is a noble and attractive place, still haunted by the memories of its long royal past and of the days when it was, in fact, the capital of France.

In 1434 King Charles VII, three years after Joan of Arc had been burned at the stake and long before the English had been forced to retire from France, escheated Amboise to the Crown, and his son, the cunning and capable Louis XI, made Amboise his principal residence until he retired to his retreat of Plessis-lès-Tours. His son, Charles VIII, was born at Amboise, and died there twenty-eight years later. Louis XII and François I spent much of their time here.

## The Conspirators of Amboise

FOR Frenchmen the word "Amboise" recalls immediately the bloody business of the *Conjurés d'Amboise,* or the "Conspirators of Amboise," in 1560. Their tale is a horrid one.

François II—a half-witted youth afflicted with adenoids—was King. The sickly lad of sixteen was a puppet in the hands of his two uncles, the Duke of Guise and the Cardinal of Lorraine, and he had been married to Mary Stuart (Mary Queen of Scots) for two years.

In this year 1560, the French Huguenots, alarmed by the dominating position enjoyed by the Guise brothers and by their hostility towards the Protestants, hatched a plot whereby the King was to be kidnapped and carried off to Blois, the Guises were to be arrested, and the government of the kingdom handed over to the Bourbons (the family next in line of succession to the throne after Charles and Henry, the King's brothers), who were to summon the States-General—the old quasi-parliamentary assembly of France.

But the secret of the plot leaked out, and the Guises hustled the King off to Amboise, a small, strong place, where an attack was hardly to be feared. The leading spirit in the plot was the *prince* de Condé (a member of the Bourbon branch of the royal family), but the ostensible ring-leader was one La Renaudie, a country gentleman from the Périgord, in south-western France, an individual as bold and dashing as he was clever and capable. The conspirators did not let themselves be discouraged by the Guises' counter-measures. Their forces split up into small detachments, and they bore down upon Amboise from different directions. But the plotters were again betrayed. The Guise brothers managed to get the conspirators cut down by strong patrols of the royal forces. In one of the skirmishes near Châteaurenault, La Renaudie was killed.

The Guises thought that all the trouble was over and published a royal decree of amnesty. But this was speedily withdrawn, since, on the 19th March, a last group of Huguenots attempted to storm Amboise. The fighting was furious, and Condé, who had gone to Court in order to allay suspicions, was obliged to stain his sword with the blood of his own captured and disarmed accomplices.

Then Amboise was the scene of a disgusting butchery, attended by the whole Court of the imbecile François II. The Guises, the Italian Queen-Mother (Catherine de' Medici)—the instigators of the St. Bartholomew massacres twelve years later—Mary Queen of Scots and the courtiers watched the slaughter as they would have witnessed a stage-play.

Agrippa d'Aubigny (the Protestant writer and grandfather of the famous Madame de Maintenon) recounts that Villemongie, a gentleman from the Angoumois province, at the moment of his execution, smeared his hands with the blood of his freshly butchered companions, and raising his arms aloft cried out, "Lord, behold Thy children's blood unjustly shed. Thou will avenge them."

Altogether more than fifteen hundred defenceless prisoners were strangled, slaughtered or hanged on gallows or from the iron balcony of the castle that is still called the *balcon des conjurés* or the Conspirators' Balcony. Thus ended the "Tumult of Amboise."

But the stench from hundreds of rotting bodies was so unbearable that the French Court left Amboise—for ever. The last two of the Valois kings lived much at Blois, higher up the river, and with the advent of Henry IV, the first of the Bourbons, the French monarchs returned to Paris. Touraine ceased to be the abode of Court and Council.

## Later Amboise

AMBOISE became a State prison. Here were shut up at various times the Cardinal de Bourbon (uncle of King Henry IV), whom the *Ligueurs,* or members of the League founded by the Duke of Guise, proclaimed "anti-king" under the style of "Charles X." Other prisoners were the *prince* de Joinville, César and Alexandre de Vendôme (sons of Henry IV and Gabrielle d'Estrées), Fouquet, the famous financier of Louis XIV's time, and Lauzun, the husband of the *Grande Mademoiselle,* whom we meet at Champigny-sur-Veude.

In 1762 Louis XV gave Amboise to the *duc* de Choiseul—whose *château* of Chanteloup is not far away—but then bought back the place in order to be able to exchange it with the *duc* de Penthièvre for the principality of Dombes.

## Ducos the Regicide

NAPOLEON allowed Ducos, his old colleague in the Consulate, to have Amboise, and the fellow mutilated the castle with astonishing vandalism.

Pierre Roger Ducos, born at Dax in the Landes, was a lawyer when he was elected to the Convention. From the first he sat in what was known as the "Plain," i.e. that part of the assembly occupied by the members who always voted with the strongest party. As his career shows, Ducos was worthy of his associates. He voted for the King's execution (and therefore technically became a regicide), and played little part in the Convention's activities. But he was a member of the Council of Five Hundred, and later was put into the executive Directory by Barras, who thought him a useful sort of stooge. Ducos accepted Bonaparte's *coup d'état* of the 18th Brumaire, and was one of the three provisional Consuls. Under the Empire he was loaded with honours, and served as vice-president of the Senate, but although characteristically and ungratefully he voted for Napoleon's deposition in 1814, he was, in 1816, exiled with all the remaining regicides. In the same year he was killed by being thrown out of his carriage at Ulm, in Germany.

Ducos was a fine example of the sort of adventurer thrown up in all countries during times of trouble. He was devoid of talent, administrative ability or intellect. His only principles and prejudices were those of furthering his own career and feathering his own nest. He was, in fact, the prototype of the professional politician.

Ducos pulled down the fine Gothic Lodging of King Louis XI as well as that of the Queen and the Great Chapel, and sold off the materials to the house-breakers.

To-day nothing remains at Amboise earlier in date than the reign of Charles VIII (1470–1498).

At the Restoration, the Duke of Orleans, the heir of the Duke of Penthièvre, got back Amboise, and Louis-Philippe had the remaining chapel admirably restored. Under the Second Empire, Amboise again became State property. Abd-el-Kader, the valiant Algerian patriot who held out so long against the French, had been imprisoned for five years at Amboise, when in October 1852, Louis-Napoleon, the Prince-President, called at the prison on his way back from the South of France, and liberated the Moslem leader, who remained a faithful friend of the French until his death at Damascus in 1883.

In 1872, after the fall of the Second Empire, the National

Assembly handed back Amboise to the Orleans family, in whose possession it has since remained. The place is excellently kept up, and is used as an alms-house ("*Hospice d'Enghien*") for pensioned-off retainers of the House of France or former French royal family.

## Town and Castle

ON the right bank of the Loire, opposite the town, is a little 15th century church known as *Notre-Dame-du-Bout-des-Ponts*, in which there is a 15th century *pietà*. It is a notable piece of sculpture. The road crosses the Loire, the two arms of which are separated by a small island known as the *Île-Saint-Jean*, from the old Romanesque Saint John's chapel you pass as you cross the two bridges that tie the islet to the two banks of the stream.

On the left bank of the Loire, the first building that strikes you is the town hall. It is an elegant mansion, put up from 1500 to 1505 by one Pierre Morin, Treasurer of France and Mayor of Tours. Later, the place was known as the "Ducal Palace," since here in 1764 Choiseul, as Lord of Amboise, housed his feudal law-court, his prison and his tax-office. The town hall was tactfully restored about 1890, and is worth visiting. There is a magnificent chimney-piece in the *salle des mariages*, or apartment where the civil marriages are celebrated.

To the right of the old Ducal Palace is the Church of Saint-Florentin, begun in 1484 by order of King Louis XI. The interesting Renaissance belfry leans a little out of the perpendicular.

There are some curious "bits" at Amboise, and it is worth while to saunter through the town and not to hurry up to the castle at once. The lodgings, cloisters and chapel of the old Franciscan monastery are fairly well preserved, and on some of the walls are 15th century frescoes.

Here and there in the town are Renaissance windows, and the so-called *Hôtel de Joyeuse* is an altogether delightful town house of Charles VIII's time.

From the little square at the foot of the castle you can walk through the old (early 15th century) Clocktower Gate or *Porte de l'Horloge*, to the Church of Saint Denys Beyond the Walls. It is a fine building in the so-called Angevin Romanesque style, and was added to and partially rebuilt in 15th century Gothic. The carved capitals of the columns are particularly noteworthy, and display curious groups of beasts and men—the wolf and the she-wolf, the bear and his companions; the farther we go back the more insistent does the bear-motif become, for it is a most ancient one, going back to the earliest times of man's art—the Massacre of the Innocents and others; the sculpture is strong and vivid and yet archaically ingenuous.

In the south aisle is a 16th century marble **Holy Sepulchre**, remarkable in that most of the faces of the figures are portraits of members of the La Bourdaisière family, some of whom we meet nearer Tours and one of whom was Gabrielle d'Estrées' mother. In a niche is a recumbent statue known as the "Drowned Woman." The figure is rather touching, and of well-preserved 16th century marble. There are a few pictures, but none of them is of any great account.

The Choiseul who was Louis XV's minister is buried in the churchyard.

Downstream, by the water's edge, is a charming leafy garden known as the *Promenade du Mail* or the Croquet Walk, in the middle of which is a pyramid (a much more tactful form of monument than the general run of statues) to the memory of Chaptal, the industrial chemist and Minister of State under Napoleon.

## *Leonardo da Vinci*

PERHAPS the year 1519 can be held to mark the end of the Middle Ages and the beginning of modern times, for this was the year that the Emperor Maximilian died and his grandson was elected Emperor as Charles V. It was the year of the Leipzig Disputation that marked the most important point in Luther's career.

And it was the year that Leonardo da Vinci died far from his native Tuscany, but in that Garden of France that was beginning to bloom with an Italianate Renaissance.

Down from Amboise castle by the Clos-Lucé road you reach the little manor where Leonardo passed away on the 2nd May, 1519. The house has preserved its 16th century oratory, but the rest of the place was rebuilt in the 17th century, and only too thoroughly "restored" in recent years. The only interest the building has for us is that it evokes the memory of Leonardo da Vinci. Goering drove to Clos-Lucé on his first visit to France in 1940.

Not far from Le Clos-Lucé, at the foot of the hills to the right bank of the Amasse stream, is the pretty little Château-Gaillard, built at the end of the 15th century, in the reign of Charles VIII. Louis XII gave this property to the cunning Italian landscape-gardener Padello di Mercogliano, who introduced the Tuscan mode into the "pleasaunces" of northern France. Later on, Château-Gaillard belonged to René of Savoy and later still to the Cardinal Charles of Lorraine, the second of the two Guise brothers who so long ruled France.

Leonardo da Vinci's body was buried in the now vanished chapel dedicated to Saint-Florentin, within the walls of Amboise castle. Some bones found during the 19th century on the site of the church have been held to be Leonardo's, and have been reburied in the Chapel of Saint-Blaise or Saint-Hubert, on the ramparts of Amboise.

But the influence of Leonardo and his countrymen you may feel at every turn. It is at Amboise that we see the first manifestations of that art which lies at the base and the source of all French architecture since the 15th century. That art is derived direct from Italy, but it is an art bearing the stamp of a genius impressed by the artists of the Loire valley.

## Castle

AMBOISE is the model and prototype of those dwellings wherein we may find mingled the charming Gothic of the fourteen hundreds with the new Italianate graces of the Renaissance. It is at Amboise that the two styles meet and merge. It is at Amboise that the French master-masons, stone-cutters and sculptors encountered the architects and artists from Italy.

Louis XI did some rebuilding here, but he was a parsimonious and cheeseparing monarch. Moreover, the wing he built has long since disappeared. Charles VIII had begun to carry on the construction of Amboise even before he embarked upon his Italian campaign. The revelation of Italy in the fateful year of 1492 astounded the French monarch and his men. Everything seemed finer than they had dreamed of; the architecture, the climate, the gardens, the elegance of the women; the French felt provincial and backward. And the King carried off a great booty for his Castle of Amboise. Most of the pillage was lost at the Battle of Fornovo in

1495, but enough had arrived at Amboise by the end of that year to stock the place. Moreover, twenty-two Italian artisans, masons, tailors, gold-smiths, parrot-trainers and architects accompanied the spoils. Fra Giocondo, Guido Mazzoni, Domenico da Cortona, Bernardino da Brescia and others collaborated at Amboise with less well known but able Frenchmen such as Senault, Pierre Trinqueau and the brothers François and Sourdeau.

These were the men who made the French Renaissance. Nothing remains of what was brought to Amboise nor of what the Italians wrought and fashioned there, though some Italian influence can be seen in some of the sculpture which has survived, but the Amboise we see is not a third of the Castle as it was at the end of the XVth century.

Charles VIII, during his short life, formed great projects. As Philippe de Commynes says:

> "He had undertaken the greatest building that any king had undertaken for a hundred years and that both in the castle and the town. This can be seen from the towers up which you may ride on horseback, and from what he undertook in the town where his plans would have entailed great works and cost and would, moreover, not have been realised for many a long day."

Louis XII went on with the building, but he did not attempt to carry out the ambitious schemes of his predecessor, and moreover, the new king made over the castle to Louise of Savoy, who raised the rear wing by a storey.

Amboise, upon its rock ridge, gives on to one of the most beautiful scenes of northern France. As you stand on the terrace and survey the broad Loire and the enchanting countryside, you feel the very spirit of the French tradition. Walk round the castle, past the delicately beautiful Chapel of Saint-Hubert, gaze at the high windows and balconies that fit in so well with the immense horizon, and then stroll in the terrace-garden with its clipped limes.

This mass of platforms, bastions, terraces, and great towers embracing a palace-castle is somehow a hospitable place—in fact, rather gay with the sober gaiety of Touraine.

The polygonal surrounding and containing wall is buttressed to the west by a huge round tower and to the Loire side by the great *Tour des Minimes*, while overlooking the valley of the Amasse is the tower called Hurault.

Of the castle, properly speaking, there remain the King's Lodging, built by Charles VIII near the *Tour des Minimes* and overlooking the Loire; another wing at right angles to the first and put up by Louis XII, and, finally, the delicate little Chapel of Saint-Blaise or of Saint-Hubert, built out, in part, over the ramparts, and formerly adjoining the now vanished King's and Queen's Lodgings dating from the reign of Louis XI.

The King's Lodging of Charles VIII is Gothic. The King began its construction immediately after his marriage in 1491. A delicate open gallery or loggia runs round under the eaves, and the roof bears graceful dormers garnished with pinnacles and gables. Within, the Lodging is rather blank and bare. The ground-floor apartment, or Guard Room, contains the pensioners' rooms, and it opens on to an arcaded gallery known as the "Summer Guard Room." Above is the "Hall of the States," occupying the whole of the first floor. Here it was that Abd-el-Kader had his prison. The apartment was in 1906 restored by the architect Ruprich-Robert. The vaulted ceiling is supported upon a row of four median pillars carved with the ermine-spots of Brittany and the fleurs-de-lis of France cut in high relief. Only the curious capitals, enriched with little figures of men and with curling acanthus leaves, reveal the new fashions coming from south of the Alps. In this great saloon is a noble chimney.

The windows give on to the "Conspirators' Balcony," whose wrought-iron balustrade is a masterpiece of 15th century smithery.

Saint-Hubert's chapel is an exquisite specimen of late Gothic that was, unfortunately, rather severely damaged during the fighting on the Loire in 1944. The bombardments of 1940 and 1944 hurt Amboise cruelly. Part of the chapel's transept was ruined and the sculptures over the entrance were mutilated. But repairs were immediately carried out by order of the Orleans family. The apse is supported by a strong buttress projecting beyond the ramparts. The external decoration is almost all modern, with the exception of the group over the entrance (showing the Legends of St. Anthony and of St. Christopher, and the Vision of St. Hubert) that is ancient. The pediment above, with the arms of France, is modern. The little steeple of gilded antlers arranged in tiers of crowns is graceful enough.

Within, the lace-like carving is all original; but the harsh, sour glass in the windows was a gift of Louis-Philippe. It was in the left transept that was buried in 1874 the leaden box containing the fragments of bones thought to be those of Leonardo da Vinci and discovered in 1869.

The chapel entrance gives on to the gardens now transformed into a lawn, and here you notice a rather elegant doorway surmounted by the royal porcupine of Louis XII. This postern is held by some to be the low doorway against which King Charles VIII dashed his head by accident and caused his death. But the door in the Haquelebac gallery, referred to by contemporary chroniclers, seems to have been, not at the north-east of the castle, but on the south side.

The Hurtault or Cæsar Tower opens on to the gardens by an entrance that is attractively arabesque. The tower, like that of the *Tour des Minimes*, has an inclined ramp down or up which one could ride or even drive. This latter tower gave, in olden days, entrance to the castle from the Loire side. The inclined ramp has fine vaultings, and up it rode the Emperor Charles V when he visited Amboise. From the outside the *Tour Hurault* is crowned with a doubly crenellated terrace that was restored in the 19th century, and lends to the whole castle a rather disturbed and unquiet look caused by the glaring contrast between the old stone and the new. Why no one has had the idea of toning down the new courses is difficult to say.

There is an inclined plane down from the castle terrace and through a vaulted corridor, under the barbican and right down into the town.

But we will not want to hurry down, but to gaze once more at the incomparable views from the terrace-garden—across the Amasse dale, the river, the town, the forest and to the Pagoda of Chanteloup, where the exiled and disgraced Choiseul entertained his friends and "philosophised" in true 18th century style.

## *Amboises and Amboises*

THE little town of Amboise gave its name to two notable families of very different origin and fortunes. And their story illustrates well enough one phase of the social evolution of the French people. Family names derived from places are, let us say, of two sorts. First and foremost the names may perpetuate the family of men who were at one time feudal lords of such and such a town, village, or castle. Family names of this origin are extremely rare in all western Europe. Secondly come the mass of men whose ancestors adopted (or were given by common consent in the haphazard way that patronymics were earned in, say, the 15th century and later) the names of towns whence they had come, where they were born or with which they had some connection. With us in Britain the disappearance of the *particule* "de" by the 15th century effaced what difference there might be between, for instance, the members of the great baronial house of Stafford and men who for some reason or another were dubbed "Stafford" because they had some connection with a place of that name. Ecclesiastics—who throughout the Middle Ages were often drawn from the humblest class of the population—retained, in English usage, rather later, a territorial designation. William "of Wykham" came from Wykham, and was not a descendant of any feudal family.

In France *particules* have been retained to this day. The tendency, indeed, has been to adopt them increasingly, as their possession was held to indicate "nobility." But although in the humbler classes a territorial name without a *particule* tended to be the rule, it was not until relatively recent times that a "de" meant anything much at all. Until the very end of the Middle Ages, indeed, and later, there could be no doubt as to the exact social status of any given individual.

In Holland, for instance, the *particule* "van" to this day conveys no suggestion of "nobility," although "noble" families do bear it as part of their names. In Germany, on the other hand, "von" has for long implied "nobility," and place-names held as patronymics by non-nobles are either just the name of the town or are in the form of an adjective. In Italy, where place-names are as comparatively rare as family names, the genius of the Italian language allows of a differentiation—"*di*," that is "of," may be taken to imply "nobility," while "*da*," that is "from," does not.

In France "*de*" means both "of" and "from." Louis XVIII made one of his very few witty sallies when he said that the

Talleyrand family was not "*de* Périgord" (with the implication that they descended from the ancient Sovereign counts of that province), but "*du* Périgord," i.e. that they originated in that part of France.

Even to-day in France there are many most illustrious-looking names, e.g. "de Valois," "de Paris," etc. (generally rightly spelt in one word—Devalois, Deparis, etc.), borne by families of no known genealogy. On the other hand, numbers of ducal and even royal names are borne among the people without the *particule*—"Bourbon," "Gramont" and the like. In a country where, despite the "democratic" spirit, a "noble"-sounding name (often to be completed by a fancy title) means something in hard cash in a marriage settlement, the temptation to add *particules,* to split names and otherwise tamper with patronymics is strong. Still, a curb is placed on such activities by French law that recognises a proprietary right in names.

But to return to our Amboises and Amboises.

When referred to without title, Christian name, or prefix of "Monsieur," etc., all French patronymics are cited *without* the "de" except those beginning with a vowel; thus *d'*Amboise is good in French usage, *de* Gaulle is not, and indeed is a vulgarism, since people of a certain social group tend to work the *particule* to death in and out of season as they do titles. In France only *duc* and *duchesse* are used by any except servants when addressing individuals, and in referring to them it is just as correct to speak of M. de Gramont as of *le duc* de Gramont. The great feudal family of d'Amboise was divided into four main branches—those of Amboise itself, those of Chaumont, of Bussy and of Aubijoux, and by a curious tradition the members of these branches were referred to, not as d'Amboise de Bussy, etc., but as Bussy d'Amboise. Of the Chaumont branch, Pierre d'Amboise had eight daughters and nine sons, the latter of whom all became illustrious, the best-known being the great Cardinal Georges d'Amboise, Archbishop of Rouen, who did much to introduce the Renaissance into France.

The other family of d'Amboise was a *bourgeois* one from the town, some of whose members were celebrated; there was a Bishop of Tréguier, the two Jean d'Amboises, father and son, who were noted surgeons.

The Michel d'Amboise, the amatory poet known as the "Fortunate Slave," was a bastard son of Charles d'Amboise, Grand Admiral of France of the feudal family.

## *"The Port of the English"*

ANDIGNÉ. Near a bridge over the Odon stream and amid a scene of sylvan quiet is the Port-aux-Anglais, whose name dates from our occupation of Maine during the Hundred Years' War. The little river-port is still sometimes used by the timber-barges. Not far away is the old priory of La Jaillette. Some arches hold in the ruined cloister. On the Saint-Martin-du-Bois road and quite near the Englishmen's Port lies hidden in trees and behind its moat the *château* de Saint-Hénis, that was for long the seat of the Andigné family, one of the most considerable of Anjou and deriving its name from Andigné on the left bank of the Odon quite near at hand. The village is sleepy and the main street severe and a little cold.

## *"Black Angers"*

ANGERS. Shakespeare's Black Angers has changed its colour, and is to-day as pale and grey as any town of the Loire's lower course. But the grim, stout walls of the old castle are dark, and must have seemed darker when the whole city was ringed with walls hewn in slaty schist from Trélazé.

Angers is a friendly if rather lifeless place, even the sloping *place du Ralliement* is generally empty, and the town sweeps away towards the Law Courts, the park and the botanical gardens in great wide streets and squares that would grace the capital of a small State. Still, the suburb of Trélazé has the most important slate quarries in France, and Angers itself is the capital of the umbrella, about two million of the useful if commonplace articles being turned out every year.

Again, though Angers is the most considerable town in Anjou—an almost wholly agricultural province—and historically and administratively its capital, it is set, not upon the lordly Loire, but upon an inferior stream, the Maine, which is only a few miles long, since it is formed, some leagues upstream from Angers, by the junction of the Mayenne and the Loir. The waterfront of

Angers is not imposing, and the suburb across the river lacks style. Still, Angers is a notable town housing notable things.

Of the castle there is not much to say. It is huge, and its high walls are fortified with seventeen great towers, but the battlements have long since been sliced off, and the whole place, for all its imposing bulk, looks truncated and shorn. But when the flared bases of the bastions bathed in the deep waters of the moat, when towers and walls were machicolated and corbelled, then Angers castle must have been one of the most formidable fortresses in Europe. The curtains of dark stone, whose harshness is a little relieved by the white circles running round the towers, are still intact.

This was the place Philip Augustus built in order to hold down his newly acquired province of Anjou which our John Lackland lost, with the rest of his Plantagenet ancestors' patrimony, at the battle of La Roche-aux-Moines nearby. St. Louis enlarged Angers castle. King Henri III had it dismantled. For a time the fortress served as a State prison, and here, after his arrest at Nantes in 1661, was incarcerated for some months the famous Fouquet, the splendid and imprudent millionaire Finance Minister of Louis XIV, before the ill-fated *surintendant* departed for his long imprisonment at Pignerol, in Piedmont, where he was, for years, the partner in misfortune of the *duc* de Lauzun, whom we meet at Champigny.

However forbidding this powerful fortress may seem, it is worth a visit, although the chapel, one of the most beautiful Gothic shrines in all Anjou and serving as an armoury, cannot be inspected by most visitors. The chapel was much knocked about during the war and must be rebuilt. Part of the castle's battlements and the *petit châtelet* or barbican were also badly damaged. There are some gruesome dungeons, and the north tower, alone among its fellows, keeps its ancient aspect, since it was not razed to the level of the curtain as were the others.

"Good King René" of Anjou was born in the castle, and a small lodging near the little chapel (built by Louis of Anjou and Yolande of Aragon his wife) is supposed to have been his birthplace. The house has been much restored.

If you walk up the Maine's banks from the castle's walls, you will see the old town of Angers rising steeply from the river. Then, looking up from the bottom of a flight of wide steps appears, framed in old houses, the west front of the cathedral. It seems narrow for its height, and although it is not one of the greatest cathedrals of France, it is a fine and imposing edifice. The elegant, towering spires flank a third tower (built in the 16th century) capped with an ugly cupola and lantern which much detract from the general effect of the building. There is only one west doorway; above it is a fine, lofty window which, in turn, is surmounted by a row of canopied niches each containing a statue. The nine original effigies of Saint-Maurice and his companions were carved in 1537, but the present figures are modern copies.

The lateral towers spring from Romanesque bases, but the spires (of unequal height, that to the south being some fifteen feet more lofty than its companion) were refashioned and rebuilt in the '30's and '40's of the last century.

The interior is light, yet its luminosity does not impair the impression of majesty and severity the great church leaves on us. The nave is roofed with Gothic vaulting of mid 12th century workmanship. The stained glass in the upper windows of the nave is all of late 12th century and is very fine. It is not easy to make out the details of the Assumption, the Legend of St. Catherine, the Passion of St. Vincent, the Virgin in Glory and other subjects, but the blaze of colour is superb, and these lights must rank with some of the finest ancient glass in western France.

Two lateral chapels open out from the lower part of the nave. That to the right (of "Our Lady of Pity") dates from the 13th century, but was extensively refashioned and modified in 1428 and then in 1622. The chapel to the north, that of St. Anne, was erected in 1467, has been much less touched, and contains a splendid Calvary by David d'Angers.

The south transept is illuminated by four fine lancets and, above them, by a superb rose window bearing the signs of the zodiac, and attributed (as is the rose of the north transept) to André Robin, master-glazier, who was working at Angers about the middle of the 15th century. In the north transept is the elaborate white marble tomb by Falguière of Mgr. Freppel, Bishop of Angers.

## A Political Prelate

CHARLES EMILE FREPPEL, one of the most notable of French bishops during the 19th century, was, by birth, an Alsatian

**Angers**    The Cathedral, West Door    **Amboise**    The Castle Chapel

"The Concert," early 16th century Tapestry, a fine Product
of the Loire Valley Looms

The *Salle David* in the Museum

The Bonchamps Monument

Panel of the Apocalypse Tapestries

**ANGERS**

from Obernheim (or Obernai). His career was made during the months he spent at Rome in 1869, when he rendered valuable services to the Papacy by his work done in the preparation for the promulgation of the dogma of papal infallibility. Pius IX rewarded Freppel by creating him Bishop of Angers in the fatal year 1870. He addressed to the Emperor Wilhelm I an eloquent protest against the annexation of Alsace and Lorraine. In 1880 Freppel was elected deputy for Brest, and kept his seat until his death. The Bishop of Angers was the first priest to be a member of the Chamber since the death of Dupanloup (the eminent Bishop of Orleans, whose opinions on papal infallibility were so different from those of Freppel), and the Alsatian prelate became the chief political and parliamentary champion of the Church. Freppel, who was in most matters a Royalist and a Conservative, was also a patriotic Frenchman. It is difficult for us now to reconstitute the atmosphere in which he moved and lived, but, in his day, the Bishop of Angers was a figure of more than local importance; his fame, indeed, spread beyond the frontiers of France. Freppel was, of course, lucky in his episcopal see, for it was (and still is) one of the more conservative and Catholic regions of France.

## The Splendid Nave of Angers

THE choir is all 13th century Gothic and the capitals of the columns bearing the vaulting are decorated with delicate and curious carvings, mostly angels' heads and ivy-leaves.

The high altar, surmounted by a great baldaquin or canopy over fifty feet high, supported on six columns of red Laval marble, is imposing enough, but out of place. The late 18th century wood panelling in the choir also lends this part of the church a heavy and dull appearance.

Behind the altar is a marble of St. Cecilia, by David d'Angers, and also a stone with an inscription giving the names of the princes of the House of Anjou-Sicily buried in the cathedral. For some reason or another, the Dean and Chapter of Angers destroyed, in the 18th century, all the fine tombs of the Anjou-Sicily family. As it happened, and as far as the preservation of the actual coffins and their contents was concerned, this ecclesiastical vandalism need not be too much regretted. The tombs having disappeared, no one thought of looking for the coffins and bodies, so they escaped profanation at the Revolution. The vaults were opened in 1895, when the sarcophagi of "Good King René" and of his wife Jeanne de Laval were discovered intact.

It is from behind the high altar that the remarkable stained glass of the choir can be best seen. It is 13th century and of gorgeous colouring. The lights present the legends of St. Julian, St. Maurille, St. Laurence and St. Thomas à Becket.

The north transept rose-window, a pendant to that in the south transept, sparkles with scenes depicting Works and Months as well as the Signs of the Times announcing the End of the World. A noble light indeed.

## The Logis Barrault

THE *logis Barrault*, one of the finest medieval town houses in France, was put up at the end of the 15th century by one Olivier Barrault, Treasurer of Brittany and Mayor of Angers. The edifice is one of those imposing, comfortable, graceful and charming houses that the new patrician caste of the cities made in the fourteen hundreds. It is a fine, big place. A little severe, perhaps, but soundly built and admirably conceived. The decoration is purely French. Nothing in the *logis Barrault* announces the coming revolution which was to sweep in from over the Alps.

The *logis Barrault* has housed illustrious guests. Marie de' Medici lived here in 1620. Later it was the headquarters of the *maréchal* de Brézé and the *duc* de Rohan, Governors of Anjou.

The staircase, as was usual in the 15th century, is sheltered in an exterior tower which in this case is octagonal below and square in its upper part.

The *logis Barrault* contains both the municipal library and museum of Angers. The museum is one of the more interesting of the French provincial collections, and is especially rich in the works of David d'Angers.

## David D'Angers

PIERRE JEAN DAVID, generally called "David d'Angers," was the son of a man who at one time was famed as a wood-carver, but he took up arms to fight against the *Chouans*, and when he returned to his home in Angers he found his customers dispersed and his livelihood gone. His son Pierre-Jean was brought up in poverty. As a consequence of his own misadventures, David *père* was most anxious that the son should get a regular job and not stray into the perilous fields of art. But young David broke away to Paris in 1807. He was just eighteen and he had eleven francs in his pocket. For a year and a half he struggled on in Paris, working at the School of Fine Arts. In 1809 the municipality of his native town voted him a pension of 600 francs (£24 gold) a year, and in 1811 his "Epaminondas" won the *grand prix de Rome*. David spent five years in the Italian capital and came much under Canova's influence. After the Restoration he returned to Paris, but disliking the reactionary and obscurantist régime of the returned Bourbons, David soon went to London, where he did not have too happy a time. Flaxman, and with him most of the English, confused him with his namesake David the painter—to whom he was in no way related—one of the "regicides," and visited upon poor Pierre-Jean's head the supposed "sins" of his supposed relation.

After his return to France from London, David's career spurted forward to great success and glory, and he must be accounted the best-known French sculptor who died in the 19th century. Though many may think that as an artist the comparatively unknown woodcarving father surpassed the famous son.

David d'Angers was a man of singularly attractive character and disposition. He was endlessly charitable and magnanimous. Many tales are told of his nobility. For instance, he much disliked Rouget de l'Isle (the author of the "Marseillaise" and a cantankerous old busybody), but when he heard that the author of the national anthem was in want, he hastened to make his bust, to put it up in a lottery, and to send Rouget the 1,800 francs the sculpture brought.

The *logis Barrault* (which contains on the first and second floors a quite interesting collection of paintings of, on the whole, rather more worth than those of most provincial museums) is a collection of sculpture unrivalled as an "artist's museum" except in Copenhagen. It was in these rooms (formerly the *École centrale* of Angers) that David received his first drawing lessons. Besides the works of David d'Angers himself, we have, at the *logis Barrault*, 153 statues, 70 bas-reliefs, 203 busts, 46 statuettes, 591 medallions, and very many drawings by artists of the rank of Pajou, Chaudet,

Delaistre, Houdon, and of David's father, the wood-carver (whose work we meet here and there in some of the Anjou country-houses).

Angers is rich in old homes, picturesque residences, ancient carvings and sculptures. You should not fail to spend an hour or two wandering in the quaint, narrow streets near the cathedral. Many of the old houses were destroyed in 1944 but much still remains. The brick and half-timber *maison d'Adam* is, probably, the best-known of the antique dwellings of the Anjou capital. It is a remarkable place, with its stout beams, corbelled storeys, lozenges, carvings grave and gay, humorous, satirical and amusing, with here and there luscious bunches of grapes reminding you of the fascinating wines of Anjou.

## *Logis Pincé*

THE *logis Pincé* lies just off the *place du Ralliement,* and was begun about 1522 for Master Jehan de Pincé, *lieutenant criminel*, or criminal law judge for the province of Anjou. The architect was Jehan de Lespine, without doubt the leading Angevin architect of his day, and Lespine's masterpiece, the *logis Pincé*, is an embodiment of the Renaissance spirit. The house encloses a square courtyard. The centre-staircase pavilion is the oldest part, and the newel of this staircase is a marvel, and the ribbing of the roof sprouts and droops like the leaves of a palm tree. Everywhere are Renaissance motifs, niches with pilasters, cartouches, scrolls, medallions and busts. The details of decoration in the rooms are excellent and the caissoned ceiling of the principal apartment is noteworthy.

In 1534 Pincé enlarged his house, a pleasure-house conceived to a 15th century plan, but decorated *à l'antique,* "in the Antick Mode," with motifs of fruits, flowers, garlands, busts of heroes and historical personages, winged genii, animals, birds . . . the *logis Pincé* is an epitome of the French interpretation of the Italian Renaissance.

The house contains a little museum left to the city by the painter Turpin de Crissé. The portraits of Charles IX and Catherine de' Medici by Clouet are interesting, while on the second floor is a really valuable collection of about 300 drawings by artists of all schools, countries and epochs—there are sketches by Rembrandt, Rubens, Van Dyck, Velasquez, the great Italians and the Frenchmen of the 17th, 18th and 19th centuries.

## The Oldest Episcopal Palace in France

THE old episcopal palace, now the Museum of Religious Art, is a noteworthy edifice. The most ancient parts date from the years 1098 and 1148 and form a huge T-shaped building. It is one of the very few Romanesque structures, other than churches, now existing. The site occupied is that of the earliest dwelling of the Counts of Anjou which Count Eudes presented in 851 to Bishop Odo of Angers. Of course, during the long ages the place has often been refashioned, added to, modified and changed a little, but it remains, essentially, what it was in early medieval times. During the years from 1868 to 1871 the palace was enlarged, and to-day at first glance, its imposing, sombre bulk looks almost modern; nevertheless, you soon realise that the majestic gravity of the façade is a heritage of the ages, and as you wander through the halls and glance from the precious contents to the splendid container, you will be able to identify, moulded into an harmonious whole, buildings of the 11th, 12th, 15th and 16th centuries. The fine staircase was ordered in 1510 by François de Rohan, Bishop of Angers.

On the ground-floor the so-called *salle des pas perdus* (formerly stables), supported by six stout columns, dates from about 1100. On the side giving on the *rue de l'Oisellerie,* the hall is supported on the old gallo-Roman city wall, here some fourteen feet thick. The improperly named "crypt," also on the ground-floor, is another noble apartment.

The Museum of Religious Art is installed on the first floor, in the great chamber known as the Synodal Hall. It is over sixty feet long by thirty feet wide, and formed the "nave" of the Romanesque Great Hall, communicating through three arched doorways with another hall, which was, in the 17th century, cut up into three apartments. Each of these two great apartments was lighted by fifteen windows.

## The Apocalypse of Angers

DESPITE all the glories of the 17th and 18th centuries, the golden age of tapestry is the age of Gothic, that is to say, the thirteen and fourteen hundreds. In those far-off days woven stuffs were used for the purpose for which they were invented. Tapestry formed the background, the trappings and the adornment of life. In the Europe of five and six hundred years ago, tapestries were woven of wool only. The few hangings which were enriched with Cyprian gold or eastern silks were felt as exotic things.

The Gothic tapestries are full of life, figures, designs, ornaments and *motifs*. There are no bare spaces. Many of the stuffs seem at first sight confused, overcharged and inexplicable. But these woven pictures are the real mirror of their times. As a matter of fact, the Gothic tapestries are charged with meaning. Nothing is mere filling or makeshift. When we have the privilege of seeing the Gothic hangings against the background they were designed to enrich, we have a glimpse of the Middle Ages which enriches our understanding of our ancestors of five centuries ago.

The city of Angers possesses a large collection of early tapestries. Of these the greatest treasure is the famous collection of the *Apocalypse*, now generally preserved in the Museum, but, at certain times of the year, still displayed against the walls, arches, columns and arcades of the city's Gothic cathedral.

The *Apocalypse* tapestries were ordered as long ago as 1377 by Louis of Anjou. Nicholas Bataille, of Paris, was the weaver, so that these incomparable woven pictures are also the most notable early tapestries of the Paris looms. Louis d'Anjou adorned with the *Apocalypse* the halls and chambers of his Castle of Angers as well as his private chapel, where was enshrined that portion of the True Cross known as *La Vraie Croix de la Boissière*.

If we would transport ourselves at times into the atmosphere of the European Middle Ages, we must not forget the part played in men's lives by relics. Relic-mongering was one of the most thriving trades of the Middle Ages. Men wished to be buried in such and such a place because they desired to lie, until the Resurrection, near the relics of some favourite saint. Relics were held to be curative, miraculous and protective. The possession of such talismans was a great privilege. Touching them, venerating them, or being interred near them afforded hope of salvation. The thaumaturgical and even magical character of popular religion in medieval times is only overlooked at the cost of a misunderstanding of our ancestors' aims, motives and actions.

But although the *Apocalypse* series were woven in Paris, the cartoons were prepared in the Low Countries and by that Jean Bandol, surnamed "Hennequin," of Bruges, one of the artists who flourished at the Court of Philippe *le Hardi*, first Duke of Burgundy of the House of Valois. It happens that we can examine the miniatures which served Bandol as model for his cartoons. The main inspiration was derived from a splendid *Apocalypse* now in the public library of the town of Cambray, but Bandol, also, used the illuminations of another precious *Apocalypse*, formerly the property of King Charles V of France and now preserved in the *Bibliothèque Nationale* of Paris.

The weaving of pieces as intricate and complicated as those of the Angers *Apocalypse* took a considerable time, and it is not clear when all the panels were finished, but, probably, before the end of the 14th century. In any case, the scene representing the Apostle John beholding in the Heavens the Seven Angels with the Seven Vials was evidently woven before 1384 (date of Louis of Anjou's death), since his monogram appears on the tapestry.

The tapestries remained in Angers castle until 1476, when they were stored, for safety, in Baugé castle. But two years before, "Good King René" of Anjou had left them, by will, to Angers cathedral, where they were exposed for the first time in 1480. By 1782 such antique "rubbish" was quite out of fashion, and the Angers *Apocalypse* was bundled away in a loft, to be gnawed by rats and pitted by moths. In 1843 the whole collection was put up for sale, and bought by Mgr. Angebault for 300 francs, or £12 gold.

It is quite incredible to us that such priceless marvels could ever have been knocked down for what to-day would not buy a chest of drawers. Seventy-two panels (out of an original ninety) of unique Gothic tapestry for 240 shillings. It is, of course, impossible to compute their sales-room value to-day, but it could hardly be less than a million pounds. We may measure the changes in taste in the price of art objects and, indeed, in the purchasing power of money if we reflect upon these two figures—£12 and £1,000,000.

We should really try to see twice the *Apocalypse* world of medieval theology and piety. We should examine and devour these treasures on the walls of Angers Museum at our leisure. And we should admire the hangings as they adorn the grey choir of the cathedral.

The magnificent designs, the faded crimsons and blues, the fantastic beasts, the imposing figures and the archaic and impressive beauty of this unique collection must be seen and seen again.

There are the Angels of the Seven Cities of Asia looming from a purple background diapered with butterflies bearing on their wings the lilies of Louis of Anjou and the ermine of his wife Anne of Brittany, Saint John drawing near to the Wise Men who count the Number of the Beast upon their fingers. The Third Angel emptying his vial and changing the Waters into Blood, and the Seventh Angel pouring out his while the lightning and hail crumble the city upon its inhabitants. Scenes that seem strangely present to our minds to-day. . . .

The Museum of Tapestry contains many other precious things— the "Life of Saint Maurille," a little later in date—perhaps the middle of the 14th century; Penthesileia, Queen of the Amazons, terribly armed against a background "semy of florets"; and the Concert of the 16th century's dawn with the sumptuously habited lady playing a hand-organ, bellowed by a page, while a gallant sings, and all against a rustic scene of blue, diapered with flowers and beasts.

## *The Duke of Wellington at Angers*

TO the south side of the castle runs the *boulevard du château,* and if you turn out of this *boulevard* to your right, you get into the *place de l'Académie,* on one side of which is an elegant 18th century building now used as a boys' elementary school. This edifice, put up from 1755 to 1761, was the celebrated "School of Equitation," kept for several generations by the Avril de Pignerolle family. We meet the Avril family again at their charming country-house of Pignerolle, not far from Angers, but here at Angers itself the Avril de Pignerolle had one pupil who interests us a good deal.

After he had been taken away from Eton (rather earlier than is, or was, usual, for the family circumstances were rather straightened), young Arthur Wesley—the change of name into "Wellesley" was an invention of some years later, about 1790— was sent to Monsieur de Pignerolle's "Military Academy" as it was generally called, at least in communications with foreign pupils and their parents. This pompously styled establishment was really a riding-school, in which some have seen the germs, or one of the germs, of the great Cavalry School of Saumur.

Young Wesley certainly improved his riding at Angers, although, having rather short legs, he was never a very good horseman. He also made some friends among the local squirearchy, with whom the Avril de Pignerolle family were pleased to class themselves. This part of Anjou, near Angers, is dotted with pleasant country-houses which, in the 18th century, were still lived in by the men who owned most of the land. Wesley, like Kitchener much later on, also acquired in France a certain ease in French, although neither man was a master of the spoken language.

Raikes shows Wesley at Angers as of "rather a weak constitution, not very attentive to his studies and constantly occupied with a little terrier called Vic." Rather a pleasing picture. By March 1787 Wesley was back in England and gazetted ensign in the 73rd or Highland Regiment. The Great Career had started.

## The Cloister of Saint-Aubin's Abbey

THERE is a good deal more to be seen at Angers, and we can only briefly mention one or two of these sights. The Prefecture is one of the finest and most imposing in France. The building lies back from a great garden and occupies the grounds of the old Abbey of Saint-Aubin, formerly the richest and most powerful of the town. The façade on the courtyard is modern, having been added in 1850, but, for the most part, the Prefecture is a late 17th century edifice. The wrought-iron railings of the courtyard come from Fontevrault abbey.

France is very rich in Romanesque wall-paintings. Most of them, it is true, lie outside the Loire country. The gorgeously painted churches that before the adoption of stained glass—and for a time afterwards—made the shrines and chapels glitter, owe their art to various sources, illuminated MSS., Oriental stuffs, Byzantine and Greek and even Persian models, the magnificence of the Cluniac school with the backgrounds of lapis-lazuli, the fierce paintings of the south-west announcing the Spanish tradition this side of the Pyrenees, the Roman frescoes of Poitiers and many others.

But the charming paintings of the Loire valley and of Touraine are, as we might expect in this quintessentially French part of France, something peculiar and of immense grace and charm.

There are Souday, with its charming Annunciation and Visitation; Areines, with its warrior saints; Montoire, with saints flying in arabesques; Thevet, with its noble ancients, and Le Liget, most touching and imposing of all. This is French art inspired by the spring-like countryside of the Loire.

Only three of the more important fall within our province in this book—Le Liget, Tavant and Saint-Aubin d'Angers.

Robert de La Tour-Landry, who was mitred abbot of Saint-Aubin abbey in the city of Angers from 1127 to 1154, was a great builder, and to his reign must be attributed the large and magnificent sculptured doorway of the chapter house and the arcades of the cloister. To-day these remains are enclosed in the building of the Prefecture. Only two of the arcades still bear their 12th century paintings. There is a Virgin and Child in a Glory supported by Angels. The colour has mostly faded. The smaller paintings are well preserved, and represent the Magi and the Massacre of the Innocents. They are of the size and style of miniatures.

If you bear north at the Prefecture and follow the wide series of avenues leading to the Botanical Gardens, you may turn off to the left a moment and get a view of the ancient Church of Saint Martin, a Romanesque and Gothic edifice, retaining some precious remnants of an earlier Carolingian church over a thousand years old.

Going north again, and opposite the public park known as the *jardin du Mail*, is the town hall, next to the ancient *Collège d'Anjou*, built in 1691 by the Fathers of the Oratory. Here and there, among less pretentious and later houses, are some fine dwellings—for instance, the *hôtel Lantivy* (1783), and nearby the house where David d'Angers was born.

The broad line of avenues sweeps on, spacious, a little dull and lifeless perhaps, but imposing and tranquil. To the left opens out the dusty, treeless *champ de mars*, leading up to the heavy, sprawling Law Courts.

### Lawsuits and Cafés

BY this time you may want to rest a while. As is not unusual in France, the neighbourhood of the Law Courts is rich in *cafés*. There is one to the left of the *palais de justice*, where the Anjou wine is very good. Take the *patron's* advice, but the bottles with green sealing-wax over the cork are generally excellent. We have known men who lost lawsuits through lingering too long at this *café*.

If you want what the French call *alcool* (i.e. liqueurs or spirits, wine is not "alcohol" in France—in fact, in Anjou, wine is looked on as a soft drink) you should always try the local *marc* and cognac from the south-west of France only if you are in a rather pretentious restaurant or hotel. At Roche d'Erigné, near Angers, you can drink the *lie,* a further and glorious distillation of the *marc,* or local "brandy" made from the residue of the pressed grapes. The *lie* is much better known in Savoy than so far north as Anjou. Angers, by the way, is the headquarters of the famous Cointreau distilleries where is fabricated that orange-flavoured liqueur often favoured by ladies.

## *The Oldest Scientist*

YOU cross the curiously named Pelican Square and pass Chevreul's statue, rising just before the ornamental railings of the Botanical Gardens.

If you walk through the western parts of the *Jardin des plantes* in Paris, near the charming Louis XVI house serving the Director of the Museum of Natural History as a residence, you will see a statue of an aged man. The pedestal bears the word "CHEVREUL" —and that will not mean much to most passers-by—followed by the figures 1786–1889. So the monument commemorates someone who lived to be 103 years of age.

But Michel-Eugène Chevreul was a noted man of science and, indeed, the longest-lived man of science of whom we have record. He was born three years before the French Revolution and lived until well after Queen Victoria's Jubilee. Chevreul was an Angevin, the son of a physician, and born in Angers. He was an eminent chemist, the isolator of stearine, the physiologist of taste and smell. He was professor of organic chemistry at the Museum of Natural History as early as 1830, director of the museum from 1863 to 1879, when he retired, but retained his chair for another ten years. Chevreul, like most men who live very long, was of an unruffled temperament, slow of speech (he was nicknamed *tardiloquus* in a country where rapidity of enunciation is often taken for rapidity of thought), weighing his words, a man of insight and sound common sense, a great enemy of humbug, charlatanism, spiritualism and deductive reasoning.

To the north-west of the Botanical Gardens is the Church of Saint Serge, which should be visited for the splendid choir built in the purest style of Angevin Gothic at the beginning of the 13th century. The columns are particularly slender and graceful, the vaulting is said to be the most perfect example of the Angevin style. Three, at least, of the lights are late 12th or early 13th century. They are in *grisaille* (or grey monochrome representing objects in relief), and are among the most beautiful of their epoch.

## The Right Bank

THE right bank suburb of Angers, though so dull to look at from afar, offers two places of interest—the archeological museum and the *église de la Trinité*.

The museum is in the old hospital, or *Hôtel-Dieu*, founded by our Henry II in 1175. The great hall, the chapel, two sides of the cloister and the storehouses date either from the time of the foundation or from a few years later. The museum houses some very fine things. There is a porphyry urn, decorated with two heads of Jupiter, and willed to the cathedral in 1450 by "Good King René," who described it in his testament as one of the wine-jars used at the Marriage in Cana of Galilee. There are other Roman and Gallo-Roman relics, and five episcopal croziers of the 12th century, a 12th century mask of an abbess in gilt bronze, the famous "Virgin of Tremblay"—a particularly gracious 16th century terra-cotta, several statues from tombs . . . and the buildings in which these things are housed are themselves "museum objects," as the collectors say.

Trinity church is a Romanesque edifice carrying an octagonal lantern-tower set up in 1540 by Jehan de Léspine, the architect of the *logis Pincé*.

## Miraculous Cures for Madness

ARGENSON. If you strike south-eastwards from L'Île-Bouchard, you cross the Sainte-Maure-Richelieu road at Pouzay, and, a few miles farther on, reach Nouâtre, where is a Gothic church whose walls are covered with 15th century (partially restored) paintings depicting the Legend of Saint-Révérend. There is also a triptych of about the same age as the paintings and probably of English workmanship. It displays five bas-reliefs, and is very like the products of the so-called "Nottingham School" of alabaster carvings.

Around the walls of the nave are iron rings fixed in this masonry. To these were chained up the madmen who were bound in the church while awaiting their cure through the miraculous efficacy of Saint-Révérend's relics.

A mile or so farther on is Maillé, and nearby the great park of Argenson castle. Of the house which was the first fief of the notable Le Voyer d'Argenson family which furnished so many notable public servants in France, little remains but a Renaissance pigeon-loft and an abandoned chapel full of tombstones and monuments.

## Peerless Azay

AZAY-LE-RIDEAU. Azay-le-Rideau (that, by the way, has nothing to do with a curtain, but is so called from the name of an ancient owner of the fief, one Rideau or Ridel, in the 12th century) has had a curiously uneventful history. The one incident in the story of the place occurred in 1417. King Charles VII, as Dauphin, was insulted at Azay by Burgundian troops. The King's men burned the town and slaughtered the Burgundians, and until the 16th century Azay was known as Azay-le-Brûlé. When we make our pilgrimage to this peerless dwelling by the Indre, we can weave any fancies and fairy-lore we like around the silvery-white image mirrored in the quiet, lily-strewn waters of the mere.

Azay lies off the main road from Tours to Chinon. After passing through Villandry, you bear to the left at Le Moulinet, and Azay is about five miles down the Montbazon road after Vallères. The little town is an overgrown village of some two thousand inhabitants. The characterless church preserves, however, set into its west front, part of the 9th century façade of the Carolingian chapel erected over a thousand years ago. Also the manorial lords' chapel (13th or more probably 14th century) is curious.

Up from Azay village the road narrows to a bridge spanning the Indre and leading into the great courtyard. The view from this side is not, perhaps, the most romantic, but you are struck with the harmony of the decoration and the balance and poise of the building framed in trees.

Azay *château* is made up of two wings at right angles, one south and one west. The foundations are, for the most part, laid on piles sunk into the bed of the Indre that bathes the walls and feeds the moat. The Indre, the stream of Loches and of Azay, seems always full to overflowing yet never overflows, but flows deep and calm between tall poplars and overhanging willows. The river, indeed, swells out before the house to form a secret and sweetly sad lake.

The architecture is quite simple. Each corner of the house is bound with a corbelled turret except on the north side, where a modern tower "in keeping with the *château*" replaced the old keep in about 1840. There are two storeys above the ground-floor and the second rises into the attic. The decoration is uniform, with a complete architectural "order" for each storey. The mullioned windows are framed by pilasters. The second-storey windows are surmounted by pinnacled gables.

The north front is the main façade, of which the most striking features are the three superimposed rows of double windows rising over the front door to a highly ornamented gable. Through that door you reach the great staircase which is the peculiar glory of Azay. Beneath a portico of great richness of sculpture and adorned with the flaming salamander that was the badge of François I, you step on to the stairs, whose carved stone walls are decorated with a profusion of fruits, flowers, ciphers, blazons and heraldic beasts: all the elegant opulence of the Renaissance, combining old and new traditions, and wedding the stern sobriety of the north to the novel graciousness from beyond the Alps. The stone roof is adorned with medallions enclosing portraits of the French kings.

At Azay you are surrounded with one of the most delicate and evocatory of French Renaissance creations. It is airy and delicate. In the pale, insistent sunlight of Touraine, it all seems to shimmer, without ever losing its crispness of outline and detail.

Within, Azay is a museum housing a collection of Renaissance furniture and works of art. Of necessity, the effect is one a little cold and lifeless. But, at least, the place is protected from "restoration." Although the structure and fabric of the house have not been much altered since the place was built, still, before Azay left private hands, it was made thoroughly comfortable and even rather too "modernised" and fitted with plumbing.

Its *confort moderne*, as the French call it, called down upon Azay the doubtful honour of being chosen in 1940 to house some of the Government departments during the flight from Paris. Fortunately, the house was only occupied by the clerks and *fonctionnaires* for a few days.

But we must not fail to wander about inside, since the views from the windows are haunting, and fill you with imaginings which, as we have said, can hardly be tied to any historical happenings as such musings could be, for instance, at Chenonceau.

And then there are one or two curious things in the little museum. There are two sculptured panels attributed to Jean Goujon, which, if not by him, are most certainly by one of his followers. None of the furniture is of the first importance, but it is pleasing and suitable to the rooms. There is some good Flemish tapestry and some paintings, one of which, representing the famous Gabrielle d'Estrées in her bath—for that charming lady took baths, a most unusual thing for anyone of her time to do—is especially curious. There is also in the Louvre a delightful painting of the "Fontainbleau" School representing Gabrielle in her bath.

But we shall want to go outside again and view the beauties of Azay from every possible angle. The house, despite all the Renaissance detail, is still a transformed feudal castle. But it is a feudal castle over which has been waved a wizard's wand. The stronghold has faded, fairy-like, into something faintly friendly and defenceless. But this custom of retaining the appearance or the suggestion of defensive apparatus long after it had been abandoned in kings' palaces was a custom not just kept alive by builders and architects, but it was a tradition clung to by landowners and lords. Letters patent were still issued (for a consideration) authorizing men to embattle their manors and country-houses for none might embattle at will. The fact was that towers and crenellations were an advertisement of "nobility" and the recognition of "nobility" not only opened paths to advancement, to government employment, to Court office, to advantageous marriages, but the recognised "noble" also secured a good deal of tax exemption. Who was "noble" paid no tallage or *taille*, the most vexatious of all the medieval imposts surviving to the end of the Old Regime. But only a shadow of ancient privilege was secured by permission to embattle. When Bernardo Salviati, Florentine merchant turned French country gentleman, got his letters patent to embattle his house of Talcy in 1520, it was specifically laid down that "by no means whatsoever must he style himself Lord Castellan nor may he have right to watch and ward."

## The Building of Azay

AZAY HOUSE is another manor that was made to the order of a great burgess. Gilles Berthelot, who was "Treasurer-General of the Finances," set up this building in the years from 1518 to 1529. The worthy Gilles had married a girl called Philippe Lesbahi, daughter of one Antoine Lesbahi and Renée Didaillon, the former of whom had bought Azay in 1504. .

Berthelot's history and fate were those of so many of the "great financiers" who throughout the French story have been called in as, or have proposed themselves as, saviours of the public finances. The list of the unlucky fellows who came crashing down in the end is a long one—Jacques Coeur whose town palace is still the wonder of Bourges, Bohier whom we meet at Chenonceau, Beaune whose fine house we used to see at Tours, Fouquet who was imprisoned until his death by Louis XIV, right down to Law of the Mississippi Bubble and to men of our time.

Gilles Berthelot was luckier than some of the big business men of his day. He was Treasurer (after Bohier) for the conquered Duchy of Milan, and did his best to find money for the King, but it was a desperate task. The financial history of the western European countries was, for centuries, one of increasing muddle. The King and his Government assumed, or were forced to assume, ever-increasing burdens, with no corresponding increase in revenue. Finally Berthelot found it prudent to flee. He took refuge at Cambray, in the domains of the Duke of Burgundy, where he was safe until his death.

The later history of Azay is that of a succession of obscure owners, and to their obscurity this priceless palace owes perhaps its preservation. But it is national property now and so had to wait two whole years, after the damage of 1944, before a pane of glass was set in its mutilated windows.

Not far from Azay is the *château* de l'Islette. It is just a wing of a house between two stout towers. There is a charming bas-relief over the entrance door but there are no pilasters framing the

**Angers**                    The half-timbered 15th century *Maison d'Adam*

**Angers**                    The Castle

**Angers**        The Cathedral

**Amboise**        The View across the Loire

Azay-le-Rideau

**Angers**              The General View

**Avesnières**

windows. The windows open on to machicolated walls free of any decoration. It is worth while going over to l'Islette just in order to realise the world that separates it from Azay—yet the two places are in time not more than a generation or two apart. L'Islette is now crushed by its disproportionately lofty roof and the towers have truncated cones of slate jammed down upon them like over-sized hats.

## The True Cross of La Boissière

BAUGÉ. We have seen, at Angers, how Louis of Anjou adorned his private chapel with the *Apocalypse* tapestries, making it a fit shrine for the precious relic known as *la vraie croix de la Boissière*. The Abbey of La Boissière was a Cistercian foundation whose ruins may still be seen not far from Le Lude. The chapel, built in the 13th century to house the True Cross, still exists on the hill-side some three hundred yards from the abbey ruins, but the little shrine has been degraded to the rank of a farm grange.

Still, the relic has been preserved throughout the ages, and is now in the *Chapelle des Incurables* at Baugé. The cross, brought back from Constantinople in the 13th century by one Jean d'Allye, is of so-called "patriarchal" form, with two cross-pieces, and is supposed to be carved entirely from wood of the Calvary Tree. In the 14th century the relic was bordered with gold and enriched with medallions set with pearls and precious stones.

This True Cross of La Boissière is of considerable historical interest, for it was taken by the House of Anjou as their badge or emblem, and was then borrowed from them by the Dukes of Lorraine. The cross, known at first as the "Cross of Anjou" and then, from the 16th century, as the "Cross of Lorraine," has been, by a pious anachronism, associated with Joan of Arc, the Lorraine maiden. During the last war the double cross of Lorraine became very familiar to us, since it was adopted as their emblem by the "Free French" of General de Gaulle.

The little Anjou town of Baugé owes its origin to Fulk Nerra, who here set up a stronghold on the right bank of the Couasnon stream about the year 1000. Baugé is a charming place full of old houses, and well worth a few hours' exploration.

The town hall is an ancient mansion rebuilt in the fourteen hundreds by "Good King René" of Anjou, titular King of Sicily.

King René, whose traces we cross so often in Anjou, was born in Angers in 1409, the son of Louis II, King of Sicily and Duke of Anjou. René visited his kingdom of Naples in 1438, but in 1441 he was ousted by Alfonso of Aragon, and never afterwards recovered his sovereignty. René, who was an amiable man noted for his charities and his patronage of the arts, was himself an amateur painter, a poet and and a writer whose memory is kept alive by a number of MSS. and pictures executed to his order, of which the best-known are the superb "Burning Bush" in Aix-en-Provence Cathedral and then, perhaps, the splendid illuminated MS. known as King René's "Book of Tourneys." René was a good representative of the open-handed, enlightened and noble Valois prince at his best.

This town castle of Baugé looks like nothing so much as a simple town house of its period, and is a one-storeyed edifice, with an attic pierced by gabled dormers. An octagonal turret, however, contains a five-flight of steps, whose vaulted roof is enlivened by radiating ribs bearing shields showing the blazons of the Houses of Sicily and Anjou.

In Saint-Joseph's hospice is a curious pharmacy with 17th century wood-panelling and a collection of glazed pottery. In the hospice chapel are two canvases attributed, respectively, to Philippe de Champaigne (the artist who, among other works, made the famous portraits of Richelieu) and to Van Dyck. The pictures are rather grubby, but certainly are of fine execution.

Baugé church, although late (16th century), has singularly beautiful Angevin vaulting.

Baugé is a typical Anjou town where Anjou cooking may be enjoyed. The *andouilles* and *andouillettes* (sorts of sausages) can be especially recommended.

The potted pork (poor name for so fine a delicacy) or *rillettes* of Anjou surpass in perfume and in taste even those of the neighbouring Touraine. The good, wholesome pork is the grand standby of Angevin cooking, pork and cream and white meat and "white butter" or *beurre blanc* which is one of the few sauces much used by the cooks of Anjou. For the Angevin *cuisine* is not, perhaps, to be set in the same class as those of the Périgord, of Lyons or of Bresse. The Anjou food is real honest-to-goodness French cooking, simple (sometimes deceptively so), fairly rich, satisfying, healthy

34

and sensible. Stuffings, elaborate sauces, spices and "made-up" dishes are not as common as you will find them at Bordeaux or Périgueux, but all visitors to Anjou will be surprised to see how much they will be able to eat and how comfortably.

## Clarence

A MILE and a half to the south-west of Baugé is Old Baugé on a hill. Saint-Symphorien church is interesting, especially for the south transept, built in 1532 by the famous Angevin architect Jean de l'Espine whom we meet at Angers. But, for us, Baugé recalls the battle here fought in 1421, when Clarence met his death at the hands of the French marshal, Gilbert de La Fayette (ancestor of the La Fayette who fought against us in the American War of Independence). On the way from Baugé to Old Baugé is a block of stone pitted with holes that are, so legend says, the hoof-marks of the Duke of Clarence's horse.

This Clarence was not Shakespeare's "false, fleeting, perjur'd Clarence," but another and earlier bearer of the title who was brother to our Henry V. After the King's return to England in 1421, Clarence rashly attacked the French and their Scottish allies at Baugé, and paid for his temerity with his life and the rout of his army.

## Jarzé

NOT far from Baugé is the Renaissance *château* of Landifer. It is a magnificent Renaissance castle, restored and doubled in size by the addition of a wing in the 19th century. The whole makes up a huge and imposing pile with six round towers. The windows, the dormers and the chimneys are adorned with pilasters in the style of Charles IX's reign (1560–74). But, perhaps, the most interesting place hereabouts is Jarzé, some seven miles away on the Angers road. Not much remains of the original castle built by the ubiquitous Jean Bourré (who we meet at Le Plessis-Bourré and elsewhere), for the house was burned in 1794 and was later restored or rather reconstituted. Still, the cellars and kitchens—great, vaulted, imposing halls—and a charming 16th century boudoir with a decoration of mythological subjects remain as evidence of what Jarzé once was.

## *Magnificent Woodwork*

BEAUCHÊNE. The country-house of Beauchêne is nothing much to look at from the outside. It is a square block with no sort of ornament, but a pediment over the main entrance door, and the house is surrounded by an incongruous Second Empire garden set with clumps of geraniums.

The *château* was begun in 1776 to the orders of René-Jacques Leclerc de Juigné, of the notable Angevin family which appears in the province of Maine from 1357. The place has not been sold since its construction and is still in the possession of the founder's kin.

The interest of Beauchêne lies entirely in its magnificent wood panelling which must be accounted the finest of its period to be found in Anjou or Maine. The fine Louis XV *boiseries* not only cover the walls of the main saloons and reception rooms, but also those of the principal bedrooms. The elegant cornices, with friezes of interlacing coils and twines freely treated, are very like those in the nearly contemporary *château* of Craon. It is not improbable that the panellings of Beauchêne and of Craon are due to the chisel of that master wood-sculptor David (the father of the more celebrated David d'Angers and one of the most consummate carvers of any age).

Perhaps Beauchêne did not possess more panelling than was usual in the 18th century, but the precious *boiseries* constituted one of the most quickly realisable assets in bad times. Countless country-houses in France have been stripped of their woodwork. That of Beauchêne has survived, and it is of exceptional quality.

## *The Dyke Road*

BEAUFORT-EN-VALLÉE. The *levée*, or dyke road, runs straight and high along the Loire's right bank from Tours to Angers. On your left you have the wide meandering stream of the great river splotched with low sandbanks, tufted with grey-green sedge and willows—sparkling, slow-moving, spacious.

To your right the ground falls more abruptly and, in most places, to the alluvial plain dotted with farms and houses. Many of the villages climb, as it were, to face the *levée*, or they are shored up where the natural level of the ground is higher than elsewhere.

They flicker past you, grey and white and orderly and calm.

Here and there is a fine doorway, an intriguing church, or a manor half-hidden in the greenery. However, there is little to distinguish one hamlet from another. The villages seem to have less individuality than those along the loftier and more broken left bank of the river.

Saint-Martin-de-la-Place, Saint-Clément-des-Levées and then Les Rosiers, which has a Romanesque church, a fine Renaissance belfry and also an excellent restaurant where you may eat *friture de la Loire* and drink the wines of the country, for the Loire, that will bear no traffic, nourishes excellent fish. Across the water is Gennes on its hill. At Les Rosiers, at Saint-Mathurin, at Saumur, at Rochefort all the bridges were blown up in 1944, as were also all those on the Maine, the Sarthe, the Mayenne and the Oudon. In Anjou alone 51 bridges were destroyed.

If you are travelling by train you will not see much on the riverside, since the line runs to the north of the *levée* and the dyke blocks the view. . . . Then comes La Ménitré and, four miles to the north-east, Beaufort-en-Vallée, a largish place in the rich meadows watered by the Authion and the Lathan streams. You can see from afar the ruins of the castle built in 1346 by Guillaume-Roger, *comte* de Beaufort, father of Pope Gregory XI, the last of the French pontiffs to reside at Avignon and the author of several bulls addressed to the Archbishop of Canterbury, the King of England and the University of Oxford, commanding an investigation into the activities of Wyclif and his followers.

King René seems to have been the first great personage by the Loire's banks to choose simple manors for his residence. At Changé near Angers he made his wine. At Reculée he had his fishponds and there he used to organise fishing parties and competitions for the anglers of the countryside. The Angevins nicknamed him *le roi des gardons*, or the King of the roaches. And the "Good King" had also two houses called La Haute-Folie and Rivette near Ponts-de-Cé as well as La Ménitré, a more pretentious place, nearby Beaufort-en-Vallée. These dwellings were all more or less on the same plan. They were small, quite comfortable and fortified in appearance only. It is said that he himself painted the "Red Currant" room at Reculée and the royal motto ARDENT DÉSIR there shown may be by his hand. René, whose thick neck, bullet head and blunt features are known from many portraits, died in

Aix-en-Provence, but his body was brought back to be buried in Angers Cathedral.

Beaufort church is rather noteworthy and, although heavily restored between 1869 and 1882, still retains much of its original Gothic appearance. The lantern-tower was put up by the noted architect Jean de l'Espine whom we meet so often in Anjou.

The local museum houses a collection left to his native town by M. Joseph Denais. The objects are rather more interesting than is usual in such circumstances. The medals and pottery and porcelains are well worth attention. Beaufort has several ancient dwellings.

Saint-Mathurin is the last place of importance before you get to Trélazé, which is really a suburb of Angers.

## Fulk Nerra's Bones

BEAULIEU. In 1870 were discovered, in the Abbey church of Beaulieu, bones which seem to have been those of Fulk Nerra, the great Count of Anjou whose name and works we meet at every turn on the lower Loire. The skull found at Beaulieu is remarkable. It is square and heavy and it is buttressed with ridges and protuberances. Fulk, in life, must have appeared as formidable a personage as we might guess him from his story to have been.

Fulk, the son of Count Geoffrey I (known as *Grisegonelle* or Greycoat), in 987 succeeded his father in the countship of Anjou (which title his ancestor Fulk the Red had usurped in the 10th century). His castle building was part of a programme for the conquest of Touraine. To expiate his numerous crimes of violence, he made no less than three pilgrimages to the Holy Land, and it was on his return from the last of these that he died at Metz in Lorraine (1040).

Of the several religious houses he founded three are notable—Saint-Nicolas at Angers (1020), Ronceray in the same town (1028) and Beaulieu near Loches, that was the earliest in date of Fulk's monasteries, for he began its building about 1007, and when he died in far-off Lorraine at the age of seventy, he ordered that his bones should lie at Beaulieu by Loches.

## Beaulieu Abbey

THE Abbey-church of Beaulieu, that Fulk's masons erected between the years 1008 and 1012, although later rebuilt, is still a noteworthy Romanesque edifice. You see from afar the tower's magnificent and daring needle piercing the sky.

Beaulieu village, or township, is a ribbon-developed place which seems, as such places will, larger than it really is. If you approach the little city-museum of Loches from the Montrésor road, Beaulieu appears as an architectural avenue leading to the Indre and over it to Loches on its hill.

As you cross the wooded, fertile plain and approach the river, to your left is the *château* de Sansac, an elegant and graceful Renaissance house, though lately restored. The Indre here widens out and encloses islands over which the bridge leads to the foot of Loches hill and the gates of the town.

In Beaulieu little remains of the old Church of Saint-Laurent, dating from the 12th century, or of the Church of Saint-Pierre or of the Queen's Lodging known as "Agnes Sorel's House." Where Beaulieu tails off on the Montrésor road is a tall, late 13th century tower known as the *Tour Chevaleau*. It is worth while walking to the top, for from it is a really magnificent view over Loches and the surrounding country of woods and dales.

As was the case with so many monastic foundations of Old France, the Beaulieu abbey conventual buildings (cells, refectory, library and so forth) were rebuilt during the 18th century with, what was for then, "modern comfort." The Abbot's Lodging—with a curious outside pulpit—is, however, fairly old, dating from the fifteen and sixteen hundreds. The rest of the monastery is to-day occupied by the municipal offices and the local elementary schools.

The abbey-church itself was ravaged and partly destroyed by the English in 1412, and although it was rebuilt, it has since the Revolution fallen into decay. Of the nave only the north wall and the belfry remain, but the belfry is a magnificent Romanesque monument with arcading and octagonal stone steeple.

The choir and transepts now serve as the parish church of Beaulieu. The choir was reconstructed during the 15th century after the destruction wrought by the English troops. The fine flamboyant windows date from the time of this rebuilding, although their glass is modern. The Renaissance choir-stalls are splendid, as is the abbot's throne, although it has been botched about during efforts at "restoration."

In the right transept is a niche marking the spot where it seems great Fulk Nerra's bones were laid to rest.

## Henry of Navarre's Patrimony

BEAUMONT-SUR-SARTHE. About half-way between Le Mans and Alençon, on the *route nationale*, lies Beaumont-sur-Sarthe. You cross the Sarthe by the suspension bridge and find yourself in a picturesque little township terraced up on the rising ground from the river's right bank and overlooking the broad stream studded with islets. An old 13th century stone bridge still spans the river and is still used for traffic.

From the middle of the suspension bridge the view is delightful. The town is overhung by the ruins of the fortress. The Romanesque keep still stands, and on the castle terrace is an inoffensive modern house in 16th century taste.

There are one or two curious "bits" to be seen in Beaumont. The church has been refashioned, but has kept its Romanesque south doorway. In one of the side-aisles is a great medallion in relief representing the Virgin of the Rosary carved by Le Brun, an excellent sculptor who flourished in Le Mans during the 18th century.

The grain market is ancient. The house of the city governors dates from the 16th century. In the *rue de Paris* is the *Hôtel* de Kaerbout, a 17th century building with fine lead finials and ornaments.

The grounds around the *Motte-à-Madame* have been laid out as a public garden. The earthwork is generally considered to be prehistoric, but it may be only of early medieval date. The line of the city's fortified walls can still easily be traced from the castle's keep to the *Motte-à-Madame*.

Beaumont was several times beseiged during the fighting which William the Conqueror had to wage in order to secure for himself the county of Maine. In 1432, nearby in the Gaudine plain, the French troops, under Guillaume de Loré, beat back and defeated the English army under the Bastard of Salisbury.

In 1562, Henry of Navarre (the future King Henry IV of France) inherited this Beaumont from his grandmother, mother of his father Antoine de Bourbon. In 1701, Louis XIV detached Beaumont from the royal domains and made a present of it to René de

Froullal, *comte* de Tessé and marshal of France, who had distinguished himself in the War of the Spanish Succession, which set the King of France's grandson on the throne of Spain. The Tessés kept Beaumont until the Revolution.

## A Queer Custom

BEAUPRÉAU. At two o'clock in the morning one day in 1608, Benjamin de Rohan, *seigneur* de Soubise, accompanied by a band of bravos, attempted to abduct the heiress of Beaupréau. The household staff of the castle managed to repulse the assailants and, by letting off squibs, frighten them into a hasty retreat.

To celebrate the victory, on every anniversary until the Revolution, Mass was celebrated at two o'clock in the morning in the Collegiate Church of Beaupréau, while fireworks were let off just outside the chapel.

Beaupréau was, from the early Middle Ages, one of the most important lordships in Anjou, and the castle commanded the highway from Saumur to Nantes. In 1540 the heiress of Beaupréau made an illustrious marriage, taking to husband no less a person than Charles de Bourbon, *prince* de La Roche-sur-Yon. Of course, in the middle of the 16th century the Bourbons had not yet inherited the crown of France, but still they were a powerful family, descended from St. Louis, and known to be in the line of succession to the throne. The lands of Beaupréau were raised in 1554 to the rank of marquisate and in 1562 to that of duchy.

In 1565, the boy-king, Charles IX, his mother, Catherine de' Medici, the Queen of Navarre and her twelve-year-old heir, Henri (afterwards Henri IV King of France) paid a visit to Beaupréau, and sat down to a magnificent banquet which was served in the park, and made so great an impression upon the childish imagination of Henry of Navarre that ten years later he paid a special visit to Beaupréau to view the site of the splendid party.

Henry of Navarre could not, however, remember his distant kinsman (and host), the *prince* de La Roche-sur-Yon, since that magnate did not attend his own party, for the good reason that he was dying in the castle and indeed died after the royal party had left the next day. The absence of the host does not seem to have damped the spirits of the guests at all.

Later on, another heiress of Beaupréau was married to the *duc* de Retz, and at the marriage festivities the bridegroom's brother, afterwards the famous Cardinal de Retz, was much struck with the beauty of the bride's only sister. He was also interested in her dowry, which amounted to the considerable sum of 80,000 *livres* income. But he was not successful in his suit, and passed on to an ecclesiastical and political career.

Beaupréau castle was "modernised" in 1775 and sold a little later. After passing through a good many hands, it became by inheritance the property of the *duc* de Blacas.

Beaupréau to-day consists of a square of three storeys, with two great round towers with conical roofs and two other towers flanking the entrance. The long, terraced façade of 22 windows and 11 dormers makes a brave if rather gloomy show. Most of the building dates from the 15th and 16th centuries. But the castle was burned in 1793 and rebuilt in the 19th century. It is an interesting place, though shorn of much of its former glory. The beautiful park slopes down to the course of the Evre.

The name Beaupréau, by the way, is pronounced Bo-pro.

## Hatters Castle

BEL-AIR. By September 1768 François Delaunay (a name he was later to spell *de Launay*—that looks much more smart), the son of a wealthy tradesman of the city of Laval, considered himself such an important person in his native province that his modest little country-house at Villeray, near the village of Moustiers-en-Cingalais, seemed quite unworthy of him. Also he was thinking of getting married.

But his fortunes were not yet grand enough to allow him to buy a really fine place, such as the Castle of La Roche-Talbot (near Sablé) which was his splendid dwelling towards the end of his career.

So, in September 1768 he took a lease of a property known by the attractive name of Bel-Air. His rent was 480 *livres* a year.

Then a month later he married Marie-Gabrielle Le Rique, and promptly assumed (from a small property of his wife's) the name of "Delaunay de Fresnay." Then he procured a patent of nobility from Louis XVI, and with a coat-of-arms from the heralds, as Monsieur François de Launay de Fresnay took his place among the landed gentry of his province.

Delaunay did a good deal to Bel-Air: he fenced, walled and ditched the park—or what was to become the park; he put some good panelling in the rooms, and he attended to his business. He was a sail-maker in a large way. He was the friend, or at least business acquaintance, of Necker, and there is extant a letter from Delaunay to the Swiss financier (who was Madame de Staël's father), a letter in which the astute upstart excused his ardent pursuit of gain on the grounds that he had seven daughters to marry off!

Delaunay does not seem to have been much disturbed by the Revolution. He was probably glad to remember his humble origins after the fall of the monarchy.

He died at Laval in 1799, leaving Bel-Air (which by this time was only an insignificant part of his property) to his nephew. The place was sold in 1872, and now belongs to the *comtesse* de Quatrebarbes, whose husband was a member of the curiously named but ancient Breton family.

Bel-Air has, unfortunately, been shorn of much of its charm. Most of the land has been sold and a railway line has been driven through the park. Several roads run near the house. But it is still an attractive place. The front curves almost like a Louis XV commode. The graceful double flight of steps up to the front door are in the authentic style of the *grand siècle*. There are enough lime-tree walks and rows of elms to make one regret the past glories of the Bel-Air gardens.

## *Bon Marché*

BELLÊME. All visitors to Paris who go shopping on the left bank of the river sooner or later end up at the *Bon Marché*, a huge department store which spreads its rather exotic architecture over several streets north of the *rue de Sèvres*. And, either coming out or going in, such shoppers will not fail to notice a rather repulsive piece of statuary in the garden between the *rue de Sèvres* and the *boulevard Raspail*. The sculpture represents a fat old woman swathed in furs and bending down most graciously towards a tattered ragamuffin standing respectfully at the bottom of a flight of steps. The portly matron was the wife of Aristide Boucicaut, founder of the *Bon Marché*. She was a benefactress of the poor. As a matter of fact, neither Boucicaut nor his spouse deserved such a vulgar monument. They were, of their kind, rather decent people.

Boucicaut, whose name for us suggests Dion, or remotedly the famed medieval marshal of France, was born at Bellême, in the Perche, and he was one of the pioneers of the new and novel department stores in France. Boucicaut, who was bred to be a salesman in a "dry goods store," early realised that the old habits of pestering customers to buy what they did not want, of bullying salesmen and saleswomen when they were unsuccessful in foisting off unwanted goods on the customers, and of pushing the sale of second-rate and shop-soiled goods were becoming woefully ineffective in a world of new social traditions and of redistribution of wealth. The story of his own success is a long one, but Boucicaut, like Chauchard and Hériot at the *Grands Magasins du Louvre*, was triumphant, and he died a very rich man, not only by French but by any standards—and there is perhaps no country in the world in which it is more difficult to make a large fortune than France, if you have to start from scratch. The *Bon Marché* has preserved its reputation (which, for long, was for selling the best and cheapest household linen in Paris) to the present day. And no rival has arisen in the southern part of Paris; all the other department stores—*Louvre, Printemps, Galeries Lafayette*, etc.—are on the right bank.

## Old Bellême

BELLÊME'S history is really bound up with that of Normandy, though the town's lords looked mostly towards the south and away from the Duchy. From the early part of the 11th to the middle of the 12th century, the lords of Bellême possessed nearly all the great territory known as the Perche. In 1082 they assumed the style of Counts of Alençon, and from the eleven hundreds that Norman city was their capital. Robert de Belesme, whom we meet in Normandy and who was a great figure in England, erected the Castle of Bellême, as well as those of Nogent-le-Rotrou and of Gisors.

The Gothic Church of Saint-Sauveur was rebuilt about two hundred and fifty years ago. Over the high altar is a picture of the Transfiguration done by Oudry, the father of the well-known painter of hunting scenes. Only the barbican remains of the old fortress. The Saint-Santin chapel is a relic of another castle.

## Bercé Forest

ON the highway from Le Mans to Tours, after Laillé, you pull up into Bercé Forest, through which the road runs for more than two miles.

Two miles to the north of the forest lies Pruillé-l'Eguillé. The Romanesque church contains a fine tapestry, splendid choir-stalls and stained-glass windows—all of the 16th century. There is an early 18th century bas-relief of the Nativity, an imposing statue of Saint Christopher, and, most precious of all, a carved wooden statue of the Virgin, about six hundred years old.

Bercé Forest, of over 15,000 acres, spreads out in a huge crescent about fifteen miles long by, on an average, only two miles wide, and over hills varying in altitude from 400 to 550 feet. The trees are mostly oaks, beeches and pines.

In the centre of the crescent lies Jupilles, whence lead off charming walks. Here and there you come upon an old church or a ruined *château*. At the *carrefour Saint-Hubert* is a rustic inn, where, if the weather is fine, you may eat out-of-doors surrounded by great trees. One of the most beautiful spots in this beautiful woodland is the *fontaine de la Coudre*, the source of the Dinan stream, whose waters splash down over an amphitheatre of rocks amid a background of tall trees.

## Clovis and Alaric

BLÉRÉ. Near the little village of Sublaines, on the road from Bléré to Loches, are two artificial mounds known as the *Danges de Sublaines*, and these hillocks are said to have been thrown up to mark the limits between the realm of Clovis, the great Frankish conqueror and founder of the Merovingian monarchy of France, and the dominions of Alaric II, the Visigothic King of the south-west, whose patrimony was eventually swallowed up by the Franks, who thus established their suzerainty over the greater part of what now is France.

About five miles north of Sublaines is Bléré, in the Middle Ages a strong fortress, but now a small town of no great interest save for its curious Romanesque and Gothic church. But Bléré is not a bad place in which to stay the night. We can then go on and see Chenonceau and Montrésor the next day, finishing up at Loches.

## Backgammon Fans

LE BOIS-MONTBOURCHER. From the high road between Lion d'Angers and Château-Gontier you turn off towards Le Bois-Montbourcher. You skirt a great mere of sluggish waters set with reeds, and there before you are the walls and high roofs of the house reflected in the lake. The path leads through an avenue of age-old lime trees to a drawbridge spanning the moat, for, on two sides, the *château* rises from the lake, and on the others it is bounded by a broad moat.

An ancient moat round a French castle means that in the Middle Ages that castle was considered as a *châtellenie* whose lord had the title of *castellan*. The seat of a simple *seigneurie* or lordship might not be moated. Thus, one can judge at a glance what was the importance, in olden days, of any ancient house in France.

Le Bois was an important place, for the lordship of nearby Lion d'Angers depended upon it. The name "Le Bois-Montbourcher" is a curious composite one adopted in the early 16th century, when the heiress of the du Bois family married a Montbourcher.

In 1711 the property was bought by a *marquis* de Charnacé. Charnacé is only about six miles away, but the old castle there was pillaged and burned at the time of the Revolution, the archives and charters were destroyed in the public square of Champigné, the tombs of the Charnacés were prised open and their bones scattered. In fact, Charnacé suffered the common fate of many French properties. The revolutionaries, from the first, made straight for the documents which, in their eyes, were the legal foundation of the *old régime*. "Burning the papers" is, of course, a regular revolutionary device, and as late as the Irish uprising of 1916 the nationalists sought to burn the land-deeds and charters in Dublin—as a matter of fact they were preserved, and what went up in flames at the burning of the Four Courts was (among other archives) the collection of the wills and other quite innocuous documents.

Le Bois-Montbourcher was rebuilt in 1589, and about all that remains of the older house is a tower rather pompously called a "keep."

There is an imposing guard-room with a very fine chimney-piece, and the walls are hung with family portraits of the Charnacés right down to a 19th century painting by Carolus-Duran, a now almost forgotten artist, but one who in his day was famous as a portraitist.

In the main saloon is a picture of Hercule de Charnacé, Ambassador of Louis XIII, to Gustavus-Adolphus; a very fine Largillière representing the first *marquis* de Charnacé as a boy of fourteen, and a pastel by Latour of one of the present owner's ancestresses who was born d'Agoult of the same family as the husband of the brilliant lady who was Liszt's mistress and mother-in-law of Richard Wagner.

Most of the inside of Le Bois-Montbourcher is in the rather sombre, dignified style of the 17th century, but there is one delightful little apartment that is a model of Louis XVI grace. It was formerly known as the "tric-trac room," for the players of the noisy game of backgammon had to be isolated from the more subdued guests. Two of the paintings in the woodwork over the doors are by Oudry, the charming artist of Louis XV's time.

## A Resourceful Husband

BONNÉTABLE. Bonnétable was originally (and until 1288) called Malestable.

The place belonged, in the 16th century, to the notable Coesmes family, for in 1520 Charles de Coesmes married Jeanne d'Har-court, who brought him Bonnétable. Charles was an uncommonly objectionable husband, who finished by losing his wife in rather obscure circumstances. She was either murdered or she committed suicide. Either explanation of her death would be probable. The poor woman was driven to distraction by her husband's brutalities and, moreover, he was just the man for assassinating his spouse. We might think that he would have hesitated to kill his wife since they had no children, and it was in her right and through her that he held the broad lands of Bonnétable. On her death they would revert to the d'Harcourt family.

But Coesmes was a man of resource. Very soon after his wife's death he abducted her younger sister—and remaining heir to Bonnétable. The girl was aged just thirteen. Coesmes married his Gabrielle at night before a hedge-priest. The couple then fled to Lorraine. The d'Harcourts—most anxious to regain possession of Bonnétable—managed to get Gabrielle back home, but Coesmes was very busy, and secured, successively, royal pardon for having abducted a minor and then papal confirmation and ratification of the marriage.

Coesmes kept Bonnétable, and lived there, it would seem, quite conventionally with his Gabrielle until his death.

Later on, Bonnétable passed by inheritance into a branch of the La Rochefoucauld family, and during the 18th century was allowed to fall into ruin. In the 19th century it was extensively restored. The great pile looks imposing enough from afar, but nearly all its medieval trappings are modern. The grounds are very fine.

Bonnétable belongs to the *duc* de Doudeauville, head of the second, or younger, of the two main branches into which the La Rochefoucauld family is divided.

The little village of Bonnétable, on the Tripoulin rivulet, is of no great interest, but if you follow the road from Mamers to Connerré-Biellé, you see Bonnétable forest sweeping in a great fringe to your left. Then comes the hamlet of Tuffé, where it is worth while stopping a few minutes to admire the old Romanesque church and a curious 16th century statue of Sainte-Barbe.

After Bonnétable on the Bellême-Le Mans highway, but a little off the road, is Torcé-en-Vallée. The church has some excellent 16th century stained glass and some good statuary. Six or seven miles farther on is Savigné-l'Evêque. The church has 18th century choir-stalls removed from the Abbey of Epau. Near Sargé (just three miles to the north-east of Le Mans) are some remains of a Roman aqueduct.

LA BOURDAISIÈRE. Two miles north-west of Véretz and on the right bank of the Cher is La Bourdaisière manor which at one time was a fief of the second *maréchal* de Boucicaut who, after famous feats of arms in the eastern Mediterranean, was taken prisoner by us at Agincourt and died in England. La

**Angers**     The St. Aubin Cloister     **Azay-le-Rideau**     The *Château*
de L'Islette

**Azay-le-Rideau**     By the Indre's Banks

The State Bedroom

The View from Moat

The superb *Château*

**AZAY-LE-RIDEAU**

Bourdaisière as we see it to-day has, however, been thoroughly rebuilt, and little remains of the manor dated 1540. By the 16th century the notable Touraine family of Babou was in possession of La Bourdaisière.

## *"The Pope's Diamond"*

WHEN young King François I held his secret conference with Pope Leo X at Bologna in December 1515, in the French monarch's suite was Philibert Babou de La Bourdaisière, accompanied by his singularly beautiful wife, Marie Gaudin, the daughter of a mayor of Tours. Either because he admired her, or because he thought that so charming a woman could not fail to have influence with the susceptible sovereign, His Holiness presented Marie with a fine diamond that, under the name of the "Gaudin Diamond," was for long preserved in the Sourdis family descended from one of Marie Gaudin's daughters.

And we can admire the effigy of Marie to this day, since in the Church of *Notre-Dame du Bon Désir* between Tours and Amboise is a sculptured group of the "Three Marys." The statue of the Virgin was carved in the image of Marie Gaudin.

Philibert and Marie had numerous offspring. The eldest son, Jean Babou de La Bourdaisière, was killed at the battle of Arques in Normandy. He left a daughter Françoise, who married Antoine d'Estrées, son of Jean d'Estrées, Grand Master of the Artillery. Françoise inherited much of her grandmother's beauty, but did not imitate her exemplary life. In fact, Françoise ran away from her Antoine d'Estrées and went to live in far-off Auvergne with a lover. Later, the guilty pair were massacred by the population of Issoire, to whom they had made themselves objectionable.

While, however, she was still living with her husband, Françoise d'Estrées gave birth, in her old family manor of La Bourdaisière, to a child, of whom it is not too much to say that her early death had an incalculable effect upon the course of French history.

## *Gabrielle D'Estrées*

GABRIELLE was born in 1573, and when she was about fourteen years of age, she and her sister were sent to the Court of Henri III. The two girls were frightened away by the troubles marking the end of that reign, and in 1588 they retired into the country to their father's estate of Coeuvres near Soissons, where Gabrielle was courted by one Bellegarde, attached to the Court of the new king, Henri IV.

In November 1590 the imprudent lover led his master to admire Gabrielle at her father's house. The girl was in the first bloom of her remarkable beauty. She was very fair, with a lovely skin, delicate and distinguished features, and was remarkable for her charming disposition. In 1591 she became the King's mistress. She was eighteen and he was thirty-eight. In June 1592 she was married off to one Nicolas d'Ameral, Lord of Liancourt, but the marriage was annulled in September. From December 1592 Gabrielle lived at the Court and with the King. Her first son César, "Monsieur" (afterwards *duc de* Vendôme and the founder of a line of notable warriors) was born in 1594. Gabrielle was created Duchess of Beaufort and of Étampes, her children were legitimised, and her furniture was upholstered in white and scarlet, the colours of the Queens of France.

## Gabrielle's Fate

HENRI'S position, although strengthened, was not impregnable. He still had to count with the antagonism of Rome that arose, not so much from hatred of a former Huguenot, but from a desire to bridle and subject the Gallican Church and the French clergy, who were suspected of separatist tendencies.

Henri, we may note, was the last French King of France. After him, the French sovereigns all had foreign mothers. Louis XIII was half a Florentine, Louis XIV half a Spaniard, while Louis XV married a Pole.

For years Henri IV had lived apart from his very unconventional queen, Marguerite or Margot, daughter of King Henri II and of Catherine de' Medici. In 1599 Gabrielle was pregnant for the fourth time. The King was away from Paris, but Gabrielle had moved to the capital to be near her sister. On Thursday, the 8th April, she supped at the house of one Zamet, a prominent Italian man of affairs. This Sebastiano Zamet, native of Lucca, who raised himself from the condition of cobbler to that of wealthy usurer and financier, was one of the Italian adventurers who, at all times, have sought, and found, fortune in France. It was Zamet who, when asked at the marriage of one of his children what were his title and style, boasted, "Write me down Lord of Seventeen Hundred Thousand Crowns."

At the supper Gabrielle ate a lemon—in 16th century Paris a rarity—and on returning to her lodging was seized with vomiting and fainting. As always, poison was suspected. It was remembered (at least afterwards) that Canon Bonciani, the ecclesiastical envoy of the Grand Duke of Tuscany and a reputed poisoner, had been present at the supper. Murder by poison is, historically, a typical Italian trick, or so the French thought. Though Ferdinando de' Medici, the then Grand Duke of Tuscany, was one of the least murderous of his family, still he had killed his own brother Francesco and that brother's wife Bianca Capello. And, in France, the stakes were high.

On Friday, the 9th April, Gabrielle's doctors decided to provoke an accouchement, and she was delivered of a dead child, *à pièces et à loppins* as the bald, contemporary account reads.

At five o'clock in the morning of the 10th, Gabrielle died in convulsions. The King, who was at Fontainebleau, had been sent for at once, but he was met on the road by messengers, who told him that Gabrielle was already dead, in order to spare him the dreadful spectacle of her living death.

It is possible, even probable, that Gabrielle died of eclampsia or puerperal convulsions and infection provoked by the manipulations of her surgeons. It is also possible that she had been poisoned at the supper. It was in the general Italian interest to get her out of the way. The divorce between Henry and Margot was imminent. It was generally believed that the King intended to marry Gabrielle. The outlook for an Italian marriage was dim.

The same year that Gabrielle died, the divorce between the King and Queen was pronounced. The blowsy, superstitious and tiresome Marie de' Medici became Queen. She and the King's new mistress, Henriette de Balzac d'Entraigues, gave birth to children about the same time. France was to be for nearly two centuries subjected to monarchs who, however they may have appeared to their contemporaries, ruined the cause of the monarchy and sowed the seeds of dissensions which still grow thick to-day.

## *The Wines of Montlouis*

ABOUT two miles to the north-west of La Bourdaisière lies the little town of Montlouis, spread over the slopes of a chalky hill, into whose flanks have been cut and carved dwellings, caves, cellars and stables. The wines of Montlouis are celebrated, although, perhaps, not so well known outside the limits of Touraine as are those of Vouvray. Montlouis is also a great place for *charcuterie* or all sorts of products made from the flesh of pig— here the *rillettes* (a delicious sort of potted pork) are particularly luscious and tasty. Montlouis is a useful kind of place at which to pull up after a surfeit of architecture and history, and indulge in a corrective in the shape of good Touraine fare and the clean, clear, white wines of the country.

## *An Unheroic Lover*

BOURGON. Bourgon is one of those delightful houses you find in the French countryside that look at first as though they were rather neglected, but that, on closer inspection, reveal themselves as just unaltered from the times when a house had to earn its keep and be the centre of an estate that was a going concern.

The nice, lively outline of Bourgon, with its high roofs, pointed gables and irregular façade, sets you imagining all sorts of hidden staircases, rather mysterious chambers and dark corners. There are no formal gardens, and if you view Bourgon from across the dried moat sprouting here and there an apple tree, the place might almost seem an overgrown farm, but it is in reality very much of a great manor. The house is built of sober sandstone, in the solid, rustic, country style of the 16th century. The courtyard looks towards the sombre woods of Bourgon forest. In the main saloon is a most imposing granite chimney-piece.

Bourgon was, in the 16th century, the scene of a tragedy whose memory long lived in local legend. Louis de Montecler, Lord of Bourgon, had a beautiful wife who became the mistress of Jean Bourré, Lord of Jarzé. Montecler's steward told the unsuspecting husband (the only man, of course, in the countryside who did not know what was going on) of his misfortune. One night, when the two lovers were in the castle and the husband was away, the steward managed to send for Montecler, who burst into his wife's apartment only to find her alone. She fell on her knees pleading for mercy, but Montecler poignarded her to the heart. And then he obtained from the King Letters of Remission for his murder.

It is worth noting that Jarzé had been let down from the window on a rope made by Madame de Montecler's maids from the sheets of the nuptial couch. The wife had thought to save her lover, and he did not stay to face her husband. An old story.

Bourgon was later sold and resold.

## The Treasures of Courland

BOURGUEIL. After Langeais, on the Tours-Angers levée or northern raised highway running downstream, you pass the Saint-Patrice road, leading in about a thousand yards up to the *château* of Rochecotte, a long, white 18th century building opening on to a buttressed terrace overhanging the valley. Rochecotte not only gave its name to a well-known leader of the "Chouans" or insurgents against the Government of the First Republic, but the house was, in the later years of his life, often a residence of Talleyrand. In the memoirs of his niece, the *duchesse* de Dino, there is much mention of the place.

Edmond de Talleyrand-Périgord, heir to his uncle's dukedom of Talleyrand, married, in 1809, Dorothea, daughter of Peter, "Duke of Courland, Semigallia and Sagan." This lady was the descendant of Ernst Johann Bühren, the grandson of a groom to one of the old Dukes of Courland. Bühren set out to make his fortune in Russia. He made it by becoming the lover of the Grand Duchess Anne, afterwards Empress of Russia. And to the end of his imperial mistress's life his influence over her was paramount. Bühren, who was a mean, vindictive, treacherous and avaricious individual, was loaded with honours, and about 1730 he impudently adopted the arms of the ancient and noble French house of Biron and took their name. In 1737 "elected" reigning Duke of Courland, he was for three weeks after his mistress's death Regent of Russia, and then was banished to Siberia, where he remained twenty years. In 1762 he returned to Court, and in 1763 the Empress Catherine restored him to his duchy, which he ruled until 1772, when he died, and was succeeded by his son Peter.

By his marriage, the *duc* de Talleyrand acquired part of the art collections of the Dukes of Courland. A portion of these collections is still housed at Rochecotte, which passed from the Talleyrands to the Castellanes—also by marriage. The Rochecotte gallery is especially rich in 17th century canvases of the Dutch school. Rochecotte now belongs to *comte* Stanislas de Castellane, a brother of the well-known *marquis* de Castellane, known familiarly as "Boni," whose matrimonial adventures and social activities kept him in the limelight for years until his death in the thirties of this century.

By the way, the names of Talleyrand and Castellane are "shibboleth" words in French. Both of them are pronounced as two syllables only: thus Talrand and Castlane. If we pronounce these two illustrious patronymics as they are written, we shall run the risk of being considered not quite the sort of people who frequent smart company!

Downstream, after La Chapelle-sur-Loire, you reach Port-Boulet, linked by a bridge with the south bank of the river. Three miles north of Port-Boulet is Bourgueil, the centre of the local wine-trade. The vineyards of Bourgueil are reputed, and their wines are held by many to be the best red wines of Touraine, but not all are of this opinion. The Bourgueil vintages have a distinct taste of raspberries. The local amateurs are apt to tell one, if one dares to mention the flavour, that they like raspberries; well, so do many of us, but not in wine. As a matter of fact, the Bourgueil vines came originally from the Chambertin district of Burgundy, a region producing most esteemed and, indeed, magnificent wines, but the Bourgueil soil has quite changed the flavour of the grapes. It is, of course, well known that not only the vines themselves but the soil they are grown in determine the quality and character of the wine. You may take vines from the greatest vineyards of France and plant them elsewhere—in Australia or America—where everything—climate, rainfall, nature of the soil—seems to favour a growth like that of the French vines, and the results will be surprising, if not startling. In Australian burgundy, Russian champagne and Californian claret, the accent should be laid very heavily upon the adjectives.

Bourgueil has some ruins of its ancient Benedictine abbey, founded in 990, but the remains are of buildings no earlier in date than the sixteen hundreds.

The Church of Saint-Germain should be visited. The Romanesque nave ends in a "Plantagenet" or "Angevin" style square choir which is most airy and gracious.

Coming down on to the levee highway again into Port-Boulet and moving towards the west, you see, about five hundred yards off the road, a charming little manor, half hidden in trees. It is the *château* des Réaux, formerly known as Le Plessis-Rideau, and built in 1452 by Jean Briçonnet, Mayor of Tours, of the noted patrician family, some members of which we meet at La Bourdaisière.

In 1650 Tallemant "des Réaux," the gossip-writer and author of *Historiettes*, bought the place. Tallemant, who was the son of a *bourgeois* of Nantes, had already decked himself out with a territorial title—Réaux was some little house he owned in his native province—so when he acquired Le Plessis-Rideau he changed its name, thereby giving himself a fine ancestral seat.

## Mary Queen of Scots' Escort

BRÉZÉ. Brézé, seen from afar, looks very lordly in its landscape of rolling hills. When we come up to the place, we may find it a little disappointing, but still it is well worth a visit.

East from Montreuil-Bellay, in southern Anjou, the Dive river calms down a little, and settles into a sort of canal back from whose right bank rise the village and Castle of Brézé.

The place was from early times the possession of a feudal family to whom it gave its name. Geoffrey de Brézé in 1110 made a gift of building-stone for the construction of the great Abbey-church of Fontevrault, where are the tombs of our Henry II and of three members of his family. In 1318 Brézé passed by inheritance to the notable and powerful Angevin family of Maillé, of whom Arthus in 1548 led to Scotland the mission to fetch Mary Stuart (Mary Queen of Scots) to France, there to marry the Dauphin. Arthus was evidently a good envoy, since the Queen-Mother, Catherine de' Medici, dispatched him to Poland in search of the heir to the French throne, Henry (afterwards King Henry III), who had been elected King of Poland. The Poles did not want to let their French king (from whom they expected considerable political advantages) go, and he had to be smuggled out of his adopted country.

Arthus' grandson, Urbain de Maillé, born in 1598, made a notable marriage. In 1615, Brézé was created a marquisate, and two years later Urbain married Nicolle Duplessis de Richelieu, sister of the great Cardinal.

## The Crazy Marquise

WHEN Urbain married Nicolle, her brother Armand (the future Cardinal) was only Bishop of Luçon.

Nicolle was, it seems, always rather strange in her behaviour, but, then, she came of a family, not only of great wits, but of the madness that is closely allied to them. And Urbain was a particularly brutal husband, who ended by getting his wife confined as a prisoner in Saumur castle, where she died. She was incarcerated, indeed, by virtue of a *lettre de cachet*. The Cardinal did not like his relations' weaknesses to be advertised. In those days, prison was considered the right place for madmen. Poor Nicolle, it appears, was persuaded that she had *le cul en verre* or, let us say, buttocks made of glass, and no haemophilic was ever more careful than she of bumps and bruises.

Urbain does not seem to have been much incommoded by his wife's troubles. He had a moderately "successful" career, was for a short time Viceroy of Catalonia, *maréchal* de France and Governor of Anjou. His daughter married the great soldier known as the *Grand Condé,* and led a most miserable life. She was ill-treated by her husband. She finished, like her mother, in prison, and she handed on to her descendants the latent madness of the Richelieu stock.

In 1682, Condé sold Brézé to one Thomas Dreux, a member of the Paris *parlement* (the French *parlements* were not parliaments in our sense of the word, but special law-courts largely concerned with the registering and promulgation of Royal Decrees under the absolute monarchy).

The *marquis* de Dreux-Brézé, who was Grand Master of the Ceremonies to Louis XVI, remained in France throughout the Revolution and Terror, living at Les Andelys in Normandy under the name of "Monsieur Evrard." He must have been a decent sort of man, for he was kept during those troublous times by money brought to him secretly by his old tenants from Anjou. When "Monsieur Evrard" came out of hiding, Napoleon, knowing that

Exterior of Megalithic Tomb

The Interior of the "Dolmen"

**BAGNEUX**

Baugé

The Castle

Beaufort-en-Vallée

The Castle

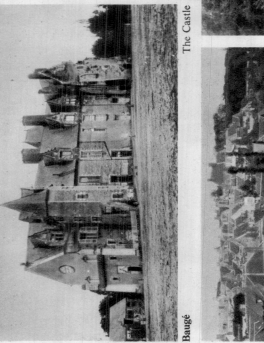

Beaumont-sur-Sarthe

Beaupréau

**Brissac**                                   The Ducal Castle

**La Belle Jonchère**                         The Manor

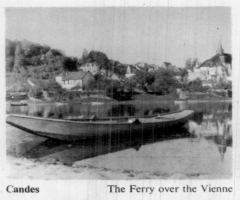

**Candes**      The Ferry over the Vienne    **Béhuard**      The Chapel

**Candes**      The Manor-House    **Candes**      The Church

**Candes**      The 12th century Porch of St. Michel in St. Martin's Church

the former Grand Master of the Ceremonies had preserved all the archives of his office, tried to get hold of these precious papers that contained, among other matters, the ceremonial ritual directions of the *old régime*. The Emperor never obtained the documents, even though he offered a very large sum for them, and his upstart Court had to get on as best it could. Napoleon was constrained to take lessons in imperial deportment from Talma the actor, who, we may suppose, found out how an Emperor should behave while he was residing with his dentist father in London. Napoleon, who was most sensitive to sarcastic remarks about his Court (he had become so imbued with the imperial tradition that after his marriage to Marie-Louise he would speak of his "uncle," King Louis XVI, since Marie-Louise was the niece of Marie-Antoinette), never forgave Dreux-Brézé, and that nobleman found it expedient to leave France and join the Court in Exile of the future King Louis XVIII.

Brézé still belongs to the Dreux-Brézé family, and it was thoroughly—too thoroughly—restored in the 19th century. On to the old feudal castle was affixed the queerest collection of "classical" façades, Corinthian columns, pilasters "in the Ionic style," including even a recumbent statue of Venus over the entrance! However, the general character of the sturdy walls and great round towers has not been altered. The inside has some interesting pictures and furniture.

From afar, in the evocatory landscape of southern Anjou, Brézé is the image of those feudal castles, strong but not severe, that we see in the miniatures of the 14th and 15th centuries.

## Ducal Brissac

BRISSAC. Brissac, although by no means the oldest, or even one of the oldest, of the inhabited houses of Anjou, does convey an impression of majestic age and dignity such as would be difficult to match.

You get out of Angers by the southern road and cross the Loire. After Les Ponts-de-Cé and Érigné, you find the Brissac road on the left. You are soon out of the little village, and there before you, in its broad, meadow-like grounds and park, dotted here and there with spreading oaks, stands Brissac's great mass. The house is towering tall; not frowning or grim, but dignified, antique, solid.

Essentially, Brissac castle is composed of two thick and stout round towers—sole remaining remnants of the 14th century castle bought, at the end of the 15th century, by the head of the Cossé family—and these two towers are joined by a lofty wing put up in Louis XIII's time. One section is over 130 feet and seven storeys high. Back from the right-hand tower, as you look at the main front, projects another wing at right angles to the main block.

Thus is the huge habitation built from 1610 to 1620 by Charles du Cossé, *maréchal* de France. Cossé employed an architect one Jacques d'Angluze, son of the man who designed the *château* of Fontainebleau, but Jacques d'Angluze was assisted by at least three other architects whose names are known, and by a number of painters, decorators and sculptors, most of them local men from Tours, Angers or Le Mans.

The northern wing, which drives back from the main façade, has high chimneys in the Louis XIII style, but it is the main front, looking towards the south-east, that is the more remarkable. The style has already something of the nobility, and even severity, which characterise the *grand siècle* or "great age" of Louis XIV. It is composed of two distinct parts. That to the left is of very simple lines. The storeys are well differentiated from one another and the tall windows are bordered with stone frames projecting somewhat from the walls. The part to the right retains Renaissance features. It is enriched with powerfully executed and bold sculpture, and contains the entrance door reached from the level of the grounds by flights of steps.

It is not easy to get permission to visit the interior of Brissac, but should permission be obtained, the opportunity of examining and admiring a great French ducal mansion which has passed from father to son for over four hundred years should on no account be missed.

Brissac has not changed its general appearance for the last three hundred years. It is still lived in by the descendants of the builder, and it is still filled with the furniture used by generations of the Cossé-Brissac family. Although there is nothing harsh or unfriendly about the apartments of Brissac, still, it must be confessed, many of them are a little dark and perhaps too great in size for modern ideas of comfort. The massive stone staircase, wide enough for a coach and four to pass up, the banqueting-hall as large as that of an Oxford college, the succession of tapestried bedrooms, the most handsome and imposing grand gallery with groups of armoured figures and suits of armour worn by dead-and-gone Cossés, banners borne in war by these same men, blazons and hangings, make up an unforgettable picture of feudal magnificence. The small chapel is untouched and unrestored. The saloons on the ground-floor, where you may be entertained to tea, are of such proportions and fittings as to make our present-day social ceremonies seem rather colourless.

There is nothing modern or urban about Brissac, for although it is a highly civilised dwelling, it is emphatically a country castle made by a great feudal magnate as the centre and capital of his duchy. The grounds are spacious but more English than French, the house stands in meadows dotted with clumps of trees and bounded with woods.

Brissac was repaired rather than restored—the place has not been transformed as Serrant has been—by the eleventh *duc's* mother, but the castle stands as it did in the reign of King Louis XIII, when the *maréchal* de Brissac gave splendid festivities here, and when the scores of Czech and Egyptian retainers clad in exotic costumes lined the stairs and waited upon the guests. A second *maréchal* de Brissac was Governor of Paris under Louis XVI, and this was the gallant but rather blundering old soldier who said when welcoming Marie-Antoinette to Paris, "Madame, here there are two hundred thousand Parisians enamoured of your person." This *duc* de Brissac died in 1780. The castle was partly pillaged at the Revolution, but some of the furnishings were recovered. In 1853 the work of repair began. Curiously enough, one of the first things done was to erect a Greek temple to serve as a family mausoleum in the grounds. The great apartments were rehung with tapestries (among them the History of Joseph and the Legend of Alexander), and the picture gallery and the private theatre were restored.

Brissac has, with all its noble air, something of the assured simplicity of France before the pretentious and pompous Court of Louis XIV influenced all the architecture and style of living throughout the land. Let us walk in the park. There will be a few hunters browsing about. A swan or two on the streams. And however far we wander, we shall still meet the view of immense

Doré-like towers, ivy-clad and imposing, enclosing the great ducal dwelling of Brissac.

## *"The Aerial Telegraph"*

BRÛLON. Most visitors to Paris used to notice a strange monument standing up isolated in the middle of a spacious crossroads, where the *rue du Bac* cuts through the *boulevard Saint-Germain*. On its high stone pedestal the bronze portrayed a man in knee-breeches and ruffles, holding and pointing to a pole, on the top of which was a queer contraption looking rather like a child's kite. To-day, and since the Germans removed and melted the bronze, the green-stained stone pedestal is bare, but you can still read the name CHAPPE cut into it.

Claude Chappe, the inventor of the "Aerial Telegraph," is for us a forgotten worthy, though the French have kept his memory green, perhaps because he was a good republican and perhaps because of his rather sad end.

Claude Chappe was born at Brûlon in 1763, and was the inventor of a device widely used in France until it was superseded by the electrical telegraph. Chappe's apparatus consisted of an upright post with a transverse bar, at whose ends moved two smaller arms on pivots. The position of the armlets indicated letters. Thus, by a succession of posts, each retransmitting the message received from its predecessor, messages could be sent about 150 miles in fifteen minutes. Such an achievement was, for the end of the 18th century, a remarkable one, and Chappe was appointed by the Legislative Assembly in 1793 "National Telegraph Engineer." But his was a melancholy and despondent temperament, and he committed suicide in 1805.

The Chappes were, indeed, an active lot. After Claude's death his brothers, Ignace and Pierre, were appointed joint administrators of the French telegraphs, and held this job until 1823, when two other brothers, René and Abraham, succeeded to the position and kept it until 1830. Ignace was, moreover, the author of a *History of the Telegraph*. But by the forties the "electrical telegraph"—as our fathers called it—was coming into use, and clumsy devices, such as Chappe's "aerial telegraph," were soon relegated to museums.

The Chappe brothers had scientific traditions in the family, since an uncle, known under the dignified name of "Jean Chappe d'Auteroche," was an astronomer who travelled far and wide. He penetrated into Siberia in 1761 in order there to observe a transit of Venus. In 1769 he was venturesome enough to make his way to California (then Spanish territory), there to observe another transit of Venus, but poor "Chappe d'Auteroche" died in the Californian wilds somewhere near where Los Angeles now stands. And all this was not two hundred years ago.

Brûlon is only an overgrown village of some thirteen hundred inhabitants, but it is the largest place in its district. The houses are perched on a hog's back overlooking the valley of the Erve, and clustering round the ruins of a feudal fortress. From the nearby Pissegrêle rocks there is a charming view over the rolling, rather wild and sparsely populated countryside.

Brûlon parish church is 12th century Romanesque and the high altar is of marble and rather fine. Two miles south of Brûlon, at Chevillé, there is an 11th century church, in which may be seen a splendid 16th century processional cross.

## The Countryside near Brûlon

IF you leave Sillé-le-Guillaume by the Sablé road, you drop down into the valley of the Ruban, and then cross the dale of the Vègre. At Parennes is an early Gothic church and a pleasing Louis XV country-house.

Two or three miles farther on from Parennes you get into the wild, rocky, jumbled country known as the *pays de Charnie*, patched with woods and interspersed with heaths. Then the forest closes in. You run through the *Petite Charnie* woods, then to the right Charnie forest stretches away. A side-road leads to Neuvilette-en-Charnie, in whose early Gothic church is a tomb with a recumbent figure of a Lord of Chaources that somehow escaped mutilation or destruction at the time of the Revolution. From Neuvilette a sylvan path winds for about a mile to the ruins of the ancient Abbey of Étival, founded in 1109.

## The Duke and Duchess of Windsor

CANDÉ. From Montbazon a charming way leads down the Indre valley that for much of the year is green and fresh. The road passes the *château* du Puy d'Artigny, a rather pleasing

18th century country-house put up about 1749. A little farther on is the Ripault national powder factory. Beyond, to the right, is the *château* de Candé.

Candé is in a small *commune* that has less than eighty inhabitants. The present house was built in 1508 by François Briçonnet, and it is an agreeable little place in the gay, light style of Touraine. For some years the house was the property of Señor Drake del Castillo, from whom it was bought by a M. Bedeaux.

Bedeaux was a Frenchman who had emigrated to the United States, and had there acquired both American citizenship and a fairly large fortune. He was particularly disliked by the American labour unions, for his name was associated with a sort of "Stakhanovist" scheme for increasing production. Bedeaux seems to have been possibly in contact with the Germans in 1940-1 and certainly on good terms with the Vichy Government. He turned up in North Africa soon after the Allied landings there. In Algeria he was arrested by the American authorities for evading military service, was then transferred to the United States, and died, from an overdose of a narcotic, in Miami prison, Florida, in 1944, and while awaiting trial on a charge of intelligence with the enemy.

It was at Bedeaux' *château* de Candé that the Duke of Windsor was married to Mrs. Simpson on the 3rd June, 1937.

### The Man who made Algiers French

CANDÉ. Legend has it that Hussein, the Dey of Algiers, annoyed by some quarrel between two Algerine Jews, his subjects, and the French Government, struck in the face with a fly-flap the French consul, one Deval. To avenge this insult, the French blockaded the port of Algiers, but nothing more was done until the shore-batteries opened fire on a French vessel—the *Providence*—flying a flag of truce and making her way into Algiers harbour.

A punitive expedition was decided upon, and the *maréchal* de Bourmont, the Minister of War, took command. On the 14th June, 1830, French troops landed at a point known as Sidi-Ferrouch. On the 19th the Dey's levies were beaten at Staouéli. On the 5th July Algiers capitulated. The Dey fled to Egypt, where he was hospitably entertained by the Khedive Mohammed Ali, and shortly afterwards died in convulsions. The French discovered in the

Dey's treasury about £2,000,000 in gold and, as the total revenues of the whole State of Algeria had not exceeded £175,000 a year, it may be inferred that piracy, the staple trade of the Dey and his men, was a rather more profitable undertaking than agriculture or commerce.

Bourmont, the man to whom the French owe their North African empire, or at least the nucleus of it, was also a man whose whole career was composed of a most curious series of defections and even of treasons, from the consequences of which he seems to have suffered little if at all.

Louis-Auguste-Victor de Bourmont, *comte* de Ghaisne and *maréchal* de France, was born in 1773. He served first as a subaltern in the French Guards under Louis XVI, but he " emigrated" and then joined Condé's anti-republican army. He was excepted from the 1796 amnesty and fled to Switzerland, but having been appointed a knight of the order of Saint-Louis by the Bourbon pretender (afterwards King Louis XVIII) and given a brigade, he headed another insurrection that collapsed—as did all those against Napoleon.

Evidently thinking that for some time, at least, the Royalist cause was a lost one, Bourmont submitted to the First Consul (Bonaparte), and was allowed to return to Paris—where he married. No doubt, Bourmont's Royalist sympathies were real, and he may have been indiscreet enough to give voice to them. In any case, he was arrested and flung into jail. Somehow or other he managed to escape. It was not always very difficult for political prisoners to break out if they had resourceful and open-handed friends. Bourmont made his way to Portugal and vegetated there obscurely for about three years. When, however, the French troops occupied that country, Junot, the Commander-in-Chief, made him a divisional chief of staff. Either, then, Bourmont was a soldier of most outstanding quality, or he had something about him that made men blind to his past.

After the Convention of Cintra, Bourmont made his way back to France, where, despite his having held high rank in the Imperial armies, he was again thrown into prison. Junot, however, seems to have taken a fancy to him, for Bourmont was released at his request and posted to the staff of Eugène de Beauharnais, the Viceroy of Italy. Bourmont's conspicuous courage at Lützen in 1813 earned him again the command of a brigade, and in 1814 his splendid defence of Nogent gained him a division.

At the first Bourbon restoration Bourmount joined the King's army, though during the Hundred Days he rallied to Napoleon. But having been given a division in the Army of the North, on the first day of the Waterloo campaign Bourmont went over to the Allies. He did not, perhaps, give them much information, and it is true that his old friends the Anjou Royalists were again up in arms and he wanted to lead them. Still, it is difficult to condone his conduct and still more difficult to understand how, during a long career, he so successfully got away with what unkind critics would call treason.

Bourmont, however, belonged to the old school of Frenchmen, and he neither explained nor excused his conduct. Moreover, he acted as prosecutor during the trial of *maréchal* Ney, his old companion in arms, who was shot as a traitor in 1815. He was not so lucky as Bourmont.

Our hero, for some time in 1824, commanded the whole French army during the miserable Spanish War. He was Minister of War in 1829, and after his success in Algiers was promoted *maréchal* of France.

Bourmont would not, however, take the oath of allegiance to Louis-Philippe after the fall of Charles X in 1830. Indeed, in 1832, this Marshal of France did not hesitate to take part in the Duchess of Berry's uprising. When it collapsed, he again retired to Portugal, where he had old friends, so that when the pretender Dom Miguel engaged in civil war with the forces of his niece Queen Maria da Gloria, Bourmont, ever on the side of absolutism, took command of the rebel Portuguese army. When the Queen's cause triumphed, Bourmont fled to Rome, where he remained until the amnesty of 1840 enabled him to return to France, where he lived until his death at Bourmont *château* at the good old age of seventy-three.

Bourmont is quite near Candé, and you skirt the park walls when you follow the western road towards Brittany. The house, though burned no less than fourteen times during the Vendean war, still has a noble air. There are a forecourt, a court of honour, still another court, towers, a keep and a chapel. In the guard-room are an English standard captured by the *comte* de Ghaisne at

**Cangé**     The old Coningham Manor near Saint-Avertin

**Bellême**  The Chapel of St. Santin  **Champigny-sur-Veude**  The Bourbon
                                Chapel

**Chênehutte-les-Tuffeaux**

**Chinon**   The Vienne

**Chenonceau**   The Gallery over the Cher

**Chenonceau**   Chapel Doors

**Chemazé**

Fécamp, the sabre of the *chevalier* de Cotignon, the sabre, tea-service and fan of the ill-fated Dey of Algiers, several portraits of the *maréchal* and the blood-stained tunic of his son who was killed at Sidi-Kalé on 24th June, 1830. The last place of any size in the department of Maine-et-Loire is Freigné, on the right bank of the Erdre. Nearby are two menhirs, and the old presbytery bears the inscription TVRRIS FORTITVDNIS, or Tower of Courage—a very suitable motto for the house of an isolated country parson—with the date 1565.

## *Where the Chouans Uprising Collapsed*

CANDÉ, at the confluence of the rivers Erdre, Moiron and the two Mandies, is a tidy little place of about eighteen hundred inhabitants that was formerly a walled fortress and, as early as the 11th century, the seat of a barony. There are one or two good 16th century houses. The church is modern, and in it are some Italian statues. The nearby pilgrimage of Notre-Dame de Beaulieu has flourished since the 15th century when a shepherd noticed that one of his sheep would not move from near a tuft of grass. He dug and found a statue of the Virgin.

At Candé was signed, on the 8th January, 1800, the agreement that marked the end of the Chouan uprising led by the Cottereau brothers, whom we meet at Laval, and by the famous "Georges" (Georges Cadoudal) who spent some time, during his plotting and fighting, in England, whence he returned to France for the last time in 1803 in order to make a fresh attempt on the life of Napoleon. French writers often assume that Cadoudal was, if not an English agent, at least supplied with English money. There is nothing improbable in this. Cadoudal was executed in 1804 with eleven of his companions.

## *An Adventurous Botanist*

CANDES. On the shaded, rather damp and overhung road along the south or left bank of the Vienne, just before you come to Candes, there is a signpost pointing up a narrow, sunken lane. The signpost reads "Le Petit-Thouars." Le Petit-Thouars is only a hamlet up in the woods of Fontevrault forest, but its name is one very familiar to French ears.

Several rather eminent persons have borne the name of "Dupetit-Thouars."

It appears that their family name was Aubert, and that the "Dupetit-Thouars" was assumed, it is not quite clear why, from the hamlet near Candes.

Louis-Marie Aubert Dupetit-Thouars, botanist and traveller, was born at Saumur in 1758. His elder brother Aristide was in the Navy, and while stationed at Brest became interested in a scheme to fit out a ship to discover the traces of La Pérouse's lost expedition. Despite a gift from Louis XVI and a vote of 10,000 francs from the National Assembly, the public of those revolutionary days did not subscribe very generously, and the Dupetit-Thouars brothers sold what land they had to further the good cause. Then Aristide told Louis that the time was come to take off. They were to meet at Brest, but poor Louis, making his way to the north-west as best he could, could not help botanising by the way, and his grubbing about on all-fours with a magnifying glass by the wayside appeared so suspicious to the local republican sleuths that he ended up in jail at Quimper. By the time he managed to get out and reach Brest, Aristide had set off in command of his ship, leaving a note for Louis fixing a meeting-place at the Île de France (Mauritius). Louis found a boat. He got aboard with a few coppers in his pocket.

But when he reached Mauritius he did not find Aristide, whom, indeed, he never saw again. Aristide had had trouble (that started, apparently, by his succouring forty shipwrecked Portuguese) at the Cape Verde Islands, was arrested by the Portuguese, and thrown into prison at Lisbon. The brothers had no sort of luck with the police. Aristide did not get free until 1783, when he set sail for the United States and there spent three years. He returned to France in time to take part in the Egyptian campaign. At the Battle of the Nile he commanded *Le Tonnant* and forced *Bellerophon* to lower her flag, but when *L'Orient*, the French flagship, caught fire, *Alexander, Swiftsure* and later *Theseus* and *Leander* concentrated on *Le Tonnant*, which surrendered only after twenty-four hours' battle. Aristide Dupetit-Thouars lost an arm and both legs and died on deck.

Meanwhile Louis, his brother, spent nearly seven years in either Mauritius or Île-Bourbon, botanising and keeping himself by jobs with planters. He brought back to France in 1802 a fine collection of plants, and lived for nearly thirty years an uneventful life of a man of science.

Another Dupetit-Thouars was a nephew—Abel Aubert. He was the man who annexed Tahiti for France, and in doing so had some trouble with one Pritchard, an English missionary. Guizot, the French minister, under pressure from London, partially disavowed Dupetit-Thouars, changed the annexation into a protectorate and got an indemnity voted for the missionary. Dupetit-Thouars became so popular for the stand he had made against the English that a sum of 80,000 francs gold (£3,200 gold) was subscribed in sums of fifty centimes to present him with a sword of honour. It must be admitted that the subscription was largely a "stunt" of the opposition to annoy the Government of the day, and Dupetit-Thouars, as a serving officer and therefore as one supposed to take no part in politics, rightly refused the gift.

## Saint Martin's Summer

FROM Chinon downstream there is no bridge over the Vienne, and you must cross to the south bank at Chinon itself and then turn left. The Vienne is a wide and muddy stream here, and far from its source fed by the melting snows of the *plateau des* Millevaches in the central mountainous mass, or *massif central*, of France. The Vienne is, indeed, rather subject to flooding, and from Chinon to the confluence with the Loire the smaller river shows a sort of bank of no man's land between the waters and the neighbouring highway.

At Saint-Germain-sur-Vienne, on the left bank, is a Romanesque church with a fine vaulted roof, all in what the French call the "Plantagenet" or "Angevin" style.

At Candes there is a ferry by which you can cross to the Véron country on the right bank. The Véron is a curious pocket or tongue of land between Vienne and Loire. It is a land of cave-dwellings, of hidden manors and of isolated farms. Candes has a church dedicated to Saint Martin, and it is erected upon the spot where the holy man is said to have suffered martyrdom.

Saint Martin was one of the great legendary figures of medieval religious tradition, and he was no Frenchman or Gallo-Roman, but a native of far-off Pannonia, or as we should say to-day, of

Croatia. However, his festival or "Martinmas," his summer, the cloak that he halved with a beggar at the gates of Orleans and his sumptuous shrine at Martinopolis have perpetuated his memory and the memory of his legend. Round his shrine outside the walls of Tours grew up a twin-city to the Touraine capital, and Martinopolis was for centuries one of the great pilgrimage-centres of western Europe.

The Church of Candes that we see to-day was built, of course, long after the time of Martin's martyrdom. The building is, in fact, of the 12th, 13th and 14th centuries. As is usual in churches which were rebuilt in those periods, the old Romanesque walls remain in parts, but the general appearance of the place is that of a Gothic shrine.

The wide and spacious monument is protected by its background of hills, and by the closing-in of the heights, and has, in this damp countryside, weathered and patinated so that the exterior is not white but grey. On the north side is a splendid portico, with a central and monolithic column supporting the vaulting.

Within, Candes church is of surprising width, and the chancel is raised high above the floor of the nave. It is a frame for scenes of ecclesiastical pomp and circumstance, such as must often have been performed here in ancient times. To-day it is just a rather large and slightly neglected country church.

There are few traces of the fortifications put up, as protection against the English, in the troublous times of the Hundred Years' War. We can climb the hill behind the church and look down upon the minglings of Loire and Vienne, one of the most beautiful waters' meet in all Europe.

## Wilbur Wright

CHAMPAGNÉ. In 1908 Wilbur Wright and his brother Orville—who had made in 1903 the first successful flight of an aeroplane—went to France. On the 21st September Wilbur Wright won the Michelin prize by a flight of fifty-six miles. In December 1908 he flew seventy-seven miles in two hours and twenty minutes. Man could fly! We may date the real beginnings of aviation from that December day in 1908 when Wright took off from the *plateau* d'Auvours, six miles out from Le Mans, and near the little village of Champagné. On the Auvours upland is the monument to the man who taught men how to fly on the battle-field where, on the 11th January, 1871, was fought a disastrous battle when Chanzy was obliged to fall back before the Prussians, the battle which really marked the end of organised resistance on the part of the French. When next French and Germans were to meet on the field of battle, in 1914–18, Wilbur Wright's invention was already a factor in warfare.

It seems a long way from the queer kite-like cotton and wood contraption or "flying-machine" of the Wright brothers to the "Flying Fortresses," "Truculent Turtles" and "Dreamboats" of our day, but the revolution in men's means of transport has been effected in little more than a generation.

Champagné parish church has some good bits of 16th century stained glass, and in the churchyard is a curious recumbent statue of a vicar, one Jean Crépon, who died in 1530.

On from Champagné towards Connerré you run past two large woodland lakes and through trees. At Saint-Mars-la-Brière is a carved wooden reliquary of fine 17th century workmanship.

## The Strong Hill

NEXT is one of the many Montforts or "Strong Hills" that lie scattered about France. This hill was fortified in the 12th century by Rotrou, Count of Perche, and King Philip Augustus stormed the castle in 1190. Of the old feudal fortress nothing much re-mains, but on its site was erected in 1820 a fine country-house in the Italian style. The place belongs to the *comte* de Nicolay, and its imposing outline dominates all the valley, while the huge park embraces nearly all the Strong Hill sides.

Follow the course of the Huisne and cross it by an ancient 15th century bridge, and you pull out of the leafy dale and leave little Montfort-le-Rotrou on its hill over three hundred feet above the river. Right along as far as Connerré, the landscape is patched and fortified by thick pine woods, so characteristic of the country-side of Maine. The woods get thinner as you approach Connerré.

## The Wines of Brézé

CHAMPIGNY-SUR-VEUDE. Champigny is quite a small village, and you somehow feel in it that you are no longer in Touraine; you are indeed on the borders both of Poitou and of

Anjou. The manner of the people seems a little more open than it is in Touraine itself. But you are still in the department of the Indre-et-Loire, though the wine you will drink hereabouts will be of Anjou vintage, perhaps from the Loire's banks between Montsoreau and Saumur, say, a bottle of Parnay, or, better still, a good year of Brézé. It is strong, or rather it is not very strong, but it has such an innocent taste that one is tempted to drink quite a lot of it at a sitting. Good Brézé wine can be got at the little café as you turn off the highroad towards the *Sainte Chapelle*.

## The Bourbons of Champigny

BUT before we prepare to visit the holy chapel, we shall get some idea of the curious history of this town if we walk round to see what remains of the *château* of Champigny. The lordship had been for some considerable time in the possession of a branch of the Bourbon family, when in the 16th century a splendid palace was put up. After the Bourbons had succeeded to the throne of France, and by a series of marriages and inheritances, Champigny came into the possession of that Duke of Orleans who was the younger brother of King Louis XIII. Richelieu, who would have no great house and great magnates living near his newly founded duchy of Richelieu, forced his king's brother to exchange Champigny for other lands. He then razed Champigny *château* to the ground, leaving standing only the pages' wing, magnificently vaulted stables and a little lodging between two towers. Some idea of the scale of the Bourbons' palace may be gained when we reflect that a relatively large and quite commodious country-house is now contained in the constructions that Richelieu disdained to destroy.

## La Grande Mademoiselle

AFTER Richelieu's death, however, Champigny was back in the possession of the Duke of Orleans' daughter, the lady who is known in French history as the *Grande Mademoiselle*, the greatest and wealthiest heiress of her day.

After the part that this adventurous woman played in the uprising known as the *Fronde,* she was banished to Champigny, and there remained for several years. About 1667 she became attracted to a member of the Gontaut-Biron family, afterwards well-known as the *duc* de Lauzun.

Lauzun, who was a rather petty-minded, spiteful and self-seeking individual, was punished for his presumption in daring to make love to a princess of the Royal House (and the richest heiress in France to boot) by being shut up for ten years in the fortress-prison of Pinerola, now in Italy, but then in that part of Piedmont annexed to France. The *Grande Mademoiselle*, who was sentimentally touched by the misfortunes of her rather unworthy lover, bought Lauzun's release by the settlement of a considerable part of her vast estates upon some of Louis XIV's bastards.

In 1681 Lauzun (aged forty-nine) and the Princess (aged fifty-four) were secretly wedded, though the marriage was never recorded in the official pedigrees of the Royal House published under the monarchy. The marriage was most unsuccessful and unhappy, as are most unions long awaited and dearly bought. Lauzun proved an insolent and negligent husband. He is even reported to have sprawled in a chair and shouted to his wife to kneel down and pull off his boots. The granddaughter of the King of France thought love too hardly won and soon discarded her Lauzun, who, after his wife's death, married, when he was sixty-three, a girl of fourteen.

The *Grande Mademoiselle* bequeathed Champigny and much other property to the brother of Louis XIV, from whom it passed to the famous Regent Orleans, who sold Champigny back to the Richelieus, with whom it remained until the tempest of the Revolution swept away all the proud duchy the great Cardinal had so laboriously constructed.

## A Peculiar Treasure

THE *Sainte-Chapelle* was begun in 1508 by Louis, *prince* de la Roche-sur-Yon (that astonishing town in the Vendée entirely reconstructed, in the First Empire style, under Napoleon), and was completed by his son, Louis de Bourbon, *duc* de Montpensier.

There is no lower church or crypt at Champigny. The exterior is not very elegant, and it is moreover weighed down by a rather clumsy Italianate portal. Within, the lofty shrine is rather bare, but full of gay light and joyous colour. There are lateral chapels, with the arms of Bourbon-Montpensier and of Longwy. Here and there are most graceful scrolls, shields and elegant blazons all carved in the soft, suave, white stone. Louis de Bourbon's monument has been smashed about, but its remains are still impressive.

But the peculiar treasure of Champigny is its windows. These eleven magnificent lights are the best-preserved of any coming down to us from Renaissance times.

The windows are a little later than the chapel building, and were executed to the order of Claude de Longwy, Duke-Bishop of Langres, generally known as the *cardinal de Givry*, in about the year 1558. The Cardinal was related to the Bourbon-Montpensiers. The windows used to be attributed to the great "enameller," Robert Pinaigrier of Tours, but now there is reason to think that they are the work of René Grézil and Armoult Terrant, *maîtres peintres et vitriers* (master painters and glazers) of Chinon.

Each light consists of three parts—a scene from the life of St. Louis, King of France, a scene from the life of Christ and a scene of Old Testament prefiguration. The apse window depicts, from top to bottom, the Creation, the Crucifixion, and over all the figure of St. Louis, upright and imperial. The whole series is a blazing hymn to the praise of the French monarchy and of the God-given ruler. We should arrange to spend several hours at Champigny, the better to study and admire these superb windows. There is nothing like them in the whole of Touraine.

The contrast between the soft, white walls and the glittering, glorious freshness and jewel-like radiance of the lights is splendid. No description can do justice to these treasures.

## Holy Chapels

HOLY Chapels—of which there are a number scattered about France, the most renowned being that of Paris, built by St. Louis himself as a shrine for the Crown of Thorns—were foundations exempt from all episcopal authority and subject only to the Holy See. Pope Urban VIII, as patron and master of Champigny, gave express orders that it should be respected when Richelieu, in his rage at anything near his Duchy recalling greater glories than his own, would have had the *Sainte-Chapelle* of Champigny-sur-Veude razed with its neighbouring *château*.

## Bluebeard's Castle

CHAMPTOCÉ. The region and lordship of Retz or Rais (pronounced Ress), in southern Brittany, gave its name to a number of families, and the title (for it is really a title and not a patronymic) was borne by at least two men of very differing fame and fortune. There was the Cardinal de Retz, a 17th century worthy descended from one of those Italian adventurers who swooped into France in the train of the Florentine queen, Catherine de' Medici. Retz was a diplomatist, an intriguing courtier, a witty man of the world and the author of entertaining and valuable *Memoirs* written with great verve and insight.

The other famous Retz was Gilles de Laval, Lord of Retz, *maréchal* of France, companion in arms of Joan of Arc, and also the infamous debauchee whose crimes led to his being strangled and burned at Nantes and to his legend being perpetuated as the story of Bluebeard.

The fine ruins of the feudal castle you see above Champtocé are the remains of one of Bluebeard's castles. There is another at Tiffauges opposite Torfou on the Sèvre Nantaise almost into Poitou.

If you are going downstream from Serrant, you pass through Saint-Georges-sur-Loire (where little is to be seen of the old abbey that was a rich and famous foundation during the Middle Ages), then, five miles farther on, begins at Champtocé the so-called *boire,* that is a broad surface of navigable water some three miles long. It merges into the Loire before Ingrandes, that is the ancient and traditional frontier of Brittany.

## *A Bone of Contention*

CHAMPTOCEAUX. The domains of the old Counts and Dukes of Anjou extended a good deal farther west along the southern banks of the Loire than along the northern. Champtoceaux looks across the river to lands which have always been part of Brittany, while the town itself, on a high wooded hill overhanging the Loire was, for generations, a bone of contention between the rulers of Brittany and those of Anjou.

Champtoceaux is traversed by a little main street running along the crest of the hill and up to the site of the ancient stronghold. An old barbican leads into a large park, in which is situated a modern *château* surrounded by ruins of the medieval fortified town that was known as Châteauceau. In olden days this castle was almost impregnable.

It was hither that in 1424 Marguerite, the daughter of the *connétable* de Clisson, lured the Duke of Brittany, John V, and kept him several months prisoner as revenge for the attempted murder of her father. In the fighting which followed this kidnapping, Champtoceaux town and castle were razed to the ground. The Loire at Champtoceaux is dotted with tufted islands and looks more like a chain of meres or lagoons than a great river, but the countryside is more often grey and serene with a lateral spaciousness that is typical of the *Val de Loire*.

If you are going downstream from Saint-Florent-le-Vieil, on the south bank of the Loire, just after Bouzillé is the *château* de La Mauvoisinière, a 17th century house attributed to the famous architect Mansart. Two and a half miles farther on is Liré, where lived, at one time, Joachim du Bellay, the poet of the *Pléïade*.

Champtoceaux and Liré, each perched on its hill and each overlooking the Loire, bound Anjou to the west. There used to be a statue of Joachim du Bellay at Ancenis, in the Breton land. During the 1939–45 war the monument was taken down and hidden. At the end of the war the statue was thought to have been lost or sent to the melting-pot by the Germans, so another statue was ordered, which was in August 1947 erected at Liré in Anjou. The pedestal bears the well-known quotation from the *Regrets*:

> *"Plus mon Loyre gaulois que le Tybre latin,*
> *Plus mon petit Lyré que le mont Palatin,*
> *Et plus que l'air marin la doulceur angevine."*

> *("More my Gaulish Loire than the Latin Tiber,*
> *More my little Liré than the Palatine Mount,*
> *And more than the sea-air the sweetness of Anjou.")*

In the meantime, the first statue turned up again, so perhaps now Joachim du Bellay will have two monuments who for so long had none but his writings. La Turmelière, where Bellay passed his childhood, now lies ruined in its park. La Varenne is the last Angevin town: Brittany lies beyond.

### Choiseul's Pagoda

CHANTELOUP. If you leave Amboise by the Bléré road, you can turn off about two miles from the former town towards Saint-Martin-le-Beau, and, at the end of an avenue, you are confronted with a most curious folly. Such things are fairly common

74

with us, but rare in France. This pagoda is all that remains of the estate of Chanteloup, where the *duc* de Choiseul, once powerful minister of Louis XV, lived in gilded exile after his fall and until 1774.

Choiseul, who was a member of an ancient and widely spread family originally from the province of Champagne, set his first step upon the ladder of promotion by marrying the rich daughter of the financier Crozat. Choiseul was a most indifferent husband, and Horace Walpole, who disliked him much, wrote that "gallantry without delicacy was his constant pursuit." Madame de Choiseul was, however, a loyal and devoted wife. When Choiseul died in 1785, riddled with debt, she spent the rest of her life in retirement in order that she might be able to pay off at least some of his creditors.

Choiseul owed his political career to Madame de Pompadour, with whom he formed what has been called an "offensive and defensive alliance," while the royal favourite is stated to have received from Choiseul *d'autres soins que ceux de la reconnaissance*. Choiseul was from 1758 to 1770 the moulder of French policy. Although the long-term results of Choiseul's administration were such as to accelerate the Revolution, his short-term policy was not unwisely conceived nor unskilfully conducted. Madame de Pompadour backed Choiseul's main plans—the "Family Compact," the alliance with Spain and . . . the suppression of the Jesuits.

If Choiseul had owed his great fortune to one woman, it was another woman who encompassed his disgrace. Madame du Barry supported the cabal which ruined Choiseul for ever.

He had to retire to Chanteloup, where he lived in great state on a relatively small fortune. Chanteloup was for four years the scene of parties, fêtes and festivities, while the fallen politician endeavoured, in the "philosophical" manner approved by the wits of the day, to weave his friendship's garlands, and give the world an edifying picture of the patriot statesman who had risen superior to his undeserved misfortunes. Such posing did not, of course, prevent Choiseul from rushing off to Paris as soon as he could and there badgering the new King Louis XIV for a job.

Of Chanteloup House itself, nothing survived the destruction of the Revolution but two small pavilions not far from the pagoda.

The folly rises beside a large lake choked with bushes and just on the edge of Amboise forest. The pagoda, which was built by Le Camus with stones from the old *château* de La Bourdaisière (where Gabrielle d'Estrées was born), was designed as a tribute to those friends and cronies who had visited and comforted Choiseul during his four years' exile.

The pagoda contains six storeys, each one consisting of a round, domed chamber, smaller in dimensions than the one below it. Four of the storeys are encircled with balconies alternately rounded and octagonal, whose balustrades are marvels of wrought-iron work. The third and fifth storeys, which have no balconies, are surrounded with a decorative frieze of sculptured laurel-leaves.

Above the ground-floor windows are slabs of black marble, upon which are engraved, alternately, two Chinese characters signifying "Gratitude" and "Fraternity."

The wrought-iron banisters of the interior are very fine. The eight windows of the third floor are arranged as a compass. From the platform on the summit is a splendid view over a sea of forests of Châteaurenault, Amboise and Blois. There is Amboise, a great stretch of the Loire and then Tours. To the north-west, the Sudaie woods, and to the east, adjoining Amboise, the Forest of Montrichard.

## *The Squire's Freehold*

L A CHAPELLE-RAINSOUIN. Furnishings of old feudal France are so rare that the Church of La Chapelle-Rainsouin should not be missed by any visitor to the eastern parts of Maine. Under the *ancien régime,* the local lords of the manor had the right to display in their churches what was called a *litre* (a word which has nothing to do with the common term for a measure of liquid) or *listre,* that is, a broad band of black paint running round the nave above the arches. On this black background were emblazoned the hatchments or coats-of-arms of the fief's lords. The higher upon the walls was the litre, the greater was the nobiliary pretension of the lords.

Of course, all such "relics of feudalism" were scraped and effaced at the Revolution. Few have been reconstituted. We may be pretty sure that any (even ancient-seeming) coats-of-arms, coronets and supporters displayed on French buildings have been "reconstituted" during the 19th century. Such things have long ceased to arouse any sort of antagonism among the people, and in the fine fever of pseudo-medievalism and "Strawberry Hill Gothick" which throbbed in France as well as in England during the last century, much "reconstitution" was achieved. But at La Chapelle-Rainsouin, the general effect is rather convincing. The place has the air (common enough with us but rare in France) of being primarily the shrine for the local bigwigs, and then, secondarily, the place of worship for the common man and woman.

The *litre* is in the choir. The north chapel, opening on the nave by three arcades, contains two superb tombs, that of Olivier de La Chapelle (*d.* 1508) and that of his wife Arthuse de Melun (*d.* 1526). It is interesting to note the change in architectural and artistic fashion that took place in the eighteen years between the deaths of the husband and wife. Arthuse's effigy is enclosed in a Renaissance niche adorned with pilasters and figures of six mourning women or *pleureuses*. Both tombs were sculptured by Gervais Duval, who was also the author of the statue of Saint-Julien de Brioude, which may be seen to the right of the altar. To the left of this 15th century altar is a charming statue of Saint-Barbara. The south-side chapel displays a little painted and gilded wood reredos of 17th century workmanship. A postern at the right of the main altar leads into the Chapel of the Holy Sepulchre, a late Gothic shrine built around an Entombment of eight figures executed to the orders of Arthuse de Melun.

This Romanesque Church of La Chapelle was almost rebuilt in the 15th century, but its recent restoration has been tactfully carried out. The not unpleasing stained glass is by Alleaume of Laval, a noted 19th century glazier.

## The Paintings of Poncé

LA CHARTRE - SUR - LE - LOIR. Mural paintings, one of the peculiar glories of French Romanesque art, are by no means scattered evenly all over the country. Many, of course, must have disappeared without leaving any trace. First, among the regions rich in these wall-pictures, comes the valley of the Loir with that of the Loire's middle course, while Poitou has preserved the greatest number of painted churches. Elsewhere the pictures are more rare, though there are enough in Burgundy, Berry, Marche, Limousin and elsewhere to attract all interested in one of the most powerful and impressive of medieval arts.

We may take it that, in some measure at least, the painted sanctuaries of the north are the humbler counterparts of the mosaic-clad shrines of the Byzantine tradition. When, in the new Gothic architecture, window space was increased and the art and craft of stained glass developed, mural painting shrank, although great representations of St. Christopher, of the Last Judgment and of the Tree of Jesse continued, almost until modern times, to illuminate the churches and chapels of western Europe.

Comparatively few of the churches of Romanesque times seem to have been entirely painted, but among them were the shrines of Saint-Savin-sur-Gartempe in Poitou, of Saint-Hilaire at Poitiers, and of Poncé in the Sarthe department.

Between Pont-de-Braye and La Chartre-sur-Loir, the highroad runs through Poncé, whose church is still entirely covered, within, with painted scenes.

The Romanesque paintings of Poncé are not, perhaps, among the finest of those in which France is so much richer than any other European country; but the impressive, exciting and evocatory effect produced by this country church, all decorated like a Book of Hours, is not to be missed. The scenes adorning the choir have been restored and retouched, as will be seen at a glance, but the general effect is that of a splendid sanctuary eight hundred years old.

When we look at the bold, majestic, but rather heavy and chilly buildings of our Romanesque (or "Norman") style, we should remember that some of their walls once glowed with colour, for if our Norman conquerors brought with them no tradition of sculptured interiors (save for capitals), they did bring with them a tradition of colour and of the sober sumptuousness of glowing, vivid walls.

## The Cavaignacs

THE cemeteries, with the possible exception of *Père-Lachaise*, are rarely explored by the visitor to Paris, yet each one of them contains some inscription to move us, some monument for us to admire and much matter for meditation. In the Montmartre cemetery, whose walls and greenery you may see northwards from some of the side-streets off the *boulevard* de Clichy, is a most noble tomb. It is simple—just a block of stone, upon which lies shrouded the body of a man moulded in bronze. The bearded head bears an expression of great majesty and pathos. This masterpiece was the work of the sculptor Rude, a Burgundian from Dijon, a town full of fine medieval carving. Rude, whose "Marseillaise" group on the walls of the *Arc de Triomphe* in Paris is perhaps his most spectacular work, may be held to have been the greatest French sculptor of his time.

The tomb in the Montmartre cemetery commemorates a man well known in his day—Godefroy Cavaignac.

La Chartre-sur-Loir, though a place of no especial interest, is prettily situated at a site where the river breaks into three arms, and as the local Jasnières wine is excellent, La Chartre is a good place for a pull-up before we move farther downstream into the classical country of the fine Loir vintages.

Down the river from Port-Gautier the highway is squeezed between stream and high cliff. If you go a little way up the vale of the Dinan (which here falls into the Loir), you will get to the *château* d'Ourne, whither, after Louis-Napoleon's *coup d'état* in 1852, General Cavaignac retired to die.

The history of three generations of Cavaignacs is a curious one. Their original home was in the south, the part of France which has supplied so many politicians and agitators. Traditionally, and thus like China but unlike most European countries, it is the south and not the north of France which is nonconformist. Grandfather Cavaignac was a revolutionary and a "regicide" (i.e. one who had voted for the execution of Louis XVI, and, as such, excluded from the amnesties). Cavaignac, after filling various minor posts under the Empire, had to flee at the Restoration and ended his days in Brussels.

His eldest son, an even more doctrinaire republican than his father, was one of the founders of the still flourishing "League of the Rights of Man." This Godefroy Cavaignac is now remembered only for his splendid tomb.

Grandfather Cavaignac's brother was a soldier who lived through all the régimes France endured, from the old Monarchy to the Second Empire. This military Cavaignac was not quite so revolutionary as his brother and nephew. He ended up as *"vicomte* de Cavaignac" and inspector-general of French cavalry.

Grandfather Cavaignac's second son became a soldier, as was his uncle, the noble *vicomte*. This younger General Cavaignac also professed dyed-in-the-wool republicanism. Most of his military career was run in Algeria, but under the Second Republic he was appointed Minister of War; moreover, during the June insurrection against the provisional government, Cavaignac was virtual dictator. Like so many men of "advanced" views, when he grasped the reality of power Cavaignac showed himself a pretty ruthless fellow. He crushed the insurgents (men not any more "advanced" than had been the cronies and pals of his old father the "regicide") in some of the bloodiest street-fighting Paris has ever witnessed, and that is saying much.

Cavaignac was a candidate for the post of President of the Republic; he was, however, overwhelmingly beaten by Louis-Napoleon, who had him arrested at the time of the *coup d'état*. He was, nevertheless, soon released, and was allowed to retire with a young wife to his *château* d'Ourne, where he survived only five years.

Now, this Cavaignac's son, grandson Cavaignac as we may call him, was the Minister of War who read to the French Chamber in 1898 the famous forged document incriminating the unfortunate Captain Dreyfus of the notorious "Dreyfus Case." Grandson Cavaignac was a man of character, since, although he had later to admit that he had been fooled by a faked letter, he sturdily maintained that Dreyfus was guilty. In fact, grandson Cavaignac was an ultra-nationalist, what, perhaps, we might to-day call a "Fascist" —but, whatever label we give him, he remains a son of the factious south.

## Secret History

CHÂTEAU-DU-LOIR. On the way from Bueil to Château-du-Loir, and just near a hamlet called Dissay-sous-Courcillon, you pass the ruins of Courcillon manor, where was born, in 1638, Philippe, *marquis* Dangeau, whose famous *Journal* is one of the most valuable contemporary documents which we possess on the doings at the Court of Louis XIV.

At Château-du-Loir was born in 1755 one Pierre Cuillier who

Bird's eye view of the *Château*

The old Tower

The Interior of the Long Gallery

**CHENONCEAU**

**Chinon**     The View from the Boissy Tower    Chimneys in the *Grand-Logis*

Hillside of the Cher Valley     **Chanteloup**     Pagoda

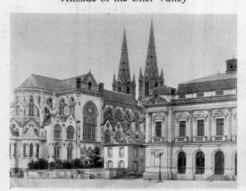

**Cholet**    19th century Church of Notre-Dame    **Chênehutte-les-Tuffeaux**

called himself Perrin. In 1780 Perrin shipped to India as a sailor and promptly jumped his ship on the Malabar coast and enlisted in the Rana of Gohao's corps under the command of a Scotsman named Sangster. By 1790 Perrin was in command of Boigne's 2nd brigade in the army which had made the Mahratta sovereign master of Hindustan. Perrin in 1796 succeeded Boigne (who had returned to France with a fortune of nearly half a million sterling) as commander-in-chief of Sindhia's army, but in 1803 Perrin deserted Sindhia and fled to the British camp. Shortly afterwards Perrin also retired to France with a large fortune and died in 1834, having outlived his old chief the *comte* de Boigne by four years.

Château-du-Loir is only three miles, or so, from Dissay, and it is a town of some size, with nearly five thousand inhabitants. As a show-place, Château-du-Loir has not much to recommend it, but it does offer one advantage—that of possessing one of the best hostelries in this part of the country. If you have a car and want to explore all the picturesque and charming region on the borders of Touraine and Anjou, you might do worse than make your head-quarters at Château-du-Loir, for you will be sure of always finding good fare, and the appetising and satisfying wines of the Loir, when you get home in the evening, surfeited, perhaps, with visions and images but rather jaded and hungry.

There is one place in this neighbourhood which we have not noted, and that is Vaas, a large village on the right bank of the Loir. Vaas is, it would seem, the ancient Gallo-Roman VEDACIUM. In the Middle Ages its Premonstratensian abbey was famed. The conventual buildings, properly speaking (they are mostly of 17th century date) have been cut up into dwelling-houses and turned into a factory, but the Gothic church is very splendid.

## A River Trip

CHÂTEAU-GONTIER. By boat you can drop down the river Mayenne from Laval, and a very pleasant trip it makes. Beyond the Bridge of Avénières, the Mayenne squeezes through a narrow valley, whose rude cliffs of dark schist are patched with broom and chestnuts and oaks. It is, for most of the way down to Château-Gontier, a fresh and picturesque scene you have unfolded before you. The landscape is even, at times, imposing, though everything is on rather a small scale.

Until you get to Château-Gontier, the country is sparsely populated. There are not many villages—or, at least, you do not see many from the river. About eight miles from Laval is the Trappist monastery of Port-du-Salut, where is made the famous and honeycombed cheese known as "Port-Salut." Of course, not all the "Port-Salut" comes from this abbey, but it is still made by the monks, and must be accounted one of the first-class cheeses of France. "Port-Salut" comes half-way between the soft cheeses, such as "Brie" and "Camembert," and the really hard cheeses, such as "Roquefort" or " Gruyère." "Port-Salut" may be especially recommended to those who are going picnicking, for it keeps well, and is a sure standby if you have to travel light.

After Origné the Mayenne twirls into a very sharp elbow, and then, just after the La Valette bridge, you can see, picturesquely perched up on its terrace set with ancient lime trees, the outline of La Rougère house.

Château-Gontier itself is about nine miles downstream, where the river flows through a narrow but verdant and fertile dale. The town, which lies on both banks of the Mayenne, grew up around a fortress founded by Fulk Nerra and a Benedictine Priory that was a daughter-house of St. Aubin's abbey at Angers, for this southern part of the Mayenne department is, historically, part of Anjou and not of Maine.

That portion of the town lying on the left bank is largely modern, with airy avenues. Trinity church (formerly an Ursuline chapel) has a notable vaulted choir. The *Hôtel-Dieu* Saint-Julien, though an ancient foundation, was entirely rebuilt in 1879.

The old town on the right bank climbs up the steep slopes of the hill, its summit crowned with the Church of Saint-Jean. The main street or *grande-rue,* as well as some of the side-streets, shows several ancient houses with columns and medallions.

The oldest parts of St. John's church date from the earlier part of the 11th century, and the edifice still has the appearance of a Romanesque building. But, unfortunately, the whole place was most injudiciously "restored" in the eighteen hundreds. The red stone of the central tower's base is ancient, but the superstructure is modern.

As it is, the crypt is the most noteworthy part of the church. This subterranean sanctuary looks very antique and primitive, with its ten squat columns bearing cube-shaped capitals. Within is the shrine of *Notre-Dame-sous-Terre*. One is reminded of the cave-temples and sanctuaries that were the earliest theatres of men's magic and religion.

North of the church is the priory (rebuilt about 1680), whose wings enclose a charming terraced garden overlooking the river. The town is rather quiet and comes to life only on market days. The peasants and the customers no longer wear their long blue blouses. The men of the Château-Gontier countryside have gone all American and favour "plus-fours" and pipes.

About a thousand yards to the north-west of the town lies Bazouges, whose 15th century church contains the tomb of one Gishwal, who died in 876. About the same distance to the south-east is Azé, in whose church are some rather fine statues removed from the nearby convent of Le Buron, now in ruins. (See p. 88.)

We can continue our river trip from Château-Gontier right down to Angers. We may take on board with us some of the gastronomical specialities of the former town, notably game-pasties, and a few of the delicious cakes known as *croquettes à l'anis*.

Although the journey downstream will not reveal much of first-rate interest, we get a good idea of the countryside, and there is always something to attract attention—churches, old castle ruins, country-houses, little manors and bright villages.

The stream is wide and its banks delightfully varied. Wooded slopes alternate with lush meadows. This is the *Craonnais* or old fief of the lords of Craon. It is an old-world region and we should get off the highroad to see this land aright. The fields of wheat waving, the fragrant expanses of clover, and then the mole-catcher at work, and a boy swinging his switch while he gazes at his cattle. But here, as everywhere else in France, the peasant is growing less wheat, there is much less money in it than in leys and pasture. On Palm Sunday all the country-people look at the vane on the church-steeple, for the wind will blow for most of the year from the quarter marked by the weather-cock during the Procession of the Palms. South and west winds bring rain and are therefore good for the meadows and bad for wheat, barley and oats; the north and east winds announce dry weather, good for cereals and bad for grass.

After Le Ménil the river takes a great bend, and to your right is the fine Louis XIV *château* of Magnanne. Seven miles down-stream you see La Haute-Roche house, on its rocky crag high above the waters. Then the river widens, the hills sink, and your eye can range far and wide over the countryside. At Montreuil-sur-Maine you pass beneath a grotto, with a miraculous image of the Virgin.

Below the Grez-Neuville bridge the right bank is bordered with abrupt cliffs scooped by quarries or smothered in greenery, for hereabouts is excavated marble and good freestone.

After Juigné the river turns sharply to the east, then, when you are past Épinard bridge, the Mayenne splits into two arms: the Old Maine, on the left, falls into the Sarthe, while the main branch of the river joins the Sarthe at Port-Mesley, to form the Maine, on whose banks stands Black Angers.

## *The Little Violet*

CHÂTEAU-LA-VALLIÈRE. Madame de Sévigné, who, with all her exaggerated maternal love for her daughter, was a rather unsentimental woman of the world, called Mademoiselle de La Vallière—

> *"une petite violette qui se cachait sous l'herbe et qui était honteuse d'être maîtresse, d'être mère, d'être duchesse."*

> (*"A little violet hiding in the grass and ashamed to be mistress, mother and duchess."*)

But, despite the retiring disposition of Mademoiselle de La Vallière, we seem to know her better than any of Louis XIV's other loves. Hers is a living memory. The fact is that she was not a complicated woman either by nature or by art.

Louise Françoise de La Baume Le Blanc was the daughter of one Laurent de La Baume Le Blanc, who took the designation of "La Vallière" from a small property he owned near Amboise. She was only seven years old when her father died and her mother married again and joined the Court of the King's uncle, Gaston of Orléans, at Blois. Later, Louise Françoise, through the influence of a distant cousin, was appointed maid of honour to Henrietta of England, who had just married Philip of Orléans, the King's brother.

The royal Court was in those days (before the removal to Versailles) held at Fontainebleau, and Louise had not been two months in residence before she became the King's mistress.

There can be no doubt that on Louise's side her affection for the King amounted to a real passion, while Louis himself was, it would seem, very much attached to her.

The pen-portraits of her are just what we should expect from her paintings. She was very fair. She was sentimental and modest in her demeanour. She remained to the end of her days slightly provincial. She lacked the sprightliness so admired in the *grand siècle*. Men—and women of course—held that she had *peu d'esprit*—that she was not very intelligent—but she was fond of reading, and was, indeed, as are so many not very bright people, serious-minded and inclined to self-improvement. All agree that she was very beautiful in a rather unvivacious way, that she had an adorable voice and that even her slight limp added to her charms.

Louise was quite devoid of any political ambition. She sought to exercise no influence on the affairs of the country, and the only enemies she made were from among those who either envied her position as the King's mistress or hated her for her very disinterestedness.

For long, the most elaborate precautions were taken to hide the *liaison* from public gaze. Of the four children she had by the King, only one, "Mademoiselle de Blois," lived to make any mark. She was the famous "Conti la Belle" we meet at Montmirail and whom the Sultan of Morocco wanted to add to his harem. (See p. 228.)

The King's devotion to Louise faded fairly quickly. She was superseded by the intriguing, strong-minded Madame de Montespan, who regarded Louise as an insignificant woman from the ranks of the lesser country gentry. There was always in the trying relations between the two women, when they were forced to live together, a little feeling of inferiority on the part of Louise.

The final rupture with Louis was marked by the famous epistle in verse sent him by Louise. The poem was, of course, not written by her, but by a poet of the day, possibly Benserade. The lines began:

*"Vous m'aimiez autrefois et vous ne m'aimez plus"*

*("You loved me once and you love me no longer . . .")*

Although her place had been taken by Madame de Montespan in 1667, it was not until 1674 that Louise was allowed to retire to the Carmelite Convent in the *rue de l'Enfer* in Paris. In 1675 she took her vows as a nun, and remained in her convent until her death thirty-five years later.

The letters patent by which the King created Louise a *duchesse* in 1667 is such a curious document that it is worth quoting in translation:

> *"We have thought by this Act not to be able better to express publicly the very especial esteem in which we hold Our very worthy, well-loved and very loyal Louise Françoise de La Vallière than by conferring upon her the highest titles of honour which a very peculiar affection aroused in Our heart by an infinite number of rare perfections has inspired Us in her favour for some years past and although her modesty has often opposed the desire which We had to raise her before this to a rank appropriate to Our esteem and to her good qualities nevertheless the affection in which We hold her does not permit Us any longer to defer giving proof of Our gratitude for merits well known to Us nor to refuse any longer to Nature the effects of Our tenderness for Marie-Anne Our natural daughter in the person of her mother We have acquired for her with Our own monies the estate of Vaujours in Touraine and the barony of Saint-Christophe in Anjou two domains considerable for their revenues and for the number of their dependencies for these reasons and for other considerations known to Us and having made communication of the whole to a Prince of Our Blood and to notable personages of Our Council and by their advice We raise the aforesaid lands to the rank of a duchy-peerage to be enjoyed by the aforesaid damsel Louise-Françoise de La Vallière and after her death by Our beloved daughter her heirs and descendants both male and female born in wedlock."*

## The Duchy of a Royal Mistress

CHÂTEAU-LA-VALLIÈRE, for a place with such a romantic-sounding name, is rather disappointing. The town was originally called Chasteaux until Louise's family territorial name was foisted on to it. There is a rather fine portrait of the royal favourite in the hospice founded by her, but she never lived at La Vallière, and the *Grand'Maison* or old ducal residence (now generally called the *château de La Roussière*) is not of any great interest. The house was rebuilt in the 18th century, but its surrounding park is beautiful.

The village, of some fourteen hundred inhabitants, spreads up the slopes of the hills overlooking the Fare stream which, as far as Vaujours, that is for nearly three miles, forms the picturesque mere of Château-La-Vallière or the Valjoyeux lake which is screened by woods and is full of fish. Château-La-Vallière church is modern, but contains one or two monuments and pictures from an older building. Three miles to the west of Château-La-Vallière is the 15th century castle of Marcilly-sur-Maulne, which has an interior of great magnificence. The saloons are adorned with fine ceilings and are full of excellent furniture. The place can be visited.

Château-La-Vallière forest, covering about 7,500 acres, comes up to the outskirts of the town. The woods are full of charming walks, and screen the picturesque ruins of Vaujours castle. The forest is inhabited by a curious population of charcoal-burners, who, in booths and huts, live their own traditional life.

On the way to Le Lude, and some nine miles from Château-La-Vallière, is the grotto or cave where, according to tradition, Jean de Daillon, the builder of Le Lude castle, took refuge for seven years (from 1461 to 1468) while he was being hunted by the police of King Louis XI (see p. 191).

South from Château-La-Vallière, on the Tours highway, you pass the *château* de La Motte-Sonzay, part of which is 12th century, and then you are soon running over a charming plateau, lightly wooded and enlivened here and there with little lakes, pools and meres surrounded with beeches, birches, chestnuts and oaks, making up the gay and sunny forest of the Touraine Gâtine. After La Membrolle you are back into the Loire valley.

## *A Restorer of Religious Peace*

CHÂTEAUNEUF-SUR-SARTHE. Châteauneuf is an overgrown village on the right bank of the Sarthe River. However, the Romanesque and early Gothic church should be visited in order to admire the daring, soaring vaulting of the roofs.

In A.D. 866 at Brissarthe, some three miles to the north-east of

Châteauneuf, Robert the Strong, Count of Anjou, was slain in combat against the Norman raiders. The fine bronze statue in the Town Hall Square of Châteauneuf is by David d'Angers, and represents the Frankish champion against the barbarous Normans, whose descendants were so soon to establish the best-governed, most orderly and powerful of all the principalities in the realm of the Franks.

On the Château-Gontier road from Châteauneuf you pass Daon, on the left bank of the Mayenne. The place is worth a thought, since here was born in 1762 Etienne Bernier, who was to become an ecclesiastic, not only adorned with the virtues appropriate to his profession, but also was to develop into a diplomatist famous in his day and time. Bernier it was who used his influence and his abilities to pacify the Vendée, put an end to the dreadful fratricidal strife which had raged so long, and to a certain extent to conciliate Republican and Royalist in the west country of France. As a matter of fact, dissensions between upholders of the old order and of the new paled and faded before the rising sun of Napoleon. Bernier put his services at the disposal of the new master, and was the principal negotiator of the concordat between the French and Papal Governments. Bernier was elected Bishop of Orléans and died in 1806.

Near Daon are several picturesque manors and country-houses —Escoublère, with its deep moat and barbican, and slender, pointed towers, is especially romantic-looking.

The road gets very attractive as you dip down to and then rise up from several tributaries of the Mayenne. At Azé are the ruins of an ancient convent, whence were removed two rather good statues now in the parish church. One is of Saint Anthony of Padua and the other of Saint Francis of Assisi.

## Cakes and Hides

CHÂTEAURENAULT. France is a country of local food specialities. Often you come across a village or town whose local patriotism seems to be concentrated in some gastronomical delicacy which, you will be told, may be imitated but cannot possibly be rivalled elsewhere.

Often there is a good deal of ballyhoo and propaganda devoted to these specialities. On the other hand, often they are incomparable in the region of their origin. Never does nougat taste as good as at Montélimar. No, not even the nougat we have just bought at Montélimar and suck stickily in the car.

Still, Châteaurenault's fame for generations past has been as much based upon its excellent cakes as upon its excellent leather. For the town is a tannery. Indeed, walking down the High Street you get the impression that there are as many tanneries as houses. Of the town's four thousand inhabitants very many are tanners or leather-workers. There still flourishes at Châteaurenault a good, old tradition of individual workmanship and splendid quality.

Châteaurenault is ancient and a fortress was set up here as long ago as 981. A good deal of the old castle has survived. The 14th century barbican and a round keep make a brave show.

## A Sumptuous Prelate

CHEMAZÉ. From the 12th century there was at Chemazé a chapel dedicated to Saint-Odon or Saint-Ouen. It was a dependency of La Roë abbey, near Craon, and this Roë abbey of Augustinian canons was established by no less a personage than the famed Robert d'Arbrissel himself, the founder of Fontevrault.

In 1493 the Abbot of La Roë was Guy Leclerc de Goulaine, of the noted Angevin family. He decided to transform the little manor at Saint-Ouen that was used as a lodging by the monks serving the chapel. And Leclerc also added on to the humble old house a building which is one of the most beautiful, of its style, in all the province of Maine. This later Gothic lodging is notable for the exceptional quality of the sculpture, the richness and sure taste of the decoration, the careful construction, and the metropolitan assurance surprising in a house set in the wilds of the country.

And this building must have cost a great deal of money, much more than the Abbey of La Roë could afford or that Leclerc could have paid out of his patrimony. But Guy was the almoner and trusted friend of Anne of Brittany, twice Queen of France as the consort successively of Kings Charles VIII and Louis XII. Anne was not a beautiful woman. She was married solely for her political importance as the heiress of the Duchy of Brittany. Nor was she a woman of any great intelligence. But she was endowed with a strong character and what one is tempted to call a truly Celtic vindictiveness and taste for revenge. On the other hand, she was true to those who were her faithful servants, and she surrounded herself almost exclusively with Bretons whom she felt she could trust amid the sombre intrigues of the Valois Court. But she made an exception in the case of Guy Leclerc, who, although an Angevin, was protected by her until her death. The lucrative and profitable jobs held by Guy over and above his abbey provided the funds for his splendid building. Guy had the advantage of being a man who knew what he was doing. He was no ecclesiastical *parvenu*, but an abbot who recognised what good living and fine housing were. He had a status beyond and in some degree above his standing. Men so situated are sometimes intelligent enough to be able to use their advantages. Leclerc did not, in all probability, carry out all his schemes at Chemazé, for the Queen died in 1514, when a great part of his income dried up. In 1515 he was collated to the see of Léon in Brittany, but did not much reside in his diocese. He returned to Chemazé, there to die in 1523.

We can understand his preference for the lordly lodging he had made for himself. We can also understand the embarrassment of the Saint-Ouen monks after his death.

Chemazé, as we see it to-day, consists of the sombre little old manor and the chapel, joined by the magnificent lodging of Guy Leclerc. Leclerc first of all put up a rectangular building of two storeys and a staircase housed in an octagonal turret whose pinnacled roof is crowned with a lead eagle with outstretched wings. The same heraldic eagle could be seen in the Leclerc de Goulaine arms inside the lodging.

In 1505 Guy added to this new house an advanced pavilion of the most gorgeous Flamboyant Gothic style, containing a winding staircase of splendid design. The main saloon is impressive, especially for its vaulting. Upstairs is the abbot's bedroom with a trapdoor leading to secret treasure-chambers. Chemazé has delightful Renaissance details and windows and carving, though, within, you have the general impression of being inside a sumptuous Gothic sanctuary.

Leclerc's building was a white elephant to his successors. The next abbot lived there, but, after him, the rulers of La Roë had neither the means nor the training or upbringing necessary to make life at Chemazé agreeable. From the latter part of the 16th century the monks put their bailiff into the house, though the Abbot of La Roë reserved for himself the use of the vaulted chamber. In the 18th century Chemazé was let and sank to the condition of a farm-house.

## Four Yoke of Oxen for a Palace

IN 1791 the property was put up for auction as the confiscated property of a religious Order. It was bought for, it is said, four yoke of oxen, by one Julien Chevrollier, a local timber-merchant in a small way.

Chevrollier, as it happened, was a man of some taste, and he took care of the place, although, of course, he defaced the Leclerc coats-of-arms with the pastoral staffs surmounting them. He also carefully chipped off the fleurs-de-lys from the pillars. But Chevrollier, who was such an ardent Republican in 1791, was by 1804 an equally ardent supporter of the Empire. Such a political and social evolution was common enough. The peasants who had become middle-class through the Revolution saw in the Empire an insurance against their losing their new status. The common French proverb runs that all the old middle-class fortunes of France were founded by the activities of an ancestor who either speculated in "national property" (i.e. confiscated lands) at the Revolution, or waged war under Napoleon. Some adventurous spirits were both profiteers during the Revolution and the favourites of Fortune with Napoleon.

## From Clogs to Clogs in Three Generations

CHEVROLLIER died peacefully at Chemazé in 1828, leaving the property to his son, a notary at Château-Gontier. This man lived a little at Leclerc's manor, and turned the chapel into a stable, ruining for ever the fine Gothic windows. Finally, the wretched scrivener, haunted by the nightmare of ruin, hanged himself under the lordly roof of the Queen's confessor. Camille Chevrollier, the son, dissipated what remained of the newly won family fortunes. From clogs to clogs in three generations.

Chemazé was later on sold to Monsieur de Sèze, the descendant of Romain Desèze. The two names Louis Seize and *comte* de

Sèze make a nice jingle in French, keeping alive the name of Romain Desèze or (later), de Sèze, the barrister from Bordeaux who eloquently—and courageously—defended his king before the Convention.

In 1880 the restoration of Chemazé was begun and carried on with taste and care.

We do not know the name of the Chemazé architect, but the chapel in plan and detail is very like that of Notre-Dame de Cléry on the Loire, and this church was devised and planned by Jehan Gobereau of Loches.

## *An Anjou Christmas*

CHEMILLÉ. Sorinière castle, a little way from Chemillé, is a simple-looking place built about 1820 or 1830, but there are two stout old towers and the house is surrounded by a quick moat. In the chapel are some curious frescoes executed between 1517 and 1540. There are three panels, an *Adoration of the Shepherds*, an *Adoration of the Wise Men* and a *Saint Christopher*. The visages of the Virgin are exquisitely beautiful. The shepherds are men of Anjou in an Angevin countryside. One of them is playing the bag-pipes, another is eating his soup out of a deep bowl, others chat, and some warm themselves before the fire with angels for com-panions whom they are entertaining perhaps unawares. It is an Anjou Christmas.

The church of Saint-Pierre in Chemillé, formerly a minster, is Romanesque, sober and impressive. The belfry is particularly fine. The town itself is a straggling place which is, in its modest way, a manufacturing centre. Blankets, rugs, mattresses and shoes are turned out. The peasants of the Chemillé countryside are great fatteners of oxen, which they buy lean in the neighbouring regions and then turn on to their meadows and in winter feed the kine on cabbage. The fields near Chemillé are covered with crops of medicinal herbs, mint, camomile, field-balm and the like, which are packed and sent out all over France.

As you come upon Chemillé from the south you pass the Gardes hill about 650 feet high. It is the loftiest point in the whole province of Anjou, and from this summit can be enjoyed on a clear day a map spread before you of the Val de Loire and the ancient Angevin land.

## An Epitome of French History

CHENONCEAU. Hardly any country-house in Touraine, or even elsewhere in France, has a more romantic, full, or inter-sting history than Chenonceau.

For some reason or another, the highway to Chenonceau is lmost always in bad repair, and it used to be a standing joke that ne road was one of the worst in France. But we must not exag-erate; if the going is a little bumpy, it is so only for a short while.

This road is a slightly winding one over the gently rolling Cher alley, then you glide into a hamlet with simple, friendly houses. he trees, tall trees, close in on either side, but in no choking, ppressive or menacing manner. A cross-roads. The highway dips own. You pass an old house they call the "Pages' Lodging"— was, perhaps, the familiar "house in the village" where, at a inch, visitors can be lodged with the servants and retainers of the nore splendid guests. At the church, a humble country church, ou turn into the wrought-iron gates of Chenonceau park. Before ou stretches a spacious avenue of tall, straight plane trees stand-ng out from the thickets that screen and isolate the place.

Ahead of you, framed in the greenery of the trees, is the pale, vory-coloured outline of a manor-house glowing perhaps in the uminous afternoon of a Touraine summer.

You step out from the vantage-shade of the avenue. Two marble phinxes guard the entrance to the grounds. To the right is the jarden of Diana, to the left is the Green Garden, backed with a urious building (containing the servants' quarters and the stables) egun, if not wholly constructed, under Philibert Delorme's super-ision for Diane de Poitiers.

You walk a little farther on the raised causeway, and you come o a terrace surrounded by a moat. Slightly to the right and mask-ng, a little, the front of the *château* is a round tower. It is a fine 5th century tower enlivened and lightened by Renaissance addi-ons, so that it fits in surprisingly well with the general scheme of he Chenonceau buildings.

It is a good idea to stop here and to sit down for a while on seat at the foot of the tower and gaze on natural and man-made eauty in a countryside that hardly has its like for softness and race and calm.

One has to be very impervious indeed to the evocatory genius

of the place if one does not start a-musing. Even Flaubert, th
author of *Madame Bovary*, fell victim to the pervasive charm o
Chenonceau.

Here in this dale of the Cher, in olden times, was a manor of
family called Marques, who had held the place at least from th
13th century. But history here goes a long, long way back. Uppe
Paleolithic tools of chipped flint made by Aurignacian and Magda
lenian man, our direct ancestors of twenty thousand years ago
more or less, show that this enchanted valley was lived in as lon
ago as the appearance of modern men in Europe. But we mus
not figure the place as looking much as it does to-day. During th
Reindeer Age, when Magdalenian men chased up and down th
Cher valley, the countryside resembled that of Siberia. The ic
walls of the great glacier rose in northern Germany, and what i
now Touraine was swept by the fierce blasts of the blizzard, an
down this delicate dale lumbered mammoth, while herds of horse
and bison swarmed over the treeless downs.

The old manor of the Marques family was razed to the groun
by the *maréchal* Boucicaut, since Jean de Marques had taken u
arms on the English side. In the middle of the 15th century th
manor was rebuilt, and to a rustic dwelling was added
manorial mill to which all the villeins had to bring their whea
to be ground. This mill was built over the stream, and had it
foundations in the granite bed of the Cher. All that remains o
this manor is the "keep" or the round tower, in whose shade w
may sit while we let our fancy wander up and down the centuries.

The latter part of the 15th century was a troublous time for th
country gentry and lesser nobility. Living costs were rising, money
and consequently power, were passing into the hands of new me
men sprung from the people, men only a generation or two off th
vagrant serfs, escaped villeins and runaway slaves who had swelle
the urban populations for the past hundred and fifty year
Already the sovereigns, ever fearing the power of the nobility an
able to neglect the lesser though they were still obliged to respec
the greater nobles, had extended their favour to these rich, cunnin
able, hard-working men of the new middle class, men who forge
the tradition of the European *bourgeoisie*.

By the end of the 15th century the heir of the Marques was on
Pierre, a fellow who did not adapt himself to the new econom

and was not sensible enough to keep quiet in the old ways. He speculated, and was soon the classical and pathetic figure of the amateur caught by the professional. The professional's name was Thomas Bohier.

Bohier came from a place called Issoire, in the far-off and mountainous Auvergne. He was the son of one Austremoine, burgess of Issoire and of Béraude Duprat, the sister of the famous Cardinal Duprat, Chancellor of France, who was the principal author of the Concordat signed at Bologna in 1516 between François I and Pope Leo X, when the Holy Father gave the "Gaudin Diamond" to Madame de La Bourdaisière, the grand-mother of Gabrielle d'Estrées, as we saw at La Bourdaisière (p. 49).

So, Bohier started out in the world as the nephew of the Car-dinal-Chancellor Duprat, and soon made his mark as a man of finance. He was in Italy in 1496 with Charles VIII and again in 1507 with Louis XII, when he was knighted at Genoa by Charles d'Amboise. In 1515 he was appointed administrator of the finances of the conquered Duchy of Milan.

Bohier married Catherine Briçonnet, of a family of Tours mer-chants, several members of which had risen to eminence in the preceding hundred years. One was a Cardinal and another had been the Archbishop of Rheims who had crowned King Charles VIII.

Such was the formidable adversary poor Pierre de Marques was up against. Bohier had already become possessed of a certain amount of property in the Cher valley. When he was not moving about with the Court or staying at Amboise or Tours, he put in a good deal of his time at his manor of Houdes, near Chenonceau. Bohier had had his eye on the desirable fief of the Marques for a long time. He intrigued, angled, plotted and contrived for twenty years before he managed to encompass Pierre de Marques' ruin and lay his hands upon Chenonceau. He hovered like a vulture over the shrinking patrimony of the decaying gentleman, and snapped up each parcel and piece of land the unhappy Pierre had to sell to keep going. Finally, in 1512 Bohier bought Chenonceau at auction for 12,540 livres. Now, his possessions by the Cher were extensive enough to form a *châtellenie*, and by letters patent of King Louis XII, dated at Blois in February 1514, Bohier's lands were united in one "faith and hommage." Bohier was Lord of

Chenonceau, of Houdes, of Bléré, of La Carte, of Infernet, of Argy and of Baigneux. The Marques disappeared and dropped down no doubt to swell the mass of the new and nameless poor.

Bohier's was, then, a typical career of a "New Man"—he soon asserted himself at Chenonceau, put in his manorial notary, set up a court-house, a prison and a market-hall, and the better to play the feudal lord he began his castle. He ripped down the Marques' old mill, and used its foundations as part of those of his new pleasure-house, which was to be so comfortable and modern while still looking as a nobleman's castle should look. Chenonceau is exactly contemporary with François I's wing at Blois, but this building had no visible influence on Bohier or his architect.

Bohier died in 1524 at Vigelli in Piedmont without having known any notable waning of his fortunes. But his son was to pay the price of his father's too rapid rise to wealth. Antoine Bohier fell the victim to his father's enemies. No man, even in the 16th century, could rise to great riches without making a host of foes, and these foes often found it easy to excite the King against a man who was not only fortunate but very wealthy. Young Bohier was condemned to pay a huge fine, ostensibly to settle the deficits reported to have been found in the elder Bohier's accounts as Receiver-General of Finance for Normandy. In 1527 Antoine Bohier had to cede Chenonceau to the Crown. The place the elder Bohier had schemed for twenty years to get was held by him and his family for only fifteen—and then the Bohiers too faded out as suddenly as they appeared.

## Chenonceau a Royal Palace

SO Chenonceau became Crown property, and although it is said that François I sometimes hunted in the woods and thickets around Bohier's house, he never used Chenonceau as a residence. When in 1547 Henri II ascended the throne, Diane de Poitiers, his elderly mistress, at once got her covetous hands upon so desirable a morsel as Chenonceau. Diane set her architect to work, that Philibert Delorme who built her great country-palace of Anet and also the old Tuileries Palace in Paris. It was he who transformed the outward appearance of Bohier's little manor and added the arches now supporting the grand gallery across the Cher, since Diane had the idea of throwing a bridge across the stream. She

**Chinon**

Old Houses in the *Rue du Grand-Carroi*

**Coëmont**      The Rock Cellars    **Cinq-Mars**

**Daon**      The old Manor-House    **Durtal**

**Chinon**   Old Houses   **Cinq-Mars**    The *Pile*   **Durtal**    The Castle

laid out the gardens, and she had planted grape-vines of the sort known as *Arbois*, whose rare and prized wine is so reminiscent of some of the vintages of Andalusia. Tradition, indeed, has it that the vines at Arbois (in the Jura department) are descended from those planted centuries ago by the Spaniards.

At the King's death, however, the widowed Queen Catherine de' Medici, who pursued Diane with undying hatred, forced the former favourite to exchange delightful Renaissance Chenonceau in its enchanted dale for grim, gloomy, feudal Chaumont on a naked hill away to the north-east on the farther bank of the Loire.

Catherine de' Medici had erected the gallery over the Cher in 1580. This building is generally attributed to Philibert Delorme, but is not his work. He did indeed draw up a plan but it allowed for a gallery of one storey only, whose modest dimensions would have made the castle more prominent. The present cumbrous edifice built by one Denis Courtin crushes the manor. The Queen's intention was to build upon the opposite bank of the river a replica of Bohier's manor, but she died before the second block could be begun, and Chenonceau remains unfinished. The great gallery, nearly two hundred feet long and rising in two storeys, is abruptly shorn off a few feet from the farther bank.

But as long as the Queen-Mother lived, Chenonceau was a very gay place. A splendid party was given, for instance, in May 1577 for the Duke of Anjou, who had just taken La Charité from the Huguenots. King Henri III, powdered, curled, painted, perfumed and pomaded, in a low-necked jacket of brilliantly coloured silks and with pearl and diamond ear-rings in his ears, presided over the festivities. The guests at the banquet were waited upon by "the most beautiful and distinguished ladies of the Court, with their hair loose and clad in the slightest of robes. . . ."

Not only did Queen Catherine construct the great gallery, but she altered, once more, the main front of Bohier's manor. She doubled the number of windows, and placed caryatids between them.

Catherine de' Medici stuffed Chenonceau with rich hangings, silks, tapestries, furniture, stained glass, statues, busts, medallions, vases and all sorts of objects both in the French and in the Italian taste. When she died at Blois, having by her influence, and by the baleful heredity she introduced, corrupted and ruined the House of Valois, she left Chenonceau to Louise de Vaudémont, widow of King Henri III. She retired to Chenonceau immediately after her husband's murder. Here the young *reine blanche*, or White Queen—for the mourning of the Queens of France was white— spent her widowhood until her death in 1601. She left the estate to the Vendôme family, and in 1732 the then owner, the *duc* de Bourbon, sold the place to Monsieur Dupin, the farmer-general and financier.

## *The Dupins of Chenonceau*

CLAUDE DUPIN was one of the richest men of business during the period of the French monarchy's decline. The Dupins, their ancestors, their descendants and their friends make up such a curious and interesting lot that their Chenonceau seems a much more real and living place to us than does the Chenonceau of royal revels and the gaudy vice and debauchery of the Florentine Queen and her painted, perfumed, effeminate and cowardly son.

Madame Dupin was Marie-Madeline Fontaine, the natural daughter of Samuel Bernard, the immensely rich speculator and financier, and of Madame Fontaine the actress.

For their son in 1747 Madame Dupin hired a tutor. His name was Jean-Jacques Rousseau. He liked his life in the Cher valley, for he wrote:

> *"We lead an amusing life in this charming place. The food is very good and I am becoming as fat as a monk. We play a lot of music, we act, compose songs, and I have written a play, but all this does not prevent me from carrying on my chemical researches."*

During the Dupin régime, Chenonceau became the home and centre of a family, and despite all the alteration, "improvements," restorations and reconstructions the house has undergone, it still retains something of the air and look the Dupins must have given it—the look of the rich country-house which is the natural centre of its countryside. The reason may be that from the death of Queen Louise in 1601 until Dupin bought it, no one had lived at Chenonceau, and the house was, by 1732, if not falling to pieces, at least in very bad repair. The Dupins spent a fortune on the place—

Chenonceau is like a beautiful woman and has always been costly —and held a sort of Court to which flocked the wits and beauties of the day, often to stay for weeks on end.

The visitors' book at Chenonceau displayed almost every name famous in the 18th century: Fontenelle, the "philosopher" who lived to be a hundred years old, and was the first writer to "popularise" science; Montesquieu, the author of the *Spirit of Laws*, which has been described as "one of the most important books ever published," which Fontenelle advised Montesquieu not to print. Then there was Buffon, the noble, handsome, wealthy author of the famous *Natural History*. And the unfortunate and kindly *abbé* de Saint-Pierre, who was ejected from membership of the French Academy because he had advocated a sort of "League of Nations" scheme. And Condillac, the philosopher, who would come over from his property of Flux, near Beaugency. Condillac (with whose uncle Rousseau had also been tutor), was the author of *The Origin of Human Knowledge*. And our Bolingbroke, who for nearly ten years lived at the *château* d'Argeville, near Fontainebleau. And Voltaire. And charming and witty women: Madame de Sabran, who married the *chevalier* de Boufflers, described as a libertine ecclesiastic, a philosophical soldier, a song-singing diplomatist, a patriotic emigrant (*émigré*) and a republican courtier. And Madame de Tencin, the mother of the philosopher and mathematician d'Alembert by the *chevalier* Destouches, and many others.

Chesterfield, of the *Letters to his Son,* as well as Bolingbroke, stayed at Chenonceau, and there met Madame du Deffand, the friend of Horace Walpole and the touchy patroness of Mlle de Lespinasse; in fact, from time to time, nearly all Madame du Deffand's "circle" was transported to Chenonceau *en bloc.* Those were the days.

## George Sand

BUT the illustrious and literary associations of Chenonceau have not all been told. Dupin's son (Rousseau's old pupil) was known as "Monsieur de Chenonceau." He was noted for his liaison with Madame d'Epinay, of which she writes at length in her *Memoirs.* But young Dupin married a lady called Marie-Aurore, the natural daughter of no less a personage than the

"Marshal Saxe" (himself a bastard of King Augustus of Saxony and Poland). The Dupins were running true to their tradition of marrying ladies of irregular parentage.

Old Madame Dupin, for all that she was the widow of a farmer-general of the revenue, was so popular and so esteemed, that she was suffered to live on at Chenonceau during the Revolution—she died there in 1799, aged ninety-three. Madame Dupin left Chenonceau to her nephew, the *comte* de Villeneuve, from whom the house and property were acquired by Madame Pelouze, the daughter-in-law of the famous chemist.

Young Dupin, however—the former "Monsieur de Chenonceau" —left a son Maurice, who took as a wife one Sophie Delaborde, the daughter of a Parisian bird-fancier. And the marriage was celebrated only a few weeks before a child was born. The daughter from this ill-assorted union was the famed George Sand, whose natural genius was probably fostered by the violent contrast between the manners, comportment and traditions of her very plebeian mother and those of her very much *ancien régime* grandmother, by whom the child was brought up. By George Sand's time Chenonceau had been lost to the Dupins, and Madame "Dupin de Francueil" had retired to her manor of Nohant in the Berri that was George Sand's home to the end of her days.

The later history of Chenonceau is soon told. Madame Pelouze had the place "restored" and repaired at great expense between 1865 and 1878 by the architect Rouguet. Catherine de' Medici's additions were removed between the chapel and the "library." In 1888 the place became the property of the *Crédit Foncier* land bank—through foreclosure. In 1891 it was sold to a rich American, Mr. Terry. From 1913 Chenonceau belonged to Monsieur Gaston Menier, the millionaire chocolate manufacturer.

## Chenonceau House

AND now let us leave our seat by the old tower and visit this most charming of the Loire *châteaux*.

Over the door of the tower is still carved Bohier's motto:

"S'IL VIENT A POINT ME SOUVIENDRA."

The causeway rises a little. On either side are the formal gardens.

You cross a bridge to the ground-floor of the house, which is all surrounded by water.

The place seems small. It is small, but appears, from a little distance, even smaller than it is because of its perfect proportions. There are two storeys and an attic with dormers set in a high-pitched pale slate roof. These dormers bear delicate and intricate gables rising almost as high as the pointed conical roofs of the corner turrets. The main block is about a hundred feet square.

The pilasters framing the front door have capitals set with figures of sirens, and the frieze joining the two uprights is adorned with angels holding scrolls and an obliterated scutcheon.

The interior is simply planned. The entrance gives into a vaulted hall. On the left is a charming sculptured doorway surmounted by figures of Saint Thomas and Saint Catherine, the patrons of the builder Bohier and his wife. This doorway leads into the so-called guard-room, which now serves as a dining-room. The ceiling bears the monogram of Catherine de' Medici and the walls are hung with Flemish tapestries. Giving out of the dining-room, and overhanging the water, is the Gothic chapel—for men kept to the old models for sanctuaries long after the new style had been adopted for secular buildings. However, here at Chenonceau, some of the details are Renaissance—the pilasters, the acanthus capitals, the shell-shaped niches. Some of the glass in the windows was old, but it was blown to bits by the explosion of a bomb which also hurt the staircase of the tower. Otherwise Chenonceau suffered little. Six hundred square yards of roof were ripped off by another bomb but the damage was repaired within twelve months.

From the left of the hall is the room of Diane de Poitiers. The magnificent chimney-piece has been attributed to Jean Goujon, the greatest of the French Renaissance sculptors. The panelled wooden ceiling is decorated with the familiar monogram of Henry II and Diane de Poitiers—the H intertwined with the three crescents. There is some good tapestry on the walls. Beyond Diane's room is the Green Room of Catherine de' Medici with Henry II furniture. Out of the Green Room gives the "Library," whose ceiling of polygonal panels and small pendants is a masterpiece of joinery.

On the south side of the house is the François I saloon. It has been very thoroughly "restored," but contains some excellent furniture and a painting of Diane de Poitiers. It is a striking portrait.

Diane walks towards you clad in a light robe, from which floats a violet-coloured scarf. In her hand she holds an arrow whose point is turned towards the ground. She is surrounded with genii and children who frolic around her and play with dogs. The picture is typical of the symbolical, allusive, timeless portraits that were so popular in the 16th century.

Louis XIII was the last King of France to visit Chenonceau. In his room hangs an imposing portrait of Louis XIV and a charming one of the famous Madame Dupin in a white robe with blue stripes.

There are some other good pictures in the house as well as a collection of historical autographs, including some of Diane de Poitiers.

## The Great Gallery

THE great gallery across the Cher dates from about 1580. The Queen, as we have seen, had planned this bridge across the river to be part of a great architectural scheme whereby Bohier's manor was to be reproduced on the other side of the Cher and the two houses joined by the bridge.

The great gallery is of simple style, within and without. The beaks of the stone piles are heightened to form turrets which, at the level of the first storey, end in balconies. Inside, these turrets are hollowed out to a depth of about six feet, and form a series of semicircular alcoves along one side of the gallery. The ceiling consists of visible rafters. There are two large fireplaces, and a remarkable staircase of two flights leads up to the upper gallery.

This double gallery, most often gay from the flickering light reflected from the river's surface, ends in a blank wall, through which a postern gives on to a rusty drawbridge spanning the few feet of gap between the gallery's end and the farther bank of the Cher, that unaccountable river, so calm as you watch it dawdling through fat meadows, but so destructive when it spreads suddenly into devastating floods. In the gallery are preserved some of the trappings which adorned the *chapelle ardente* or funerary chamber of Queen Louise, who died here in 1601.

But we shall not want to leave Chenonceau after a visit to the house. We shall want to stroll in the park, wander through rays of the stars in Diana's garden, and sit in Catherine's garden. And we shall feel, rather than be able to explain, the pervasive charm and the slightly melancholy beauty of this most lovely of Loire *châteaux*. Even from the air Chenonceau seems enchanting. A gallery spanning a stream, a castle at the gallery's head, a drawbridge and its arches, an oblong terrace bearing a tower and surrounded by water, another bridge from this oblong terrace to dry land and beyond the terrace a great formal garden set as a star, and nearer to you on this side of the island-terrace another garden more discreet, more modest and half-swathed in trees. It is a fairy palace leading nowhere but to a land of dreams.

## From Chronicler to Historian

CHINON. The Church of St. Etienne at Chinon bears over its grey portal a stone-carved and painted coat-of-arms that, at first glance, you may take to be that of the City of Plymouth or, more familiarly, of a well-known brand of cigarettes. As a matter of fact, this shield of "Three Castles" has nothing to do with the West Country, but was the blazon of the famous Philippe de Commynes, at one time governor of Chinon town and castle for King Louis XI living nearby at Plessis-lès-Tours. But Commynes was something more than an adroit courtier and an able administrator. He was the first chronicler to write in the French language chronicles that are also history.

He is, indeed, the first French historian and, moreover, an historian who was a man of affairs, and had studied the business of State under such a master as King Louis XI.

## Nationality Long Ago

COMMYNES (whose name made Cummings with us at a time when men translated their names) was born near Hazebrouck, in Flanders, about the year 1445. He was therefore by birth a subject of the "Grand Duke of the Occident," or the famous *Philippe le Bon* (or "Philip the Good," but his contemporaries mostly called him *Philippe l'Assuré* or "Philip the Confident"), Duke of Burgundy. The Burgundian dukes were, to all intents and purposes, independent sovereigns, though they owed homage (a purely formal rite) to the Kings of France for some of the Burgundian domains and to the Emperors (of the "Holy Roman Empire" or of "Germany") for other lands and provinces.

But a man such as Commynes could hardly look up farther than to his great Sovereign-Lord Duke. Commynes, however, having started his career at the Brussels Court of the Burgundian duke, left the employ of Duke Philip while serving as that potentate's ambassador at Paris or elsewhere at the Court of King Louis XI of France. The King always recognised a smart man when he saw him, and Commynes was a fellow after his own heart, cunning, secretive, able and full of insight, foresight and judgment. Commynes did well enough by the change-over (that no one of the time apparently found at all odd), but it is fair to say that we must not compare Commynes' action with that of a man in modern times who might shift from one nation's service to another. Commynes lived in a world on to which had not been imposed the blessings of "nationalism." We should rather seek for parallels to Commynes in the careers of those Germans who, only a few generations ago, switched about from the service of the King of Prussia to that of the Emperor in Vienna and then to that of some smaller prince.

The French king appointed him councillor and chamberlain, and arranged for his marriage to a rich heiress, by name Hélène de Chambes, Lady of Argenton (and of the same family as the Lords of Montsoreau we may read about in Dumas' pages), and the lucky Fleming was even awarded the principality of Talmont (confiscated from the ill-fated family of d'Amboise), but this piece of preferment was contested by the La Trémoïlle family, and after the death of his protector King Louis XI, Commynes had to discard his principality. Indeed, after having been accused of plotting to kidnap King Charles VIII, the temporary "Prince of Talmont" was for a time imprisoned in the most uncomfortable fortress-prison of Loches, but in 1492 he was summoned to Court again and given some employment. He died at his fief of Argenton in 1511, and his magnificent tomb, adorned with the castles' shield (such as we see at Chinon), is now in the Louvre.

And, if we would understand something about the life and times and curious character of Louis XI of France, the man who really welded the French realm into one, if we would realise to what depths our English Court had sunk under Edward IV, and if we would learn many more things that cast a clear light on the history and development of the English and French peoples, we must read Commynes. Compared with Commynes, Froissart is a mere gossip-writer, and moreover a man, like most gossip-writers, living upon the fringe of the society he sought to portray. Commynes was at the heart of affairs, trusted councillor of the most successful and able monarch of his day, ambassador to England, statesman, politician, diplomatist, dispenser of secret funds and careful architect of his own fortune; Commynes was also a vivid, accurate and penetrating writer.

## Saint Mexme's Cope

A FEW steps lead down under the blazon of Philippe de Commynes into the single-naved Church of Saint-Étienne. The building was begun at the time when Charles VII of France was holding his Court at Chinon, and the church was completed under his son Louis XI when Philippe de Commynes was governor of the town and castle.

There is at St. Stephen's—or Saint-Étienne's—a curious 14th century tomb put up to the memory of two members of the Paumard family.

But the treasure of the church is the vestment known as "Saint Mexme's Cope." Christianity came to these parts late, and although there are traditions of a Saint-Gatien in Touraine by the 3rd century, there are no sure traces of any ecclesiastical organisation before the 4th century. Saint-Mexme was the legendary Apostle of Chinon, and his memory is kept alive, not only by the ruined church of his name, but by the cope preserved in the Church of Saint-Étienne.

The cope is, of course, of much later date than any in the 4th century. It is of splendid Oriental brocade—probably of the 11th century—and is a relic worthy to be compared with any piece of ancient silk in Europe, such as the splendid shroud with spread eagles from Sens, or even the imperial coronation robe at Vienna. These Moslem-woven stuffs bore often most unsuitable quotations worked into their substance. It sometimes happened, during the Middle Ages, that the vestments worn by great prelates and ecclesiastics bore prominently displayed the inscription THERE IS

NO GOD BUT GOD, AND MOHAMMED IS THE ENVOY OF GOD, but as no one could read the Arabic lettering, all was well.

This "Cope of Saint Mexme," however, is certainly, after some of the buildings, the most interesting thing in Chinon. The local museum is hardly worth a visit.

Saint Mexme's old church, formerly collegiate, and the most ancient and celebrated of Chinon, was secularised in 1790, and was allowed to fall into a ruinous condition. Of this notable 11th century and Romanesque building, only the atrium (narthex or vestibule), the two towers and the nave are standing. The nave serves as the local elementary school. The west front has preserved some interesting remains of early 11th century sculpture and ornamentation. The northern tower is Romanesque, and within it are some curious 12th century mural paintings.

## The Town

CHINON is a sleepy little place squeezed into a ledge between the Vienne's banks and the hills. The ramparts and battlemented walls formerly ran right down to the water's edge, but now the north-bank road widens out at Chinon to a tree-lined promenade. Chinon itself is confined to the right bank of the river. A stone bridge, however, joins both right and left banks to a central island in the Vienne and leads to the southern suburb of Saint-Jacques.

There are a few old houses in the town, but the sights of the place, apart from the famed castles, are soon dealt with. The Church of Saint-Maurice has a fine "Plantagenet" Romanesque nave, on to which, in the 16th century, was added another nave with fan vaulting. The 12th century vaulting is interesting, and the keys are finely carved and, with the knops, are painted and gilt. All the wall-paintings are modern. There are some indifferently preserved old stained-glass lights, and there is a large, dingy painting optimistically attributed to Rubens.

Chinon is a place to pass through rather than to stay at. The accommodation is mediocre, the restaurants rather indifferent. But the town is at the heart of a countryside rich and beautiful, full of interesting houses, charming villages, important monuments and beautiful scenery, and a countryside, moreover, producing bread and wine, meat and fruits in abundance; all the fruits of Touraine and Anjou are excellent and Anjou is about the most northerly region of France where peaches ripen out-of-doors in all their perfumed perfection. Apricots are especially fine in the Loire valley, as are also the raspberries, strawberries, cherries and melons, especially those known as orangines.

And here, again, we are struck with one of the deep mysteries of Touraine. Why, amid such abundance, are there so few good restaurants? In neighbouring Anjou you may eat well almost everywhere. Still, things are not so bad as one might imagine. There are some notable places in Touraine all the same. But the meat of Chinon, the produce of the famous Saint-Louans dairy nearby, the fruits and vegetables of the countryside are unrivalled. You can pluck tomatoes weighing a pound apiece and grown out-of-doors as late as November . . . a speciality of the town is its *rillettes d'oie,* or potted goose. The local red wines have their admirers, but the more esteemed of the two vintages (that made from the so-called "Breton" grapes) has rather a flavour of raspberries—or so it seems to some of us.

## *Where our Henry II Died*

THE enormously strong strategic site now crowned by Chinon's castles was occupied by a Celtic *oppidum* or stronghold and then by a Roman *castrum* or walled town. Legend has it that in A.D. 426 Saint-Brice built the first parish church of Chinon and Saint-Mexme a little later on founded a monastery and put up a second church.

Clovis made Chinon one of the principal strong-points of his Frankish realm. In the 10th and 11th centuries Chinon belonged to the Counts of Blois, one of whom, Thibault III, ceded, in 1044, Chinon to Geoffry Martel, Count of Anjou. Thus, in the 12th century Chinon was part of the patrimony of our Henry II Plantagenet, who often lived in the castle where, also, he died, a man still defiant but disappointed and troubled by the defection and rebellion of his sons and their mother.

There is no truth in the local legend that Richard Coeur de Lion, after having been mortally wounded at Châlus in the Limousin, was transported to die at Chinon castle.

Chinon held out for more than a year against the forces of the French king, Philip Augustus, in 1204 and 1205, during the campaign against our King John, a campaign by which Anjou and

Touraine were definitely reannexed to the French Crown. In 1308 Philippe IV (*Le Bel*) obtained from the Pope a Bull permission to try the Grand Master of the Order of Templars, Jacques Molay, who with 140 of his followers was imprisoned at Chinon. The next year Molay and 54 others were burned alive in Paris.

In 1321 under Philippe V (nicknamed *le Long* or the "Tall") 160 Chinon Jews (and the presence there of so many Jews is a sure proof that the place was more prosperous than it has ever been in modern times) were accused of having poisoned the town water-supply. As a matter of fact, the lower parts of Chinon, to this day, tend to be flooded at times during the spring or autumn, and we may easily imagine that in the 14th century sewage and water-supply got rather mixed up. Anyway, the Jews were fair game in those days, and the 160 of them were burned alive on that island in the Vienne lying between Chinon town proper and the suburb of Saint-Jacques.

## Joan of Arc

IN 1428, Charles VII was still known generally only as the Dauphin, since his nephew, our Henry VI, had been held (at least by the English, by their Burgundian allies and by those French who were on the English side) to have succeeded in 1422 on the death of his grandfather, Charles VI of France, to the throne of France. Our Henry V had married Catherine, the daughter of Charles VI, and our Hotspur had been proclaimed heir to the throne of France to the exclusion of his brother-in-law, who was, conveniently enough, found to be of doubtful parentage.

In 1428 the Dauphin, whose troops precariously held but a few provinces of his kingdom, was moved to summon a meeting of the States-General. This vague "popular" assembly of the three "States" of the realm had never in France developed (as it did in England) into a regular parliament. The sovereigns summoned the States-General when they felt right up against it, and did not know which way to turn for money, men or defence. It will be remembered that Louis XVI resolved to summon the most famous of all the States-General—that of 1789—only when all other devices for remedying the sorry financial and social plight of the realm had proved useless.

In 1429 the English were besieging Orléans, only a hundred

miles or so away up the Loire. And it was in this year 1429 and during the sitting of the States-General (a much-reduced and not very numerous States-General by the way) that Joan of Arc was introduced into the Dauphin's presence at Chinon castle, and persuaded him to succour Orléans.

It was, in fact, at Chinon that the fortunes of the French turned, and the place deserves to be remembered as the birthplace of French independence after the Hundred Years' War.

In 1498 Chinon Castle was the scene of a brilliant ceremony, the last great occasion in the place's history. King Louis XII here received the Papal Legate, no less a person than the magnificent Cæsar Borgia, son of Pope Alexander VI. Cæsar was the bearer of a Bull dissolving the marriage of the King and his Queen, for at the age of fourteen years Louis had been married off to the daughter of King Louis XI, the "Universal Spider." This lady had two humps on her back, was afflicted with a disease of the hip and had a face much like that of a female monkey. The marriage lasted twenty-three years, but when Charles VIII died his successor, Louis XII, must, by the terms of Charles's will, marry his widow, Anne of Brittany, whom Louis happened rather to like. Moreover, such a marriage would secure that Brittany remained a French province. Louis XII, therefore, celebrated the arrival of the liberating Bull with great rejoicings and with splendid feasts in honour of Cæsar Borgia.

Chinon, like neighbouring Tours, and indeed the whole of Touraine, declined in importance and in prosperity from the end of the Middle Ages. In 1633 the fief of Chinon became the property of the Cardinal de Richelieu, and his family retained the place until the Revolution swept away all the old feudal system. In the 17th and 18th centuries the eldest sons of the *ducs* de Richelieu often bore the courtesy title of *comte* de Chinon. The castles were demolished at the beginning of the 19th century.

## The Historic Castle

YOU go up the street from the river-side and then climb until you have the main entrance to the castles on your left. To your right are the blurred remains of the St. George's fortress built by our Henry II. Although it is the latest in date of the three Chinon strongholds, it is also by far the most ruinous, and nothing much of it remains beyond an outer wall which has been razed to the level of the soil that fills the site of the Plantagenet buildings.

The castles follow each other from east to west on a long, narrow ridge of rock falling steeply to the river and dropping, though not quite so sheer, on the opposite side towards the fringe of great Chinon forest. This natural stronghold ends westwards in a sharp spur or bow. It would be impossible to find a stronger position for miles around.

The entrance to the Middle castle or *château du milieu* is to your left when you have climbed to the crest of the ridge. Before you towers the lofty *Pavillon de l'Horloge*, or Clock Pavilion, more than a hundred feet high, and you reach this barbican by a slender arched bridge spanning a deep dry moat or ditch that cuts the castle ridge of rock transversely.

The Middle castle was erected on the site of the original Roman *castrum*. Parts date from the 11th, 12th and 13th centuries, but the whole was rebuilt and restored under Kings Charles VI, Charles VII and Louis XI. However, with a little imagination, we may reconstruct, in our mind's eye, the fortress as it was when, over five centuries since, the Girl from Lorraine was led hither.

The containing walls of the Middle castle are, of course, oblong, since they follow the outline of the crag. These walls enclose little now but a straggling, ill-kempt, tree-grown plot pompously styled a *jardin anglais* ("English Garden" is a favourite French euphemism for neglected grounds). On the town side and commanding Chinon and the broad, far-reaching Vienne valley are the crumbling walls of the *Grand Logis*, or Great Lodging, that has preserved some rather fine chimneys. It was here, overlooking the smiling and gracious countryside of Touraine, that our Henry II Plantagenet died. It was in this Great Lodging that Charles VII and Louis XI often stayed. And it was in the throne room of the Great Lodging (all that remains of this room is the west corner enclosing still a splendid chimney-piece, and this poor fragment we have watched steadily diminish during the last generation) that Joan of Arc was, on 9th March, 1429, presented to the Dauphin, afterwards King Charles VII, and said to him:

*"Gentil Dauphin, J'ai nom Jehanne la Pucelle. Et vous mande le Roi des cieux par moi, que vous serez sacré et couronné dans*

*la ville de Reims, et serez le lieutenant du Roi des cieux qui est le Roi de la France."*

*("Gentle Dauphin, My name is Joan the Maid. And the King of Heaven tells you by me that you will be consecrated and crowned in the town of Rheims, and that you will be the lieutenant of the King of Heaven who is King of the Land of France.")*

Just outside the Great Lodging rises a square tower well enough preserved. On the Middle castle's façade overlooking Chinon is another tower, and on the opposite side, towards the Tours road, are two more towers known as the *Tour des Chiens* and the *Tour d'Argenton* (named after Philippe de Commynes, who was Lord of Argenton) and under both towers are dungeons.

The *château* du Coudray, that occupies the western spur of Chinon ridge, is separated from the Middle castle by a deep dyke. Within, Coudray castle is also a "garden," but this most westerly portion is also the best preserved of all the three fortresses. At the corner of the dyke or moat is the magnificent Boissy tower of oblong ground-plan. The "crenellated" platform at the top of the tower is a crazy "reconstruction" by some local antiquarian, and it is unlike anything known in the Middle Ages.

The fine vaulting of the guard-room has also been restored, but tactfully and in good taste. In the stout, round 13th century *Tour du Coudray*, looking west, Joan of Arc was, it is supposed, lodged from 9th March to 20th April, 1429. During this time she was questioned and examined by doctors and divines to discover if she came from God or Devil. The Dauphin was a prudent man. He called in the experts. During the time she was the Dauphin's guest, Joan was under the guard of one Guillaume Bélier, lieutenant to the captain of Chinon castle. Near to Coudray tower rose the now vanished Chapel of St. Martin, where Joan would pray.

In this Coudray castle, indeed, Joan of Arc passed some of the most critical days of her short life, those in which she swayed the Dauphin, gained her will, and prepared herself for the triumph of Orléans, the Coronation at Rheims, and even for the final tragedy when she was callously left to her fate by the man she had made King of France. Put not your trust in Princes.

At the south-western corner of the Coudray castle is the

well-preserved *Tour du Moulin*. It is the loftiest and slenderest of
all, and formerly was used as the watch-tower. Nearby is a fine
vaulted chamber on the ground-floor of a 16th century bastion,
and herein is housed a small collection of objects dug up in the
grounds, but there is nothing of any real interest.

The curtain or containing wall on the western side reveals in
places masonry laid when the first Coudray castle was constructed
by Thibault le Tricheur or the Trickster, Count of Blois, in about
954. Of the rest of the Chinon towers, none now remains above
the level of the terrace.

For their historical associations, for their interesting medieval
architecture and for the views they afford over one of the most
delightful countrysides in northern France, the Castles of Chinon
must figure as something not to be missed on the list of all
pilgrims to the Garden of France.

## *Down the Vienne*

BEHIND Chinon, towards the forest, are vast subterranean
quarries and stalactite caves known as *Les Vilains*.

The Vienne, or as it used to be called the "Little Loire," winds
for weary miles through the arid heaths of the Sainte-Maure country, but by the time it reaches Chinon the Vienne is a friendly river,
wallowing in a wide yellow bed with green fringes. The
right-bank road following the Vienne stream is bordered to
the north by hill-slopes that, in places, straighten up to form low
cliffs. This highway, for many months out of the year sunny and
sheltered, is set, here and there, with terraces bearing pleasing,
white, tree-shaded houses. About a mile and a half from Chinon
is the modern Convent of Saint-Louans, whose chapel is, however,
built upon a crypt, in which are to be seen four antique sarcophagi
containing, it is said, the bodies of Saint Lupentius (Saint-Louans)
and his three principal disciples who, in the 7th century, founded
an abbey here in the Vienne valley.

As you move westwards the slopes are often scored with vineyards facing almost due south. A little over a mile from Saint-
Louans is the attractive late 15th century country-house of
Coulaine. It is not always easy to visit, but is worth while seeing,
since from the road little or nothing can be glimpsed of it through
a walled park of thick trees stretching up the hilly slopes.

Craon                                    The Magnificent *Château*

Cinq-Mars                                The Guard-Room

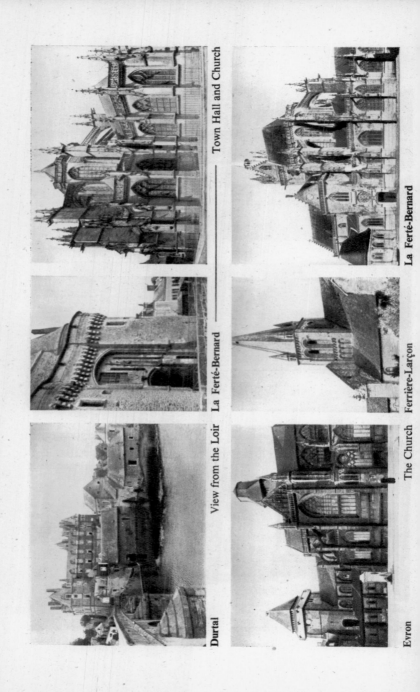

Durtal     View from the Loir     La Ferté-Bernard     Town Hall and Church

Evron     The Church     Ferrière-Larçon     La Ferté-Bernard

Farther on the road leads into the Véron, past Razilly, where was once a royal "love-nest," to the curious dwellings of the Véron troglodytes. You can then swing round through Avoine, where there is a large but neglected Louis XIII brick palace in a ravaged park, and through Huismes to hit the Chinon forest road again. Everywhere the gently rolling land is rich and fertile, everywhere you turn are manors, large farms, old *châteaux* and ruined castles.

One realises that for long France was the richest and most populous land of Europe.

## *Chinon Forest*

NORTH-EAST from Chinon and cut through by the Chinon–Tours highway, stretches the great Forest of Chinon, covering more than 13,000 acres.

In Chinon Forest Louis XI had two lodges where he often stayed. They were Little Bonaventure and Forges. Nothing now remains of them but a few stumps. It was at Forges that the King had his first stroke, after which he removed to Plessis-lès-Tours, which he hardly left until his death. In the Forest also was great Turpenay Monastery, a Benedictine foundation whose lands and domains stretched far and wide. But the trees have gathered over the abbey long since. On either side of the highway rise the great trees, noble oaks, dark pines—sometimes there is thick undergrowth, sometimes you can glance along the rides. Then the road dips, and you feel the forest close about you; then, at the crest of a hill, you view the sea of greenery billowing away to the horizon. These mighty woods are friendly places—Chinon is not one of the gloomy northern forests. Not a hundred yards off the highway you are enclosed in a sylvan world of peace and delight. Here and there are the foresters' huts and cottages, but the forest is not inhabited or cut through with pretty walks, "picturesque" sites or "old-world" villages with fake hostelries where you pay dear for a poor meal, as so often in the woodlands near to Paris. Chinon forest is still a piece of the old, forested, medieval France, where you can for a few fleeting minutes be alone with your thoughts and fool yourself that you have outwitted the planners, the millennium-mongers and the snoopers of our brave new world.

## A Much-burned Cabbage Patch

CHOLET. A Gallo-Roman town seems to have existed on the site of the modern Cholet, and the old name was CAULETUM, that means a cabbage patch. Little or nothing is known of the place's early history, but it was from the 11th century a town of some importance, lying in the south-west of Anjou.

Cholet is one of the few manufacturing towns of the Loire region, and owes its industry to Colbert "de Maulévrier," one of the lucky Colberts whose rise to fame and fortune was due to the outstanding merits and the spectacular career of the famous minister of Louis XIV. Colbert de Maulévrier was one of the last feudal lords of Cholet, and he imported a number of weavers into the Anjou town, where, in a short time, their wares became renowned. To this day, the cotton stuffs, cloths, handkerchiefs, table-cloths and fabrics of Cholet have throughout France, but especially in the West, a deserved reputation for strength and lasting qualities, making them very fit for the use of hardy peasants and country-people.

Cholet, lying spread up the right bank of the Moine's leafy valley, has a 19th century appearance. The long streets and factories string along above the course of the Moine river. There are few monuments of any account. The only ancient monuments are a bridge and a turret in the Church of Saint-Pierre. The only building that can be called old is the hospital erected in 1642. The main square or *place Travot* is bordered by the theatre, the town hall and the modern Gothic Church (1865) of Notre-Dame. To the west of the square opens the bustling, busy and commercial *rue nationale*, for not only is Cholet a textile centre, but it is also a capital of the meat trade, and every Saturday the streets are thronged with men and beasts.

The food is good at Cholet, and the local *charcuterie* or pork products—*rillettes, boudins* and the like—are famous.

In the building of the post office is a small museum, with some collections of local products, souvenirs of the Vendean wars, etc., but there is nothing of any moment. The *jardin du Mail* occupies the site of the old castle terrace.

The reason for so ancient a settlement looking so new is that the unfortunate inhabitants of Cholet had their city burned about their ears three times in a few years.

On the 15th March, 1793, Stofflet's peasants seized the city, and two days later the most murderous engagement of the whole civil war was fought on the Bégrolles heath, then outside the city gates, but now covered by the railway station. The Republican armies were led by Kléber, Marceau and Haxo. The Vendeans, under Bonchamps, were defeated and their leader killed. The town had been burned in the fighting. On the 10th March of the following year Stofflet again occupied Cholet and burned it. Later it was burned again.

For over two years the charred ruins of the once prosperous manufacturing town were entirely deserted. It is not surprising that Cholet seems new, but it is a pleasing, clean and rather attractive little city. The new Church of the Sacred Heart on the Terre-Jaune plateau is an astonishing creation, very "modern-style," and must be seen to be believed. The surroundings are charming—woods, heaths and dales, studded here and there with megalithic monuments, menhirs and dolmens.

## *A Favourite's Fate*

CINQ-MARS. To all those interested in French literature the name of Cinq-Mars recalls Alfred de Vigny's novel. The poet romanticised the tragedy of a vassal's rebellion against his sovereign (and his sovereign's all-powerful minister), but Cinq-Mars' rebellion was, indeed, the last uprising of the *noblesse* in France.

The next time there was a rebellion it was a Revolution, and this was made by the people and not by a privileged caste.

Henri Coiffier Ruzé d'Effiat, *marquis* de Cinq-Mars, was the second son of a Marshal of France, and was introduced to the Court by his fellow-countryman from Touraine, Cardinal de Richelieu (who had been the old Marshal's friend) with the rather questionable aim that the young man's influence should supersede that of Mademoiselle de Hautefort (who afterwards married the *duc* de Schomberg), then much in favour at Court. The handsome lad soon became a favourite with the King, Louis XIII. His fortune, founded on his sovereign's caprice, did not satisfy him. He wanted a high military command, and in 1642 he became party to a hare-brained scheme for bringing in the Spaniards to overthrow Richelieu. The misguided youth was merely a stooge of wilier men, such as the *duc* de Bouillon and even Gaston of Orléans, the King's brother. Cinq-Mars was, moreover, in love with a lady called Louise-Marie de Gonzague, afterwards Queen of Poland. Richelieu had no great difficulty in breaking up the plot. Cinq-Mars was arrested and executed at Lyons in 1642. He was just twenty-two years of age.

Of the *château* de Cinq-Mars, that was splendidly rebuilt in the 16th century, little survived Richelieu's vengeance (and the pillage of the neighbouring peasants) but two stout towers which rise imposingly from beside the high-road about twelve miles downstream on the right bank from Tours. Inside, however, are large apartments with rib-vaulted ceilings. The castle is well worth a visit and the huge moat is said to be the finest in all France. Just before you come to Cinq-Mars village is a square tower, over ninety feet high, terminating in four small pyramids, and known as the *Pile de Cinq-Mars*.

## The Plantagenet Tradition

CIZAY-LA-MADELEINE. What the French call the Plantagenet or Angevin style of architecture is a thing peculiar to the country around the middle reaches of the Loire.

The essentials of the style are the (remotely) Byzantine cupola borrowed from the south of France (where it may be seen at its best in the great churches of Périgord and the Quercy, e.g. at Périgueux) and Gothic vaulting borrowed from the Île-de-France (the region around Paris) and especially from the Abbey-church of Saint-Denis, the first Gothic edifice of any importance. Now, while the Gothic vaulting of the Île-de-France (and of those provinces which imitated the Île-de-France style) remains almost unchanged throughout the 12th and 13th centuries, the Angevin style of vaulting passes through a series of transformations, resulting in a type of vault very different from that of the classical Gothic of the north-east.

There still remains in Anjou a number of buildings (dating from the first half of the 12th century) whose roofs are formed of cupolas in the Byzantinesque tradition of the Périgord. Among such edifices are the Church of Saint-Martin and the Abbey-church of Le Ronceray at Angers. But the chief specimen of this style is the splendid Church of Fontevrault Abbey. Then, by the middle of the 12th century, we find the peculiar Angevin vaulting exemplified in the Cathedral of Angers.

This vaulting went through a surprising number of transformations, all, apparently, of local origin, so that the study of the Angevin style is one of endless interest. It is possible to date a building of Angevin style to within a few years—once we have sorted out the phases.

If you leave Saumur by the national road No. 160, the Cholet highway branches off about a mile and a half after the Thouet bridge. Five miles farther on you pass one of the innumerable Montforts of northern France, and to the south-east lies Cizay-la-Madeleine, whose church has a fine 13th century choir, and contains furnishings removed hither from the old Abbey of Asnières, and this abbey should, if at all possible, be visited by anyone travelling in this part of the world.

The abbey-church was unfortunately mutilated in 1853, when the nave was pulled down, but, as it stands, the building is a remarkable specimen of the Angevin style. The south transept dates from the 12th century, the north transept and the choir from the following century.

The choir is splendid, and forms a huge rectangular hall supported by two columns, from which spring light and elegant vaults whose key-stones and knops are carved with scenes from the Life of Christ.

From the south-east corner of the choir you go into the abbatial chapel, a charming oratory dating from the thirteen hundreds.

But little remains of the conventual buildings—a wall of the chapter-house, and some scattered and isolated rooms, granges and halls in the neighbouring farms.

## Scarron's "Comic History"

CONLIE. Scarron's *Comic History* is not the history of his own life, which was more tragedy than comedy, but the title of his best-known book. Scaron or Scarron was a man whose literary works would by this time be forgotten had he not been an actor in one of the most extraordinary dramas of French history. Scarron's father, who was, at one time, in enjoyment of the profitable and honourable post of councillor of the Paris *parlement* (that was not a parliament in our sense of the term, but a judicial body charged, among other duties, with the registering and promulgation of royal decrees), had the misfortune to fall foul of the Cardinal de Richelieu, who deprived him of his job and exiled him to Touraine. The younger Scarron had a detestable stepmother, and he was forced also to be the helpless witness of his family fortunes' collapse. He had to find some more or less suitable employment, and managed to procure his appointment to a canonry in Le Mans cathedral. Under the old *régime* canonries (and many other pieces of ecclesiastical preferment) were often regarded as sine-cures to be distributed to persons in need of pensions or at any rate desirous of getting pensions. Such "canons" were not necessarily in holy orders, even of the most minor sort, and, as a matter of fact, Scarron, though known until his marriage as the *Abbé* Scarron, remained a layman. These lay "canons" could not, how-ever, marry and their status was not unlike that of Oxford dons in the 18th century.

Scarron led a gay life in Paris, interspersed with periods of residence at Le Mans, where his conduct was also not wholly befitting his quasi-ecclesiastical profession. When he was twenty-eight years of age, a terrible misfortune overtook the *abbé*. He became partially paralysed, and was so martyred by an affection of the joints that his head sagged on to his chest and his legs dragged behind him. Various explanations have been given for Scarron's sudden affliction. The classical story is that one carnival-day in Le Mans he daubed himself with honey and rolled in a ripped-up feather-bed until he resembled a wild man of the woods. He then rushed out into the streets and joined the merry throng of holiday-makers, but he was so mobbed by the crowd that he ran off and flung himself into the river, there remaining in the water until everyone had gone home, when he made his way back to his house, only to find that in the morning he was tortured with pain and a physical wreck. As a matter of fact, Scarron's disease, though rare, is known as Rhizomelic Spondylosis, it is a complaint practically speaking confined to men between the ages of 20 and 40. It develops very slowly, but little by little in excruciating pain the wretched victim is hardened as it were into a block of stone.

His disabilities did not prevent him from resuming, more or less, his old life in Paris and continuing his satirical writings. Someone had suggested to him that the climate of America might cure him (strange idea!), and one day a friend of his brought to his house a young woman called Françoise d'Aubigné, who had returned from Martinique some time before.

## The Beautiful Indian

THIS girl, of a well-known but quite impoverished family, was strikingly beautiful, and her friends called her *la belle Indienne* ("Indian" in those days meant generally American Indian). Scarron was captivated by the graces of Françoise and touched by her indigence and helplessness. He offered to marry her. She accepted. Scarron lost his canonry by his marriage, and was reduced to literary hack-work, until a pension paid by the famous financier Fouquet eased the couple's circumstances a little. The Scarrons maintained a sort of semi-Bohemian *salon* in the Marais quarter of Paris, a *salon* where met the most diverse sorts and conditions of people—famous courtesans such as Marion Delorme (who had been Richelieu's mistress) and Ninon de Lenclos; eccentrics such as Madame de La Suze, who changed her religion so that she might be certain of never seeing her husband again in a future life; Saint-Evremond, the wit and writer who ended his days in England; courtiers, men of fashion and adventurers.

The Scarrons lived on the fringes of the Court, and were favoured by the Queen-Mother (Anne of Austria) and by Mazarin.

Scarron died in 1660, leaving nothing but debts and a considerable number of writings, among which were a rhyming will by which he gave his wife permission to marry again (he could little have thought who would be his successor) and a pathetic epitaph for his own tomb.

Madame Scarron was lucky enough to get transferred to herself her husband's pension paid from the Queen's Privy Purse.

## Uncrowned Queen of France

MADAME SCARRON'S later career belongs to general history. In 1669 she was chosen to bring up in secrecy at Vaugirard (then a suburb of Paris) the children Louis XIV had by Madame de Montespan. In 1674 the widow Scarron removed to Court at Versailles with her charges. She had made enough money out of her job to buy the property of Maintenon, not far from Paris, on the Chartres road. In 1678 the King raised Maintenon to the status of a *marquisat*.

The Queen, Maria-Theresa of Austria—whose miseries and humiliations are summed up in her own pathetic words, "Since I have been Queen I have not known one day's happiness"—died on the 31st July, 1683, rather suddenly, of an anthrax, or malignant boil, which the royal surgeons, after the fashion of the day, treated by profuse blood-lettings.

Louis XIV affected nothing but the most perfunctory mourning for his ill-used spouse, and he scandalised by his indifference even the easygoing members of his Court.

On the 9th October of the same year, the King returned from a sojourn at Fontainebleau, and, according to latest researches, he married Mme de Maintenon during the night from that Saturday to Sunday, the 10th October, 1683. Mgr. de Harlay, Archbishop of Paris, performed the ceremony in the chapel of Versailles *château*. There were few witnesses and the secret was well kept. So great, indeed, was the terror inspired by the King's threats, that no one during the King's lifetime dared to refer (at least in writing) to the marriage.

Mme de Maintenon would, doubtless, have liked a little less discretion, but she was powerless in this matter, though her influence in many other directions was great and became greater with the passing of time. However, she was always, in phrase at least, of becoming modesty. As she wrote to her niece (afterwards her heiress and *duchesse* de Noailles), who was showing, in her aunt's opinion, a little too much of the bumptiousness of youth, "I am of not much account, whereas you are of no account at all."

At the time of their second marriages the King was forty-five and his Mme de Maintenon forty-eight. It seems probable that the ceremony regularised a long-standing, if, possibly, intermittent liaison. Louis XIV was rather promiscuous in his amours, and did not, for instance, disdain to favour with his attentions Mlle Desoeuillets, Mme de Montespan's chamber-maid.

As the morganatic wife of Louis XIV, Mme de Maintenon was to play a considerable rôle in the history of the French monarchy and, therefore, in that of the French people during the latter part of the Sun-King's reign.

Her first husband, poor Scarron, in his *Histoire Comique*, could

**La Ferté-Bernard**                    Old House

The Plantagenet Tombs

Henry II—Henry II and Eleanor of Guyenne—Richard Coeur-de-Lion

The Minster

The Cloisters

The Chapter House

**La Flèche**

The Castle and Gate of the *Prytanée*

**Fontevrault**                The Kitchen    **Le Grand-Pressigny** The Keep

Fresnay-sur-Sarthe     Town Gate

Gennes

Le Grand-Pressigny     The Castle

Jublains     The Roman Camp

Château de la Côte

Fresnay-sur-Sarthe

have imagined no more improbable story than that of his widow's remarriage.

The scene of parts of Scarron's *Comic History* are laid in and around Le Mans. Domfront-en-Champagne is famous only because it figures in Scarron's work, and the country hereabouts is as much Scarron's country as is the region across the Vienne from Chinon Rabelais' land immortalised in *Pantagruel*.

## Scarron's Country

IF you leave Le Mans by the Sillé-le-Guillaume road, you pass, at La Chapelle-Saint-Aubin, the ruins of an old leper-house, founded, it is said, by a St. Christophe in the 13th century. Farther on, near La Milesse (whose church contains some good statuary), lies Aigné, with some brass, or rather copper, tomb-plates which, though common enough with us, are rather rare in France, since most of them were ripped off and melted down at the time of the Revolution.

The highway takes a series of dips down to Domfront-en-Champagne, near which is an artificial mound nearly 100 feet high and dubbed "Cæsar's Camp," but the name is probably no older than that of most other places associated in popular legend with the Conqueror of Gaul.

Conlie is some three miles from Domfront, and its church has some fine furnishings. In the churchyard there is a granite calvary erected over the common grave of 118 Breton soldiers who died in the Conlie camp during the years 1870 and 1871.

## The Magic of the Megaliths

CONNERRÉ. One of the most complicated phases of the pre-history of Europe is that covering the activities of the people we know as "megalith builders." Several intersecting and crossing streams of culture, characterised by the erection of megalithic or large-stone monuments—cists, dolmens, gallery-graves, passage-graves and the like—swept through and around western Europe in New Stone Age times. We may take it that most of the builders of the megalithic monuments we meet with in and around the Loire valley came up the river from the coast. It seems clear that the megalith-builders were men wielding a powerful magic, practising an elaborate, and doubtless impressive, cult of the dead, and depending for their material welfare upon a sea-borne commerce.

Megalithic monuments are met with, however, at considerable distances from the coast (though the most famous monuments, such as the "alignments" of Carnac in Brittany, are by the seashore or not far from it) and, for instance, quite near Connerré (about fourteen miles from La Ferté-Bernard) is a magnificent gallery-grave known at *La Pierre Couverte*. It is composed of six slabs of sandstone, the longest of which measures twenty-five feet. About a thousand yards from *La Pierre Couverte* lies *La Pierre Fiche*, a "menhir" or tall upright stone, which is pierced with a circular hole in its upper part.

When we reflect on the riches of south-western France in traces of early man and on the evidences of his passage nearly all over the country, we shall visualise the history of the country we call France as a very long tale indeed. We are coming more and more to realise that between pre-history, proto-history and history itself there are no gaps and intervals at all save such as are due to our ignorance. The long story of man stretches back, in our western European lands at least, through incredibly remote ages.

You can reach Connerré down the Nogent-le-Rotrou to Le Mans highway and through some picturesque villages with old churches. At Duneau there is the tomb of Catherine d'Illiers, Lady of Monterel, who died in 1417; this antique monument escaped the damage of revolutionary times.

Connerré itself lies in the pretty valley of the Dué stream. The Church of Saint-Symphorien has a fine Romanesque belfry, and there are some traces of the old town-walls, for Connerré has known better (or more distinguished) days, and was once a little fortress.

## The Englishman who Taught the Franks Latin

CORMERY. Our Alcuin, born at York in 735, the greatest scholar and the most eminent figure of the revival of learning under Charlemagne—a revival known as the "Carolingian Renaissance"—was, for a time, Abbot of Cormery, a Benedictine foundation established in the late seven hundreds by one Hitier, Abbot of Saint-Martin's at Tours and chancellor to Charlemagne, Emperor of the West.

Cormery abbey survived until the Revolution. Then, after a thousand years of corporate life, the monastery was dissolved, and the buildings fell into ruin. Of Cormery there remains to-day the *tour Saint-Paul* (built from 1026 to 1048) that was the belfry. The first storey forms a chamber with a rib-vaulted roof divided into sixteen compartments. Then there are the 14th century refectory, the abbot's lodging and its chapel (about a hundred years later in date), parts of the Gothic cloisters, and the *tour Saint-Jean*, which formerly marked the south end of the transepts.

The parish church of Notre-Dame-du-Fougeray is Romanesque, and in its churchyard is an early Gothic Calvary.

Only about three miles from Cormery, in the direction of Tours, and down the Indre valley, you reach Esvres, where is a good 12th century church and, not far off, the *château* of Couzières, which is, in part, five hundred years old. The highway up the Indre valley is delightful.

## Rabelais Country

L E COUDRAY-MONTPENSIER. If you cross the Vienne stream by the Chinon bridge, and instead of taking the Richelieu road to the left or following the course of the river you strike to the right, you are soon in the delightful rolling, wooded country of western Touraine, a land of old manors, fairy-like castles and hidden villages. It is a land with all the exciting quality that comes from a rather restricted horizon. You never know what you will come upon next. We have halted by the way-side to picnic, and found ourselves in the tangled grounds of a deserted Renaissance manor with graceful Italianate carvings, crumbling caryatids, and spacious halls still showing in places a superb flooring of white and black marble.

Quite near Seuilly, immortalised by Rabelais, lies the village of La Roche-Clermault—you are in the country of *Gargantua* and *Pantagruel*. Soon, afar off, on its hill, rises the proud outline of Le Coudray-Montpensier.

The place was begun towards the end of the thirteen hundreds. The castle was greatly enlarged after 1482 by Louis de Bourbon, Lord of Montpensier and of neighbouring Champigny-sur-Veude. Here the influence of the new style of defensive architecture is clearly visible as at Le Plessis-Bourré (see p. 247). Louis was a

natural son of the first *duc* de Bourbon and had married Jehanne
the bastard daughter of King Louis XI by Marie de Sassenage. A
marriage with a natural daughter of the monarch was considered
a great honour calling for a display of pomp—hence the lordly
residence of Le Coudray, renamed Le Coudray-Montpensier.

For some generations now Le Coudray has been in the possession of the La Motte-Baracé family, the head of which, some years
ago, was an eccentric old *marquis*, one of whose hobbies was
resoling his own boots.

The main wing of Le Coudray is three storeys high, and is
flanked with huge round towers. It is a most imposing place.

### *A Fisherman's Retreat*

COURÇAY. As a relief from architectural exploration or even
from sight-seeing in general, nothing could be more agreeable
than a short stay at Courçay, on the right bank of the Indre.
Here are simple, good inns, delicious wine, plain but satisfying
Touraine fare and excellent fishing. This is just the place to laze
about in for a few days. You can loll in a boat, tie up under the
overhanging trees, or paddle about the leafy, twining reaches of
the river. From almost anywhere you choose to land, charming,
lazy sorts of walks lead into a countryside full of sleepy, picturesque
villages and ruins and old churches. If you row up to Azay-sur-
Indre, you can make your way by road as far as Genillé, in the
Montrésor direction. Genillé church has some of the furnishings
formerly gracing the nearby Abbey of La Bourdillière.

### *Louvois' House*

COURTANVAUX. A creature of Mazarin's, Michel le Tellier,
was by his patron's protection appointed Secretary of State
for War. He proved an efficient administrator. Later he was
Chancellor of France, and one of the instigators of the Revocation
of the Edict of Nantes, the Act that caused such grievous loss of
France by the emigration of thousands of Huguenots. Le Tellier
amassed great wealth, and arranged for his elder son (the younger
became Archbishop of Rheims), François-Michel, a marriage with
the sole heir of Charles de Souvré, Lord of Courtanvaux.

This François-Michel Le Tellier, *marquis* de Louvois, was,
perhaps, with the possible exception of Carnot, the greatest War

inister France has ever known. He died at the early age of fifty
only six years after his father), leaving a widow of whom Saint-
mon says much in praise—"She had the finest mien in the
orld, the most lovely . . . figure . . . she was dark and beautiful."
er son by Louvois was known as the *marquis* de Courtanvaux.
ater, Courtanvaux passed to a branch of the Montesquiou family,
' which was that Robert de Montesquiou, a real though rather
diculous poet, whose affectations, pretensions, misfortunes and
elations with Marcel Proust have been vividly and attractively
ld by Madame Elisabeth de Gramont.

Courtanvaux is rather a melancholy place nowadays. The por-
ait gallery of the Montesquious is no more. The furniture has all
een auctioned off. The house is a husk, but as you look through
he huge vaulted doorway surmounted by the chipped and effaced
scutcheon of the Le Telliers, the old mansion seems noble
nough, its great façade and grey towers merging into the dark
oods of its neglected park.

Courtanvaux' village is little Bessé-sur-Braye, whose 15th cen-
ury church contains a Montesquiou chapel with some family
nonuments and the family vault.

### *"An Emissary of Satan"*

CRAON. Readers of Borrow's *Bible in Spain* will remember
the incident at Evora, in Portugal, when our traveller fell into
conversation with Geronima, the kitchen-maid, who would not go
o Mass, and gave as her reason that she had been converted to
'free-thinking" by reading Volney's *Ruins of Empires.* Borrow
nduced her to produce the detestable volume, characterised its
author as an "emissary of Satan," and solemnly burned the book
while the chastened Geronima sat by telling her beads.

Volney is a now almost forgotten worthy, but he was a prominent
figure in his day, and must be accounted the most famous son of
the town of Craon, where he was born in 1757. Constantin François Chasseboeuf was in his youth called "Monsieur de Boisgirais,"
and only later adopted the style of "Monsieur de Volney," that is
perpetuated in the *rue* Volney (and in the *cercle* Volney) in Paris.
Volney saw life for about four years in Syria and Egypt, and then
returned to France, and became a member of the States-General.

It was in 1791 that he published his famous *Ruin of Empires* which so horrified Borrow. Like other men who have been deeply impressed in youth by contact with alien faiths and manners and customs, he constructed a sort of synthetic "philosophy" of religions, a "philosophy" in which he claimed to have embodied the "underlying truth" of all confessions without, of course, any of the "overlying falsehood." Volney's pompous synthesis is hardly readable to-day, and we are inclined to wonder at the violent and adverse criticism the book aroused. In 1792 he bought an estate and tried to put into practice the political and social theories he had evolved, but he was thrown into prison at the time of the Jacobin triumph. On his release he tried his hand at teaching, and was for a time professor of history at the *École Normale* (or special school for the training of high-school masters), but in 1795 he thought it advisable to move to the United States—then, in the imagination of many Frenchmen, a sort of promised land, not of wealth perhaps, but of freedom and liberty—but three years later the Americans unkindly expelled him as a "French spy" that he was almost certainly not. He rallied to the imperial cause (as did most prudent Frenchmen in Napoleon's time), although he remained a moderate. The Emperor, however, created him a *comte*, and gave him a seat in the Senate. Under the Restoration he was made a Peer of France. So his unorthodox opinions had either died down or they did not prove very offensive to the ultrareactionary and clerical government of King Louis XVIII.

## Short Shrift for Wantons

CRAON is the centre of the Craonnais, one of the richest agricultural regions of France. The town has an ancient wooden covered market. For the rest Craon is famed for two things—first its excellent breed of pigs, and secondly, for its magnificent *château*. The little town, on the Oudon, with Volney's statue by Dénecheau on the main square, is, otherwise, not remarkable, but the *château* should not be missed by the visitor to Anjou.

There was a Gallo-Roman villa at Craon and in the 9th century the Count of Nantes here built a castle. The powerful family of the Counts of Craon lasted through the Middle Ages. In the 14th century the lordship of Craon passed, through marriage, to the La Trémoïlle family. In the time of King Louis XI

Georges (II) de La Trémoïlle appears to have made an unfortunate marriage, since by letters patent dated from Amboise, 25th August, 1471, the Lord of Craon was authorised to keep his wife:

> "*Enclose et emmurée en quelque lieu seur de manière qu'elle ne puisse converser avecques personne afin que les adultères, cas, crimes et inconvenances . . . ne puissent advenir.*"

> ("*Imprisoned and shut up in some sure place so that she may be able to have no converse with any person in order that the adulteries, scandals, crimes and misdemeanours . . . cannot take place.*")

The straw that, apparently, broke the camel's back was an attempt to poison her husband, and that in collusion with one of her lovers, a man called Ambroise Roichelle, who, being a low fellow, did not get off so easily as Marie de Montauban, widow of Louis de Rohan and wife of Georges de La Trémoïlle, Lord of Craon.

Roichelle was publicly executed at Tours.

Georges and Marie de La Trémoïlle had no children, and on his death an interesting inventory of the contents of Craon was drawn up in connection with the inheritance of the estate (which passed to a brother).

We get some idea of how a great feudal castle was furnished in 1481.

There were very many tapestries, and these hangings constituted, we may take it, the greatest luxury of a great house and also the most obvious sign of wealth and fine living. Then come beds, nine mantles (clothes and furniture are all grouped together in the lists), two *veluz*, that is thick-pile and not tapestry carpets—probably imported from the East and evidently objects of great value, since only two are recorded for the whole great house—two cushions or pillows of brocaded silk, two cushions of black velvet and two of yellow.

Kitchen utensils, sheets and various other pieces of furniture.

Twenty pipes of wine—white, red and *clairet* (i.e. not what we call claret to-day, but rather *rosé* or pink and light wine). There was a regular small arsenal in the Great Tower and plenty of hunting-gear.

In one of the bedrooms there was a "basin for washing the hands"—an unusual luxury.

When the widow of Louis (II) de La Trémoïlle died, and before her body was enclosed in a wooden and then in a leaden coffin, plaster casts were taken of her face and hands, and these were fixed on to a dummy which was then gorgeously apparelled and placed upon a catafalque, before which for thirteen days and thirteen nights seven chaplains said Mass.

The bells tolled continuously for three days. Mourning was distributed to all the dependants and tenants. It was a very gorgeous funeral.

Craon old castle was much damaged in the Wars of Religion, and in 1604 Henry IV gave orders for its complete demolition. The name, indeed, recalled unpleasant memories to the King, for here in 1592 Merceour defeated his troops and d'Aumont and his cavalry had to be sent to clear up the situation.

## The New Château

IN 1701 François de la Forest d'Armaillé bought Craon, and in 1760 his grandson commissioned Pommereul to design and build a fine country-house in the style of the day.

Craon is rather low and all executed in Saumur stone. The main block has two slightly projecting wings and a central forepart also advancing a little. The whole is a model of elegance and good taste. The fine *boiseries* or panelling within are probably the work of David *père*. The decoration, with masks, garlands and floral motifs, is very like that of woodwork known to have been executed by the father of David d'Angers (see p. 36).

In the first half of the 19th century Craon was for years the home of the widowed *marquise* de Champagné, who was much under the influence of Louis Veuillot, the extravagantly ultramontane polemist, journalist and author. Dom Guéranger, the restorer of the Benedictine Abbey of Solesmes, was also a frequent visitor to Craon.

## A Church over a Thousand Years Old

CRAVANT. Most of Cravant church is in characteristic Carolingian style; the south wall, especially, displays what is called *petit appareil* or courses of small blocks, with layers or

La Guerche          The Fortress

L'Ile-Bouchard       Apse of St. Leonard's Church

The Castle     Landifer     and the Mayenne River     Laval

The Ducal Palace     Laval

The Layon Stream

chains of *grand appareil* or large blocks, while in the upper portions there is *appareil réticulé*, or masonry arranged in interlacing rectangles. This latter style is directly derived from Roman architectural traditions.

Farther down the Sainte-Maure road lies Panzoult, a village immortalised by Rabelais. The church, Romanesque and Gothic, contains a number of interesting statues. The neighbouring Pressoir manor has a charming Renaissance pigeon-loft.

Nearby is a grotto whose walls bear traces of paintings. This, by tradition, was the case of Rabelais' *Panzoult Sybil*.

## The Most Magnificent Romanesque Building in Anjou

CUNAULT. If you leave Saumur by the left-bank road, which is much more picturesque than, if not so good for speed as, the billiard-table surface of the right-bank *levée,* you run through Saint-Florentin that is really a suburb of Saumur. Here much of the "champagnised" wine is fabricated.

Chênehutte-les-Tuffaux, on the river's banks, has a restored Romanesque church. The pale grey cliffs are all pitted and bored with cellars, habitations and store-rooms. Sometimes a masonry cottage-face is stuck against the escarpment while the dwelling extends backwards into the rock. On the crest of the hill is Chênehutte castle, with the ruins of a 16th century priory.

Two miles farther on you pass the magnificent feudal keep of Trèves. It towers up a full 100 feet high, all that remains of a castle set up in 1435 by one Robert le Maçon, Chancellor of France. It is composed of a round tower flanked with a square block surmounted by a polygonal edifice bearing crenellations and machicolations. The inside of the keep is worth visiting, and is admirably preserved. There is at Trèves a splendid Romanesque church containing the tomb of Robert Le Maçon; his recumbent statue is mutilated but the monument is surmounted by a Flamboyant 15th century carved stone canopy.

A mile away is Cunault, famed for its magnificent Romanesque church.

On the north side is a tower (more ancient than the rest of the building), terminating in a stumpy spire added in the fourteen hundreds.

The western façade is fortified and over the door is a superb and archaic crowned Virgin in Majesty, adored on either side by converging angles of great elegance and beauty. The interior is very imposing. It is about 225 feet long by 75 broad and 66 high. There are more than 200 carved capitals. Three bays of the nave have "Angevin vaulting" that we see so well displayed in Angers Cathedral, that is to say vaulting which rises up so as to form a kind of dome. There are, here and there at Cunault, traces of the painting which in the heyday of Romanesque architecture illuminated the interior of churches and cathedrals. There is a fine Descent from the Cross (15th century sculpture) and the treasure of the sanctuary is the shrine of Saint-Maxenceul in carved, painted and gilded wood. The reliquary has the form of a church and dates apparently from the eleven hundreds. Reliquaries in wood are extremely rare and almost all the ancient ones which have survived are in metal.

The general impression made by this noble church is one of antique and austere majesty.

## *Rabelais*

LA DEVINIÈRE. We have no sure proof as to where Rabelais was born, except that he was born in Touraine and somewhere near Chinon. There is, however, a fairly reliable and ancient tradition that would set his birthplace at what has been often, but rather pompously, called the "Manor of La Devinière." Rabelais' father may have been a lawyer of some sort, or, on the other hand, he may have been a vintner and wine-merchant. In the 16th century, occupations were often not very clear-cut, especially with men who sold their own produce. A man might be, at once, a butcher and a large stock-raiser, he might keep a pub and also own wide acres of vineyards. He might also combine various callings, and be both a lawyer and a vintner. One story has it that Rabelais' father was the "lord" of a little property called Chavigny-en-Vallée. There is, however, no suggestion that he was of "noble" origin.

The "manor" at La Devinière, about a league from Chinon on the other side of the Vienne, is nothing but a cottage with a steep, slate roof. You go up four steps to the front door that leads right into a lower room occupying the whole of the ground-floor.

A staircase of thirteen scooped and slippery steps leads to the upper room (also occupying the whole storey), where, tradition has it, Rabelais was born. But the tradition is highly suspect.

It is, however, clear that Rabelais knew this part of Touraine well, and it is even probable that he here spent his childhood—or part of it; Lerné, Seuilly, La Roche-Clermauld and Panzoult, all names familiar to readers of *Pantagruel,* are villages quite near to La Devinière.

As a matter of fact, little is known for certain about the life of Rabelais at all. He was a doctor of medicine of Montpellier. He was a Franciscan monk. He held several country livings, notably that of Meudon, near Paris. But the description of him as the *curé de Meudon* (as he is often called by the French) is hardly justified. He held the benefice for about two years, and it is more than probable that he never went near his *cure.* In fact, Rabelais' "life," as generally received, is all fable and legend. There is no foundation for the silly story that has given rise to the proverbial saying *le quart d'heure de Rabelais,* or Rabelais' quarter of an hour. It is not very likely that, if a wandering monk had in the 16th century declared his intention of poisoning the King, he would have been transported from Lyons to Paris. He would have been dealt with on the spot. And had Rabelais been brought to Paris, he would hardly have been pardoned for the sort of joke that the Valois kings hardly found amusing.

The corner house, No. 15, of the *rue de la Lamproie* at Chinon bears a plaque indicating that the dwelling was that of Rabelais' parents, but Rabelais was born in 1495 and the Chinon house is not 450 years old. However, the inn-keeper, vintner, apothecary or lawyer father of Rabelais may well have had a house in Chinon town, and it may well have stood upon the site of that now bearing the inscription. Local legend has it that it was from the first-floor windows of his father's house that Rabelais fished for lampreys in the flooded streets of Chinon. There is nothing inherently impossible in the tale. We have seen the lower town of Chinon with three feet of water in the streets. Four hundred and more years ago we may be sure that lampreys did sometimes wriggle up the alleys of the little township, but we need not suppose that Rabelais made a practice of fishing from his mother's drawing-room. If the tale had any foundation in fact, it would fall into the class of those legends that swell out the occasional and exceptional into the frequent and usual.

## The Tiers Livre

RABELAIS lives in his books or rather in his book, and nothing we may surmise or guess or even learn about the conditions of his life will tell us as much about him (and about ourselves) as will the reading of his deathless human comedy.

In 1546 Rabelais published his *Tiers Livre des Faits et Dits héroiques du bon Pantagruel* (or "Third Book of the Heroic Deeds and Sayings of the Good Pantagruel." The *Tiers Livre* may not be the most-read or the best-known of Rabelais' volumes, but from many points of view it marks the climax of Rabelais' art. About a dozen years had passed since *Gargantua* had been printed, and now Rabelais dared to drop his pseudonym of "Alcofribas Nasier" and to let his real name appear on the title-page. The writer, in fact, thought that he was sure of the royal protection of François I, who was, indeed, well enough disposed towards him, and an admirer of his works, but the King was getting old and tired, and did little or nothing to shield Rabelais from the arrows aimed at him from the Sorbonne, or University of Paris, whose professors were outraged by the satirical allusions and by the direct attacks contained in the *Tiers Livre*.

The central theme of the *Tiers Livre*, however—the tragi-comic uncertainties of the married state—was not one to astonish or to perturb the theologians.

Briefly, the story is that the crazy Panurge suddenly decides that he must get married, but greatly fearing conjugal misfortune, he wants to take out an insurance against being deceived. So he sets off on a series of consultations. One after the other he questions Pantagruel, the old soothsayer of Panzoust or Panzoult, near Chinon, then he sees what he can get out of Nazdecabre, the mute who gives his answer by signs. Then come Raminagrobis, "the old French poet," Epistemon, the astrologer Her Trippa, Brother Jean des Entommeures, Hippodathée the theologian, Rondibilis the doctor, Trouillogan the philosopher, Bridoye the judge, Triboulet the fool. But all in vain. So Panurge persuades Pantagruel to go forth upon a pilgrimage to consult the oracle of the *Dive Bouteille* or the Divine Bottle, and the story of this pilgrimage is the subject of the *Quart Livre*.

During his account of Panurge's search for matrimonial wisdom Rabelais allows himself violent attacks on women. Such antifeminine literature was nothing new. It was, indeed, in Rabelais' day quite common, and had been a feature of French writing ever since the medieval days of the *Roman de la Rose*. But it is to be noted that Rabelais dedicated his *Tiers Livre* of brilliant and rather brutal satire on women (whose wits he claims are *abstrait, ravi et extatique*) to Marguerite of Navarre, one of the most intelligent, cultivated and able women of her time.

In this *Tiers Livre* of one great Touraine writer we may see a resemblance to the work of another great Touraine writer generations later. In fact, Rabelais, long before his fellow-countryman Balzac, was the first to publish a *Physiologie du Mariage*. The book of this Franciscan monk is an amazing and revealing and exciting medley of medicine and philosophy, through which runs, like bright thread, Rabelais' conviction that the highest manifestations of human genius are bound up with a physiological act.

And the prose and the style of the *Tiers Livre* are different from those of its predecessors *Pantagruel* and *Gargantua,* which are written in what is, essentially, a popular and somewhat "vinous" manner. The *Quart Livre* smacks of the sea, and is illuminated by a sort of marine iridescence. But the *Tiers Livre* is more finely drawn. The fooling and clowning harden into irony. There is as much of the Greek spirit as of the coarser Gallic and, together with play and fantasy, much serious and penetrating thought. Pantagruel represents, in contrast to the scatter-brained and wrongheaded Panurge, wisdom and serene reason. The matrimonial confusions of Panurge illustrate and even illuminate the mighty problems of man's liberty and destiny.

"Pantagruelion" is the name of the magic herb of which Pantagruel takes a good cargo when he sets off to consult the oracle of the Divine Bottle, and "pantagruelion" is a symbol of man's technical progress, thanks to which, thought Rabelais, men would become masters of the most secret forces of nature, and would eject the gods from their celestial abodes. In an almost lyrical outburst Rabelais throws off the prejudices of his time and looks far forwards in words which seem to us strangely prophetic. And yet all the *Tiers Livre* is full of the acutest observation, of a rich comic humour, and of all the sharpest and wittiest raillery and satire.

In the descriptions of the men Panurge consults, Rabelais presents us with a veritable *Comédie Humaine* ("Human Comedy"), sketched with a sure hand—a trait, an observation and the man is pinned down for us. Nothing could be more thought-provoking than the description of Bridoye the judge, who delivers his judgments on a throw of the dice.

We can well understand how the men of the Sorbonne were alarmed and why they secured that the *Tiers Livre* should be suppressed. The reign of the libertine François I was closing under the shadows of a harsh, fanatical piety. And in the same year that Rabelais published his *Tiers Livre*, Etienne Dolet, the scholar and printer, was burned as a "relapsed atheist" on the *place* Maubert in Paris.

## The Fountains of the Douet

DOUÉ-LA-FONTAINE. The famed "fountains" giving their name to Doué-la-Fontaine are great basins, about 140 feet long by 80 feet wide, hewn out of the living rock. Round them runs a tree-shaded terrace that is the public promenade of the town. Doué is a place of some size, although it is so straggling that it appears smaller than it really is. With the neighbouring villages of Douces and Soulanger, the population of the town is above five thousand souls. Doué is built, very largely, over old and deep quarries, which until comparatively recent times were lived in.

## Subterranean Houses

THE subterranean "house" under the *maison Lyonnet* (*place de La Halle*) can be visited. Several rooms lead out of a main hall, and in some of the walls sepulchres are hollowed out.

The so-called "theatre" of Doué, long attributed to the Romans, is nothing else than another old, abandoned quarry which was worked in terraces, giving the place something of the appearance of a Roman amphitheatre, an appearance which was accentuated by the cutting of the terraces into seats for the use of audiences at stage-plays given here as long ago as the 15th and again in the 17th centuries.

The Church of Saint Peter is Gothic, and nearby are the ruins of the old collegiate Church of Saint-Denys, but neither place is of much interest. The remains of the old fortress walls rise on a height above the town, and enclose an 18th century lodging of pleasing, but not striking, appearance.

Not far from Doué is Nueil-sous-Passavant, whose church contains some tombs, a few statues and, notably, an abbot's throne from the ruined Abbey of Asnières, a mile and a half away. Nueil was, during the Vendean wars, the scene of a notable feat. On the 28th May, 1794, Pilet, the republican mayor of the place, together with twelve good men and true, held out in the church against a siege by Stofflet and six hundred insurgents. Pilet, alone, of the defenders was killed.

## French Schombergs

DURTAL. At Durtal, the village is of small account; you see only the supple, smiling Loir, and then the bold outline of an imposing castle.

Around a fortress set up here on the bluff by Geoffrey Martel, son and emulator of the great Fulk Nerra, in the middle of the 11th century, grew gradually a settlement of houses.

The great castle we see to-day was, however, rebuilt in the reigns of Henry IV and of Louis XIII by Henry de Schomberg and Françoise d'Espinay, his wife. This Henry de Schomberg, *comte* de Nanteuil and Durtal, *maréchal* de France, and Grand-Master of the Artillery, came from the branch of the Saxon Schönburgs, who were of the same stock as that Duke of Schomberg well known in our history. Schomberg's wife had inherited Durtal from her mother, the heiress of the Vieilleville family.

Durtal consists of three wings buttressed and flanked by two stout, round towers, which are the only remains of the ancient feudal fortress. The southern wing facing on the Loir is a regular and noble façade of brick and stone in the style of the Touraine tradition prevailing during the middle years of the 15th century.

## A Public-spirited Duke

LATER on, Durtal belonged to that *duc* de Liancourt of whom we read in Young's *Travels in France*. Liancourt was a social reformer who was impressed by a visit he paid to England in the years just before the Revolution. He was a member of the States-General and an acute observer of events. He uttered a warning to the King, who remarked to him (three days before the fall of the Bastille), "This is a revolt." Liancourt countered, "No, Sire, it is a Revolution." In 1792, Liancourt was the guest of Arthur Young in England, and then, like so many other Frenchmen of the revolutionary times, he proceeded to the United States, but returned to Paris in 1799. As what in those days was considered a "revolutionary" (what we should to-day think of as an old-fashioned Liberal) Liancourt got no kindness, consideration or compensation for his financial losses from the restored monarchy of Louis XVIII. Still, Liancourt devoted his life to social welfare, promoting vaccination, agricultural reform and to furthering the work of the Academy of Medicine. He was certainly the most useful and distinguished of Durtal's masters, and he deserves to be remembered among a host of frivolous and inconsequent men, both of his class and of others, who cram and jostle their way through the fifty feverish years from 1789 onwards.

Higher up the curling course of the Loir from Durtal lies Bazouges, whose fine barbican is defended by imposing towers. Bazouges is, approximately, of the same date as Durtal.

Moving down the Loir from Durtal you pass the *château* of Le Plessis-Greffier. It is a fine 17th century house. And four miles farther downstream are the ruins of Le Verger (see p. 352).

Then comes Seiches-sur-le-Loir (note the insertion of the word *le,* so that when the name is spoken there shall be no confusion with the greater Loir*e*) with, nearby, the *château* d'Ardenne, whose keep and chapel date from the thirteen hundreds.

Pellouailles church, a mile and a half before you reach Angers, is worth a short visit, since it houses a very fine painted panel of the Entombment–it is probably French work, and dates from the 16th century.

## How Mansart Worked

ÉCHAILLY. Échailly lies about fifteen miles from Saumur and on the boundaries of Poitou. In 1730 the property was bought by one Jean de La Selle and his descendants kept the lands until 1900.

La Selle erected, in the first half of the 18th century, a large country-house, for which the plans are said to have been "drawn up by Mansart." There is nothing improbable in this. The most fashionable architect of the day maintained a large office, with draughtsmen engaged in preparing drawings, just as the fashionable artists and painters often had most of the work done by apprentices and pupils while they filled in or executed the more "showy" parts of the picture. Mansart would sell plans to a customer, and they would be carried out by local architects and, indeed, often by master-masons. It was only the most important places which received the personal attention of the great man himself.

Échailly is a fine, classical Louis XV house of particularly beautiful clear grey stone. The decoration of the windows is strictly "classical," but very well executed. The mansion has escaped all mutilation, "restoration," "improvement" and "adaptation."

The main saloon is a magnificent octagon with two fine chimney-pieces and furniture covered with Aubusson tapestry.

After the marriage of the *marquis* de Chabrignac with Mlle Hennessy, Échailly took on again much of the appearance that it must have had in Louis XVI's time.

## The Mansarts

WE are always meeting the name of Mansart or Mansard when we read about French architecture or when we travel through the land of France. There were, indeed, two Mansarts (the name gave us an English word "mansard" for the curb roof, in which each face has two slopes, the lower one steeper than the upper); first of all there was François Mansart (1598–1666), the inventor of the mansard roof and the architect of the Bank of France and parts of the *hôtel* Carnavalet (the municipal museum) and the Val-de-Grâce in Paris; and then there was Jules Hardouin, his great-nephew by marriage (1646–1708), who took his great-uncle's name, and was known as Hardouin-Marsard or "Mansart," and he it is who is generally meant when the architect of that name is spoken of. This Mansart was the reputed designer of Versailles *château*, of the dome of the *Invalides* in Paris, of the *Grand Trianon* and many other buildings.

We are lucky enough to possess a portrait of Mansart from the acid pen of the *duc* de Saint-Simon, who in his *Memoirs* treats the man, whose professional reputation stands so high to-day, as a very second-rate fellow indeed. Doubtless, much of Saint-Simon's sarcastic comment was dictated by his absurd nobiliary and snobbish prejudices, offended by the considerable position Mansart enjoyed at Court and in the favour of Louis XIV. Listen to what the noble Duke writes:

> *"Hardouin, first of all drummer-boy, then stone-cutter, apprentice to a mason and finally groom, managed somehow to get close to the great Mansart, who procured him a job in the department of Royal Works . . .*

According to Saint-Simon, Mansart's plans were really drawn up by a less-known worthy called Lassurance, who was kept more or less sequestered so that he might not blab out what he knew to the detriment of the King's architect.

> *"As Mansart had no taste and as the King had none either, nothing beautiful or even comfortable was erected, despite enormous expense."*

It is strange to note also that many other contemporaries of Mansart were severe critics of his work, and also it is odd that for the exhibition organised at the Paris *Bibliothèque Nationale* to celebrate the tercentenary of Mansart's birth, no plan, nor even a text, by the hand of Mansart himself could be found.

Two of Mansart's works have always been admired—the Versailles orangery and the dome of the *Invalides*. Rumour has it that the former was built to a plan conceived by Le Nôtre (more famous as a designer of gardens), while the latter, it seems, was inspired by a drawing of François Mansart, the uncle, for a Bourbon chapel at Saint-Denis.

Mansart's appearance is rather familiar to us by portraits due, one, to a famous painter—Rigaud—and the other to a sculptor of the first rank—Coysevox. The man's face might well be that of a humbug and cunning courtier, just the sort of man to show Louis XIV intentionally imperfect plans, so that the "Sun-King" might have the satisfaction of correcting them. Anyway, whatever were his real merits as an artist, Mansart certainly "got away with it." His story leaves us wondering how many other great reputations were just a little usurped.

### Berengaria of Navarre

ÉPAU. Berengaria, the wife of Richard Coeur de Lion, is perhaps the most shadowy figure of all the Queens of England; it may be because she never set foot in our country. She married Richard in Cyprus, was with him at Acre, but for the rest of her life lived in Italy and France. Le Mans was her home for the time of her widowhood, and she survived the Lion-Heart by many years.

In 1230, when she had already been a widow for over a generation, she founded the Cistercian Abbey of Épau, on the left bank of the Huisne, some two and a half miles to the east of Le Mans. In 1365 the men of Le Mans destroyed the abbey for fear that the English might seize the place, fortify it and use it as a base for an attack on Le Mans town. But at the end of the 14th century Épau was restored.

Épau abbey to-day consists of the cloister arcades, the sacristy (whose walls bear very effaced 14th century paintings), the chapter-house, divided into nine bays by columns whose capitals are finely carved with floral motifs, the cellars, the kitchens and the refectory. They are all of the 13th or 14th century.

The Cistercian abbey-church is a noble ruin. At the east end is the skeleton of a magnificent rose-window. A plaster-cast marks the site of Queen Berengaria's tomb which, in 1821, was removed to Le Mans Cathedral.

### A Strange Life and a Strange Wife

ERNÉE. The great Cardinal Mazarin, the wily Italian who succeeded to Richelieu's office as chief minister of the French Crown, had a bevy of nieces whom the wits of the day called the *mazarinettes*. Mazarin's sister, Geronima, was married to a Roman by the name of Lorenzo Mancini, by whom she had eight children, who were all transported from Rome to Paris as their uncle's fortunes rose to unexampled heights. Of the three sons only one, Filippo, *duc* de Nevers, survived childhood. The five nieces, however, were all married off to illustrious personages. Laura became *duchesse* de Mercoeur, Olimpia, *comtesse* de

Soissons, was the mother of the famous soldier Prince Eugène of Savoy. Maria married in Italy and was the wife of the Constable Colonna, while Maria-Anna had for husband the *duc* de Bouillon.

The most attractive of the family was, however, Ortensia or Hortense, her uncle's favourite. Hortense was brought to France in 1653, and after a few years at a convent to learn French and a smattering of polite accomplishments, she was presented at Court in 1657. Her arrival created a sensation. She was known to be the heir to most of her uncle's enormous wealth, and she was very beautiful, and although not especially witty or brilliant in conversation or of any great intelligence, she was no fool. Her languid and rather nonchalant airs masked a considerable strength of will which, had it been allied to a little more common sense, would have saved her from a good many of the disappointments of her adventurous though by no means unhappy or uninteresting life.

Hortense was courted by innumerable suitors, including the Prince of Wales (afterwards Charles II), always, of course, at the French Court known as the King of England. Charles and his mother pressed his suit, but Hortense would not hear of him, or rather Mazarin himself would not hear of the marriage. Eventually, when she had reached the ripe age of fifteen, she espoused one Armand-Charles de La Porte, eldest son and heir of the *maréchal-duc* de La Meilleraye, a man of no great family but of very considerable wealth. This Armand-Charles was such a queer character that he merits a few words on his own account.

Saint-Simon, in his *Memoirs*, reports that young La Meilleraye, before his marriage, was well-read, clever, witty, open-handed, gracious, affable and polite and, indeed, possessed of almost all the virtues. Contemporary opinion in France commiserated with La Meilleraye on his conjugal misfortunes and laid all the blame upon his wife. She does not appear, in our later-day judgment, to have been wholly to blame. However, Saint-Simon reports that La Meilleraye (or Mazarin as he called himself after his marriage) in mature age, "despite his misfortunes, was a tall, healthy-looking, fat man, and seemed cheerful."

Hortense and Armand-Charles were married on the 28th February, 1661, and by the marriage he obtained the title of *duc* de Mazarin (with the *pairie*) and the Governorship of Alsace. On the 9th March the same year Cardinal Mazarin died, leaving Hortense about twenty-eight million *livres* and all sorts of sinecures, pensions and "charges," one alone of which, the governorship of Haguenau, brought in thirty thousand *livres* a year.

Armand-Charles appears to have been of a disposition little fitted for Court life under Louis XIV. Mazarin was passionately in love with his wife, and the attentions she received from King and courtiers made him insanely jealous. For five years he dragged his Hortense about the country, avoiding the Court as much as possible. His jealousy, of course, bored his Hortense exceedingly, and her boredom increased his jealousy and gave it, indeed, a twist and a turn leading to something very like madness. He became involved in numerous lawsuits, in fact, he sought them out. He was a lawsuit fan, having contested, it is said, no less than three hundred of them. Although rich himself, he had, of course, according to the customs of the time, the complete control of his wife's fortune, but this fortune, he maintained (rightly enough), had been ill-gotten, and before he could enjoy any piece of it he would fight a lawsuit over it.

The more important decisions in life he settled by a throw of dice—there may be worse ways of making up one's mind—and Voltaire in verse has satirised the *duc's* manias:

> *"On conte que l'époux de la célèbre Hortense*
> *Signala plaisamment sa sainte extravagance:*
> *Craignant de faire un choix par sa faible raison,*
> *Il tirait au trois dés les rangs de sa maison.*
> *Le sort d'un postillon faisait un secrétaire,*
> *Le cocher, étonné, devenait homme d'affaire;*
> *Un docteur hibernois, son très-digne aumônier*
> *Rendît grâce au destin qui le fit cuisinier."*

> ("*They say the husband of the celebrated Hortense*
> *Showed pleasantly his crazy eccentricity:*
> *Fearing to decide anything by his feeble judgment,*
> *He arranged his household by the throw of three dice.*
> *So a postilion might have the luck to become a secretary,*
> *The coachman to his astonishment a man of affairs;*
> *A Hibernian doctor, his very worthy chaplain,*
> *Gave thanks to Providence for having made him a cook."*)

In 1664 the old *maréchal-duc* de La Meilleraye died, but his son continued to call himself *duc* de Mazarin. Two years later—Hortense was just twenty—husband and wife separated. In 1668 Hortense, rather foolishly, fled from Paris, and as no settlement had been made, her husband kept what was left of the Cardinal's inheritance. After seven years' wandering in Europe, the beautiful Hortense landed in England, where she remained for the rest of her life. King Charles II was delighted to meet his old love again, and graciously accorded her a pension of £4,000. In 1776, however, one of Hortense's old lovers, the *prince* de Monaco, having turned up in London, Charles was so annoyed that he cut off the pension, but Hortense was soon forgiven and granted rooms in St. James's Palace, where her *salon* became one of the most agreeable in London. In the *duchesse* de Mazarin's drawing-rooms there reigned an atmosphere of gallantry, gaming and wit. Saint-Evremond (like herself an exile in England and the most faithful of the Mazarin *salonnards*), has left a pretty picture of the easy, free and unconstrained tone of Hortense's parties. Indeed, the beautiful *duchesse* had nothing much to regret. She was free, she was rich—or she lived as though she were—she was loved and admired.

From time to time there was a little trouble. A young Swede named Banér (grandson of Gustavus Adolphus's famous general) loved her and was loved by her. It happened that Hortense's nephew, the *comte* de Soissons, was in London at the time. He called out Banér and ran him through the body. Hortense was much put out. In 1687 her sister the *duchesse* de Bouillon spent some time with her in London, and then it was that La Fontaine wrote a rhyming epistle to Saint-Evremond, beginning:

> *"Hortense eût du ciel en partage*
> *La grâce, la beauté, l'esprit, ce n'est pas tout."*
>
> *("Hortense had as gifts from Heaven*
> *Grace, beauty, wit, and that is not all.")*

And ending:

> *"L'Angleterre en ce point le dispute à la France,*
> *Votre personne rend nos deux peuples rivaux."*
>
> *("England on this point competes with France,*
> *Your person makes our two peoples rivals.")*

The fall of the Stuarts, of course, brought poor Hortense's pension to an end, but William III gallantly (though prudently) restored the allowance—at half its former rate.

Hortense used to spend the summers in the sylvan retreat of Chelsea, and here it was she died in 1699 aged fifty-three. A few days only before her death she exclaimed:

"I have never felt so well. I have never been so beautiful."

Her body was taken back to France, and the eccentric husband, who had not contributed anything to his wife's support for thirty years and had not allowed her a penny of her own money, was so overwhelmed with grief at her death that he carried her body about with him for a twelvemonth.

Hortense had had, before her separation from her husband, four children—a son and three daughters. Armande, her son's daughter, married Louis de Mailly, and was by him the mother of four girls—the *comtesse* de Mailly, the *comtesse* de Vintimille, the *duchesse* de Lauraguais and the *marquise* de La Tournelle—all of whom were successively the mistresses of King Louis XV. Hortense's charms lived on in her great-granddaughters.

While she was still residing in France, or at least before she had settled in England, Hortense made over an old *château* and some land, near Ernée, in the province of Maine, to the ecclesiastical authorities in order that they might use the proceeds of the sale of the estate for the construction of a church. And this church, which was finished in 1697, two years before she died in Chelsea, is about the only monument Hortense has in the second of her three countries, Italy, France and England.

The rather fine stone cupola of Ernée church is a landmark some time before you reach the little town, which, rather exceptionally for rural France, is a comparatively modern place. It lies in the charming valley of the Ernée stream, which winds through rich meadows dotted with giant beeches. On the hills above the river is the fine 17th century *château* de Panard.

Two miles east-south-east is the prehistoric site of Montenay; while the same distance to the north is the megalithic covered alley of La Contrie, some twenty-two feet long.

On the Mayenne road, to the east of Ernée, you pass the manor of Loré, where in 1396 was born Ambroise de Loré, companion in arms of Joan of Arc.

## A Superb Church

ÉVRON. Évron, on the Laval-Sillé-le-Guillaume high road, is a place of note. It is a pleasing little town of some three thousand five hundred inhabitants. It has several good inns where you can stay while exploring the eastern part of the Mayenne department and making excursions to the walled town of Sainte-Suzanne or to the curious Saulges grottoes. There is an ancient covered market. At the corner of the road, leading to the church, is a house whose façade bears strange finials and crockets of tin.

But these curiosities do not really amount to very much. The interest of Évron centres entirely in its superb church.

There is no west front, for at the west end the building abuts on to the 18th century (1726) convent (now occupied by Sisters of Charity), whose imposing classical façade gives on to a "French" garden. Here there was, it seems as early as 648, a church founded by St. Haduin, Bishop of Le Mans, in honour of a miracle attributed to the virtue of a few drops of the Virgin's milk brought back by a pious pilgrim from the Holy Land.

However, the tower and the old nave, the most ancient parts of the present church, are not earlier than the 12th century. The battlements and other military trappings of the tower, giving it so secular an appearance, were added during the fifteen hundreds. The windows of the nave were enlarged in 1666. The rest, conceived and executed in the finest style of *rayonnant* Gothic, was put up in the 13th and 14th centuries. These Gothic additions consist of two bays of the nave (with side-aisles), the transepts, the spacious choir and ambulatory, with seven radiating chapels. The whole is on a grand scale.

You enter through a south-side door surmounted with shields bearing the arms of the Bois and Châteaubriand families.

Although the sturdy, Romanesque nave is impressive enough (despite the filling-in of the side-aisles' bays), the eye travels at once to the wonderful choir. However, in the south side-aisle are two 14th century tombs of knights and their ladies with recumbent effigies. On the north side is an interesting Renaissance window representing the life and deeds of Haduin, the sainted bishop of Le Mans and founder of the church.

The organ-loft surmounts the Abbot's throne, that is 18th

**L'Ile-Bouchard**                                        **St. Leonard's Church**

**La Haye-Descartes**                          **The Interior of Descartes' House**

**Langeais**     The Garden Front of Castle     **Langeais**     Battlements

**Langeais** ——————————— The Courtyard of Castle and Drawbridge

**Ligueil**     The Esves Stream     **Loches**     Agnes Sorel's Statue

century work, while nearby is a particularly fine carved wooden credence of about the same date as the throne. Very often in the church are exposed four magnificent 17th century tapestries from the Aubusson looms. The great stuffs portray "Jacob's Dream," "Hagar and Ishmael," "Lot Guided by the Angel" and "The Sacrifice of Abraham." Despite the collecting into museums of so many of the ancient tapestries of France, still, it is no such unusual thing to discover, here and there, even comparatively humble sanctuaries whose walls are sumptuous with ancient hangings. The abundance of old, and, indeed, less old, woven stuffs still surviving in France denotes, almost more clearly than anything else, the riches of the country in the Middle Ages and later. For France, until about 1750, was not only the most powerful State, the most populous land, but also the home of the wealthiest people in Europe.

Above the arches of the choir's five windows runs a most delicately carved frieze harmonising with the charming and gracefully sculptured capitals of the pillars. Much of the glass in the lights is of the 14th and 16th centuries.

The high altar is wrought in *turquin*—that magnificent Italian blue marble with white veins. The chiselled bronze features, the rich candelabra all combine to make up a picture of 18th century ecclesiastical pomp. The choir-gates are of iron elegantly fashioned, and are surmounted with the blazon of the Abbey's arms.

The seven radiating chapels are not only of architectural magnificence, but they house a wealth of statues, carvings, paintings and stained glass of unusually high quality and of great variety.

In the third chapel, for instance, is the tomb of Dom Chastelet, the Abbey's Treasurer in the 14th century. Nearby, in the fourth chapel, is a superb Gothic (13th century) statue of the Virgin known as "Our Lady of the Thorn." In a silver-gilt reliquary is preserved a leaden ampulla containing the drops of the Miraculous Milk of the Virgin.

Behind the high altar are ten statuettes arranged in groups representing the Annunciation, the Circumcision, the Nativity and the Flight into Egypt.

Saint Crespin's chapel, on the north side of the choir and dedicated to that popular personage who was the patron of cobblers and shoemakers, is an interesting 12th century Romanesque shrine. The barrel roof is supported on brackets with interesting capitals. At the entrance of the chapel lies, beneath a canopy with three pendants, the recumbent effigy of Jean de Favières, who died in 1484, the last regular abbot. At Évron, as in so many abbeys, there succeeded a line of commendatory abbots. Above the tomb are two gables in the Flamboyant style.

Really quite a good deal remains of the early wall-paintings. The niche of the apse is adorned with frescoes divided into scenes by brown borders. An oval glory in the middle encircles a colossal Christ surrounded by the symbols of the evangelists, while, to the right and to the left, are Saints Benedict and Haduin upon their knees. Their heads, however, have been wretchedly repainted. Above, five arches display a curious ornamentation of rounded corner-stones. The same motif is repeated in red granite on the outside of the Romanesque doorway. These rounded corner-stones are said to symbolise Saint Crespin, the patron of cobblers— possibly they represent his mallet.

The statue of the Virgin above the altar is ancient—perhaps 14th century, while the carved wooden crucifix on the altar is 13th century.

In the sacristy leading out from Saint Crespin's chapel is the old Abbey Treasure—or what has survived of it; the most remarkable piece is a 16th century reliquary.

A notable place.

## A Kingmaker's Grandfather

LA FERTÉ-BERNARD. The fortified castle of Ferté, in the Perche, is mentioned as early as the 11th century, and the feudal family of Bernard owned the fief until the thirteen hundreds. Ferté, lying on the borders of the Norman Dukes' domains and those of the French Kings, was, during the 12th century and the expansion of the French sovereignty westwards, often the theatre of interviews between the monarchs of France and England.

In 1424, after a four months' siege, La Ferté was captured by Thomas de Montacute, Earl of Salisbury (whose second wife was Chaucer's granddaughter), grandfather of the Kingmaker and the most skilful commander we had in France after the death of Henry V.

Richelieu bought La Ferté in 1642, and his family held the town until the Revolution, when, in common with all privately owned villages or cities, La Ferté was freed from feudal lords. La Ferté is a curious little place surrounded by streams and intersected by canals.

A bridge over the Huisne leads up to a 15th century fortified city-gate and into the barbican—the only part of the old fortifications now well preserved. The streets are quaint, and show, here and there, carved and painted façades and a few Renaissance medallions. There is a charming 17th century fountain formed by a polygonal basin, out of which rises a granite obelisk. But La Ferté is most notable for its church.

## A Splendid Shrine

NOTRE-DAME-DES-MARAIS, or Our Lady of the Marshes, consists of two architecturally distinct parts. The nave, the transepts and tower were put up from 1450 to 1500 in Flamboyant Gothic taste and to rather a small plan, whereas the choir (erected from 1500 to 1596) is a monument of capital importance, showing a transition style from Flamboyant to Renaissance, and richly decorated, finely carved and blazing with magnificent painted windows.

Even from the outside the view of the choir is imposing, with its flying buttresses set with crocketed and pierced pinnacles and rimmed with delicate balustrades, the lower series of which (finished about 1540) bear, on the southern face, curious statuettes of the Kings of France and their Peers (i.e. the Peers in the old feudal sense of the term, the sovereign Dukes of Burgundy and Normandy, the Prince-Bishops and so forth, the great magnates who were, in France, the peers of the Electors in the Holy Roman Empire) and also the symbols and designs of the seven planets and images of Jupiter, Mercury and Venus. Elsewhere the balustrade spells out the letters REGINA COELI—Queen of Heaven. Below, amid charming arabesques, are busts of Roman Emperors and of Cæsar and Cleopatra. The upper balustrades of the apse date from the end of the 16th century, and their scrolls and motifs are interspersed with the letters AVE REGINA COELORUM, "Hail, Queen of the Heavens."

On the south side of the nave is a gracious Renaissance chapel, while the 16th century west entrance has carved doors in the Flamboyant taste.

The interior is splendid. The three absidial chapels have roofs with carved and pierced stone pendants. The finest of the stained glass is in the central chapel, five of the windows in the choir are ancient.

What was formerly the covered market (built in 1536 by Claude of Lorraine and his wife Antoinette of Bourbon-Vendôme) is now an assembly-hall. The monumental and classical façade adorned with lions supporting shields is fine. On the first floor is a remarkable chimney-piece of Renaissance workmanship.

Altogether, La Ferté is not a place to miss out from a trip through western France.

## *Treatise of Human Nature*

LA FLÈCHE. David Hume, the Scottish philosopher and historian, was among the most pro-French of his traditionally francophile nation, and he had, at one time, the intention of settling in Paris for good, since he found there, he said, the most entertaining, stimulating and agreeable society it would be possible to imagine. During the three years Hume spent in France from the summer of 1734, most of his time was passed in quiet study at La Flèche, a town sacred to all philosophers as having been the school of great Descartes himself.

It was at La Flèche that Hume wrote his *Treatise of Human Nature*, his first work, the one which lies at the base of all his later writings and is really the fundamental exposition of his philosophical views.

## *A Famous College*

LA FLÈCHE straddles the Loir River where it divides into several branches, and the place offers the pleasing aspect of an old town with unexpected views of running water and bridges.

The fortress around which La Flèche grew up was founded in the 11th century. In the fifteen hundreds the lordship passed to the Bourbon family, and the father and mother of Henry of Navarre left the town only a few months before their famous son was born. In 1604 Henry IV gave his castle of La Flèche for use as a college, which was conducted by the Jesuits until their expul-

The Portal of St. Ours Church

The King's Lodging

**LOCHES**

Castle Entrance

*Porte des Cordeliers*

The King's Lodging

The *Tour Saint-Antoine*

**LOCHES**

sion from France in 1762. Under the able direction of the Society of Jesus, La Flèche college became one of the most renowned in Europe.

After the expulsion of the Jesuits, their college was turned into a preparatory school for the *école militaire* in Paris. In 1776 Louis XVI restored the La Flèche foundation to its status as a school for civilians, but the place was closed down in 1793. In 1808 Napoleon established at La Flèche in the old buildings the so-called *Prytanée militaire*, or school for the sons of soldiers, where they are prepared for a military career up to the age when they can enter one of the special military colleges.

The *Prytanée* (this queer word is derived from the Greek and meant, in ancient Athens, the house reserved for the use of senators) has a fine façade on the street, and is composed of five buildings erected from 1620 to 1653 and separated from each other by spacious courtyards. To the north of the *Prytanée* are fine grounds. The chapel is a splendid 17th century church, with imposing statues and a superb reredos of coloured marbles.

In a niche is preserved a gilded leaden box containing the ashes of the hearts of Henry IV and Marie de' Medici. The relics were burned in 1793.

## Fine Tapestries

THE principal church of the town is modern, but encloses the transept of the old 13th century edifice. Within is some excellent statuary, but the chief adornment of St. Thomas's is the collection of eleven 16th, 17th and 18th century tapestries that is hung in the nave and the choir.

The town hall is housed in the old convent of the Carmelites, but the building was burned in 1919, and has been restored without much taste.

## Coppélia and Sylvia

A MILE and a half to the north of La Flèche lies Saint-Germain-du-Val, where was born in 1836 Leo Delibes, the author of some of the most delightful ballet-music of the 19th century. *Coppélia* and *Sylvia* are, perhaps, the best known of his light, graceful and pleasing compositions.

The *château* d'Yvandeau, by Saint-Germain, was Hume's residence during the time he spent at La Flèche. The manor is surrounded by caves, one of which is known as the *Trou d'Enfer* or Hell's Hole—it is tempting to imagine that the philosopher may have been inspired to write some of the chapters of the *Treatise of Human Nature* in or near the *Trou d'Enfer*.

## Plantagenet Tombs

FONTEVRAULT. The magnificent, austere Abbey-church of Fontevrault bears a name familiar to us from childhood's days as that of the burial-place of the Plantagenets.

Fontevrault is a shrine for all English visitors to France, and it is in itself a superb building. It is not only in planning, proportions and conception most satisfying, it is not only an architectural curiosity, but it is, unchanged, the image of its old self in Plantagenet days.

The vast, triple-domed nave, lighted only from high-perched clerestory windows, is divided from the eastern end by walls, which narrow the view of the much more luminous choir to a lofty panel framing and heighten the majesty of the sanctuary.

But beyond taking in a general impression and being struck by the strangely timeless effect produced by the even and regular blocks of light-coloured stone divided from each other by courses of dark mortar, we will want to leave a closer examination until we have looked at the Plantagenet tombs.

They lie two on either side of the nave, and beneath the most easterly of the three cupolas at the entrance to the sanctuary. Most of the flooring of the church is but sand and earth, but under the last cupola there is a pavement on which are set the low monuments, each consisting of a stone pediment surmounted by a recumbent figure. Until you are right upon them the tombs seem absurdly small for so spacious a building which, beyond them, contains no monuments or furnishings at all.

But the tombs are, of course, no longer in their original positions. Until towards the end of the Old Régime the recumbent statues were collected together in an elaborate wall-niche, apparently of 17th century workmanship. The statues were arranged so that the four of them sloped down one beneath the other on an inclined plane. The general effect as shown in Gaignières' engraving was most clumsy and almost ludicrous.

These recumbent effigies are among the oldest still existing, although they are not, it would seem in all cases, datable to the year of death of the personage represented. The effigies seem to be early 13th century, and therefore those of Eleanor of Guyenne (wife of our Henry II) and of Isabella of Angoulême (wife of our King John) were probably carved and placed in positions soon after those queens died. The effigies of Henry II and of Richard Coeur de Lion may have been prepared at the same time.

The statues of Henry II (*d.* 1189), of his wife (*d.* 1204) and of Richard Coeur de Lion (*d.* 1199) are of stone painted in polychrome. The effigy of Isabella of Angoulême (*d.* 1226) is of wood, also painted in several colours. All the figures have been much restored. The faces, as were those of all tomb-effigies for long afterwards, are idealised or, rather, stylised. Richard Coeur de Lion at Fontevrault looks a little mild and benign and very different from the Richard of his Great Seal, where his face conveys an impression of strength and cruelty.

The remains of Henry II, of Richard and of Eleanor were, in the 17th century, apparently at the time when the effigies were collected together under the canopy, removed from under their monuments and conveyed to another part of the church. And to this transfer is due their preservation during the troublous years at the end of the 18th century. The dust and bones of Isabella of Angoulême (who when she was rid of her wretched King John married her old lover Hugues de Lusignan) have vanished, and no trace of her relics was found when the remains of the other three Plantagenets were discovered during the restoration of the abbey in 1910.

Fontevrault was founded by Robert d'Arbrissel, whose Pastoral Staff—a plain stick with a handle of crystal—is preserved in the Chapel of the Fontevristes at Chemillé. The ancient and, formerly, most wealthy Abbey of Fontevrault has, since revolutionary times, suffered much degradation. The bulk of the conventual buildings is still used as a prison for men serving long sentences, and the whole place is what is euphemistically called in France a *Maison Centrale* or "Central House."

Fontevrault is an undistinguished village and about the only thing which will strike us as strange will be the large number of men bicycling about and all wearing flat caps adorned with silver stars.

These men are the prison warders. The prison, the abbey and the church lie, indeed, over a mile from the village.

It was in 1810 that Napoleon ordered the old conventual buildings to be changed into prisons. Fontevrault is, to this day, what it was in Napoleon's time. The inmates of the jail are rather a tough lot, some of them being prisoners condemned to penal servitude for long terms (since transportation to Devil's Island has now been abolished). The men serving penal-servitude sentences wear red stars, the men condemned to terms of hard labour have yellow stars and the simple, short-term prisoners have to wear white stars. All the inmates are clothed in the same drugget costume.

The prison is supposed to hold 600 men, but in 1947 when we visited Fontevrault there were 1,200 inmates. All the prisons of France are crammed since much room is taken up by political prisoners, "collaborators" and men condemned for offences committed during the war and the German occupation. The dormitories of Fontevrault are jammed and although work is not obligatory most of the prisoners choose to work in order to escape, in some measure, from the dreadful boredom of prison life. The prisoners work in a drugget factory and they must neither speak nor smoke while the machine-tools set a pretty quick pace. Even in France where, when men do get sent to jail, conditions are particularly harsh, it is now proposed that prisoners should work outside the prisons in "free" workshops and only return at night. Some attempts at re-education are to be made and there is a little reaction from the old practice that offenders against the sacrosanct laws of property must be shut away for as long a time as possible and be treated as wild beasts. The greatest objection which could be made to prison conditions in France in 1947 was that all sorts of prisoners were mixed up together, if not always in the cells, at least in the corridors, the exercise-grounds, and the work-shops. Political prisoners had to live side by side with hardened old lags.

We can visit the church, the cloisters, the kitchens and a few other apartments, and these are by far the most interesting.

Fontevrault was for many generations a convent, whose abbess was a woman of high birth, and most of whose nuns were drawn from families of the *noblesse*. The coat-of-arms you see over the chapter-house entrance is that of the ducal house of Mortemart. Gabrielle de Rochechouart de Mortemart, a sister of the famous

Madame de Montespan, was, through her sister's influence, named Abbess of Fontevrault only a few years after she had taken her vows. The *Grande Mademoiselle*, whom we met at Champigny, not so far away, was also, for a time, Abbess of Fontevrault. The foundation was therefore one of the most important in the realm, as well as one of the most wealthy. As a consequence, much rebuilding was undertaken. Luckily, the abbey-church was spared.

For years, however, the church was divided up into cells for the prisoners. France was so rich in churches, monasteries and convents and the Revolution and Empire needed so many buildings for barracks, police-courts, prisons, schools and the innumerable offices demanded by the modern centralised State, that a sad tale of degradation and destruction must be told in every province of France.

Fontevrault church is about 270 feet long, and it was put up in two "spurts" at the beginning of the 12th century. As we said, it is an architectural curiosity, since the doming of the nave with cupolas, although common enough in the south-west of France (and especially in the Périgord), was unknown in the north until the fashion set by the Fontevrault architects spread in Anjou.

The sanctuary at Fontevrault is not unlike that of Saint-Benoît-sur-Loire, that is one of the most splendid in all France.

After the church, the rest of the Fontevrault abbey buildings produce rather an impression of anticlimax, but there is a fine 16th century cloister whose east side opens through a splendid doorway into the chapter-house. The refectory's roof is elegantly vaulted, and is a little earlier in date than the chapter-house—possibly about 1515.

The so-called *Tour d'Evrault* is a 12th century building which formerly served as the kitchen. It is of curious design, being octagonal, and each side being set with a niche whose conical roof is pierced to serve as a chimney. The tower is capped by a high pyramid covered with the typical "Angevin" fish-scale tiling. The tower terminates in a 13th century lantern covering the main chimney of the kitchen. Altogether the *Tour d'Evrault* is one of the strangest buildings in Anjou, and has something very southern about it, reminding us of Cintra Palace in Portugal.

Beyond and around Fontevrault stretches its open, friendly

forest, along the higher ground to the left bank of the Vienne. There is no more charming place hereabouts to eat a rustic meal. If you do not feel inclined to picnic, then you can move down the road towards Montsoreau and the Loire, and order a *brochet au beurre blanc* or a pike done in the Anjou mode with a shallot sauce. The right drink with this will be an Anjou white wine. Any of the local growths are good—Parnay, Brézé, Saumur and so forth.

## A Swan Lake

FOULTORTE. Foultorte is an enchanted place, half-rustic, half-legendary.

The castle dates from about 1590 and, seen from across the swan-haunted lake that serves it as a moat, the old house, irregularly regular, makes a brave show. Not a little of its charm is due to the uneven courses of its dark stones set in thick layers of lighter mortar. The whole looks something like a leopard's skin.

The old Angevin family of Vassé held Foultorte for many generations, until one of their creditors, a financially-minded ecclesiastic, the *abbé* Hardy, foreclosed on the place in 1709. Since Hardy's day, Foultorte has not been sold.

The main and central wing is of considerable beauty and simplicity of line, nobility of proportion and sobriety of decoration.

The great staircase within it is broad enough for a coach and four to drive up, yet each step is hewn from a single stone.

The dining-room is a particularly attractive apartment hung with Louis XVI *toile imprimée* or chintz of most graceful, airy and delicate design.

One wing collapsed in 1839, dragging down with it the chapel. What remains you will long remember—the strange outlines of the roofs, the high chimneys, the delicate patina—and the clear image in the Swan Lake.

## Murder in the Bois de Boulogne

ONE evening in April 1564, when that poor creature, Charles IX, was King of France, Pierre Belon had been in Paris visiting his friend Jacques de Bueil. Belon had been given by the King a lodging in the *Château de Madrid*, but then known rather as the *Château de Maldrie*. The *Château de Madrid* we see to-day is a pretentious, pseudo-antique building, housing a fashionable restaurant and a rather discreet hotel at the corner of that old-world bit of Neuilly which cuts into the Bois de Boulogne.

Four hundred years ago, more or less, Belon's lodging must have seemed far away in the country, since the walls of Paris were no farther out than the line of what is now the *grands boulevards*.

Belon had a good three miles to walk to get home. And he never was to get home, for in the morning his body was found slashed with wounds and lying near a footpath through the woods. Why Belon was murdered has never been discovered. Possibly it was just an ordinary crime, since the *Bois de Boulogne* in the fifteen hundreds—and for long afterwards—was a regular Hounslow Heath of footpads, cut-throats and thieves.

When we hear the word "Belon" now we are apt to think of those particularly succulent, fawn-fleshed oysters that are among the best France has to offer; but our Pierre Belon, who was born at Soulletière, a hamlet near Foulletourte, in about 1517, is a man with some real title to fame, since he was a founder of the science of comparative anatomy.

Belon took his doctor's degree at the University of Paris, and while he was living in the Latin Quarter became a friend of Ronsard the poet. Belon then removed to Germany, where he studied under the botanist Valerius Cordus at Wittenberg, and travelled with him to several of the German seats of learning.

On his return to France, Belon found powerful patrons—the Cardinal de Tournon of rather sinister and persecuting memory, the Chancellor Cardinal Duprat (uncle of the builder of Chenonceau) among others. Through his patrons he managed to finance a scientific Grand Tour which, for the times, was a long and rather daring one.

Belon was absent from France for three years—from 1546 to 1549—and he visited Greece, Asia Minor, Palestine, Arabia and Egypt. Our hero was wise enough to hold out an attractive bait to his backers. He would bring back with him *substances médicamenteuses*, by which we may understand drugs, spices, powdered mummy, and any other of those strange products so sought after by our forefathers as stimulants, flavourings, medicine or for quasi-magical ends. Ronsard celebrated his friend's adventures in verse:

*"Combien Belon, au prix de luy*
*Doit avoir en France aujourdhuy*
*D'honneur, de faveur et de gloire*
*Qui a veu ce grand univers*
*Et de longeur et de travers*
*Et la gent blanche et la gent noire."*

(*" How much should Belon have in France to-day, honour,*
*favour and glory, who, at what cost to himself, has seen this*
*great universe, in length and breadth, and peoples both white*
*and black.")*

Belon, in 1553, published of his travels an account which is full of
acute observation and interesting notes on plants and animals. He
also wrote volumes on "strange fish" and on birds, and in 1557 he
gave the world the first French book to describe in detail the
people and products of the Near East. The volume, entitled
*Pourtraicts d'oyseaux, animaux, serpens, herbes, arbres, hommes*
*et femmes d'Arabie et d'Egypte*, makes entertaining reading.

In all his works, Belon shows what for his time was a remarkable foretaste of the scientific attitude; indeed, after him, until
Cuvier's time, little progress towards a system of comparative
anatomy was made. Belon was not neglected in his own lifetime,
and was in favour both with Henry II and Charles IX.

## The Twin Town

THE twin-town of Cérans-Foulletourte is to be found on the
Le Mans–La Flèche road, and it is built by the banks of the
Fessard stream. The 16th century choir stalls in Cérans church
are well carved, and in Foulletourte church there is a curious 17th
century panel of the Ascension. Belon is commemorated by a
statue in Foulletourte main square.

## A White and Red Marvel

FRESNAY-SUR-SARTHE. The word "Fresnay" (in many
different spellings and even forms) means "a place planted
with ash trees," and is a common name in France. This Fresnay
on the Sarthe is a picturesque little town on a rocky crag overhanging the left bank of the river.

View from the Air

The Banks of the Indre River

**LOCHES**

**Loches** — The King's Lodging

**Loches** — Tomb of Agnes Sorel

**Loches** ———————— The Royal Apartments and Town Hall

**Loches** — from the River

**Le Lude**

Fresnay is still walled and has been walled—and fortified—for nearly a thousand years. The town suffered similar ups and downs of fortune to those endured by most of the settlements in this border-land between Normandy and the Loire. Fresnay was twice seized by William the Conqueror, occupied by us, after much fighting, during the Hundred Years' War, and sacked by the Huguenots in 1568. The place also suffered much during the Chouans' rising (see p. 175).

The pride of the town is the splendid Romanesque Church of Notre-Dame, constructed of alternate courses of white stone and reddish rock (known as *roussard*)—the effect is striking, and reminds you rather of the Lombardo-Genoese architecture of northern Italy rather than of anything this side of the Alps.

There is a fine octagonal lantern-tower and the west front has a magnificent portal. The carved doors date from 1528, and display a Crucifixion, a Tree of Jesse, and images of the Twelve Apostles in shell-shaped niches.

The nave and transepts are covered with fine ogival vaulting, but the effect of the whole is rather marred by an abundance of modern paintings with gilt backgrounds.

In the right transept are statues of Saint Leonard (the patron of the priory founded at Fresnay by the Viscounts of Le Mans) and of Saint Bonaventura, the patron of the old-established and still flourishing Fresnay textile trade, as well as of Blessed Marguerite of Lorraine, *duchesse* d'Alençon and *vicomtesse* of Fresnay.

Giving on to the *place du château* is the arcaded market, and nearby is the barbican of the old fortress flanked with two great towers and bearing an inscription to the memory of Ambroise de Loré, captain of Fresnay and companion in arms of Joan of Arc. On the right-hand side is the town hall and on the left the museum and library.

Through the barbican you get into the castle enclosure, now set out as a public garden.

From Fresnay to Saint-Léonard-des-Bois the road rises, allowing splendid glimpses of the winding Sarthe valley. The highway then dips down to the Roussette stream and up again to Sougé-le-Ganelon, whose church houses a fine "Death of the Virgin," painted in 1584 by François Dionis.

## The Fine Food of Gennes

GENNES. The picturesque south-side road along the Loire's banks humps up to Gennes, overhanging and overlooking the whole expanse of the river's spacious valley. The view is magnificent.

On your way towards Gennes, following the south bank of the river, you see the white cliffs of *tuffeau* or micaceous chalk, carved with the cave-houses of the wine-growers and peasants. The doors and windows are embowered with purple clematis with azure wisteria and with rambler roses. Some of the troglodytes' dwellings have masonry façades making you think at first sight that houses have been taken up and thrust into the rock-face. Of such cottages and their inhabitants, René Benjamin has written:

"There the inhabitants are neither cold in the winter nor hot in the summer. There also they are near their barrels so that they can take a drink whenever they feel like it. Sometimes you see chimneys pushing up through the fields. You are taking a walk in a vineyard when suddenly you feel smoke under your feet, a good housewife down below is cooking her soup. As Théophile Gautier said, in such a fairy-land the rabbits must just fall into the pots."

There is an excellent restaurant at Gennes. It is by the roadside and you can sit on the terrace, shaded with and framed by trees, and, after you have eaten and drunk, survey the scene from Saumur to Angers. The *beurre blanc* of Gennes is famous. When the pike are fresh and not too big, a *brochet au beurre blanc* is a noble introduction to a meal. For wines you may drink the vintages either of the Saumurois or of Rochefort. Maybe it will be well to begin with some fresh Saumur vintage and finish up with an old bottle of *Côtes du Layon,* say a *Quart de Chaumes 1921* if you can still find one. Failing the '21, try any other *good* year; and the old saying holds, generally speaking, when it's a really good year in any of the French vineyards, then it is good everywhere.

The graciously wooded heights around Gennes have that air of lightness, almost of gaiety, coming from a predominance of birch and beech. Near Gennes village is the old disused Church of Saint-Eusèbe. It is crumbling and uncared for, but since the choir was built in the fourteen hundreds on to the old Romanesque nave, nothing much has been done to the place. The spire was demolished in 1940, rebuilt in 1941 and again destroyed during the bombardments of 1944.

From Gennes downstream the road moves away from the riverside. After Coutures, you see the imposing feudal fortress of Monsabert. Once you are through Saint-Saturnin-sur-Loire, the descent is steep, but you have before you the distant prospect of "Black Angers," on the far side of the great river.

## The Tombs of the Du Bellays

GIZEUX. The fine Romanesque Church of Gizeux, in the valley of the Changeon and on the Bourgueil–Château-La Vallière road, is adorned with two Renaissance chapels, one on the north and one on the south side. Each encloses a monumental tomb with white marble figures attributed to Guillain (of Cambray) and put up during the fifteen hundreds. The tomb on the north side is to the memory of Martin du Bellay and Louise de Sapvenières his wife, while the monument on the south side is to René du Bellay and Marie, titular "*princesse* d'Yvetot," his wife.

Gizeux manor, built by the du Bellays in the 15th and 16th centuries, was refashioned in the 18th. Gizeux is worthy of a visit to view the fine pieces of sculpture and also the house of the notable du Bellays, one of the foremost families of Anjou, and not only illustrious because of the Joachim du Bellay, of the *Plêiade*, who wrote the *Deffense et Illustration de la Langue françoise* and was one of the fashioners of modern French, but also on account of a number of men who served their king and country in positions of trust and eminence.

About seven miles from Gizeux northwards lies Rillé on the Lathan, formerly a barony and still walled and moated. In the church, that is partly Romanesque and partly Gothic, with 17th century additions, are the relics of Saint-Urbain, brought hither by Hardouin de Maillé (of Maillé, now Luynes) in 1213, and also the relics of Saint-Loup, Bishop of Angers.

## A Partisan of the Boers

GREZ-EN-BOUËRE. If you leave Sablé by the Château-Gontier road, you run along a hog's back between the dales of the Vaige and the Erve. Then you cross the former stream and reach Grez-en-Bouëre, some ten miles from Sablé. Grez is quite a small place of some thirteen hundred inhabitants, but it is the centre of the Mayenne marble industry. Nearby are numerous quarries, whence is hewn fine marbles of various colours. At Grez half the population is engaged in the sawing sheds, polishing shops and carving studios. Many of the elegant marble chimney-pieces, still so much used in France, come from Grez.

In the town square is a bust of a local worthy, one Colonel de Villebois-Mareuil, who was killed while fighting against us, on the side of the Boers, during the South African War. This sort of monument makes us realise how startling and novel a thing was the Franco-British *Entente Cordiale*, concluded only two years, or so, after the end of the Boer War.

### Agnes Sorel's Bower

LA-GUERCHE-SUR-CREUSE. Agnes Sorel, *dame de Fromenteau et de Beauté-sur-Marne*, the King's favourite whose tomb we find at Loches, was the earliest in date of a series of royal mistresses from Touraine, which was the province also of Gabrielle d'Estrées and of Françoise de La Vallière. Agnes's royal lover, King Charles VII, is said to have built for her the *château* of La Guerche-sur-Creuse, which remains one of the more imposing of the Loire castles.

By the water's edge, and surrounded by greenery, the massive old walls of La Guerche rise buttressed by stout towers, whose modern conical roofs are, however, rather too low. To get the best view of the place we should walk out on to the bridge over the river. The castle towers up over a hundred feet from the banks, and the façade is pierced only by small windows. To the right, you can see stretching backwards another façade with towers flanking the main entrance, since the *château* is four-square and built of stone set in small blocks to resist the ravages of time.

On the river-side there are no less than six vaulted storeys—counting the cellars.

On the inside walls, here and there, is the monogram of Agnes, and you are shown the place where her body was first interred, since after her death at Jumièges in Normandy her remains rested some time at La Guerche before they were transferred to the Collegiate Church of Saint-Ours at Loches.

La Guerche was, at one time, the property of the notable

Touraine family of Le Voyer d'Argenson, whom we meet so often in this part of the country. From the d'Argensons, La Guerche passed into the hands of the princely family of Croy, who still own it and by whom the castle has been repaired.

La Guerche village is a tiny place with a fine Romanesque church. The bridge over the Creuse links the hamlet with another called La Petite-Guerche, nearby which are vestiges of Roman baths.

Here we are on the southern borders of Touraine. To get back northwards towards La Haye-Descartes we can follow either the left or right bank of the river. The former is the more picturesque —through Leugny, where is the Romanesque Chapel of *Notre-Dame de Prélong* and the Fountain of Saint-Hilaire, which is miraculous and a pilgrimage place. About three miles farther on, under the *château* de Chaloupy, is a subterranean refuge carved out of the rock—the sort of cave that may be in the future as useful as it was in the past. As you enter La Haye, you pass by Descartes' birthplace. It is a house of no great distinction except for the memories it evokes.

## The Home of the Coesmes

LE GRAND-LUCÉ. There are few more melancholy regions in northern France than the vast moors of barren, sandy soil stretching on either side of the high road leading from Le Mans to Le Grand-Lucé.

Quite suddenly the scene changes. The dreary heaths drop away and roll back before trees bordering the refreshing valley of the Veuve. You are on to Le Grand-Lucé park. Here was the seat of the Coesmes, *barons* of Lucé and Preuillé, of whom was that Charles de Coesmes who kept Bonnétable in such strange circumstances. A later Coesmes, Louis, married in 1545 Anne de Pisseleu, the niece of the *Duchesse* d'Etampes, the mistress of François I. This second Anne de Pisseleu is none other than the Mlle d'Heilly of whom we get some amusing sidelights in Brantôme's *Life of Gallant Ladies*.

In the 18th century Le Grand-Lucé was the property of the *marquis* de Dangeau, a witty courtier who left a valuable *Journal of the Court of Louis XIVth* (see p. 80).

But nothing remains of the old manor of the Coesmes. In 1760, therefore, in the reign of Louis XV, Jacques de Viennay began building the present imposing house. It is in the classical good taste of its epoch, and consists of an oblong block composed of roughly three cubes set end to end. There are two storeys and attics. The central cube has a fine tympanum. Up to the basement windows the material employed is hard sandstone, the rest is an excellent Vouvray rock, with white tuffeau (micaceous hard chalk) details. The contrast between the greyish—"French greyish"—mass and the white *tuffeau* is striking. A notable place.

Le Grand-Lucé belonged in recent years to the *vicomte* d'Avenel, the economist, financier and author of that revealing and witty book *Les Français de mon Temps*.

## A Prehistoric Manufacturing Town

LE GRAND-PRESSIGNY. Much farther back in the dim ages of prehistory than was formerly thought possible, men not only made and used stone implements, but they also exchanged, bartered, traded and exported them. Men tried all sorts of materials for their tools. The earliest of all were possibly sticks and beasts' bones and antlers. But, from very remote ages, from the early Old Stone Age, hundreds of thousands of years ago, men made and used stone implements. When men could get flint, they discarded all other substitutes—obsidian, chert, chalcedony, quartz, etc.—so there was rather a tendency for men to settle near where flint could be worked. Of course, flint is a widely distributed substance; still there are many regions of the earth's surface where it is not to be found.

Round Le Grand-Pressigny was an abundance of flint, and stone instruments have here been discovered in such quantities, instruments of many different types and of differing ages, that we must conclude that the Pressigny area was from very early times an active centre of human industry. From the times of the New Stone Age, at least, Le Grand-Pressigny seems to have been a sort of prehistoric manufacturing town, and its characteristic honey-coloured flint was exported far and wide. The beautiful, blond stone occurs in lumps, locally known by the attractive name of *livres de beurre* or "pounds of butter." Of course, "New Stone Age" sounds very antique indeed, but most of Europe was living in the New Stone Age when the civilisations of the Near East were already flourishing.

Le Grand-Pressigny, near the junction of the Claise and Égronne streams, lies at the foot of, and up, a hill crowned by the considerable remains of an ancient fortress, partly in ruins and partly in sufficiently good preservation to serve as home for several families. The buttressed, square 12th century keep is in a rather remarkable state of preservation. The corbels are intact. We may, by the way, note that we can always guess at a French keep's age by its shape. If it is square, it will be 11th or 12th century. If it is round, it will be later.

The "New Castle" built by the *marquis* de Villars is a charming 17th century building now occupied by the local *gendarmerie*. Nearby is a now isolated polygonal staircase-tower called *la tour Vironne*, evidently the remains of a 15th or 16th century dwelling.

Le Grand-Pressigny church is a worthy building of the usual Romanesque nave and Gothic choir type.

On the Preuilly road, after you have crossed the Égronne and the ruins of the feudal Castle of Étableau, you come successively on the church of Saint-Martin and that of Chaumussay, both Romanesque.

## *"I think, therefore I am"*

LA HAYE-DESCARTES. The little township of La Haye, in south-western Touraine, was the birthplace of the illustrious philosopher Descartes, and it is interesting for almost nothing else. But there is no museum in Descartes' birthplace, and only an inscription over the entrance. Nothing has been done to make a pilgrimage-place out of La Haye. The local bookshop, we noted, had none of Descartes' works, nor indeed any books about him.

Although Descartes' name is famous all over the world, although we have most of us seen copies of his portrait showing him a man of curious, lined features and grave expression, although some of us may have beheld—or even handled—his skull that is on exhibition at the Museum of Man in Paris, none of us, outside France, can quite realise what the name "Descartes" means for a Frenchman or what an immediate response is awakened by the use of the adjective *cartésien* to designate an impeccably logical piece of reasoning or of deduction or of induction. Touraine has given to France one of her greatest, if not her greatest, novelist —Balzac; her greatest statesman—Richelieu; her greatest satirical and humorous writer—Rabelais; and her greatest philosopher— Descartes. Not only in its scenery but in its sons is Touraine the fruitful garden of France.

Descartes was born in 1596 at a small manor or farm some three miles from La Haye; the place is called *Les Cartes*, and his parents belonged to the class of the semi-nobility of the law. When he was a young man, Descartes was known as "Du Perron," from a small lordship he possessed. It was in those days the fashion for all who were, or affected to be, "noble" to assume a territorial name for any fief they might possess, however humble, since such an assumption was a public advertisement of their "nobility."

Descartes received his schooling at the famous Jesuit college at La Flèche. Descartes had, from his youth up, poor health, and he always spent a good deal of his time in bed. Later, René made his way to Paris, and there took his part in the pleasures of the capital. Here his friends included Mersenne the friar, who was to be his life-long friend. In 1617 Descartes most unexpectedly enlisted as a volunteer for the war in the Low Countries, and after two years in Holland he again volunteered for service in Bavaria, and it was at Neuberg, on the Danube, shut up as he expressed it "in a stove," that he was led into the meditations that formed the basis of his chief work, *Le Discours sur le Méthode*. Three dreams were said to have given him much insight into the problems he was turning over in his mind. After some travels, he settled in Holland in 1625, and until 1649 was only thrice in France. In 1630 he paid a flying visit to England.

It was in 1649 that he left, by invitation of the Swedish Court, for Stockholm, where the climate killed him.

Of Descartes' philosophy we cannot speak here, but we may note that his was what we like to think of as the modern spirit— eager for knowledge of man and of the world he lives in. The influence of Descartes has been capital in the history of human thought.

In 1692 there was published *chez Claude Cellier*, rue Saint-Jacques, at the sign of the "Big Ship," Paris, a little book by one

Baillet. It has now become very rare, and it gives us a curious description of the great philosopher. We read:

*"Monsieur Descartes was of a height a little above the average. . . . He appeared to have a head rather large for his body. . . . He had on his cheek a little pimple which was often scratched but always came up again. . . . His eyes were dark grey, his face always serene and his appearance affable. The tone of his voice was soft and neither loud nor low, but too weak to allow him to go off into a long speech without pauses. . . . His way of life was always very regular and set. He was naturally sober. He drank little wine and often went months on end without tasting any at all. But, as he was lively and charming during meal-times, his sobriety did not make his friends feel ill at ease. He was neither finicking nor exacting in the matter of his food, and he had trained his taste to accept everything which was not harmful to his health. . . . He slept much."*

Descartes was economical. His income was between six and seven thousand *livres*—in those days a very comfortable fortune—and he lived decently, being neither misanthropic nor melancholy. But he disliked writing and was negligent in answering letters. He was of a cheerful disposition and, moreover, practised cheerfulness as part of philosophy, since he was convinced that cheerful people have better health than melancholy ones.

Descartes was a man of secretive temperament, and no doubt his natural inclinations were strengthened by prudence. Philosophers and "free thinkers" were marked men: in Holland he was far freer than he would have been in France, but, all the same, he changed his abode twenty-four times in twenty-four years. He lived in thirteen different towns. He would not reveal his addresses. His motto was LARVATUS PRODEO—"I go forward masked."

He was almost extravagantly discreet and reserved,

*"not unsociable enough to consider that if people thought about him that they should think ill of him, but still much preferring that they should not think about him at all. . . ."*

## The "Father of French History"

L'ÎLE-BOUCHARD. André Duchesne, generally called the "Father of French History," was an infant prodigy if we may judge from his first work published when he was eighteen years of age. Richelieu, who was a fellow-countryman of Duchesne's, got him appointed geographer and historiographer to the King. In fifty-six years of life Duchesne was a most prolific and hard-working author. Books poured from his study: biographies, genealogies, translations of the classics, editions of standard authors, works of history, archeology and geography. And when he died he left behind him more than a hundred folio volumes of MSS.

Duchesne, who was born at L'Île-Bouchard in 1584, was killed in 1640 by being run over by a carriage when he was on his way from Paris to his country-house.

Duchesne's home-town is a place one has a tendency to rush through on the way to Champigny and to Richelieu. It is, however, worth some attention.

L'Île-Bouchard itself is an island at the junction of the rivers Manse and Vienne. On the left bank of the latter stream lies the suburb of Saint-Maurice, while on the right bank is that of Saint-Gilles. They are joined by a bridge supported on the island. Saint-Maurice grew up round the church of that name. It is a building with a fine late Gothic hexagonal tower and stone spire remarkably lofty and elegant. Of the ancient Priory of Saint-Léonard, behind the railway station, there is still standing a magnificent Romanesque sanctuary with an ambulatory and radiating chapels whose great arches rest upon splendidly carved capitals. In another Romanesque church nearby there is, set into the north wall, a curious bas-relief depicting the Miraculous Draught of Fishes.

On the Saint-Gilles side, the church (the earliest parts of which date from about 1067) was enlarged in the eleven hundreds. The choir, dating from 1540, was refashioned in 1620.

About a couple of hundred yards beyond the suburb of Saint-Gilles is a fine dolmen, one of whose roofing stones is over twenty-two feet long.

If you take the road towards La Haye-Descartes, you pass Crouzilles, whose 12th century church has seven Romanesque statues. Some miles farther along is Nouâtre, on the Vienne. Here both the 15th century church and the contemporary ruined manor are worth a visit.

## The Heart of the Mauges

JALLAIS. At Jallais we are in the heart of the Mauges country. If you crossed the Loire at Ingrandes by the first great suspension bridge and then climbed the Montjean cliff, that was one way into the Mauges country. But the better way lies through Vihiers if you come from the *Saumurois* and the east. To the west the Mauges reaches right to Brittany. This *pagus medalgicus* derived its name, they say, from the iron and lead mines once worked hereabouts. The Mauges was, before the Revolution, a province apart, but neither Cholet, nor Vihiers nor Chemillé were counted in it though now they pass for Mauges towns.

The Mauges is rather a harsh land and it was here that the Vendean war, or uprising, had its origin. If you ask, hereabouts, where are the old houses, the old churches and the old castles you will be told "Burned down in the Great War." And you will wonder when war raged so fiercely in this western France. But these western Angevins mean by the "Great War" not that of 1914–18 or that of 1939–45 but the Vendean war of 1793. For to suppress the uprising the Convention sent down to Anjou and the Vendée the so-called "infernal columns" commanded by Turreau, whose orders were to instil terror by massacres and fire. The "Great War" began on 12th March, 1793, and Cathelineau took Jallais the next day. To the original 27 insurgents flocked thousands, but the horde of peasants could not stand against the republican troops. Hoche settled the war and gave the Angevins and Vendeans liberty of conscience by the treaties of La Jaunaie and Saint-Florent.

In some parts of the Mauges you may still see hand-looms in the "cave" or ground-floor room of the cottages, but the looms have become rather rare and you may more often hear the hammering of leather, for many of the peasants work in their own homes for the shoe manufacturers. The men get a fixed sum per week during the months when out-of-doors work is at a standstill. Many of the so-called *façon bottier,* or "hand-made style" shoes, sold in Paris come from the Mauges, that is a region almost entirely inhabited by small peasant farmers.

Near Jallais village is a farm called La Chaperonnière, which was from the 16th century a manor-house famed in Angevin folk-lore.

One of the Chaperons, Lords of the place, on returning from the wars found his wife married to another. As Chaperon's steed was piebald, that is *pie* in French, the ballad about this worthy's conjugal misfortunes is known as the *Complainte de la Pie*, or the "Complaint of the Magpie" (for "*pie*" means magpie as well as "piebald").

La Chaperonnière was also the scene of an historical tragedy. On 27th May, 1832, during the uprising fomented by the scatterbrained *duchesse* de Berry, German daughter-in-law of King Charles X (and mother of the *comte* de Chambord, pretender to the French throne, who, said M. Thiers, looked from a distance like a German and from near at hand like an idiot), Jacques Cathelineau (following in his father's footsteps) was "out" against the régime of Louis-Philippe. Jacques was hidden with some friends at the farm when a platoon of soldiers surrounded the place. The farmer refused to talk, but Jacques hearing the threats came out, saying "Don't shoot, we surrender." He was shot dead.

## A Roman City

JUBLAINS. Jublains is the finest example remaining in France of a Roman fortified town. There is an outer enclosure, built of small stones alternating with bricks, and flanked with two round, more than half-ruined, towers. The second enclosure is an earthwork, within which are the ruins of public baths or *thermae*. There are four stone sarcophagi in the building, and sections of the terra-cotta pipes used for conveying the hot air; steam and water can also be seen.

In the centre of the camp is a *castellum* or "keep" of masonry, into which you walk through gateways formed of huge superimposed blocks of stone. The walls are about six feet thick, and in each corner is a storeroom, entered by an arched door. In the middle of the court is an *impluvium*, or drain, through which rainwater was collected into two subterranean cisterns.

There are a few jumbled vestiges of an earlier Roman town.

You cannot help thinking, as you look about this Roman settlement, how lasting was the Roman tradition. The barbarian invasions may have swept over Gaul, they may have, for a time, submerged Roman civilisation, but that civilisation lingered on, coarsened, degenerate and decayed, and when men began again to organise their lives, they began to copy Roman monuments and

Le Lude

The Castle Front as it is Today

**Luynes**                                  A Bird's-Eye View

**Luynes** ——————————————————————— The Feudal Fortress

**Luynes**        Old Houses in the Village     **Mamers**        The Church

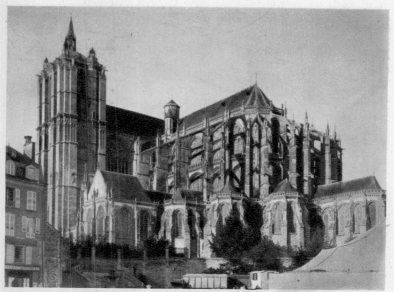

The graceful Gothic Choir of the Cathedral

The *Notre-Dame de la Couture*       "The House of Queen Berengaria"

**LE MANS**

Scarron's House

Renaissance Mansion

Half-timbered Dwelling

The "Adam and Eve" House

**LE MANS**

Roman architecture. A town like Jublains, a fortress if you will, is the ancestor of the strong castles of centuries later.

This Jublains, it seems, was originally a Gaulish settlement which the Romans, when they took it over, called NOEODUNUM. But it was not fortified, and was sacked by the barbarians during incursions in the 3rd century. It was later that the *castrum* was constructed. Some time in the 4th century probably, another barbarian raid ruined the place for ever.

But the Roman stones were used, and Jublains church is said to have been built with them. Jublains is only a small hamlet, and it lies some four hundred and fifty feet above sea-level. As you leave the village you can see more ruins and stumps of building piercing the soil and dotted with wild flowers and herbs—bluebells and thyme and yellow St. John's wort . . . and just beyond the church, on the Évron road, are the half-buried tiers of a Roman amphitheatre.

If you come this way from Évron, on the Mayenne road, in three miles you are in La Roche-en-Mézangers, where we meet the "Green Lady." Then the road skirts the west side of the lake known as Le Gué-de-Selle. In front of you is the range of the Coëvrons Hills, on whose highest peak, the Montaigu or the Sharp Mount, is perched a little chapel. It is a rather wild and desolate countryside, but charming in a melancholy sort of way.

## Five Hundred Pigeons

LANCHENEIL. In the commune of Nuillé-sur-Vicoin, just off the Château-Gontier high road, lies Lancheneil, an ancient fief whose lords enjoyed hereabout the rights of High Justice, Middle and Low. These old Mathefelons (whose cradle was near Durtal) seem to have used their privileges rather freely, since the old chroniclers tell us that the country round about Lancheneil was dotted with gibbets.

The Mathefelons claimed that they had been granted the lordship of Lancheneil by the great Count of Anjou, Fulk Nerra, himself. What we can still see to-day is a feudal castle, though a late one. The irregular outline, the surface of dark stone and white bonding and courses, the steep roofs and the air of antique inevitability combine to make Lancheneil a notable monument.

And there is still the old pigeon-loft for five hundred pigeons

—a number that even the powerful Lord of High, Middle and Lower Justice must not exceed.

During the 19th century Lancheneil was allowed to fall into ruin, but since 1908 has been restored.

Within are some charming portraits of the Préaulx family (who acquired the place by marriage in 1718). On the first floor is a saloon, with fine Louis XVI panelling; and on a commode, with metal-work by Caffieri, is a bust of Louis XV by Coysevox, the celebrated sculptor who, among other works, was the author of the "Mercury and Fame" now in the Tuileries Gardens in Paris.

## Alangavia

LANGEAIS. Langeais was a township as long ago as the 5th century, when it was known as ALANGAVIA, a fortified post on the high ground between the Loire and the little Roumer stream. Later on here, as at so many places in Touraine and in Anjou, we meet our old friend Fulk Nerra, the formidable Count of Anjou, who about 990 erected a fortress at Langeais, a fortress whose blurred ruins can be seen near the existing castle.

The fief of Langeais was, in the 13th century, owned by Philippe des Brosses, surgeon-barber and minister of State to King Philippe *le Hardi*. But Brosses' fortune soon faded.

Jean Bourré, one of the wily "new men" with whom King Louis XI delighted to surround himself, was the builder of the present castle. Much of Bourré's rapidly acquired wealth must have been invested in houses, since he built or rebuilt Longes, Longué, Jarzé, Vaulx, Coudray, Le Plessis-Bourré and Antrammes near Laval. Langeais must have been finished about 1470. But Langeais was put up on the King's orders and presumably the castle was not wholly paid for by Bourré.

Later, the place passed into the possession of the famous Anjou family of du Bellay and then into that of d'Effiat de Cinq-Mars. The *ducs* de Luynes owned Langeais from the 17th century to the Revolution. The estate was bought and sold, as so many others, in Revolutionary times, but was rarely, if ever, lived in. Towards the end of the last century it was bought by Monsieur Jacques Siegfried, who had the whole house very skilfully restored about fifty years ago. He filled it with fine furnishings and, by his will, left the place to the *Institut de France*, the organisation that includes the French Academy and the four other academies of arts and sciences.

## Where Brittany became Part of France

LANGEAIS is a strange and impressive place, but neither from the outside nor from the inside does it convey the impression of a house that was ever much lived in. Indeed, despite its size, its convenient position on the Loire and the great personages who were its lords, Langeais has not been the scene of any great historic event except that of the marriage of Charles VIII of France with Anne of Brittany, heiress of the duchy of Brittany. By this alliance the ancient and independent duchy was united to the Crown of France.

Langeais is dark and grey, massive and lofty, overlooking and dominating a little town of narrow alleys whose houses huddle up to the castle's walls. This rude fortress never had anything of the fragile superstructures which made Saumur almost a fairy-story castle.

The plan of the place is curious. It consists of two wings—one of which is considerably longer than the other—set at right angles. Seen from the side of the township, the castle has all the appearance of a great feudal fortress, but when you go round to the back, or garden, side, you see that either the building was never completed or that it was never intended to be more than a fake fortress, since the garden front consists of an irregular façade of a sobre, simple and, indeed, forbidding architecture, but one that is quite unmilitary, and suggests a peaceable country-house of the 16th century. It is probable, however, that at first it was intended that Langeais should be a stronghold, but before the place could be finished the conditions of warfare had changed and the social and political situations of France had altered.

The "fortress" side of the house has few windows, three enormous towers with conical roofs, machicolations and battlements nearly a hundred and fifty yards long. There is no moat. The road runs close to the walls that, between the two main towers, are pierced with a portcullis gateway, to which access is had from the street up two flights of steps and over a drawbridge. This arrangement seems to be relatively modern, since in olden days a moat, fed by the waters of the river, washed the foot of walls and towers.

Despite the general rather bogus impression made by the contrast between the front and the back of Langeais, the northern tower is a real keep capable of sustaining a siege. And, compared with the modest royal manor of Plessis-lès-Tours, bourgeois Langeais seems royal indeed.

Again, Langeais has not suffered any mutilation, rebuilding or modification. As we see it to-day, so it was in 1470—at least in all essentials.

The garden front, as we have noticed, is less severe than that giving on to the town, but it is still exceptionally formidable and forbidding for a Touraine *château*. The stone is not the pale, charming *tuffeau*, but a hard, dark limestone that has weathered into tones like those of an elephant's hide.

There is no "decoration." The windows are "functional," and have not been grouped or arranged with any regard for symmetry or grace. They bear little moulding beyond drip-stones familiar to us from Tudor buildings at home. The gables of the dormers are adorned with crockets, and three pentagonal staircase turrets break up the monotony of the façade.

The gardens are laid out in formal parterres bordered with box, and their pleasing geometrical patterns fit in well enough with the impressive and rather mysterious bulk of the great house beyond them.

Within, Langeais is a rabbit-warren of passages, corridors, stairs up and down, rooms of all sizes and shapes. There are one or two splendid apartments with magnificent chimney-pieces, the finest of which is in the guard-room. Here the mantel is (as in *bourgeois* Jacques Coeur's house at Bourges) carved with a representation of a feudal fortress manned by defending troops. Another chimney-piece adorns the Great Hall—where, they say, took place the marriage between Charles VIII and Anne of Brittany on the 16th December, 1491—this monumental fireplace is cunningly sculptured with foliage.

Langeais is full of interesting furnishings, many of them of contemporary date with the building, some later and some, indeed, reproductions of old pieces. There are Flemish tapestries, there are beds, busts, hangings, paintings, coffers, chairs and every other sort of object that would grace a great house in the 15th and 16th centuries.

Although Langeais is emphatically a place not to miss visiting, it is not an agreeable house, though a most interesting one.

## Ubu-Roi

LAVAL. The sleepy, provincial town of Laval has given the world three strange sons, of whom the most curious in his life and ways was Jarry, the author of that satirical masterpiece *Ubu-Roi*, a work perennially topical as only classics are. Jarry brought with him to Paris the rough draft of his book that was inspired by the men and women of his native town. The people of Laval still do not like being reminded of *Ubu-Roi* and it is hardly tactful to mention the work when you are in the capital of the Mayenne department. Jarry, who was also the author of *Ubu-Cocu* and of *Le Sur-Mâle*, lived miserably in Paris and died young. Endless tales are told of his eccentricity and mordant wit, as also of his habit of breeding owls in his garret. Perhaps the birds of Minerva were living symbols.

Jarry seems to-day an author of great significance since he was, with Rimbaud and the man who wrote under the name of "Lautréamont," among the first of what we might, to-day, call the "superrealist" writers. To their contemporaries, however, Jarry, Rimbaud and Lautréamont displayed a peculiar humour which was sign and evidence of terrorist and "nihilist" revolt against the established order. And in a country where mental incoherence and especially incoherence of expression are felt as the greatest of moral and intellectual crimes, the fantasy, the satire and the wit of the early "superrealist" men of letters were held in horror. There is no monument to Jarry at Laval.

## The First of the Superrealist Painters

THE second strange son of Laval was Henri Rousseau, better known as the *douanier* Rousseau, although he was never a customs-house official but only an employee of the *octroi* or Paris excise administration, since still, even to this day, small taxes are levied on the importation of some articles, notably food-stuffs, into the French capital.

Rousseau was the first of the superrealist painters, at least of those in modern times since Breughel and Hieronymus Bosch and others were, in their way, superrealists, and there has always been a superrealist or subjective tendency running through pictorial art. But Rousseau's work was so strange, so subversive of received art-traditions that during his life-time he was hardly taken seriously by any except a small coterie of admirers and, it must be admitted, boosters. Five French writers have sung his praises—Alfred Jarry, Rémy de Gourmont, Max Jacob, Guillaume Apollinaire and Salmon, but still the *Petit Larousse*, the pocket encyclopædia of the average Frenchman, does not mention Rousseau's name.

Rousseau was the painter of such marvels as the *Charmeuse de Serpents* in the Louvre; of *La Noce*, astonishing with its cubist architecture, the blue blouse of the peasant in the foreground answering the blue of the sky, the white bride like a wraith against the dingy black frockcoats of the guests and the decorative, medieval-seeming background of verdure with the leaves arranged in tiers, the biggest below, the smallest above. Then there is *Les Joueurs de Ballon*; and *La Carriole du père Juniet*. It is like a snapshot of a fair, or a still of a swift-moving film. Just a minute's, a second's stop, and then . . . With Rousseau the old sentimental syrup is dried up, no more silly anecdotes, no more patronizing smiles. We cannot say, of course, whether Rousseau's reputation will remain as high as it is now. Perhaps to our grandchildren Rousseau's importance will seem largely to have been that he broke violently away from a tradition they will know of only as a faint echo.

Laval has treated Rousseau's memory more kindly than that of Jarry. The painter was buried in a pauper's grave at the Bagneux cemetery near Paris, but in 1947 the body was removed to Laval and reinterred in the middle of a square now bearing the painter's name. There has also been removed to Laval the tombstone put up at Bagneux by Quéval, Rousseau's friend and on which Brancusi, the sculptor, carved in 1913 the epitaph by Guillaume Apollinaire beginning:

*"Gentil Rousseau, tu nous entends . . ."*

## *"The Father of Surgery"*

BUT the third famous son of Laval is still he of whom the men of the city are most proud—*Ambroise Paré*, the "Father of Surgery." He came of a poor family and his father was a carpenter. He himself had little education and never mastered Latin—in the 16th century still the universal language of science and learning. Paré was apprenticed to a barber (the barbers were the surgeons of the day), and when he had learned the trade moved to Paris, where he exercised his art on the patients of the *Hôtel-Dieu*. In 1536 he was received "Master-Barber and Surgeon." Paré accompanied the *maréchal* de Montjean on his campaigns, and then it was that the "barber-surgeon" began to practise his most revolutionary method of tying arteries, rather than pouring boiling oil into shot wounds in order to "counteract the poison in the blood." Paré it was who removed the piece of lance-blade from the forehead of the *duc* de Guise who, thereafter, was known as le *balafré*, or "the slashed." Paré was soon the most eminent surgeon in the kingdom —and in Europe, surgeon-in-ordinary to the King, and specially excepted from the slaughter of Saint-Bartholomew. As the old chronicler puts it: "The King, who was crying Kill! Kill! made an exception for Master Paré."

Paré, a man of most pious disposition, grave and dignified, was a resolute Huguenot, and nothing would induce him to change his religion. He is an important figure in the history of medicine. Ambroise Paré has a noble monument at his native place in the shape of a statue done by David d'Angers.

## The Owl's Whistle

IF, however, Jarry and his *Ubu-Roi* and his owls are not commemorated, owls have played a great part in the history of this part of the world. It was in the neighbourhood of Laval that the Cottereau brothers organised their bands of *Chouans*. *Chouan*, or *Chat-Huant*, means an "owl," and Jean *Chouan* (so called from the owl's whistle, which was his signal), whose real name was Jean Cottereau, was the eldest of four brothers who lived in a humble cottage known as the *Closerie des Poiriers*, some ten miles from Laval. Jean and his brothers and a party of followers—mostly made up of former smugglers who had found much of their living gone with the abolition of the internal customs' barriers—carried on irregular warfare against the Republicans during the Vendean rising. Jean, after the defeat of La Rochejaquelein's arms at Le Mans, sought refuge in the Misedon woods, where he was found and killed on the 28th July, 1794. Of the brothers, René only survived the troubles, and returned to plough his lands at the *Closerie des Poiriers.*

## The Old Castle

LAVAL, the chief town of the Mayenne department, lies in a charming site on both sides of the Mayenne River. On the right bank the old quarters cover the slopes of a steep hill, while on the left and lower side are the more modern streets. About thirty thousand people live in the clean and rather friendly city, which is cut through with many leafy, shaded walks. The northern part of the town was much knocked about in the 1939–45 war.

From the middle of the bridge you can look up at the imposing mass of the Old Castle with its sturdy round tower, while farther on, to your left, but adjoining the ancient building, is the whitish façade of the New Castle. You are standing on the *pont-vieux,* whose pointed arches span the stream. The bridge was cut in two during the late war but has been patched up. This part of Laval has much changed in recent years, and when we first visited the place, the old fortress still rose above a jumble of antique wooden houses jostling each other on the river-front. Nowadays it is all swept and garnished and rather cold.

The New Castle, or "Galleries of the Counts of Laval," is a huge Renaissance palace now housing the Law Courts. There is an elegant arcaded gallery on the ground-floor of the garden front, the first floor and the attic have mullioned windows, between which are garlanded medallions enclosing swags of fruit. The lofty left wing was added after 1850.

The Old Castle is a much more interesting place. Its foundations go back to the 8th or 9th century. The building has often been refashioned, modified and altered, but the bulk of it is still the 11th and 12th century Romanesque fortress of the Counts of Laval, great barons of the west. The Old Castle suffered some damage during the fighting.

For long it was believed that the original Castle of Laval—*vallum guidonis,* later, Laval-Guyon—had been erected by one Guido (a contemporary of Charlemagne) in order to hold up the forays and incursions of the plundering Bretons. However, the real history of Laval begins with Guido or Guy, who seems to have laid the foundations of the fortress about 1020.

**Le Mans** The Poplar-plumed Highway to Laval

**Marcilly-Sur-Maulne**   The *Château*

**Montbazon**   The Keep

**Mayenne**   The Church

**Montbazon**

**Mayenne**   View from the River

**Montsoreau**   The Manor-House

The barony (later countship) of Laval was one of the most famous and important fiefs of medieval France, and was held successively by families as eminent as the Montforts, the Montmorencys and the Colignys.

When, at the commencement of the 15th century, we occupied nearly all the strong points in Maine, Laval alone held out against the English, thanks largely to the energy of Anne de Laval. However, "Old John Talbot" stormed the town on the 13th May, 1428. Soon, nevertheless, the French regained possession of the stronghold, and that by a stratagem well remembered in French history—the miller Jehan Fouquet hid some knights with his sacks of flour and the town was taken from within.

Laval changed hands several times during the Wars of Religion, but from 1594 enjoyed peace and prosperity, until in 1793 La Rochejaquelein, the Vendean leader, carried the city and defeated the Republican army commanded by the incapable Léchelle, despite the efforts of his subordinates Kléber and Marceau. Some time later La Rochejaquelein evacuated the place, and the Repulican National Guards then seized the *prince* de Talmont, *comte* de Laval (a young man of twenty-eight), and executed him before the door of the castle in which his ancestors had lived as lords for eight hundred years.

Laval castle is indeed an antique place. When we reflect that the lower chapel and the keep date from the ten and eleven hundreds, that the principal lodging is seven hundred years old, and that the latest parts were put up before America was discovered, we expect to find something of interest. We are not disappointed.

The fortress served as a prison from 1792 until 1909. Since the latter date the place has been thoroughly reconditioned, but not over-restored. The collections in the art and natural history museums are being arranged in the castle's apartments.

The inner façades on the courtyard were pierced, in Renaissance times, with fine, long windows framed with richly decorated sculpture. The bronze statue in the courtyard is of Béatrix de Gavre, the wife of Count Guy IX of Laval. She brought from her Low Countries' home Flemish weavers to Laval, where they established the industry which was to become and remain to this day—the principal one of the town.

The 11th century Romanesque chapel is archaic, but the four

granite columns were added in the eleven hundreds. On the first floor is the great Hall of Honour of the Counts of Laval, and it is nearly a hundred feet long.

The keep, on the other hand, is over a hundred feet high and its walls are more than twelve feet thick. From one of the rooms on the ground-floor you can get by steps in the thickness of the wall down to a dark dungeon. A staircase winding upwards, and also in the thickness of the wall, leads to three storeys, the top one of which has a fine and very ancient (12th century) open-work wooden roof.

The Church of *Notre-Dame des Cordeliers* was formerly the chapel of a Minorite priory, built in 1397 by Count Guy XII of Laval. The building was much refashioned in the 15th century and again in the reign of Henri IV, when the splendid portal was erected.

The Church of Saint-Martin is more interesting. It is a Romanesque building whose interior walls are covered with paintings ranging in date from the 12th to the 17th century. Unfortunately, they were all botched and ruthlessly "restored" about 1883. However, the magnificent head of the Christ in the *noli me tangere* scene of the north transept is of pure 12th century workmanship. The allegorical calendar (originally painted in the same period) on the choir arch has been much retouched.

## The Cathedral of the Holy Trinity

SCATTERED about Laval's streets are some old houses, but of the ancient fortifications nothing much remains but the so-called *Tour Renaise,* together with the *Porte Beucheresse* barbican, flanked with two stout towers, which is near the cathedral.

Laval is one of the very few modern sees in France where, ever since the Revolution, the tendency has been to reduce the number of bishoprics (there are sixty-nine dioceses and seventeen archdioceses in metropolitan France alone, and these for a population of barely forty millions, of whom the majority cannot be held to be Catholics other than in name only). But the bishopric of Laval was constituted in 1865 by carving the new see out of the diocese of Le Mans.

The oldest part of Laval Cathedral dates from 1070, but the

present nave was put up in 1160, and the building was often re-fashioned and added to, right up to the last century.

The vaulting of the nave is of primitive Gothic type (dating from about 1185) and in the typical Angevin style of the day.

Although Laval Cathedral is a fine and even imposing building, it cannot vie in interest or in importance with those of Le Mans, of Tours, or of Angers.

There are one or two good pictures on the walls, and the nave is often adorned with six great hangings of Aubusson tapestry (17th century), depicting the Legend of Judith and Holofernes.

## Guy's Vow

THE Laval art museum is a rather pleasing modern edifice in classical Greek style, and it houses a few good paintings, mostly by later French masters, such as Isabey, Meissonier, Oudry, etc. There is a "Virgin and Child" of the Flemish School. The panel has been, without much justification, attributed to Jean Breughel.

Sloping down from the museum is a charming garden known as *La Perrine*, through which you may reach the river-side and then the Old Bridge.

Just on the other side of the Mayenne lies the late Gothic Church of Saint-Vénérand, with a fine Flamboyant west entrance; but the most noteworthy church hereabouts is not in the town of Laval itself, but some thousand yards south of the walls. It is known as *Notre-Dame-d'Avénières*.

It is said that Guy V of Laval, while crossing the Old Bridge on horseback, toppled off into the water, though, owing to good luck or the most eminent horsemanship, he remained seated. Horse and rider were swept along the stream while Guy made a vow to the Virgin that if he managed to reach the banks he would, where he landed, raise a shrine to Our Lady. The date of this incident is set about 1140, but, alas for the story, Avénières church was founded at least a hundred years earlier.

Avénières is a Romanesque building, but its architecture is late enough in date to give a hint at the transition to Gothic, and we may set some time between 1140 and 1170 for the erection of the present church, so that it is possible that Guy rebuilt an existing shrine after his adventures in the waters of the Mayenne.

The vaulting of the nave and the capitals of the columns are early Gothic, but the choir, ambulatory and radiating chapels are in very pure Romanesque tradition. The building suffered some damage in the 1939–45 war.

Above the high altar and embedded in an oak-tree trunk sprouting golden leaves is the venerated statue of "Our Lady of Avénières." The image, wearing a swelling, flounced skirt in the Spanish mode, is, according to a modern legend, the same effigy which Guy found in an oak tree when he scrambled ashore.

## Painted Pritz

A MILE and a half to the north of Laval is a hamlet bearing the very Germanic-seeming name of Pritz. No visitor to Laval should fail to make a pilgrimage to Pritz church, to reach which you have to pass through a farm-yard and into a leafy garden. Much of the masonry of the nave and transepts must be Carolingian work and may date from about 880. The rest of the building is probably 11th century. The interior of the place was, at one time, entirely covered with mural paintings. The oldest are the "Legend of Saint Catherine" and the "Works and Days" calender. These are of 13th century date. The "Legend of Saint Hubert" and the "Life of Saint Christopher" are later, the former 16th and the latter 15th century. Unfortunately, all the pictures are in bad condition, but the calendar over the choir-arch is the best preserved of the Pritz frescoes.

## Incomparable Romanesque Paintings

LE LIGET. The round shrine near Chemillé-sur-Indrois is one of the main sights of Touraine.

About 1170 a chapel was set up in Loches forest, but the trees have been driven back. To-day the little shrine stands in the fields though near the wood's edge. Originally the whole of the inside walls, including the dome, were covered with pictures.

You can enter either by a main door or by a postern whose lintel is surmounted by a bust of Christ. Seven small windows let in plenty of light. In the embrasures of each of the windows are two figures of saints, face to face.

Between the windows are six great panels. To the right of the main door is a *Tree of Jesse*. To the left is the *Nativity*, then follow the *Presentation in the Temple*, the *Descent from the Cross*, the *Holy Women at the Tomb* and the *Dormition of the Virgin.*

Above these six scenes runs a decorated scroll, on which are set, in rectangular frames, bust-portraits of the Prophets holding phylacteries with inscriptions.

The paintings of the dome have quite disappeared.

The colours of the Le Liget frescoes are soft, clear and bathed in light—the colours (with a predominant note of white) are yellow ochre, six shades of red, three of green and, here and there, a touch of blue, limpid as a Touraine sky after rain.

The figures do not lend themselves to description. There emanates from them an atmosphere of sweetness and humanity that is overwhelming.

How human is the figure of the Virgin pressing her sad face against her Son's arm as the lifeless, limp body is taken down from the Cross! How serene is her visage in the scene of her Dormition when Christ receives her soul in His hands! This most moving picture of the Virgin's death we may compare with the 12th century mosaic at La Martorana, in Palermo, or with a later window in the Cathedral of Chartres.

At Le Liget, in the last years of the 12th century, we see already the calm, reassuring, serene grace which later informs the sculpture and the stained glass of the French Gothic cathedrals. As M. Paul Deschamps has well written:

*"In the list of French masterpieces the paintings of Le Liget must be considered to hold one of the highest places."*

## Macaroons and Goat's Cheese

LIGUEIL. Ligueil town, a small place of about two thousand inhabitants who make the most excellent macaroons and goat's cheese, lies in the valley of the Esves, an affluent of the Creuse. There is not much to see in Ligueil except some old houses and a fine 17th century reredos of gilded wood in the parish church, but out from the town and on the Sainte-Maure road, about seven miles away, you should stop and have a look at the notable *château* de Bagneux. It is now a farm, but it still makes a fine show standing on rising ground. The building dates from the fourteen hundreds, and the two round towers, corbelled and machicolated, are in excellent preservation.

## The Craonnais

LE LION-D'ANGERS. Going northwards from Angers you are in the Craon country, or the *Craonnais,* as soon as you reach Avrillé. Here and there are the shrunken patches of the ancient forests—Longuenée, Ombrée, Chemazé or Rouvrais, but the woods of the *Craonnais* are far from being as extensive as those, for instance, in the Baugé region. The *Craonnais* is a land of hedges, hedges set often with tall trees such as we are familiar with in the English countryside. And these hedges of oak, chestnut, elm and dogwood and brambles are wide and thick, making strips of woodland with a distinctive character of their own.

The *Craonnais* is watered by the Mayenne stream and it is a country of little hidden manors and country-houses, nearly all of them now used as farms. But there are also fine castles and *châteaux* which have managed to survive. Only until yesterday, indeed, Anjou was essentially a land of small and middling country gentry living in their unpretentious manors and on the produce of their own acres. Times have changed, but they have changed perhaps less in Anjou than in any other part of northern France. The little squires, despising commerce and ignoring industry, still linger on.

The towns of the *Craonnais* are small—Segré, Craon and Château-Gontier. It is a province of broad meadows. At La Meignanne, ten miles from Angers, is a megalith, and in the Colleterie-Wood near Saint-Lambert-la-Poterie is the "Fairies' House," screened with tall trees and set by a mirror-like mere. The "House" of two chambers, one formed of four stones and the other of six, is all that remains of what must have been an important barrow-tomb.

Then we come to the old posting-town of Le Lion-d'Angers.

## The Seven Deadly Sins

ON the nave's walls of Saint-Martin's church in Le Lion-d'Angers are traces of some ancient mural paintings. There is a gigantic, sturdy Saint-Christopher, and more notable still, near the organ-loft, a vivid seven-headed hydra symbolising the Seven Deadly Sins. In execution and spirit this awesome monster reminds us of the apocalyptic seven-headed beast to be seen on the Gothic tapestry of Angers museum in the "Revelation" series.

Saint-Martin's was, originally, the chapel of a Benedictine priory. The nave and belfry are Romanesque, but the spacious choir is quite modern, though you have to glance at it twice to realise that it *is* modern, so cleverly and successfully has the 13th century style been imitated.

Le Lion-d'Angers is a charming little town situated on the right bank of the Oudon and a little over a mile upstream from the *Bec d'Oudon* where it falls into the Mayenne. Between the left bank of the Oudon and the Mayenne is a large estate known as Isle-Briant, surrounding a country-house rebuilt in the 18th century.

North of Le Lion-d'Angers on the Segré highway you pass through Andigné, with the ruins of the 15th century *château* des Vents, and when you are only a mile from Segré town, you can stop a few minutes in order to look at the Chapel of La Lorie house. The little sanctuary has two painted glass windows dating from Renaissance times and an impressive 17th century reredos.

## *Loches*

LOCHES. Loches leaves on its visitor one of the strongest impressions he will take away from Touraine. The most attractive way to come upon Loches is to drive on the poplar-plumed pathway through Beaulieu on the other bank of the Indre, which here divides into several arms. The highway through Beaulieu is bordered by lush meadows set with willows. You cross several bridges and reach the foot of Loches hill.

There may have been a Roman or Gallo-Roman settlement called LUCCAE or LOCCAE, but Loches grew up around a monastery founded by Saint-Ours or St. Ursus, who came hither in the 5th century from Cahors, in the Quercy, far away to the south. In the troublous times of the 6th century Loches hill already boasted a fortress, for the height affords a strategic position of great strength. During the Middle Ages, Loches was, as we shall see, both a prison and a royal residence. Kings, in those days, rather liked to have their victims near them, if underground. Charles VII (the "fair Dauphin" of the Joan of Arc legend) often stayed here with his mistress Agnes Sorel, whose tomb was made in the Collegiate Church of Saint Ursus. Louis XI enlarged the prisons. The last royal visitor of note was Marie de' Medici, widow of

King Henry IV who, having escaped from enforced residence at Blois, made her way to Loches, whose governor, the *duc* d'Epernon, furnished her with the means to reach Angoulême and continue her campaign against her son the King.

## A Town within a Town

LOCHES consists of a fortified town—the castle—within a walled town. Let us visit the town first. From the *quai de la Filature,* just across the Indre from the Beaulieu road, you can walk up to the *Porte des Cordeliers,* an exceptionally fine example of a 15th century city-gate set with turrets. In the *rue Saint-Antoine* is an interesting Renaissance house and, a little farther on, is the Tour Saint-Augustin, a Renaissance tower on a Gothic base, all that remains of the old Church of Saint-Augustin.

The town hall is a rather meagre Renaissance building put up during the years from 1535 to 1543. Although it was thoroughly restored about a generation ago, the apartments are interesting, and the library contains a number of volumes formerly at Le Liget monastery. The *Porte Picoys* adjoins the town hall, and through the gate you reach the new town.

In the Church of Saint-Antoine is a magnificent triptych of the Passion. The panels were formerly at Le Liget, and the painting appears to be by a follower of famous Jehan Fouquet of Tours, the author of that glorious Virgin and Child (much restored) now in Brussels, for the central figure of which picture Agnes Sorel is said to have sat as a model. Certainly the Virgin's face is not unlike that shown on Agnes's tomb at Loches, or in portraits reputed to be of her.

In the *grand'rue,* leading up towards the castle, are some notable Renaissance dwellings, the most remarkable of which is the so-called "Chancellery," built about 1531. Among the sculptures of classical subjects are figures of Hercules, Dejaneira and the centaur Nessus of the charmed shirt. Here and there you can make out the royal motto, IVSTITIA REGNO PRVDENTIA NVTRISCO ("I reign by justice, I am nourished on prudence"), disposed among the "antique" orders of Doric and Ionic columns.

The former collegiate Church of Saint Ursus, or Saint-Ours, has its apse abutting on the eastern rampart of the castle. The building was formerly dedicated to Our Lady, and its name was changed at the Revolution, when the old Church of Saint-Ours (which lay under the King's Lodging) was destroyed.

The first bay of the nave belongs, it is said, to a church built in 965 by Geoffroy Grisgonelle, or "Grey-Mantle," Count of Anjou, but the bulk of the edifice is of considerably later date. To the west front was added in the 12th century a porch. In it is a Gallo-Roman altar now serving as a holy-water stoop. The main entrance is also 12th century work, and has a magnificent though much-damaged carved arch. The tower and steeple are Romanesque. The nave is covered by curious stone pyramids and the central tower is stout and square. It is a place of odd outline.

In the crypt is a large mural painting of Saint-Brice. In the treasury is preserved the Virgin's girdle, to house which relic the church was erected. It is not clear what relation this girdle bears to that of Puy-Notre-Dame.

Before we examine the castle we may mention that Loches is famed as a gastronomical centre. The poultry is excellent. The legs of kid (*gigots de chevreau*) are a speciality of the town, and although this tender, white and succulent meat is known and highly appreciated by most gourmets who like Italian food, kid's meat (or at any rate that avowedly such) is rare in France. The *gélines* or boiling fowls of Loches are splendid, and there is a delicious local cake known as *corde*. There are no particularly reputed local wines, but all the good Touraine vintages can be found in the town.

## Castle

LOCHES castle was, in the Middle Ages, one of the strongest and largest in all France. The fortress occupies all the summit of a hill dividing the valley of the Indre from a lateral dale. As they exist to-day the castle walls measure about two thousand yards in length. You enter a gate defended by two towers, and make your way up to the *Logis du Roy,* or Royal Lodging. Unfortunately, in this building are housed the quarters of the local sub-prefect as well as his offices, so that the place is only accessible in part.

The King's Lodging consists of two distinct portions. That to the left, or "Old Halls," is crenellated and the façade bears four turrets whose conical caps do not reach as high as the steep, plain roof of the building. The right-hand portion, or "New Halls," is more richly decorated, and bears elegant, gabled dormers. The Old Halls must have been put up before the reign of Charles VII for the building is typical of the 14th century. The architecture is sober and stern with just a little sculpture at the base of some of the turrets. The New Halls, on the other hand, are clearly of 16th century workmanship and this part of the Lodgings is later in date than the Louis XII wing at Blois.

Within is the renowned oratory of Queen Anne of Brittany. It is a closet built by Charles VIII for his consort, and the walls are covered with ermine spots and knots in low relief. The oratory is unrestored, the stone altar and its canopy are graceful and the loops and curls of the knotted ropes over the entrance are soberly elegant.

### La Dame de Beauté

IN the ground-floor of the highest tower is the beautiful tomb of Agnes Sorel. The recumbent figure is of 15th century workmanship. The *Dame de Beauté* (she was so called, not because of her beauty, but because she was the Lady of the fief of La Beauté-sur-Marne) lies, her head supported by angels and her feet reposing against two lambs—emblems of Saint Agnes. The face of Agnes is serene and rather lovely, with the prominent forehead characteristic of the Gothic cathedral statues. A long Latin inscription on the monument invokes, successively, God Almighty, Apollo, Diana and Isis.

Agnes Sorel, the famed mistress of Charles VII, on whom she exercised an influence on the whole happy, though far from being as great as has been often stated, was a Touraine woman, born at Fromenteau, near Loches, in 1422. She died at Jumièges in Normandy when she was but twenty-eight years old, and while her heart was interred in the Norman shrine, her body was brought eventually to Loches and buried in the collegiate Church of Saint-Ours (the old church and not the present one of that name), on which she had showered many benefactions. Her tomb bore the inscription, *en son vivant Dame de Beauté piteuse envers toutes gens et qui largement donnait de ses biens aux églises et aux pauvres.* "In her lifetime Lady of Beauté pitiful towards all men and who gave freely of her goods to churches and to the poor." The ungrateful canons who were ready enough to take Agnes's money did not want her body to pollute their shrine, and after many attempts to have the coffin removed, at length obtained permission from King Louis XI for the transfer of Agnes's remains. In 1793 a detachment of republican soldiers belonging to the Indre battalion trooped through Loches and, taking the monument for that of a saint, hacked it about. The broken fragments were stowed away in a store-room until 1806 when the tomb was repaired by the sculptor Beauvallet, who had to provide the nose, the hands, part of the robe, the wings and heads of the angels and the head of one of the lambs. In 1806 the prefect of the Indre-et-Loire department was one Pommeuil, who chose its present resting-place for the tomb. Pommeuil also wished to adorn the chamber with sprightly mottoes of his own devising, the first of which was to be:

> *"Je suis Agnès,*
> *Vivient France et l'Amour."*

and all in rather questionable taste. However, the Archbishop of Tours got wind of the project and scotched it.

## Cages for Men

THE south side of the castle walls is the strongest part of the fortifications, since here the natural defences are weakest and the castle rock joins the neighbouring plateau. Here, on this south side, is the keep. Within it is the keep, properly speaking, consisting of two rectangular towers of 12th century workmanship. The towers are joined together. The larger of the two was divided into four storeys, and here were kept notable prisoners. On the second storey of the smaller tower was the chapel. It was in the 15th century that the old castle was developed into a large fortress. After the realm had been pactified by Louis XI, Loches became a State prison.

Louis XI put up another tower called the New or Round Tower, and this building, with its adjoining structures, was designed to defend the keep to the west. Within the New Tower are some fine chimney-pieces. In the Question (i.e. Torture) Chamber are preserved some of the racks, thumbscrews and other instruments used for putting the Question.

Of the famous Cages of Loches it seems that there were two. Each was about six feet square and made of wooden trellis-work strengthened with iron bolts, stanchions, bars and brackets. There was a small hutch for passing food and drink, while a hole in the bottom of the rounded door served as a lavatory. One cage was kept in the Round Tower and the other in the *Martelet*. The latter trap enclosed for some time Lodovico il Moro, while the former contraption was used for our old friend Philippe de Commynes during his misfortunes, and for many other worthies including Geoffroy de Pompadour, Grand Almoner of France, and Georges d'Amboise, Bishop of Montauban. In the 15th and 16th centuries there was not much doubt as to who was master—King or Bishop. And the most famous prisoner to be hung up (for the thing was suspended from the roof like a canary's cage) was the Cardinal La Balue.

Both cages were destroyed in 1790 at the demand of the "Loches Patriotic and Literary Society." The wood was distributed to "two or three of the most necessitous families of the town," but four pieces were kept back to be burned on the bonfire of the 14th July.

## *Dungeons*

THE dungeons of Loches lie under a 15th century edifice known as the *Martelet,* whose upper storeys have disappeared. In these subterranean prisons was apparently the cell of Lodovico Sforza, known as *Il Moro,* Duke of Milan. He painted pictures and designs on his prison-walls—a sundial, two portraits of himself—they are all much effaced. When, in 1508, he was finally released, he dropped dead from emotion at seeing the light and knowing himself free.

Farther down are other dungeons still more murky and grim. Here is the "Bishops' Cell," wherein are carved rough representations of the Stations of the Cross. In another dungeon was incarcerated Saint-Vallier, the father of Diane de Poitiers. There are, hewn in the rock, still other cells dropping down to deep *oubliettes,* or shafts, wherein men fell to perish of hunger, thirst and wounds.

The Good Old Times.

Out into the light again you may peep into a corridor leading to the Round Tower and take in the significance of the maxims engraved upon the walls, such as:

ENTREZ MESSIRES CHEZ LE ROY NOSTRE MAISTRE
("*Enter, Gentlemen, into the house of our Sovereign Lord the King.*")

DIXISSE ME ALIQVANDO PENITVIT TACVISSE NVNQVAM

(*"I have sometimes regretted having spoken, never having kept silence."*)

Seen from without and below, the battlements, walls and towers of Loches are impressive, and especially so on the southern face, where rise three great towers generally known as *tours à bec,* since their ground-plan, instead of being circular, projects into an angle, giving such towers a prow or beak. Loches, despite its extensive restoration, offers a striking image of the late medieval fortress.

A mile and a half south of the town-fortress is the square Mauvrière tower, put up in the 14th century as an advanced defence for Loches; this Mauvrière tower communicates through subterranean passages with the dungeons of the Martelet inside Loches castle.

## Della Robbia in Touraine

SANSAC, quite near Loches, is a small, much-restored manor-house which, in its present form, seems rather shapeless and awkward, but it shows, all the same, resemblances to Azay-le-Rideau in its staircase front. The doorway is charming and bears the date 1529. The medallion over the door enclosed formerly a terra-cotta bust of King François I. 1529 was the year that the King visited at Suresnes near Paris the workshop of Girolamo della Robbia (great-nephew of the famous Luca) where he was making enamelled terra-cotta medallions for the *Château de Madrid* in the Bois de Boulogne. Girolamo was an architect and sculptor in marble and in bronze as well as a fashioner of enamelled clay. The medallion at Sansac (now removed) was almost certainly made by della Robbia.

## Love and Madness

LA LORIE. La Lorie seems a most attractive place as you approach it up the sweep of the main drive. The formal gardens, with lawns set with conical-cut yew-bushes, stretch beyond a containing balustrade of Italian taste. A poetical French writer has described La Lorie as "an eagle spreading its wings to alight on a garden of flowers," and the rather severe mass of the buildings curving round from a central wing—defined at either end by pavilions with pointed roofs and then prolonged on either side—does give an impression of movement.

For a time La Lorie was in the possession of a Le Pelletier family, but one Le Pelletier ran away from his wife in order to live with a maid-servant, who so encouraged his expenditure that when he owed the enormous sum (for those days) of eight million francs, his family got him shut up in prison, and his son-in-law became possessed of the property. Since the Revolution La Lorie has passed through many hands, but as it stands to-day it is in much the same state as it was when it had been partially rebuilt and redecorated about 1780.

There is a magnificent ball-room that is, perhaps, a little incongruous in an Anjou country-house. The room seems transported from a Venetian palace. The floor is superb, and made up of flags of grey, salmon pink, black and red marbles. The walls are of grey Sablé stone, with decorations in red Laval stone, with white pilasters of Baveno marble. The chimney-piece is of salmon-pink marble set with mosaics. The hangings, the furniture, the mellow gilding, all combine to make a picture of Italian splendour.

Here and there in this apartment are inscriptions such as

ENTRE L'AMOUR ET LA FOLIE CE PAUVRE MONDE EST BALLOTTÉ
(*"Between Love and Madness this poor World is tossed."*)

L'UN EST LE DOUX SOMMEIL ET L'AUTRE EST L'ESPÉRANCE
(*"One is sweet Sleep and the other is Hope."*)

During the 19th century an owner of La Lorie, having bought the fine wood panelling which formerly adorned the country-house at Vitry-sur-Seine belonging to Cardinal Dubois (the cunning Minister of Louis XV), decided to add a wing to house the *boiseries,* so he set up the large dining-room that is, in a way, a pendant to the great drawing-room. The dining-room is filled with the rich patina of the carved panels, and the only touches of colour are provided by two canvases by Van der Meulen—the Flemish painter of Louis XIV's time who was famed for his battle-pieces —and a superb Louis XIV clock.

## Seven Years in a Cave

L E LUDE. Perhaps one of the things striking us as most strange about the lives of men in the Middle Ages, and even much later, is the apparent unconcern with which they underwent long terms of imprisonment or concealment, and then stepped out to take up their lives where they had, so to speak, left them off. It may be that men had better nerves than we have to-day, or it may be that men were so accustomed, from early youth, to a world full of violent hazards, that imprisonment affected them less. Yet we find it hard to understand, for instance, that a brilliant courtier like the *duc* de Lauzun, whom we met at Champigny, after spending ten years in a fortress, should, on his release, at once go back to Court, take up his private life as though he had only been away for a few weeks' travel, and marry the lady who was foolish enough to let him make love to her.

In 1457, many years before the time of Lauzun, one Jean de Daillon, a man from the province of Berry, bought the fief and Castle of Le Lude. As early as 976 there had been a fortress at Le Lude put up to defend the Loir valley against Norman incursions. The place held out against the English in 1370, but we carried it in 1425, and held it until two years later, when Ambroise de Loré, the Angevin companion-in-arms of Joan of Arc, dislodged the English garrison.

Jean de Daillon, at the time he bought Le Lude, had already made his peace with the King, Charles VII. Earlier on, Daillon had been a crony and confidant of the Dauphin (afterwards King Louis XI, and always on bad terms with his father), but the wily adventurer thought there was more to be gained from the father who was king than from the son who might be king one day.

When in 1461 he came to the throne, Louis XI did not forget his former friend—he rarely forgave and never forgot real, or fancied, slights and injuries; Daillon quickly felt how the wind was blowing and, leaving his castle, his estates and his belongings, disappeared from the sight of man.

For seven years he lived in a cave and nourished by a peasant-woman. Then he was pardoned, if not forgiven. Louis XI had a pressing need of just such fellows as Daillon, new men, men owing everything to royal favour, and men without friends or relations among the stiff-necked and half-rebellious feudal nobility. And Daillon was a man after the King's heart—cunning, resourceful, dissimulating, clever, suspicious, ruthless and patient. Louis nicknamed him *maistre Jehan des habilités,* or "Master John of the clever tricks."

Daillon had himself done some rebuilding at Le Lude. The old lodging was pulled down. The towers were refashioned and the northern wing of the existing castle was put up. But Jehan de Daillon did not live to see his plans carried out. He died far from Le Lude, in the Catalonian province of the Roussillon.

Daillon's son, Jacques, was the real creator of Le Lude. He built the original east wing and, above all, the south wing which remains to this day, one of the most remarkable achievements of French early Renaissance architecture.

Kings were entertained at Le Lude—you can still visit "Henry IV's Chamber," but that gallant monarch was always on the business of peace or of war, travelling up and down his realm, so that his "bedrooms" are as common in France as are those of Queen Elizabeth with us.

Curiously enough, Daillon was one of the few "new men" created by the Valois sovereigns whose family lasted long and took its place among the *noblesse* of France.

Henry de Daillon, Grand-Master of the Artillery in the 17th century, married Eléonore-Renée de Bouillé, the "Red Lady" whom we meet at Rocher-en-Mézangers. This Daillon was created a *duc,* but he left no children. With him the main line of the Daillon family became extinct. Le Lude passed into the possession of the Vieuvilles who, during the 18th century, restored Le Lude that had been allowed to fall into decay. Le Lude was sequestered at the Revolution, but the Vieuville heirs managed to regain the place, which later passed by inheritance to the Talhouët family, with whom it still remains. In the middle years of the last century, the *marquis* de Talhouët expended large sums on the repair of his magnificent castle.

## A Palace in a Fortress

LE LUDE hamlet, set at the intersection of the Tours-La-Flèche and the Château-du-Loir to Baugé high roads, is a nice enough little village. The church has a Romanesque choir and

The Castle of the Bastarnays

View from the Castle Grounds to the Collegiate Church

**MONTRÉSOR**

**Montrésor**  Collegiate Church     **Marmoutier**                    The Abbey Portal

**Montrésor**                       **Montmirail**                     The *Château*

**Mézangers**                                                          The Romantic Castle

two charming Renaissance chapels. But Le Lude is noteworthy for its castle and for nothing else.

The castle is perched upon the stump or foundations of the ancient feudal fortress, and has a dry moat on three sides, while the east wing gives on to a terrace that falls down to the river's banks. Le Lude has the classical ground-plan of a French castle —three wings with a tower at each corner and enclosing a central courtyard. And the courtyard is closed on the west side (where there is no wing) by an arcaded portico.

As Le Lude is one of the most magnificent and important of French *châteaux*, it merits detailed notice. The best way to approach the place is from behind rather than from the main entrance.

An elegant, yet sturdy, balustrade in the Italian taste borders the moat. The great towers, impressive and massive, are enlivened by Renaissance windows, graceful gables and high chimneys.

Here, you feel, is something different from what you have experienced before. There has been no violent transformation. There has been no juxtaposition of old and new. It is as though an Italianate spring had charmed a grim old fortress to blossom into Renaissance grace, preparing you for the splendours within.

When you are in the Court of Honour you are faced by three wings of three different styles of architecture but each, in some way, harmonising with the other, so that the whole makes up, not only an imposing palace, but a living museum of French architecture.

The façade of the north wing dates from the last quarter of the 15th century, and is a beautiful example of late Gothic secular style. The two storeys are carried upon a lofty arcade. Some of the high mullioned windows are, in accordance with the tradition of the style, only one-half as wide as others. A large niche in the first storey shelters an equestrian statue of the very unmilitary Jehan de Daillon, the founder who spent seven years in a cave. At the base of the roof run corbels and machicolations, while above them rise three beautiful dormers surmounted with carved and crocketed gables in the Flamboyant style. Still higher are fine chimneys.

The south wing was put up in the time of François I, and must be accounted one of the classical examples of its period. An elegant, unstrained effect is achieved by harmonious simplicity.

This wing has only one storey, surmounted by an attic, lighted by high gabled dormers.

The eastern wing was finished under Louis XIV by the Vieuvilles, when they restored the place in the 18th century. This façade is in good classical taste, although it is rather disappointing after the other two.

The towers communicate with and form part of the living-quarters of the mansion.

The interior of Le Lude is so magnificent and interesting that all those who visit the Loir valley should allow several hours for their appreciation if they manage to get permission to view the apartments.

## The "Angel of Le Lude"

THE most precious thing from Le Lude is no longer there, or even in France. We must go to New York to see it, in the Frick Museum. It is the renowned "Angel of Le Lude," a copper statue dated 1475 and signed JEHAN BARBET DE LYON on the underside of one of the wings. In elegance of outline, simplicity and beauty of drapery and in excellence of execution, the "Angel of Le Lude" must be accounted one of the finest and most important pieces of French (15th century) metal-work.

## A Tuscan Villa in Anjou

LE LUDE is full of fine things—furniture, tapestries and pictures. There is an imposing ball-room. In one of the towers is a library whose vaulted roof is supported by a single pillar.

The jewel of Le Lude will seem to many to be the painted chamber, whose beauties were revealed only in 1854. The apartment is not only in the Italian taste, but it is clear that the decoration must have been executed by an Italian artist. You are transported to a Tuscan villa; the shallow, ribbed vaulting, the coats-of-arms encircled with laurel-wreaths, the scenes of sacred and profane story—and the deeds of Jehan de Daillon's life duly romanticised and idealised—framed between pilasters, the dado of Florentine ease and elegance and urbanity—everything combines to take you far away from France . . . yet from the window you look down over the smiling, northern valley of the Loir and the Garden of France.

For the splendid gardens and park of Le Lude follow the leafy course of the river for more than a mile and a half.

## The Architect of Le Lude

QUITE near the entrance to the *château* is a small, graceful 16th century house (now used as a post office) which may have served one of Le Lude's architects as a lodging. It was the custom in bygone days for the architect (who was generally master-mason, clerk of the works, *entrepreneur* and what you will, as well as what we should call "architect" to-day) to put up for himself a comfortable little house before he began what might be a good many years' work on his job. The Le Lude post office is still called "Jean Gendrot's House," and Gendrot, at one time overseer of the "Good King René," was, at the end of the 15th century, architect for the rebuilding of Le Lude. We also happen to know the name of another architect who worked here. He was one Turbillon, who in 1470 underpinned the castle-towers for the original Jehan de Daillon.

## Heterodox Opinions about the Devil

ALTHOUGH the direct male line of the Daillons came to an end with the *duc* du Lude in the 17th century, branches of the family survived, and some members of them were most unlike their ruffianly ancestor, the servant of King Louis XI. One branch of the Daillons were Huguenots, and two of them took refuge in our islands. Benjamin de Daillon (who died at Castlelough, in Ireland, in 1726) was a Protestant theologian who held what are (or were) unorthodox opinions about the Devil. Daillon, indeed, maintained that the Devil was one, that there was no multiplicity of Devils. Benjamin propounded his views in several publications and was seconded by his brother Jacques de Daillon. Jacques was, for a time, a beneficed clergyman of the Church of England, but he lost his living, partly, indeed, for his political views, but also because of his obstinacy in upholding, in and out of season, brother Benjamin's detestable heresies.

The British Daillons had travelled a long way from the founder of Le Lude.

## To La Flèche

NEARLY all the little villages along the Loir's banks have restaurants where can be drunk some of the excellent wines of the *côteaux du Loir*; but, if you are headed in the La Flèche direction, it will be as well to push on to that famed gastronomical centre where, together with a bottle or two of Huillé, Durtal, Briollet or Lézigné wine, you will get a La Flèche capon. . . .

From Le Lude to La Flèche you follow the *route nationale* No. 159 (the Tours-Laval high road), which runs through the perfumed pine forests on the left bank of the river. In fifteen miles you are at La Flèche. And as you pass along the Loir's course, you will see the chalky cliffs hollowed out with stores and dwellings as are those of the greater Loire. Men have lived in the caves of these rivers' banks for thousands of years.

## Family Fortunes

LUYNES. The Luynes family, whose name is in France a synonym for ancient nobility and ultra-royalist traditions, owes almost all its eminence, not, as in the case of the Richelieus, to one man's genius, or, as in the case of other families, to a slow climb. The Luynes great fortunes were due, as those of the Bentincks with us, to a sovereign's whim and affection.

The family tree of the Luynes goes back, it seems, to one Thomas Alberti, said to have been of Italian origin, who died in 1455, owner of a number of small properties in Provence. He may have been one of the many Italian adventurers who sought a career in France from the conveniently placed centre of the so-called *comté Venaissin*, or Papal Domain round the city of Avignon. This province formed no part of the French King's dominions, and was an integral part of the Papal States until the Revolution at the end of the 18th century. Anyway, Thomas Alberti was not a personage of any great account, and although he was "lord" of a number of fiefs, he was not of notable lineage.

After a few generations of obscurity, the descendant of Thomas Alberti, one Honoré d'Albert (note the "amelioration" of the name) served faithfully and successfully the last three Valois kings, and also the first Bourbon sovereign, Henri IV. Honoré spent much of his time in northern France far away from the relatively humble associations of his ancestors, although towards the end of his life he was "Captain" of the southern fortified town of Beaucaire.

When Honoré died in 1592, he had been able to place his eldest son in the Royal Household. So it came about that the real founder of the family fortunes, Charles d'Albert, was brought up with and became the fast friend of the Dauphin (afterwards Louis XIII). Such friendship brought both wealth and power. In 1619 Charles bought the rather dilapidated but very feudal-looking fortress of Maillé in Touraine. The Albertis, or d'Alberts, often styled themselves "d'Albert de Luynes" from a small town of that name in the "deep south" of France. Motorists on the road from Avignon to the Riviera through Aix-en-Provence will see Luynes as just another dusty, provinçal village shaded by immense plane trees. No sooner had he become possessed of the ancient cradle of the baronial race of the Maillés than Charles d'Albert obtained royal permission to change the place's name to that of "Luynes."

Charles d'Albert's rise was rapid enough. By 1615 he was Governor of the Louvre, in the next year Grand Falconer of France. He it was who, with Vitry, arranged for the latter to assassinate (with the consent and indeed at the instigation of the King) the Italian adventurer Concini (generally known in France as *le maréchal d'Ancre*), a close associate of the Queen-Mother, Marie de' Medici. In 1617 d'Albert was Captain of the Bastille and Lieutenant-Governor of Normandy. He then married Marie de Rohan, daughter of the *duc* de Montbazon. D'Albert was the principal author of the Treaty of Angoulême, whereby the Queen-Mother was allowed almost complete liberty, since her star was on the wane. In 1619 d'Albert was Governor of Picardy and, then, Constable of France. Since Concini's death he had been, in effect, First Minister of the Crown. After his appointment as Constable he felt a need to justify his new honour, and engaged in an expedition against the French Protestants, but in 1621 he died of fever at Longueville, in Guyenne. Charles d'Albert (who had been created *duc* de Luynes in 1619) possessed no sort of practical ability. He was a muddling Minister, an amateur soldier and, generally, a poor creature. He was soon forgotten under the rising sun of Richelieu. But Luynes had done well by his family. His second brother was created *duc* de Chaulnes and his youngest brother *duc* de Luxembourg-Piney. Both were married off to great heiresses. Neither of the younger d'Alberts was at all an outstanding figure.

But, as so often happens, in the next generations, the d'Alberts, favoured by wealth, opportunity and influence, did throw off some rather eminent men. The second *duc* de Luynes distinguished himself as a pietistic writer and friend of the Jansenists; he was a man of severe principles and exceedingly unlike his father (did not the Borgias, only a generation or two after Cæsar, Lucrezia, Pope Alexander VI, produce the great ascetic saint and duke of Gandia?). A later d'Albert was not only a Cardinal-Archbishop, but an astronomer of note. Another, the *duc* de Chaulnes, wrote on mathematical instruments. His son was a chemist, and the *duc* de Luynes who flourished in the first half of the last century was a noted author of works on archeology.

For many generations past the d'Albert de Luynes have not lived in Touraine. The main seat of the family is lordly Dampierre, in the Chevreuse valley (not far from Paris), and well known to all visitors to that most charming part of the Île de France.

## Old Maillé

IF, after crossing the Loire bridge at Tours, you turn left down the north bank of the river, you pass through Saint-Cyr, squeezed between the great stream and chalk cliffs. Saint-Cyr church is worth a few minutes' visit, if you have the time; it is supposed to have been founded by Louis XI. It contains a rather fine font and an admirable terra-cotta, polychrome statue of the Virgin. In the villa de La Grenadière, nearby, both Balzac and Béranger stayed at different times. Béranger, although born and bred a *gamin de Paris*, often lived in Touraine, where the amiable and popular creator of incomparable *chansons*, clear, sparkling, witty and profoundly human, sometimes sought inspiration away from his hand-to-mouth existence in Paris.

Where the hills scoop back from the Loire, about eight miles from Saint-Cyr, rises Luynes, with many of its houses carved out of the rock, and dominated by the frowning, dark and impressive mass of its old castle. On its rock was a Roman *castrum*, and from early feudal times Luynes, then called Maillé, was the seat of the Maillé family, premier barons of Touraine. Hardouin IX de Maillé, having sold his estate of Les Motils, near Tours, to King Louis XI, who there made his manor of Plessis-lès-Tours, devoted the money he received to the repairing and the strengthening of his ancestral fortress, which had hardly been touched since the 13th century. He partly rebuilt the towers and established in the Court an elegant and comfortable lodging much more pleasant to live in than the cramped cubicles and draughty halls of the ancient castle.

As we have seen, in 1619, the Maillé of the day sold his home to Charles d'Albert, and then the new designation of "Luynes" quite effaced the old name of Maillé, although the Maillé family continued to flourish, and is to-day represented by a *duc* de Maillé.

Luynes castle stands four-square. Its high walls are six hundred years old, although they are, here and there, pierced with trumpery little windows, cut, probably, in the 15th century.

You enter from the east side over a drawbridge. A simply constructed lodging, put up about the same time that the windows were pierced in the walls, is perched against the outer wall and the south-east tower. It is between the north-east and centre towers that the main entrance opens.

In the inner court are two lodgings of very different styles. That to the right is the one put up by Hardouin de Maillé about 1465. Hardouin copied his master, and built a little Plessis-lès-Tours within his old fortress. It is an elegant house in the new red brick and white stone fashion of the day. This Maillé wing resembles lodgings put up at about the same time at Amboise and Loches and elsewhere in the Loire valley. There is only one storey. The high, steep roof is set with fine dormers and a lofty square chimney, the staircase is enclosed in an octagonal turret projecting from the façade. The decoration is very sober and restrained—the framework of the windows in white stone, a few mouldings and a balustrade running under the eaves, the gables of the dormers and the ornamentation at the angles, also in white stone, of the staircase turret.

The lodging on the left-hand side is of later date. It is less elegant in design and less sober in execution. Again, there is only one storey, except for a southern-projecting wing of two storeys. This house was built to the order of the first *duc* de Luynes in the time of Louis XIII by Pierre Le Muet (who was also the architect of the west front and the vaulting of the "classical" Val-de-Grace church in Paris), but he was not a great artist, and at Luynes his style is, perhaps, seen at its worst.

One of the curtains of Luynes has been razed, and from the court you get a magnificent view over the historic Loire valley. Eastwards, on a plateau, you can see a 15th century chapel with a carved wooden roof. Beyond is old Maillé church and the Priory of Saint-Venant, nearby which are some Gallo-Roman ruins. Less than a mile to the north of Luynes village are the forty pillars and six arches of a Gallo-Roman aqueduct.

You climb down a series of staircases and steps and over old walls into Luynes village, where there is a curious covered market-place with a steep roof.

## The Devil of Bressault

MAGNANNES. For about three hundred years from 1429 Magnannes was held by the family of Récappé, of old Breton stock. In the 16th century Magnannes had to suffer from the depredations of one René de La Rouvraye, known as the "Devil of Bressault," a Huguenot leader who mingled very effectively religious fanaticism with personal ambition. René was, however, eventually captured and executed. In 1572 his head—stuck on a pole above the main entrance-gate of Château-Gontier—reassured the Lord of Magnannes. Thenceforth Magnannes was peaceful. In 1701 the chief of the family obtained—at considerable expense—the title of *marquis*.

The present house is a fine building in the Louis XIV style. It stands on the banks of the Mayenne, about six miles from Château-Gontier. The place is constructed on old foundations and makes a brave show, though it has been, perhaps, a little too much restored.

The plan is that of a square block with two projecting wings of less height than the main building. A splendid oval granite *perron* or flight of steps leads up to the main entrance.

Inside is some excellent furniture. In the dining-room are four decorative panels after Lancret (the National Gallery has his "Four Ages of Man"). There is French *Regence* (i.e. early 18th century) panelling, and there is some remarkable Gobelins tapestry on the chairs of the great saloon.

## Caillaux's Fief

MAMERS. If, to most Frenchmen—outside the department of the Sarthe—you mention the name "Mamers," the chances are that they will nod "Oh yes, that's where Caillaux came from." As a matter of fact, the late M. Caillaux was not a native of Mamers, but the town was his electoral fief for many years of his strange and variegated career. Caillaux was the man who, when Prime Minister in 1911, negotiated directly with the Germans over the head of his own Minister of Foreign Affairs, the colourless M. de Selves. Caillaux was a politician of great ability, for whom circumstances were too strong. He was an excellent financier (he it was who, after great opposition, managed to saddle the French with an income tax), and he was persuaded that "even a victorious war would be fatal to France owing to her low birth-rate," and he consistently sought some "arrangement" with the Germans. He passed for being anti-British, and probably was so, in the sense that he maintained that an Anglo-French *entente* or alliance spelt war. On the eve of the 1914–1918 conflict Caillaux's wife murdered Calmette, the editor of the *Figaro* newspaper. She was acquitted, but Caillaux dropped out of office, though not out of political life. Towards the end of the First World War his old enemy, Clemenceau, had him tried before a High Court, and condemned to a term of banishment that he served in Spain. Later, he returned to France, and even was, for a time, Finance Minister. He died just before the Liberation of 1944. Caillaux is an example of a very clever man who failed in all he undertook.

Mamers, famed for its potted pork and cider, is a small place of less than five thousand inhabitants, and like most of the towns in the Sarthe, shows a northern face, very different from those of the smiling Loire valley.

Of the old Mamers relatively little remains. The city-walls have disappeared. The Romanesque and Gothic Church of Notre-Dame was thoroughly restored in 1801, and later on in the 19th century was enlarged. It is of no great interest. The 14th century Church of Saint-Nicholas was rebuilt in the fifteen hundreds. The former Convent of the Visitation now houses the town hall, the library, the sub-prefecture, the headquarters of the *gendarmerie*, and a small museum of no consequence.

The road northwards to Alençon cuts through the magnificent Forest of Perseigne. Just before the woods begin lies Neufchâtel-en-Saosnois, whose Romanesque and Gothic church contains some furnishings from Perseigne abbey, ruins of which rise at the end of a long, narrow piece of water and at the entrance of the *Val d'Enfer*, about a mile and a half north-east of the village.

After Neufchâtel there is a long pull up of some three miles on to a plateau of very ancient rocks—sandstones, schists and porphyrys—whose boulders, bluffs, crags and hills vary in height from five hundred to eleven hundred feet. You are nearing the borders of Normandy.

## A Historic City of the West

LE MANS. Le Mans is, for the French provinces, a large city, since it has some seventy-five thousand inhabitants. The town spreads on both banks of the Sarthe River. It is, however, on the left bank that are found the old streets, the cathedral and the principal sights. Round the cathedral hill—pierced by a tunnel— has grown up a sort of garden-city, a pleasing settlement full of villas set in greenery.

Le Mans has factories and manufactories. The Léon Bollée automobile works—the oldest in France—are here. Agricultural instruments are made. There are important tanneries. Le Mans is, in fact, a prosperous place in a provincial, conservative, un-hustling way.

The town was the ancient capital of the Duchy of Maine (practically conterminous with the modern department of the Sarthe), and before that it was a Gaulish city which the Romans enclosed within walls. The episcopal diocese dates, it would seem, from the 3rd century, when Saint-Julian here preached and converted. The Bishops of Le Mans, as bishops in so many places, gradually acquired great power, and they were often men of more account in their province than the "Counts" (or viceroys) appointed by the Frankish sovereigns.

In Charlemagne's time Le Mans was one of the very few industrial cities of his realm. The town was pillaged by the Normans, as were nearly all the towns of north-western France. In the 11th century William the Conqueror seized the place, but, after several revolts, the heir of the old Counts of Maine recovered his heritage. Philip Augustus annexed Maine and Le Mans to the French Crown, but he ceded the city, for her life, to Berengaria, the widow of our Richard Coeur de Lion. Later, Queen Marguerite (of Provence), the consort of Saint-Louis, held Le Mans as part of her jointure.

In 1392, while marching on Le Mans to give battle to the Duke of Brittany, King Charles VI was seized by the madness that was to be so fatal for France.

## The Madness that Ruined France

ON the 14th June, 1392, disturbing news reached the Royal Court at Paris in the *Hôtel Saint-Pol* (between the *rue St. Antoine* and the quays)—the Constable of France, Olivier de Clisson, had been grievously wounded by Pierre de Craon, and the assailant had taken refuge with the Duke of Brittany. King Charles VI, then a handsome, strong, active, cultured and warlike man, promptly set out at the head of his troops to avenge the outrage. When the royal forces had reached the plain near Le Mans and the outskirts of the forest, a strange thing happened. The old French chronicler tells the tale in these words:

> *"When the King of France . . . was about to enter the Forest of Le Mans, on the fifth day of August, there came unto him a man with a distorted countenance crying: 'King, if thou enterest the Forest to go unto Le Mans, there will be misadventure.' Then came up a madman with contorted face who, seizing the bridle of the King's horse, said to him: 'If thou proceedest thou art a dead man!'*
>
> *"The King wished to free himself from the madman, and advanced towards his page to get his sword. But the page was afraid and ran away, and the King ran after him. And the King took the sword and fell mad with anger and vexation, having been made desperate, or poisoned or bewitched or possessed. For when he had got the sword into his hands he turned upon those around him and killed many of them. And no man ever knew what became of the aforesaid messenger or of the madman.*

*And the King was only with difficulty overcome, for no man
dared to approach him until he was at length taken by a knight
from Caux."*

Such is the tragic story. Charles had, as a matter of fact, an
heredity of madness: his mother suffered from bouts of prolonged
insanity, and he again, like most manic-depressives, had lucid
intervals, but they became shorter and shorter until the King of
France, the man upon whom all the authority of the country
rested, fell into a state of drivelling idiocy. In 1402 Charles VI
appointed his wife, Isabeau of Bavaria, regent. By this time the
King was helplessly insane. The next year was born the Dauphin,
afterwards Charles VII, whom the enemies of the French monarchy
declared to be a bastard, and in view of the notorious misconduct
of the Queen it may well be that they were right.

France was to be plunged into the horrors of war that so nearly
led to her extinction as a sovereign State, while the crazy King,
pallid, filthy, ragged, covered with boils, wandering with vacant
eyes and matted hair about his prison-palace, lingered on until
1422.

## Later Le Mans

LA ROCHEJAQUELEIN and his Vendeans entered Le
Mans, but the Republican generals Marceau and Westermann
drove him out. For three October days of 1795 the Chouans held
the town.

In 1870 Chanzy took up his quarters in the city, while to the
east and south of it was fought, on the 11th January, 1871, the
disastrous battle sealing the fate of France and securing the final
victory of the Prussians.

## Kitchener's First Campaign

KITCHENER was, in part, educated at a French school in
Switzerland, and there he learnt enough French to enable him to
carry on a conversation, although either he never was really at
home in French or had forgotten most of what he had learned in
the circumstances of his life in the East, for, in later years at any
rate, he could certainly not be said to be what his biographers
have often claimed, "a perfect French scholar." He did, however,
retain for the French and for France very friendly feelings, in some

measure, no doubt, conditioned by a rather romantic episode of his youth.

Kitchener's parents, after his father's retirement from the Army, lived at Dinan, and, strangely enough to our modern ideas about "total war," went on residing at that Brittany seaside, or rather river-side, resort right through the Franco-Prussian campaign. Young Horatio Kitchener passed out of Woolwich in December 1870, and while staying with his father and mother at Dinan and waiting for his Gazette, he slipped away and spent a few weeks serving with Chanzy's "Army of the Lower Loire" which was making a fighting retreat to the west. Since he fell sick Kitchener did not stay with Chanzy's forces to the end. Despite a reprimand on his "improper" conduct, as a neutral, in joining up in the French Army, Kitchener got his commission in 1871, and left for the East, where most of his professional life was to be spent.

## The Battle of Le Mans

THE Battle of Le Mans, fought on the 10th, 11th and 12th of January, 1871, was the culminating point of General Chanzy's fighting retreat into western France after the early winter campaign in the Beauce and the Perche.

Chanzy, who was still a young man of under fifty, was summoned from Algeria, after the fall of Napoleon III, by the Government of National Defence, to command the XVI Corps on the Loire. With his numerous, ill-equipped and ill-trained levies, he won the greatest French success of the war at Coulmiers and another victory at Patay.

Then, in command of the "Second Army of the Loire," he slowed up, if he could not hold up, the Prussian advance from Beaugency on the Loire to Le Mans and to Laval.

The German Second Army, under the command of Prince Frederick Charles, and consisting of veterans of six months' fighting experience, advanced in three Army Corps in first line and with one in reserve.

On the 9th January, the III Prussian Corps drove an advanced French division from Ardenay (thirteeen miles east of Le Mans), and on the following day Chanzy's main defensive position was attacked. Chanzy's right wing was east of the River Sarthe—about three or four miles from Le Mans; his centre held the heights of

Auvours, with the Huisne River behind it; the French left was scattered along the west bank of the Huisne as far as Montfort, east-north-east of Le Mans, and then tailed off into the countryside for some miles more.

On the 11th January Chanzy tried a counter-offensive, but his raw levies flinched and broke. Chanzy fell back under German pressure, then, as Prussian cavalry began to appear beyond the extreme left of the French, Chanzy retired during the night of the 11th January on Laval, and the Prussians occupied Le Mans on the 12th. The French defeat was due solely to the misconduct of the Breton "mobiles" who, after falling back before the appearance of the Prussian infantry, fled in disorder, infecting with their panic the men in the reserve training camps, who in their turn broke and ran. As a matter of fact, the Prussian army was at this time very exhausted, as the events of the next few days showed clearly enough.

The indomitable Chanzy drew off his field army intact to Laval, where he was joined by a freshly raised corps. The enemy could not deliver another blow and retired. In fact, the Prussians considered the situation of the Loire so threatening that Frederick-Charles hurried back to Orleans, there to assume command. By this time Chanzy was at the head of 156,000 men, and was about to take the offensive against the 40,000 Prussians left in the Le Mans region when he had to submit to the armistice of 28th January, 1871.

Chanzy, who later in 1871 fell into the hands of the Commune and had to be ransomed for a million francs by the Republican Government, was, before his sudden death in 1883, Governor-General of Algeria and then, successively, Ambassador at St. Petersburg and commander of the VI French Army Corps at Chalons.

## 1944

THE Americans, in their drive to the east from the positions they had conquered in Brittany, Normandy and the lower Loire valley, swept forwards into the departments of the Mayenne and the Sarthe in two directions. The VII Corps struck along a line to the west of the Mayenne-Alençon road to Argentan and Chambois in Normandy. The XV Corps followed the road from Laval to Le Mans, and then turned sharply north along the Le Mans-Alençon highway, north of which latter town the corps divided, one detachment bearing westwards to join forces with the VII Corps south of Argentan, and the other detachment turning eastwards towards Dreux.

The XII and XX American Corps (which had followed, as far as Le Mans, the same line of advance as the XV Corps) continued due east from Le Mans, the XX following the line Chartres-Étampes-Fontainebleau, while the XII drove ahead to Châteaudun, Orleans and Montargis.

After the closing of the Falaise Gap and the crushing of German resistance in southern Normandy, the German retreat hurriedly became a rout, and France was cleansed of the enemy in a surprisingly short time.

Although the fighting north of the middle reaches of the Loire and south of the Norman border was not to be compared with the fierce struggle in Normandy itself, Le Mans, in 1944, as in 1871, proved to be an important strategic point in the battle for France—luckily the outcome was more satisfactory in the last war than it had been seventy-three years earlier. And, when we try to understand the point of view of the French people as a whole, it is well to remember that not a few men still living have known their country three times invaded, ravaged, sacked, pillaged and persecuted by the Germans, who in the years from 1945 onwards were learning what their ancestors had not known from Napoleonic times.

Our Henry II Plantagenet was born at Le Mans, as also was King John *le Bon* or the "Good" of France. This was the monarch who was taken prisoner by us and held as such until his ransom could be raised. Why he was dubbed *le Bon* passes the wit of man to say. Perhaps it was sought thereby to arouse sympathy for his misfortune and thus to facilitate the collection of the ransom-money. As a matter of fact he was a callous, feckless, incompetent, selfish, extravagant and sullen half-wit, and, if we may judge by a contemporary and unflattering panel-portrait of him, a most unprepossessing individual.

From Le Mans, also, came Joachim Bouvet, a Jesuit who was sent to China by Louis XIV, there to study the arts and manufactures of the Middle Kingdom. The 17th century was still a time when Europeans could travel about in China, for they had not as yet aroused the suspicions of the Chinese Government. Moreover, the Government of Louis XIV was enlightened enough to realise that we had something to learn from the Chinese. Dom Prosper Guéranger, the famous Benedictine whom we meet at Solesmes, was also a son of Le Mans. But for us, perhaps, one of the most significant men coming from Le Mans was Michel Denisot.

## The Man Who Lost Us Calais

WE all learned at school that "Bloody Mary," when she lay dying, exclaimed that the word "Calais" would be found engraved upon her heart when she had ceased to live.

Now the man who more than any other one person was the instrument of our losing our last possession in France was Michel Denisot or Denysot, who was born at Le Mans in 1515. Denisot was a minor poet, and one of the *Pléiade*, whose productions have been so much overrated largely because of the happy influence their writing had, not upon French poetry, but upon the French language.

Denisot, in his thirties, migrated to London, where he became tutor in French language, literature and manners to the daughters of the Protector Somerset. Denisot acquired a good knowledge of the English language and, apparently, not much sympathy with English policy, for in 1558, when the *duc* de Guise was preparing his attack on Calais, Denisot made his way into the town, took sketches of all the defences, notes of the garrison and supplies and arms—our intelligence service must have been very poor—and then made his way out with his booty to the French commander who, as we know, employed an army of thirty thousand men for seven days against the very small English garrison of about eight hundred men.

Denisot may have been an indifferent poet, but he seems to have had the making of an excellent "agent."

## The Couture Church

LE MANS is a city where there is a good deal to see, but the sights are rather hidden in the newness of a prosperous and spreading country-town.

On the main square is a monument to Chanzy and his Second

**Nogent-le-Rotrou**                    The Great Duc de Sully's tomb

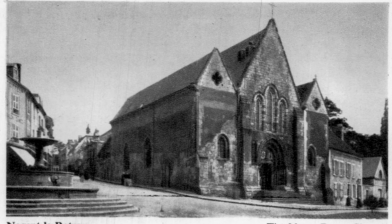

**Nogent-le-Rotrou**  The Notre-Dame Church

**Nogent-le-Rotrou** —————————— *Rue Saint-Léonard* and the Keep

**Montreuil-Bellay**  The Town Gate   Main Front of Castle

Loire Army, while on the west side of the *place* lies the Church of the Visitation, adjoining the old convent buildings now occupied by the Law Courts and the *gendarmerie*. The church was built about 1730 to the plans of an architecturally minded Visitandine nun, and the plans were carried out by two local men, one Riballier and his son. The result was a much finer building than might have been expected. The white interior is spacious and imposing. The carving on walls and vault was executed by pupils of Robert de Cotte (the author of the *Invalides* dome in Paris and of the chapel of Versailles), and a lofty gallery adorned with a wrought-iron balustrade runs round the church. The choir and transepts are divided from the nave by a splendid wrought-iron grille.

The Prefecture is housed in the conventual buildings of Couture abbey, dating from about 1770, and standing in a fine park. Between the Prefecture and the Church of Notre-Dame-de-la-Couture is a doorway leading to the cloisters, whose arcades have, unhappily, been filled in with glass. Through the cloisters you reach a monumental staircase with a fine wrought-iron balustrade. At the head of the staircase is the entrance to the library, containing, among other volumes, nearly 500 MSS. removed, during Revolutionary times, from churches and convents in the diocese of Le Mans.

The yellowish-brown, imposing, but truncated west front of the Couture church is executed in a noble and simple style of 13th century Gothic, but the two flanking towers were never built up above the level of the façade, and one is capped by an inelegant and clumsy pointed roof, while the other shows a jagged outline to the heavens. The splendid porch between the towers is, however, of great interest, and the six statues of the Apostles are among the masterpieces of Gothic statuary. The canopy covering the figures, and representing walls and houses, is clearly of Byzantine inspiration. The tympanum of the porch is filled with a Christ seated between the Virgin and Saint John, and presiding in Last Judgment over the weighing of souls.

The Couture church owes its curious name to a Benedictine abbey known in Latin as *Abbatia SS. Petri et Pauli de Culturā Dei*—"the Abbey of Saints Peter and Paul for the Service of God" —and the monastery appears to have been founded in the 6th century by a Saint-Bertrand. Of the original edifice nothing, of course, remains, but some portions of the existing church go back to the end of the 10th century.

The aisleless nave is Romanesque, and has fine ogee vaulting in Angevin style. The double lights lend the interior a gay and serene air, and the nave's walls are covered with paintings, none of which is, however, earlier than the 16th century. "The Sleep of the Prophet Elijah," by Philippe de Champaigne, is possibly that artist's masterpiece.

The transepts, the choir and the crypt are built in a heavy but majestic Romanesque style, and (in so far as they have not been rebuilt) date, it would seem, from the 995 church. The rectangular chapels are a later edition, but the whole of the east end of the church was tinkered about with (often rather cleverly) right up to the fifteen hundreds, and it is often hard to tell what piece belongs to which period. The sanctuary is raised nine steps high above the level of the nave, and it is encompassed by a superb sweep of thirteen pillars and arches dating (at the latest) from the 11th century. Under the altar is the shrine of Saint-Bertrand, while the crypt's eight columns have antique sculptured capitals.

The ambulatory has preserved its 11th century vaulting, and in the chapels are some interesting statues. The five paintings by Parrocel (1718) were formerly in the refectory of the abbey.

One of the greatest treasures of the Couture church is the white marble Virgin and Child by Germain Pilon. Pilon's work was inspired by a new Renaissance. His figures are Gothic in their profound, moving and quite untheatrical expression and gestures, while the draperies, suggested by antique and Italian models, are wonderfully decorative and quite peculiar to Pilon's genius. This Virgin and Child at Le Mans is worthy to rank with the sculptor's most consummate achievements, the *Vierge des Douleurs*, in the Church of *Saint-Paul-Saint-Louis* in Paris, or the statuary of the tomb of Henry II and Catherine de' Medici at the Abbey of Saint-Denis. There are other paintings—by Restout, Van Thulden, Jouvenet, G. Seghers and Lodovico Caracci. There are two 17th century Flemish panels and a "Jesus in the House of Mary and Martha," by one of the younger Parrocels, though it is not clear which.

And this bright, coloured nave of painting and light is generally enriched and adorned with a splendid series of 16th and 17th century tapestries which, without being as fine as those at the cathedral, are very noble stuffs, lending the Couture church a peculiar air of elegance and grace. And the biblical scenes are nicely interspersed with those drawn from mythology and the chase, or with those panels termed by the French *verdure* representing greenery, leaves, trees and glimpses of the countryside. The "Toilet of Diana" adjoins "Moses saved from the Waters," and the "Adoration of the Golden Calf" hangs next to a spirited stag-hunt.

In the treasury are a 16th century gilt reliquary of Saint-Calais, and a superb piece of Oriental silk known as the "Shroud of Saint Bertrand."

A very notable church.

## Geoffrey Plantagenet

THE Archeological museum is in the crypt of the ancient collegiate Church of *Saint-Pierre de la Cour* (partly 11th century) that was the "Sainte Chapelle" of the Counts of Maine.

There are fine recumbent statues from the tombs of three *vicomtes* and a *vicomtesse* de Beaumont (12th and 13th century work). One of these statues of the beginning of the 12th century is perhaps the oldest piece of French secular sculpture.

There is some good furniture, a collection of Gallo-Roman bronzes, a parchment drawing of the 15th century by an architect of the original rood-screen of Le Mans Cathedral, an excellent Roman marble statue of a dancing satyr, a fine series of enamels and a good coin collection.

In the Jacobins garden, laid out in 1798 by Bruyère and full of old trees, you can reach the Municipal museum in the old Bishops' Palace, whose pleasing garden joins that of the Jacobins. There are some excellent pictures—a Ribera, a Louis David and a Le Sueur— some sculpture and a few pieces of fine 18th century furniture. The chief piece of the museum is the famed enamel plaque in *champlevé* representing Geoffrey Plantagenet, Count of Anjou and Maine, father of our Henry II.

## The First Plantagenet

A CHRONICLER records that when our Henry I knighted his newly married son-in-law Geoffrey, called "Plantagenet," Count of

Anjou, in 1127, the King hung about the young man's neck a shield of arms painted with golden lions. No blazon of a seal has been proved earlier than 1136. Geoffrey died in 1151 and was buried in Le Mans Cathedral. The plaque now in the Museum was made in the year of Geoffrey's death (or earlier) and used to hang above the tomb.

The plaque is a splendid thing. Against a background of diapered gold, Geoffrey the Handsome, or Plantagenet, with flowing hair and sparse beard, stands casting his large eyes upwards and towards his left. On his head is a cap of maintenance, in shape rather like the Phrygian bonnets worn during the French Revolution. Geoffrey's headdress is blue and shows one golden lion. The Prince is habited in a long blue and gold mantle over which is a green and gold surcoat, while over his shoulders is a blue mantle lined with what in heraldic jargon is called "vairy of silver and blue," a conventional representation of *petit gris* or squirrel fur. In his right hand Geoffrey holds upright a great sword. His left hand is hidden behind his huge body-shield of arms. It is blue and shows clearly four rampant lions, but since we see only half of the shield no doubt the full blazon was six rampant lions in a blue or azure field.

Geoffrey is thus the earliest recorded bearer of a coat-of-arms in any country. But we must hardly think of coats-of-arms as being hereditary at this early date. Such insignia were purely personal as were the nicknames (improperly called surnames) used by or attributed to great personages of the same period. For instance, "Plantagenet" was Geoffrey's personal nickname, as also was "Beauclerc" the nickname of Henry I or "Curtmantel" that of Henry II.

Geoffrey would wear, they say, in his cap a sprig of broom, or *genêt,* the brilliant plant which in early summer "makes the open country of Anjou and Maine a blaze of living gold."

This Geoffrey the "Handsome" (1129–51) was the son of Fulk V (1109–29), son of Fulk IV *le Rechin,* the "Harsh-faced" (1068–1109), son of Geoffrey, Count of the Gâtinais, by Ermengarde, daughter of great Fulk Nerra. Geoffrey was, therefore, the direct descendant of Fulk the Red who, in the 10th century, has usurped or assumed the title of "Count of Anjou."

Geoffrey, when only seventeen, was married to Matilda, widow of the Emperor Henry V and only heir of our Henry I. She was ten years older than her second husband and outlived him by thirteen years. Geoffrey in his short life showed himself a ruler and warrior of indefatigable energy, and he it was who, by leaving his son, our Henry II, a strong, united realm in the Loire valley, made possible the establishment of the great Anglo-Norman empire of the Plantagenets.

There are also in the Museum some good Italian pictures as well as a Breughel, a Ruysdael, a Rubens, and two particularly fine pieces of furniture, a superb Louis XV commode in marquetry and a Louis XV piece by Crescent.

From the road facing the museum you can reach the old Abbey of Saint-Vincent, rebuilt under Louis XIV and XV. It now houses an almshouse and the municipal and departmental archives. The staircases and apartments of the Louis XV wing are superb.

No. 1 of the *place Saint-Michel* is the 16th century house where it is said Scarron lived in 1646 (see p. 169). There are several old houses and an especially fine Renaissance façade in the *rue des Chanoines*. The *Hôtel du Grabatoire*, in the *place du château*, was once the infirmary of the canons, then the residence of the Governor of Maine and until quite recently the Bishop's palace.

## Academical Honours

THE present Bishop of Le Mans, Mgr. Grente, is the only representative of the French episcopate to sit as a member of the French Academy. That august body, to which are elected some, but not all, of the leading figures in French literature, has a strongly conservative tinge, although it is always reported that there is a "left wing" as well as a "right wing" among the members. The academicians, however, mindful of the royal and ecclesiastical traditions of their company's foundation (Cardinal de Richelieu was the author of the academy), generally manage to have among their number an outstanding churchman, a duke or two, an eminent soldier, and one or more of the less illiterate politicians. Although it is still true that a successful candidate for a seat in the Academy must have published *something* (though there have been cases of men elected who have been guilty of no printed works), the literary output of some of the academicians may be very meagre indeed if it is thought that they are, for other reasons, suitable. A duke with two volumes of "memoirs" or vague "historical studies" to his credit may be preferred to a writer of greater professional, though less social, distinction. It has sometimes been difficult to discover a prelate whose claims to an Academy seat can be based on his literary, as distinguished from his pastoral, activities. For prominent soldiers a slim volume on *New Tactics* or *How Napoleon Won his Victories* has often been considered to constitute a qualification for Academical honours. And the members of the Academy do not like innovators, daring probers into things better left secret, or social revolutionaries. Many of the most noted French men of letters—among others Balzac and Proust—have not been members of the Academy, and it is edifying to reflect that to-day M. André Gide, by common consent one of the most eminent writers of his generation, is not of the choice company, while some others perhaps authors of a number of half-forgotten novels, are *membres de L'Académie française*. Still, membership of the Academy, besides conferring upon the lucky few the right to wear a becoming green-embroidered uniform, also enables them to earn much more for their writing than they could before they were elected, and, furthermore, to claim, and be accorded, a flatteringly high precedence at dinner-parties.

## The Superb Cathedral of Saint-Julien

LE MANS cathedral of Saint-Julien is one of the most magnificent in France, and although not quite in the rank of, say, Rouen or Coutances in Normandy, it is worthy of the most careful study.

Le Mans cathedral is, on a large scale, what we so often find exemplified on a small scale in the parish churches of western France; that is to say, there is built on to and, as it were, there soars out of, a comparatively low, antique, archaic-looking and majestically massive nave, a Gothic choir of the most elegant, imposing and satisfying pattern.

The Romanesque cathedral was begun on the site of the original church founded by the first Bishop of Le Mans in 1060. But no sooner had the building been completed than it was ravaged by two fires.

Bishop Guillaume de Passavant (who held the see of Le Mans from 1145 to 1187) restored his cathedral just at a time when the Gothic vaulting had been developed in the Île-de-France region. He adopted the new style to roof his repaired church.

Excited, however, by the marvels of the new architecture and moved to rivalry by the rising glory of Chartres, the Bishop and Chapter decided, in 1217, to rebuild in the Gothic mode the choir of their cathedral. The transepts and the central tower are a good deal later in date, and were put up at the end of the thirteen and the beginning of the fourteen hundreds.

The west front has kept its archaic Romanesque appearance. A very Byzantinesque Christ the King sits enthroned, surrounded by zodiacal signs and fantastic animals. On the other hand, the south entrance, though still Romanesque (it is 12th century work), has statues reminding us of those at Chartres. The Christ in Bene-diction standing amid the symbols of the evangelists is essentially French and northern.

The interior is striking.

The Romanesque capitals of the pillars are carved with baskets of leaves interspersed with human heads and birds. The columns of the side-aisles are composed of alternate layers of white and red stone. The great west window (much restored) has some late 12th century glass and several windows of the side-aisles contain early 12th century glass—the most ancient in all France. The lights glow in reds and blues, and in the figures and the design a clear Byzantine influence can be seen.

The windows of the south transept are a blaze of colour. The wall fades around these marvels, so that you have almost the illusion of gazing on to a vast expanse of jewelled glass.

The vaulting springs up to the choir, and you are looking into another world, from the massive majesty of the Romanesque to the daring beauty of early Gothic. Hardly a hundred years separates the two styles, yet they have little in common.

In order to examine the architecture of the choir and, above all, to enjoy the magnificent lights, you should go up into the gallery and look through field-glasses.

The choir, with its double ambulatory, its radiating chapels (built from 1217 to 1254), is one of the glories of France, rivalling the choirs of Bourges and Coutances. The seven arcades of the apse are long and sharp as blades. The upper lights represent standing figures (the tenth light is modern). In the first ambulatory above the triforium, whose bays are very elegant with rosaces and foliage, the figures are smaller and rather difficult to distinguish, but all these windows blaze with crimson and azure, deep, sonorous and impressive, and comparable to the splendours of Chartres.

The radiating chapels are all interesting, but in the Lady Chapel the vaulting is covered with late 14th century paintings executed to the orders of Bishop Gonthier de Baigneux. The glass is all 13th century, and the Tree of Jesse window is especially magnificent. The rose in the north transept and the lesser lights below are of considerably later date than the windows of the choir—the designs and drawings are simpler, the figures are more transparent and are more clearly visible, but this 15th century glass hardly impresses and moves us as much as does that of the sanctuary. In the Baptismal chapel are two fine monuments. To the right is the marble tomb of Charles IV of Anjou, Count of Maine (1414–72). It is Italian work of the 15th century by Francesco Laurana. Charles is lying, his hands crossed and his feet touching his helmet. To the left is the monument of Guillaume du Bellay, seigneur of Langey (d. 1543), viceroy of Piedmont under François I, and brother of the Cardinal de Langey, Bishop of Le Mans. The white marble tomb is supported by two black marble sphinxes. Guillaume, with books on his knee, holds his sword in his right hand and rests his left elbow on his helmet. The decoration is all "profane" and Renaissance. Caryatides support a white, marble frieze figuring the sports of naiads and tritons.

Against the west wall of the north transept is the sarcophagus of Queen Berengaria of Navarre, widow of our Richard Coeur de Lion. The recumbent effigy of the queen is a remarkable specimen of 13th century sculpture. The tomb was formerly in Épau abbey, the queen's own foundation not far from Le Mans (see p. 139).

The cathedral treasury contains a series of superb tapestries which, at some seasons of the year, are exposed and displayed in the nave and choir. The six panels representing the Legend of Saints Gervase and Protasius and the 16th century series of the Legend of Saint-Julien are noteworthy.

## Queen Berengaria's House

IN the *grand'rue,* or main street, is the so-called House of Queen Berengaria. Just why the place is so designated is not easy to say, since the existing dwelling was put up from 1490 to 1515 by a rich alderman of the city named Robert Véron. It is possible there may have been a tradition that the queen's mansion stood upon this site. The first storey of the house is enriched with wood carvings. "Queen Berengaria's House" and that next door to it now serve as a Museum of Ancient Art. There is a good deal of interesting furniture, and a really magnificent collection of old faience and pottery—Rouen, Nevers, Strasbourg and Delft.

On your way to the town hall (built from 1760 to 1764 on the site of the palace of the Counts of Maine) you will notice not a few ancient dwellings, and near the *Hôtel de ville* are some vestiges of the original Roman wall. Of the Gallo-Roman city-walls enough remains to enable us to trace their circuit, which formed a parallelogram measuring some five hundred by two hundred yards.

The Church of *Notre-Dame-du-Pré* is a restored though fine Romanesque edifice, with 15th century Gothic vaulting. Under the sanctuary is an ancient crypt, whose flooring shows traces of a still earlier crypt, where it is said Saint-Julien, the evangelist of Le Mans, was buried.

In the modern Church of Saint-Benedict are the remains of Saint-Scholastica, Benedict's sister, whose body was brought hither from Monte Cassino in Italy towards the end of the 7th century.

The newer sections of Le Mans stretch southwards as far as the banks of the Huisne. The so-called *église de la Mission* was formerly the Great Hall of the Coeffort Hospice, erected by our Henry II about 1180. It is one of the earliest buildings in the Angevin-Gothic style.

Le Mans is an altogether notable place, where we may do worse than spend a few days, making it our headquarters for exploration of eastern Maine. And, then, Le Mans shares with La Flèche the enviable reputation of furnishing the best capons and chickens in all western France.

## Our Lady of Anjou

MARILLAIS. In no other provinces of France, perhaps, are there so many pilgrimages in honour of the Virgin as in Anjou. Marillais seems to be the most ancient of these pilgrimages, for in 430 the Virgin appeared to St. Maurille, Bishop of Angers, and bade him celebrate at Marillais the festival of her Nativity. This pilgrimage of the 8th of September is known throughout the Anjou land and even in Maine as *Notre-Dame Angevine*, or *L'Angevine*.

In a valley turned towards the Loire and scored with rivulets which are crossed by little bridges stands Marillais church. It is a skimpy, tasteless, tall edifice, but it and the countryside around it blaze into life, colour and movement at the festivals. In olden days the pilgrims came to Marillais by water and landed near Saint-Florent on the boundary of Anjou where the land merges into the luminous horizons of Lower Brittany. Nowadays, less picturesquely, the pilgrims pile up in motor-buses.

## The Seven Sleepers

MARMOUTIER. The Loire's banks to the north and opposite the town of Tours rise in wooded slopes set with villages and villas, which in recent years have merged into a straggling suburb of the Touraine capital.

If you cross the stone bridge which prolongs the main street of Tours, when you reach the right side of the stream you have the hamlet of Saint-Symphorien before you and that of Saint-Cyr to the left. Saint-Symphorien church was originally Romanesque, but was rebuilt in the 16th century. A slender, lofty spire dominates the place. It is a most graceful building, conceived in a style similar to that of Ussé chapel (see p. 346), or to that of Montrésor church. Here we meet again the Italian decoration which soon becomes so familiar in the Loire valley.

If you turn upstream from Saint-Symphorien you pass Sainte-Radegonde, rising up the hills in terraces. After Sainte-Radegonde parish church is a fine 18th century entrance-gate into Marmoutier abbey.

The Abbey of Marmoutier—that is, MAR(tini) MO(nas)TER(ium) or Monastery of Martin—was reputedly founded by Saint-Martin himself, and during the Middle Ages it flourished as one of the most wealthy and powerful of all France. Here in 1095 Pope Urban II preached the First Crusade. The abbey-church—now almost entirely destroyed—erected in the 13th century to the plans of Etienne de Mortagne, was one of the most magnificent of all the Loire valley.

What remains of the old abbey is soon seen.

Looking towards the Loire's course is the Portal of the Pastoral Staff, so called since it was opened only for the mitred Abbot of Marmoutier himself. This portal is a charming little early Gothic construction with a row of miniature windows (giving on the guard-room) and a pyramidal watch-tower.

The abbey domain is bounded by a steep wall of cliff, at whose foot rises a high tower, at once belfry and keep. The rock-face is hollowed out with tombs, chapels, sanctuaries and chambers. A winding staircase leads to the cruciform "Chapel of the Seven Sleepers" hewn in the stone. The tombs of the Seven Sleepers are in a grotto where, it is said, Saint-Gatien, Apostle of Touraine, celebrated his first Mass in the country, and established the cult of the Virgin, always so flourishing in the diocese of Tours. The Seven Sleepers were seven cousins and brothers, disciples of Saint-Martin and, like him, coenobites, who all died on the same day and at the same hour exactly twenty-five years after Saint-Martin himself. The bodies of these Seven Sleepers not only suffered no corruption, but their faces were preserved with the blush and full-ness of health, and their bodies wrought miracles.

## Magic Feet

LE MAS. Once upon a time the young Lord of Le Mas had a most beautiful wife though none knew whence she had come and some said that she was a witch. Before the marriage, she had made her lord swear that he would never look at her feet:

"If ever you look at my feet, all our happiness will suddenly disappear for ever."

The Lord of Le Mas swore and thought no more of his oath, the couple lived in bliss, but, as time went on, the young man's happi-ness grew perhaps not less but more accustomed, so he gradually came to be more and more tormented with the thought of his wife's strange request. One night, coming home from a long day's hunting, he found his wife sleeping profoundly, so he scattered all round the bed a layer of ashes from the hearth. The next morning he feigned to be still asleep until his wife had arisen, then he peered out of the bed and on to the ashes where he saw the imprints of two webbed goose-feet.

"What have you done, my Lord?" cried the lady, and as she spoke, the thunder crashed and the earth opened swallowing up all the castle. And where once was Le Mas was a lonely mere. This sort of taboo story is, of course, widely spread.

This curiously southern-named place, for *mas*, that is ma(n)s(io), is Limousin, Catalan and Provençal for country-house, you find on the left bank of the Oudon stream as you move up the valley from Le Lion-d'Angers on the old high road to Brittany.

## The King and the Queen of Maulévrier

MAULÉVRIER. Every year, until the Revolution, there was held at Maulévrier the festival known as *La Bachellerie*. On Whit-Sunday, the bailiff of the castle chose from among the tenants a "King," and on Whit-Monday the "King" and the bailiff attended at Granges farm where was held merry-making, including a race known as the *course à la pelote* and choral contests of couples who had been married during the preceding twelve months. Then a "Queen" was selected. On Trinity Sunday, after evensong, both "King" and "Queen" and their retinues had supper at Touche-Manor-farm. They they proceeded to Echaubroges, a neighbouring village, where the "King" exacted a tribute of wine from the inn-keepers. The next day the "Queen" led the "King" and his suite to La Roalière, where the farmer had to serve a luncheon, of which the main dish was junket. In the evening the whole company repaired to the kitchens of Maulévrier Castle where they found prepared thick cakes (*fouaces*, still a delicacy of the countryside), wine and minstrels. The dancing and feasting went on far into the night.

## Stofflet's Master

MAULÉVRIER is a small town on the Moine stream of western Anjou, but the place does not offer much to interest us apart from its castle which stands upon a high hill. A fortress was erected on this height by the orders of Geoffrey Martel, son of the redoubtable

Fulk Nerra. The house was entirely rebuilt in the 18th century by the famous Colbert, minister of Louis XIV, and one of his sons took the title of *comte* de Maulévrier (a name, by the way, which has given us our English patronymic Mauleverer). Until the Revolution the *comté* of Maulévrier was a large and wealthy fief. The castle was burned down during the Vendean war but the house was rebuilt in 1830 by the Colbert of the day. A fine park surrounds the building, while before the main entrance stairway is a French garden set with clipped yews and formal parterres. In an enclosure adjoining the courtyard is an obelisk erected to the memory of Stofflet, the leader of the first Vendean insurgents. We cross Stofflet's traces here, there and everywhere in Anjou and here, at Maulévrier, we track them to their source, for Stofflet was gamekeeper to the Lord of Maulévrier and, like most gamekeepers, he was a strong upholder of the established order, of property rights and of the privileges of the landed gentry.

## The First Catholic Bishop of Boston

MAYENNE. Jean-Louis-Anne-Madeleine Lefebvre de Cheverus was a man who had what the French call an "exceptional destiny." He was born (the son of a judge) at the town of Mayenne in the year 1768, bred to be a priest, and, at the early age of twenty-three, was appointed, by family influence, a Canon of Le Mans Cathedral. It was the year Louis XVI and his family endeavoured to flee from France, but there was, as yet, no Terror, no overthrow of the monarchy. However, in 1792, the year of the Battle of Valmy and of the proclamation of the Republic, young Lefebvre de Cheverus thought it prudent to emigrate. He came over to England, but his stay here was for him, as for so many other continental Europeans since his day, but a prelude to emigration across the Atlantic. In 1796 Cheverus settled in Boston. Here, among a population traditionally opposed to the members of his Church (times have changed and Boston is, to-day, one of the principal centres of the Catholic Church in the United States), he laboured and soon became generally respected for his uprightness of life and purity of purpose. In 1808 the Pope created the See of Boston, and appointed Cheverus its first bishop. On 1823 Louis XVIII insisted upon Cheverus's return to his native country. He left America, after twenty-seven years' residence, during which time he had lived through an astonishing social and political and economic evolution, and had seen his Church set upon the road along which it has since travelled so far. Among the eminent men who have been responsible for the Catholic community of the United States increasing in numbers from a few thousands to over twenty-five millions in less than one hundred and fifty years, Cheverus must take high rank.

The peculiar and leading position Boston occupies in the Roman Catholic religious life of the United States must be attributed to the Frenchman from Mayenne.

The rest of Cheverus's story is soon told, since, although the latter part of his life was passed amid honours and high ecclesiastical office, his real work was done when he left the United States.

In 1823 he was collated to the see of Montauban, in France, where he distinguished himself by his tolerant attitude to his Protestant fellow-citizens. In 1828 he was preferred to the archbishopric of Bordeaux, and in 1836, a few months before his death, he received, at the special request of King Louis-Philippe, a cardinal's hat.

## Battered Mayenne

MAYENNE is a town of some nine thousand inhabitants in a picturesque site on two hills overlooking the Mayenne River that is here canalised and made navigable. About half the town was badly knocked about during the late war. Mayenne owes its origin to a castle built in the 11th century and besieged in 1068 by William the Conqueror, who managed to reduce it by ruse. In 1425 Mayenne fortress held out against four successive attacks by the English army under the Earl of Salisbury. The French recovered the place in 1448.

In 1654 Mazarin acquired the duchy of Mayenne. During the Revolution the town was occupied by the Vendeans under La Rochejaquelein and then by Generals Hoche and Kellermann.

Mayenne is cut through from south-east to north-west by two parallel streets, one ancient and very steep that crosses the river over the *Notre-Dame* bridge, the other modern that crosses the Mayenne over the *Pont-Neuf*.

From the *quai de la République*, or left embankment, there is a fine view of the right bank, with the apse of Notre-Dame and

**Montreuil-Bellay**                    View from the River

**Montreuil-Bellay**                    The Thouet Stream

**Montrésor**          The Old Castle

"The Fallen Angel"

**Paulmy**          The Manor-House

**Le Plessis-Bourré**

**Mortiercrolles**          The Barbican

**Paulmy**          The Ruined Tower

condemned by the courts but acquitted as having acted "without discernment." The colony covers about eighteen hundred acres on a plateau. There are ten "family houses," each containing fifty children.

About fifteen hundred yards to the north of Mettray and on the right bank of the Choisille there is a splendid gallery-grave about thirty-five feet long, composed of twelve stones regularly squared; it is one of the finest megalithic monuments in France (see p. 121).

## A Feudal Stronghold

MONTBAZON. Two miles south of Tours lies Joué-lès-Tours, famed for its red wines. Six miles farther on you dip down into the valley of the Indre, cross the river at Monts and along the leafy valley reach Montbazon.

The village is charmingly situated by the river's banks, and is overshadowed by the huge keep of Montbazon castle rising on the heights behind the houses. The rectangular tower is over ninety feet high, and is, for the most part, of 12th century workmanship, with traces of still older masonry. The copper statue of the Virgin that surmounts the tower was put up in 1866.

There are crumbling ruins of two concentric fortress-walls, but the remains of three of the ramparts' towers are still imposing.

Montbazon was, for several generations, a duchy in the Rohan family, and a mile and a half to the north-east of Montbazon is the *château* de Couzières which from the 16th century was the seat of the *ducs*. The house was rebuilt at the beginning of the 17th century. A marble slab let into the walls records that here, on the 5th September, 1619, Marie de' Medici and her son King Louis XIII met in a (momentary) reconciliation which led to the confirmation of the Treaty of Angoulême (arranged by Richelieu), marking one phase of the troublous course of French affairs before the Cardinal took complete control of the situation.

## Dignified Decay

MONTCLER. Montcler House dates from about 1500 and from the early part of the 16th century belonged to a family which held the place until the 18th. The house was spared at the Revolution and is a most picturesque place, especially if viewed from across the now dry moat towards the bridge and the bold, tall, isolated entrance-gate, now all covered with creeper and ivy that swarm and straggle down into the deep ditch and up the stone embankment, forming the boundary of the great courtyard. And there, on two sides, is the regular, imposing façade, a little lifeless, perhaps, to-day, but dreamy and dignified. The third side of the square has crumbled and is no more, but the trees and the thickets screen the mutilation and merge old Montcler into the landscape.

## The Châteaubriand Blazon

MONTGEOFFROY. Montgeoffroy is said to take its name from that Geoffroy de Châteaubriand, remote ancestor of the famous René de Châteaubriand, writer and statesman. Geoffroy, so the story goes, was wounded at the Battle of Mansura while serving in the armies of Saint Louis. Family legend has it that the King, to reward Geoffroy, changed his coat-of-arms to that still borne by the family—"gules semy of fleurs-de-lis or," that is, a red shield covered with fleurs-de-lis, and added the motto, "My blood stains the banners of France."

The Montgeoffroy of to-day has not a very "feudal" appearance. It is indeed a Louis XVI house of classical design, set between two round towers of the old castle. To the left-hand side, as you look at the place, a wing projects at right angles to another round and conical-roofed tower, while on the right-hand side the chapel raises its rather higher roof above the level of the wing leading to a tower similar to that on the left. A balustrade skirting the ditch of the old moat forms the boundary of a splendid, spacious court in front of this notable house.

The modern history of Montgeoffroy begins in 1676, when Erasme de Contades, Lord of La Roche-Thibault in Anjou, bought the estate. This Contades was a trainer of performing dogs, some of which he presented to the King, who was much pleased with them. There is at Montgeoffroy an amusing painting by Pourbus, representing Louis XIII with one of these remarkable dogs.

## A Choleric Marshal of France

THE great man of the Contades family was Louis-Georges, *maréchal* de France, who bore the Crown at Louis XVI's coronation and rebuilt Montgeoffroy in 1775. To get the stone for his new house the Marshal did not hesitate to pull down La Roche-Thibault in Jarzé, the first property to be owned by the Contades in Anjou. Our ancestors had very little of the present-day reverence for "antiquity" as such. In the olden days and under the rigid social system of pre-Revolutionary France, men of the privileged classes felt no need to reside in "historic" houses. They preferred "fashionable" (and more comfortable) ones. They did not have to bolster up the good conceit they had of themselves by living in real (or fake) medieval settings.

At the Revolution, Contades' sons and grandsons emigrated, but the old man stayed on. He was, however, suspect to the revolutionaries as a relation of so many men who had left France. He found it advisable to take refuge in a small house at Livry, and here he died at ninety years of age, carried off in an attack of apoplexy induced by the explosion of rage at what he considered was the modern and revolutionary insolence of his servants. Nothing could, however, show more clearly the essentially *bourgeois* nature of the French Revolution than the fact that a great nobleman such as Contades could go on living in the country and continue to have servants at all. The Revolution was, in fact, except for moments and in some towns and places, a much less violent change than is often imagined. Lesser men than Contades—but still men of the "privileged" classes—lived right through the troubles almost undisturbed. Indeed, some men and women in out-of-the-way places hardly knew that there was a Revolution going on.

There are some fine things inside Montgeoffroy, including a Brussels tapestry (acquired by the Marshal in Belgium), representing the Tunis Campaign of the Emperor Charles V, and then there is the Marshal's portrait by Rigaud, the magnificent portrait-painter of the reigns of Louis XIV and Louis XV.

## The Sultan's Quest

MONTMIRAIL. Montmirail, from early medieval times, formed one of the five great baronies of the little land known as Perche-Gouët, and on the 9th January, 1169, at the old fortress of Montmirail, our Henry II, with Thomas à Becket in attendance, met the French king to discuss terms of peace.

Later, Montmirail passed into the possession of the family of

Bar. At the end of the 17th century Montmirail was the property
of Louis-Armand de Bourbon, *prince* de Conti, whose wife was
Mlle de Blois, the daughter of Louis XIV and the *duchesse* de La
Vallière (see p. 84).

The *princesse* was famed for her beauty, and was known as
*Conti la belle.* In 1698 the Moorish Sultan, Moulay Ismail, sent
an embassy to Versailles in order to demand that *Conti la Belle*
should be added to the Sherifian harem. The Embassy was not
successful, and the wits of the day wrote this sort of verse about
the ridiculous affair:

> *"Votre beauté, grande Princesse,*
> *Porte les traits dont elle blesse,*
> *Jusqu'aux plus sauvages lieux,*
> *L'Afrique avec vous capitule*
> *Et les conquêtes de vos yeux*
> *Vont plus loin que celles d'Hercule."*

> ("Your beauty, great Princess,
> Bears the features wherewith it strikes
> As far as the most savage regions.
> Africa capitulates to you
> And the conquests of your eyes
> Go farther than those of Hercules.")

In 1719 the *princesse* de Conti sold Montmirail, as she preferred
to live in her charming house at Choisy-le-Roi, near Paris. Later
Montmirail passed through many hands.

The main front, as we see it to-day, dates from about 1450, the
octagonal tower in the middle is a little later—possibly about 1490,
as is the other façade. There are very large cellars—probably the
remains of an older building. Within are fine apartments, and the
main drawing-room is said to have been decorated and arranged
by *Conti la Belle* herself. Among the pictures is a portrait of Sir
Thomas More—said to be by Holbein.

## Walled Montmirail

MONTMIRAIL town, on a high hill rising to the west of dark
Montmirail forest, has now no more than six hundred inhabitants,
but the place is surrounded by its picturesque ramparts and
one of the barbicans still stands. The church has some fair stained

glass, and in the choir is a rather fine tomb, that of Madeleine-Françoise Leboucher, *dame* de Guillebon, who died in 1761.

## Polish Treasure

MONTRÉSOR. On leaving Loches you run through Beaulieu and then the State forest of Loches. About five miles after Le Liget and its frescoed chapel, you come upon Montrésor, huddled on the banks of the Indrois, under the shadow of its old *château*.

For about a hundred years the house was in the possession of the Polish Branicki family, and it sheltered what was often rather pompously called the "Polish Regalia." As a matter of fact, what were preserved at Montrésor were some pieces of plate, mostly from the collection of King Jan Sobieski, the hero of the defence of Vienna against the Turks.

The Branickis of Montrésor were, moreover, not descendants of the ancient Polish family of that name, but of one Branetzki (of obscure and probably Tatar origin), who appears in history about 1762 and rose to the rank of "Grand-General" of Poland. He was, throughout most of his career, in reality a Russian agent, and he died at a good old age on his estates of Biala-Cerkiew in 1829. But his descendants were Polish nationalists who found it convenient to settle in France, where, in 1849, Count Xavier Branicki bought Montrésor.

There is some good furniture in the place, that is full of other Polish relics and souvenirs besides the Sobieski plate. Montrésor to-day belongs to the *comtesse* Rey.

Montrésor *château* is a pleasing Louis XII building still surrounded by double walls attributed to the famous Fulk Nerra, Count of Anjou. This Renaissance lodging was put up by Imbert and François de Bastarnay, whose tombs are in Montrésor church. The *château* is a rectangular building with a high turret at each corner. The simple façades are pierced with mullioned windows, and the dormers are surmounted with high gables decorated with pinnacles and crockets.

## A Renaissance Marvel

THE collegiate church that the Bastarnays constructed at Montrésor is, however, in every way a more important monument than their manor. Montrésor church is, indeed, one of the marvels of the French Renaissance, and no visitor to Touraine should fail to see it.

The church was begun some time soon after 1520, but was not completed until 1560. However, despite the length of time taken for its building, the church was constructed on a Gothic plan, but with decorative motifs in the most delicate spirit of the Renaissance.

The west front is supported by buttresses surmounted by pinnacles carved with foliage and Flamboyant fleurons. Above the entrance door is a sort of portico, divided by pillars into recesses, each one of which bears a statue. The whole façade is delightfully fresh and friendly. The entrance on the south side is also gracefully ornamented and adorned with little figures. It is a mass of festoons, garlands of flowers and fruits, floral motifs and leaves and roses, carved in low relief with the greatest art. This beautiful doorway is seen at its best when gilded and enlivened by the afternoon sun. Here we have art of the real Renaissance of the Loire valley, of the real French Renaissance, exquisite in taste and masterly in execution.

At the entrance of the nave are the Bastarnay tombs. They have been badly botched and "restored," but they still show something of their former grandeur.

The road eastwards from Montrésor runs through Villeloin, where are remains of a Benedictine abbey. The last place of any interest in this part of Touraine is Nouans, with a fine Romanesque church in which on the north side of the nave may be seen a French primitive of the school of Jean Fouquet.

## Balzac's Père Grandet

MONTREUIL-BELLAY. The model Balzac took for Eugénie Grandet in his masterpiece by that name is said to have been the daughter of one Jean Nivelleau. Nivelleau's career was typical of those of many cunning fellows of revolutionary times. He was born at Saumur and started buying up land in the first years of the Empire, when things began to look safe for big business. As early as 1807 he acquired Vélon, in the Véron region, that tongue of land between Vienne and Loire. In 1810 he was owner of La Tour de Menìves, a charming hexagonal keep at Saint-Hillaire, near Saumur. In 1822 he bought Montreuil-Bellay for 180,000 francs from one Glaçon. Montreuil had been sold in 1662 to Charles de La Porte, *duc* de La Meilleraye, whose descendants in the female line, the La Trémoïlles, sold the place on 6th Thermidor, Year IV of the Republic, for 74,699 francs to Glaçon. But we must not imagine that Nivelleau tried to ape his "betters" and set up as a country-gentleman. He was first and foremost a shrewd peasant and a man of affairs. In those early days of the 19th century—as to-day and for the same reason—stoppage of building—there was a housing shortage, and Nivelleau let out the feudal apartments of Montreuil-Bellay as lodgings. The place, even in those days, was a tourist resort, and Nivelleau, in his usual peasant's garb, used to hang about, show visitors around and take the tips.

He had, however, one weakness: his daughter should be brought up as a lady. She was sent to the school kept by English Augustinian nuns in the *rue des Fossés-Saint-Victor*, in Paris, a school described by George Sand in one of her books. It was a sort of French "Ladies' Eton," as a contemporary establishment in London was nicknamed. The years of social readjustment after the Revolution were times when there was a steady demand for schools where the sons and daughters of the new rich could be turned into "gentlemen" and "ladies." The same sort of phenomenon was observable in early 19th century England. Anyway, the relics of the *old régime* earned a living by educating their new masters.

Mademoiselle Nivelleau returned to the tarnished splendours of Montreuil-Bellay an "accomplished young lady" and, since she was sole heir to her skinflint father's considerable fortune, she did not lack admirers. Eventually she married a curly-haired, bewhiskered ex-hussar called Alexandre Millin, *baron* de Grandmaison. He was thirty, she was nineteeen, and she led a thoroughly unhappy life. When her only son died she left Montreuil to the grand-nephew of her husband, a Monsieur de Grandmaison, later a French senator, who restored Montreuil to something of its former state.

## A Fairy-story Castle

IF you leave Saumur by the high road called *route nationale 138*, just after the Fouchard bridge and near the village of Bagneux there is a megalithic monument known as *Le Grand-Dolmen*. It forms a corridor about sixty feet long and some twenty-three wide, and it varies in height from seven feet to ten feet. This is one of the best-preserved structures in northern France left by the Megalithic Builders, the adventurous colonisers who penetrated into north-western Europe through Spain in New Stone Age times.

After crossing the Thouet River again, and in a few miles, the stream widens, and you are in one of the most charming villages of Anjou. The rippling rivulet, the well-wooded hills, the mild and smiling landscape all combine to make up a scene the finishing touch to which is given by the dark, feudal fortress whose pointed roofs and towers rise above the encircling trees.

Great Fulk Nerra had a stronghold here, but nothing remains of his fortress. Most parts of the picturesque and irregular pile we see to-day were probably erected by order of Guillaume d'Harcourt, who was lord of the place from 1428 to 1484. Further additions did not rob the place of its fairy-story look.

This is no fake castle, such as Langeais, or a disguised country-house. It is a real fortress made for defence. The terraced tops of the towers bore no machicolations but were adapted to use by the new artillery. Still, despite its imposing appearance, the place is somehow elegant and civilised. It is surrounded by a great wall strengthened by round turrets. Within, you see that the castle is really double. There is the Old and there is the New. It is true that the New is five hundred years old.

The Old castle is made up of a small and narrow lodging, flanked by two sturdy round towers, capped with conical roofs whose outline is almost hidden, when you look up at them, by lofty dormers. From the river-side, as you look upwards, all you can see of the New buildings is the two round towers.

The inside courtyard is as fantastic as a stage setting. There is the little 15th century barbican bristling with turrets, there is a huge kitchen whose cupola is mounted on four pillars, there is a wing with pinnacles and gables surmounted by high chimneys, there is an octagonal staircase tower whose steps are alternately of grey sandstone and white limestone and whose vault is emblazoned with the coats-of-arms of most of the owners of the place—but not with that of "*le père Grandet*." And there are creepers and greenery and flowers. In moonlight, just the setting for cloak-and-dagger drama.

## Bibulous Canons

IN 1484 a collegiate chapel as large as a parish church was consecrated in the castle and Montreuil-Bellay castle maintained two canons, who kept the archives and served the chapel. The job of Canon of Montreuil was sought after. Not only did the ecclesiastics enjoy the fare prepared in the great kitchen (comparable with those of Cintra in Portugal or with those of neighbouring Fontevrault), but they had a reputation of being topers. In fact, there was a local saying that the canons of Montreuil

*"drink better than they write."*

Well, the local wines are very good, but, as we saw at Champigny, are also insidious.

Montreuil village also offers some curiosities—the Romanesque and Gothic church, the 17th century cloister, the town gate with flanking towers set with stone bosses like lumps on a crocodile's hide, the remains of the old walls . . . it is a delightful place.

## Ruins of Charlemagne's Time

MONT-SAINT-JEAN. The Forest of Sillé is cut through by the road joining Sillé-le-Guillaume with Mont-Saint-Jean. At La Rotonde the longitudinal road crosses the transverse way, leading to the very picturesque Defais pool, by whose banks are what seem to be Carolingian, that is early or middle 10th century, ruins.

Mont-Saint-Jean is a small village with a rather interesting church, Romanesque, of the 11th century, with 16th century additions. Inside is the tomb of the famous *marquis* de Dreux-Brézé who died in 1829.

## Mirabeau's Challenge

DREUX-BRÉZÉ is not famous for anything much that he did, but for something that was told him.

The Dreux family, though descended from a 15th century commoner, one Thomas Dreux, affected to trace its pedigree from the illustrious race of Dreux founded by Robert de Dreux, the legitimate brother of King Louis VII of France. However, Nicolas Dreux, *Vidame* (i.e. representative of a Bishop, as the Viscount was of a Count) d'Esneval and Baron of the same, did marry Catherine, an heiress of the old Brézé family of Anjou. Not only did the Dreux-Brézés take their place among the first nobility of France, but for over a hundred years before the time of Henri Edouard, *marquis* de Dreux and *marquis* de Brézé, his ancestors had held the illustrious office of Grand-Master of the Ceremonies at the Court of France (see p. 56).

The date is the 23rd June, 1789. The *salle des menus plaisirs* at Versailles had been prepared for the *séance royale* (the "royal sitting"). At the *séance royale* Louis XVI made known that he willed the Estates to sit and to deliberate apart. He then left the hall. Thereupon most of the *noblesse* and some of the clergy retired to their separate chambers. But the rest, with the Third Estate, remained.

Then it was that the *marquis* de Dreux-Brézé addressed the Assembly, requiring its members to obey the royal injunction. Dreux-Brézé, according to Court etiquette, for he spoke in the King's name, advanced into the hall wearing his hat. There were shouts ordering him to uncover. This he refused to do. Thereupon Mirabeau apostrophised him in words which have been quoted in different versions, but that, according to Dreux-Brézé's son (who told that his father had always wanted, after the Restoration, to give his own version but was forbidden by the King to make any public declaration), were as follows:

*"Nous sommes ici par le voeu de la nation, la force matérielle seule pourrait nous faire désemparer."*

*("We are here by the Will of the People, material force alone could make us leave the place where we are.")*

During the next few days many of the clergy and nobles, including the Archbishop of Paris and the *duc* d'Orléans, joined the Assembly. The King accepted his defeat. The French Revolution had begun.

## The Will of the People

AT the Restoration Dreux-Brézé got back his old job as Grand-Master of the Ceremonies, but in a very changed world. He died just a year before the fall of Charles X and the end of a disastrous experiment to restore the *old régime* and to ignore the Revolution. Near to Mont-Saint-Jean is the *château* de La Lucazière, where the Grand-Master of the Ceremonies died and where his descendants still live.

## St. Bartholomew, 1572

MONTSOREAU. There are few incidents in French history better known and worse understood than the Massacre of St. Bartholomew. To begin with, the numbers of the victims have been greatly exaggerated. It is not probable that more than seven thousand persons perished. Again, the massacre was inspired, not by religious, but by political motives. The French Protestants were a strong political force thought to be dangerous to the dynasty. The Queen-Mother, Catherine de' Medici, prime mover in the outrage, was the daughter of that Medici to whom Macchiavelli dedicated "The Prince." With her the reason of State outweighed any other considerations. It is, indeed, arguable that the massacre achieved some, at least, of its objects. French Protestantism, as a political movement, was dealt a blow from which it never really recovered.

Great care was taken not to implicate directly King or Court. The orders for the slaughter were sent to the provinces by word of mouth. The provincial governors received letters enjoining them to obey the instructions given to them by the messengers, but no mention was made as to what those orders were. Some of the provincial governors refused to accept such irregularly issued commands. In Burgundy, for instance, there was no massacre.

## The Lady of Montsoreau

BUT in Anjou, a home of Huguenots, the slaughter was widespread, and of all the sadistic murderers of the province, none was more hated than Jean de Chambes, Lord of Montsoreau. Chambes was no novice in the art of assassination. We need not believe all the legends concerning him or his wife famous from Alexandre Dumas' novel *La Dame de Montsoreau*, but there seems no doubt that the Lord of Montsoreau did use his spouse, in a particularly revolting way, to lure his enemies into his power. Then he would strangle them and throw their bodies into the Loire from the windows of Montsoreau *château*, whose walls in those days were washed by the waters of the river.

The most famous of the Chambes murders was that of Bussy d'Amboise, the favourite of King Henri III's brother, the *duc* d'Alençon. Bussy was renowned as a dueller. Chambes did not want to meet him in open fight. It seems certain that Chambes forced his wife to fix an assignation with Bussy at the *château* de La Coutancière (on the opposite side of the Loire), where Bussy was assassinated. After this incident Chambes and his wife lived together on excellent terms, had a large family and did not die until about forty years after Bussy's disappearance (see p. 13).

But there was an earlier Lady of Montsoreau who also was mixed up in tragic events. This Madame de Chambes was the mistress of the *duc* de Berry, brother of King Louis XI. Berry and his love were the prime movers in the "League of Public Welfare," which the King was able to suppress only by the murder of his brother and of the Chambes lady.

On the road from Candes you round a projecting beak of hill, and then follow the Loire's southern bank for a mile or so. The rather narrow highroad now cuts between the castle walls and the shelving banks of the broad Loire. And the castle abuts almost upon the cliff-face behind. However, in medieval and later times, Montsoreau was an island. There are, indeed, old prints showing it as such. The waters surrounded it, lapping its foundations. A bundle flung out of the window soon went slithering down the river. A strong place. Montsoreau was no "new man's" ostentatious dwelling. The Chambes held Montsoreau long before and long after the building of the house we see to-day, a house which is remarkable for the picture it affords a fairly rich feudal magnate's stronghold in the times when, if houses had begun to be livable, they were still castles and used as such.

The façade on the Loire is imposing: two storeys of mullioned windows, dormers and some decoration, but also machicolations and battlements. Back from the river and at right angles to the main wing two shorter wings project towards the cliffs. Each of the smaller wings ends in an octagonal staircase-tower. The one on the right as you stand in the courtyard was added about 1520. Its doorway is surmounted by four windows, each above the other, and adorned with elegant motifs. A bas-relief between the third and fourth storeys displayed the motto so grimly lived up to by Jean de Chambes: IE LE FERAY—"*I will do it.*"

## *Squatters*

AFTER the Revolution, Montsoreau, like so many manors, castles, *châteaux* and country-houses, became the home of squatters. People just moved into empty houses, and after thirty years' possession and residence were held to have acquired a title. Until comparatively recently Montsoreau was a rabbit-warren of mean lodgings. From 1804, at least fifteen poor families occupied the half-ruined manor. In 1911 the place was bought by the State. It had, at last, been realised that this splendid house, almost untouched since 1455, was a priceless national possession. Repairs began in 1919. The squatters were only got out with great difficulty. As recently as 1930, when we spent some time at Montsoreau, three recalcitrant squatters refused to budge, while scaffolding, planks, boards, masons' saws and blocks of stone cluttered up the whole place. Now all the squatters have left, and the house has been restored to something of its old nobility. No attempt has been made to "reconstitute" it by filling the place with furniture. Woodwork has been fitted where it was lacking. All the repairs have been done by local men, the worthy descendants, it may be, of those capable and honest artisans who built Montsoreau in the 15th century.

It is endlessly pleasing to watch the subtly changing colours of the landscape through the mullioned windows, framing one of the most peaceful and yet grandiose views in northern France. The pale-yellow sands, the shifting, scrub-tufted islets, the white or silvery-grey houses, and then, far away, where the Loire bends, the noble outline of Saumur castle on its rocks. The sky is high and generally of a pale, luminous blue.

You can make a good, long halt at Montsoreau, or run up to Fontevrault and back again, for the local inn is excellent. The speciality is *brochet au beurre blanc*—pike with shallot sauce; it is a culinary masterpiece, never so good as in Anjou. Then there will be the good wines of the Saumurois or of Brézé. They are unlike the Anjou vintages of farther west, but they have the same sparkling and greenish freshness.

## A Queen's Rancour

MORTIERCROLLES. The *maréchal* de Gié, whom we meet at Le Verger and elsewhere, the faithful servant of Kings Louis XI, Charles VIII and Louis XII, rebuilt the old manor of Mortiercrolles, some seven miles from Craon. If we wonder why even so wealthy a man in his day as this Rohan magnate should spend so much time and money in building, we may imagine that houses were one of the safest forms of investment. It is true that they could be confiscated by a jealous, covetous or wrathful sovereign, but, then, life was cheap, uncertain and hazardous; anyway treasure—in the sense of gold and silver and jewels—was difficult to amass, as the supply was far less than the demand, and America had not been discovered, or at any rate had not begun to pour her flow of poisoned gold. Houses, too, could serve for daughters' dowries. . . .

Anne of Brittany, Queen successively of Kings Charles VIII and Louis XII, pursued the unfortunate *maréchal* de Gié with a real, passionate, 'Celtic' hatred. And poor Gié himself had done nothing to merit in any way the rancorous Queen's dislike (see p. 354).

François II, last independent Duke of Brittany, was, perhaps by temperament, but certainly also from necessity, a temporising and rather slippery individual. He was surrounded by enemies. It was obvious that, sooner or later, Brittany would be united to the Crown of France. This wild, rocky peninsula could not become another Portugal: the centripetal force of a united France was too great. The Duke had two daughters. Not unnaturally, they had many suitors, or, rather, many men wanted them. Among the people to whom the Duke had promised one or other of his daughter's hands in marriage was the father of the *maréchal* de Gié, Louis de Rohan, of the ancient and illustrious Breton family of that name. But Louis de Rohan did not want the Lady Anne for himself, but for his son—the future *maréchal* de Gié. Later, Anne became Queen of France, and not once but twice. She never, however, forgave poor Gié for his father's presumption. Anne of Brittany persecuted and maligned the poor fellow to the end of his days, although for some time before his death he had retired to the country.

Of Gié's country-houses, Le Verger was almost a royal palace. La Motte-Glain was also a great place, but Mortiercrolles was unique in its graceful union of Gothic and Renaissance beauty.

The great twin towers, with crenellations and machicolations, rise from among the trees, and on either side of a fine gateway. The alternate courses of brown and white stone give these towers a rather civilised and southern air, though they look medieval enough.

The last of the Rohans at Mortiercrolles was Anne, one of Brantôme's *dames galantes*. She was an unlucky and unhappy woman. Most of the men who loved her perished on the scaffold or by sudden death. Her elder son was executed. Her younger was such a hopeless prodigal that, with him, his family was reduced to poverty. Mortiercrolles was sold in 1783.

It is when you are about half-way from Segré, on the Craon road, that you see to the right a superb avenue of trees leading to Mortiercrolles. You turn into the drive, and the imposing mass of the place, with its four tall towers rising from the waters, comes gradually into view. It is not a sight to miss.

MOULIHERNE. About three miles off the Noyant-Saumur road lies Mouliherne, whose Romanesque and early Gothic church preserves in the walls of the nave a not inconsiderable amount of *petit appareil* or "small masonry" work, which must be dated, probably, as far back as the nine hundreds. The vaulting of the nave and the transepts is particularly interesting as showing the evolution of the Angevin style during the 12th and 13th centuries. The roof of the nave is especially light, airy and daring.

## Ambassador to Queen Elizabeth

NEUVY-LE-ROI. At La Mauvissière, near the village of Neuvy-le-Roi, was born, about 1518 or 1520, Michel de Castelnau, *Sieur* de La Mauvissière. There is a rather large number of places throughout France called Castelnau, and the several families of this name have no common origin. These Touraine Castelnaus have no connection with the Curières de Castelnau stock from the south, of which one was the celebrated general of the 1914–18 war.

Michel came of a large family, but, owing probably to his showing while young exceptional promise, he was, for his day, very carefully educated both in France and in Italy. He was for a time in the army, but having been taken into favour by the Cardinal of Lorraine, the brother of the *duc* de Guise, Castelnau was introduced to the Court, and his first diplomatic mission was to carry royal dispatches to Scotland for Mary Stuart, then betrothed to the Dauphin. From Scotland he travelled down into England, and conducted some negotiations with Queen Elizabeth respecting her claims upon Calais. He then was employed in Germany, in the Netherlands, in Parma and in Rome. On his return to France, he managed to get wind of the preparations for the Amboise conspiracy, and passed on his knowledge to the Court (see p. 3).

On the death of King François II, Castelnau it was who was chosen to accompany Mary Queen of Scots to her native land and to meet her fate. He it was who stood by her while she sobbed her farewell to France and all the way of life that she loved:

*"Adieu, charmant pays de France."*

Castelnau stayed with the Queen of Scots for a year, during which time he made several journeys to England in an attempt to bring about a reconciliation between the two Queens. He took part in the fighting during 1562 and 1563, and then for ten years was employed in a variety of diplomatic missions.

In 1572, King Charles IX sent him to London as Ambassador in order to allay, if he could, the resentment and excitement caused in England by the massacre of Saint-Bartholomew. We know from a famous picture the circumstances in which he was received. The Queen was seated on her throne, in a hall draped in black hangings. Gloriana herself was in deep mourning, and all the members of her Court were in sable garments. Elizabeth, as we see her, turns her head and holds a handkerchief in her hand. Castelnau, in rather flashy, light-coloured array, advances, making a very low bow. The atmosphere was chilly. The Ambassador's job was thankless. But neither the Queen nor her people was prepared to do anything much more than make a demonstration. The prudent and cunning policy of Elizabeth and her servants moved into no unconsidered acts. But Castelnau was a decent fellow, an honest man and a devoted servitor of his sovereign. He was the sort of man the Queen understood and instinctively valued.

In 1574, Castelnau (who had been recalled after a short time in

**Les Ponts-de-Cé**

The Castle Bastion

**Plessis-lès-Tours**      Louis XI's Manor

Le Plessis-Bourré      Façade of Court

Poncé-sur-le-Loir      The *Château*

Le Plessis-Bourré      View across the Moat

England) was reappointed Ambassador in London, and remained with us for no less than ten years. During these ten years his task was not easy. Our relations with the French had drifted into that state of latent hostility and suspicion that was to characterise them for generations. Castelnau did his best to promote the ill-found scheme for a marriage between Elizabeth and the Duke of Alençon. But, at long last, the Ambassador realised that he was being made a fool of, and ended by refusing to accept or to transmit to France the many contradictory promises proffered by the Queen. He returned to France, only to find that his manor of La Mauvissière had been sacked and ruined in the Civil War. He was not re-employed, lost his various jobs, including the governorship of Saint-Dizier, and was reduced almost to destitution. But Henry IV, on his succession, did something for the poor old man, and eased his later days with various employments. Castelnau's valuable *Memoires* were written in England during the last years of his mission, when he had very little else to do, but they cover a period from 1559 to 1570 and therefore treat of events anterior to his first embassy here.

## *An Unfortunate President*

NOGENT-LE-ROTROU. Monsieur Paul Deschanel, who was for many years an elegant if not very authoritative president of the Chamber of Deputies, was preferred by the French parliament to Clemenceau as President of the French Republic. Deschanel, only a few months after his election, made headline news in the world's press by falling out of the presidential railway-train and by walking in his nightshirt along the permanent way into the arms of an astonished, and, indeed, incredulous, platelayer. It was soon realised that the President of the Republic was in a poor state of mental health. After he had startled his staff by walking through the ornamental fountains at Rambouillet while he was clad in frock-coat and top-hat, he was prevailed upon to resign his high office. But he had quite lucid intervals, and when the select committee of the Chamber and the Senate waited upon him to secure his signature to the act of resignation, the eminent parliamentarians wondered, for some time, whether they had not been too precipitate. However, the ceremony proceeded, and the President signed with good grace. The Paris wits maintained that no doubt as to the propriety of the politicians' action remained after the signature had been examined. It was NAPOLEON. *Se non è vero* . . .

Deschanel was for many years deputy for Nogent-le-Rotrou, and his bust adorns a square of the town. Nogent, though in the modern department of the Eure-et-Loire, is historically a capital of the Perche. It is a largish place of over seven thousand inhabitants who mostly live on the left bank of the Huisne at a point where the valleys of the Rhône, the Cloche and the Arcisse converge with that of the Huisne. The town is built to a curious plan consisting, essentially, of four long streets enclosing what was until recent years an open space of meadows and trees. Now the new section of the town had grown up inside the old quarters.

Novigentum was a Gallo-Roman settlement, where Rotrou, first Count of Perche, set up his stronghold in the 11th century. In 1449 the place was burned on the orders of King Charles VII, who thought it could not be defended against the English. Later, Nogent was rebuilt, and its lordship was bought in 1624 by the famous *duc* de Sully, who had been Henry IV's minister.

There are some notable buildings. The Church of Saint-Hilaire, originally Romanesque, was rebuilt in Flamboyant style in the 15th century. The polygonal 13th century choir is remarkable. The Church of *Notre-Dame* (mostly early Gothic) was formerly the chapel of the *Hôtel-Dieu*, or public hospital, which was enlarged and endowed by Sully. Adjoining *Notre-Dame* church, and in the courtyard of the hospital, is a small hexagonal building, erected by Rachel de Cochefilet, the great man's widow, and containing her tomb and that of her lord.

## Sully

MAXIMILIEN DE BÉTHUNE, *duc* de Sully, the faithful and trusted collaborator and friend of Henry IV, is a man whose influence upon French history it is rather difficult to estimate. His career was not as spectacular as Richelieu's, nor was it mainly devoted to foreign politics, but it is possible that, taking the broad view, Sully was one of the statesmen who left the deepest imprint on his country.

In every direction he fostered, encouraged and healed the economy of France so grievously battered by lengthy civil war.

However, Sully was eminently fortunate in serving a master such as Henry IV, to whom must probably be ascribed most of the credit for the major policies and programmes adopted during his reign. In any case, we may say that, together, the master and the servant restored France and prepared that country for the rôle it was to play under Richelieu's guidance, that is to say, the part of the leading Power in Europe.

Sully (an ardent or, at least an obdurate, Protestant) was not a very attractive sort of man. He was overbearing, rude, as parsimonious and grasping in his own affairs as he was careful and honest in those of the State. He was, however, a man of outstanding executive ability, self-confidence and character.

As Sully and his second wife were Protestants (she changed her religion to please him), their remains could not be buried in a Catholic church or cemetery. Hence the shrine put up in the *Hôtel-Dieu* at Nogent-le-Rotrou.

The monument to the *duc* and *duchesse* was executed by Boudin in 1642. On a stone pedestal, painted to imitate green marble, are two magnificent statues in white marble. The figures, in State costume, kneel on cushions. Below are the arms of Sully. The tomb was rifled at the time of the Revolution and the relics of the Sullys dispersed. In a black marble coffer on the monument are what are supposed to be such remains of the bones as could be recovered.

Nogent castle, or the *château-de-Saint-Jean,* was the ancient dwelling of the sovereign Counts of Perche. Sully sometimes resided here, and the place remained the property of his descendants until 1789. The keep (built from 1003 to 1030) is about eighty feet high, and its walls, at the base, are not less than ten feet thick. The tower (dismantled in 1378 on the orders of King Charles V) is in an excellent state of preservation, though disfigured with poor modern "crenellations." The keep backs on a 15th century lodging set between two machicolated towers. The containing wall of the castle enclosure is set with half-round 12th and 13th century towers.

## A Punning Inscription

IN the *rue du Capitaine-Renot* is the late Gothic church of *Saint-Laurent,* while the nearby hall of the boys' school is the Romanesque and Gothic choir of an old church. The school itself is housed in a fine town mansion, over whose doorway is the inscription:

DE PIERRE BLANCHE—DURANT FEBVRIER—JE FUS FAICTE, 1542
*("Of White Stone—during February—was I made, 1542.")*

But as the builders were Pierre Durand and his wife Blanche Febvrier, the old Nogent worthies perpetuated a pleasing little rebus, or pun, for the delight of passers-by and generations of *Percheron* schoolboys.

## Louis XIV's Chief of Police

PAULMY, Marc René Le Voyer, *marquis* de Paulmy, was the third member of the notable Le Voyer d'Argenson family to attain distinction. He was for twenty-one years, from 1697, "lieutenant-general of police," that is, not only the head in Paris of the royal police, secret and otherwise, but also the controller of the corporations and gilds, of the printing press and of the provisioning of Paris. He was a man of great ability and strength of character, as Saint-Simon describes him, "ever inclined to the mildest measures, but courageous, bold and audacious . . . and consequently the master of the people." During the long term of his tenure of office he was privy to all the secrets of Court and Cabinet, and he was one of the most influential men in France.

Later he was appointed by the Regent to reorganise the finances of the country—perennial and hopeless task!—and although he helped John Law, of the "Mississippi scheme," to apply his "system," he also quarrelled with him and prepared his downfall. But to cover himself, the Regent threw the blame for the collapse of Law's schemes on to Marc-René. When he died in 1721, the people of Paris broke up his funeral procession, pelting his coffin with stones, and shouting that he had ruined the country.

The Paulmy, from which Marc-René Le Voyer d'Argenson took his title, is Paulmy on the Brignon, whose 16th century church contains the family vault of the d'Argensons. Downstream from the village and to the right of the valley is the old Castle of Paulmy. About a mile farther on is the ruined *château* du Châtelier, a huge fortress dating from the eleven and twelve hundreds, and during the 16th century in the possession of a celebrated Huguenot captain known as Lanoue *Bras-de-Fer*. Later, the place was bought by the Le Voyers, whose ancestral fief, Argenson, is not far off.

The walls of Le Châtelier are still intact: they rise from a deep moat crossed by a drawbridge. Inside, little remains of former glories. There are several lodgings and buildings used as granges, stables and barns. One of the houses has a 16th century polygonal staircase-tower. The keep still stands over ninety feet high but is rent from top to base.

## A Family of Noble Horse-masters

PIGNEROLLE. In the middle of the 18th century a report on the Angers "Academy of Equitation" ran:

> *"The Academy is the best conducted in the Kingdom, and it is there that foreigners study for preference, for Messieurs de Pignerolle attract them, not only by the excellent qualifications of the masters, but also by their own good temper and fine manners."*

It was to this "Academy" that the future Duke of Wellington was sent to learn French and riding in 1785 (see p. 24).

The little property of Pignerolle was bought in 1680 by François Avril de Pignerolle—who had been appointed by the Governor of Anjou "Equerry of the Great Royal Stables"— *"Écuyer de la Grande Écurie du Roy"*—and then set about organising the *Académie d'Equitation d'Angers*.

Pignerolle soon became famous for—

> *"the great care he exercised in guiding the studies of those who came to him to learn, and for the extraordinary expense that he incurred in attracting to his establishment the most competent masters in the sciences and arts."*

So we can see that M. de Pignerolle was no novice in the art of publicity. Soon his establishment became an essential part of Angers' prosperity. It was estimated that at one time in the 18th century Pignerolle's pupils spent no less than four hundred thousand *livres* a year, to the great joy of the Angers tradesmen, hotel and lodging-house keepers, and of the general population of Anjou's capital and its countryside.

In 1724, so great was Pignerolle's fame that the Prince of Lorraine enticed him away to run the riding-school at Lunéville. But Pignerolle left his brother Bernard to carry on at Angers, and Bernard in 1743 made his nephew Charles his partner. And in 1761, Charles, having become sole owner, took in his own brother Marc-Antoine. These were the "Messieurs de Pignerolle," famed for their "good temper and fine manners," who were the directors of the "Academy" while the young Arthur Wesley or Wellesley was at Angers, not very attentive to his studies, but spending much of his time looking after his terrier Vic.

When the Revolution broke on France, the school was being run by Marc de Pignerolle. On the 1st August, 1792, a municipal report was made on the establishment and we read that there was only one pupil, and that Pignerolle had not only not taken the oath of allegiance to the nation, but that he steadily refused to.

Poor Pignerolle was arrested at his house of Pignerolle in the Year II of the Republic, One and Indivisible, and sent to die in the cellars of a house in the Angevin village of Doué-la-Fontaine.

Pignerolle was confiscated and sold, and that was an end of the famous dynasty of Angers horse-masters.

## A Beautiful House

PIGNEROLLE is for French ears a familiar name. It is reminiscent of Pignerol (that is, the French form of Pinerola), the Piedmontese fortress, once belonging to France, where many State prisoners, including the famous Fouquet and the "Man in the Iron Mask," were incarcerated (see p. 71).

But the Pignerolle in Anjou, that lent such an aristocratic touch to the family of Avril, is not so well known. Yet the house, even in its present state, is most attractive. The architect was one Bardoul de La Bigottière, a pupil of the famous Gabriel who built the *Petit Trianon* at Versailles and the *École Militaire* in Paris. Bardoul was worthy of his master, and to his plans were erected the pleasing and graceful *Hôtels* de Livois, de Lantivy and de La Besnardière at Angers, as well as the little pleasure-house of Châteaubriand, near Angers, and at the confluence of the rivers Maine and Loire.

Pignerolle is, however, Bardoul's masterpiece. It is a compact house, rather deeper than it is broad. It looks as though it might have been the prototype of some of the more elegant of the American "colonial-style" country homes, with its slender columns, perfectly proportioned outline and gracious, white-stone façade.

The exterior walls are adorned with two bas-reliefs which have been attributed (of course) to David d'Angers. A statue or two set on the lawns lend additional lightness and 18th century charm to this delightful house.

Inside, the vestibule is a marvel of classical grace, and all the original decoration has been preserved. The panellings were, however, stripped from the saloons and sold to a dealer. These *boiseries* have never been traced. The house is well kept up, and is surrounded by a pleasing park.

Pignerolle was put up at a time when the aristocratic horsemasters of Angers were riding on the full-tide of their prosperity, and when they were considerable personages in the county. At Pignerolle were given parties where the "young gentlemen" of the Academy could meet the youth and beauty of the local squirearchy. For, in its way, the Angers Academy played quite a part in the social life of 18th century Europe. We may imagine the youthful Arthur Wesley making his acquaintance with the Anjou gentry in the genteel saloons of Pignerolle.

For some months in 1940 the house was the residence of the President-in-exile of the Polish Republic.

## *"The Saint of Anjou"*

LE PIN-EN-MAUGES. The Old France of before the Revolution preserved, together with a mass of other anachronisms and cumbersome relics of the past, a burdensome and vexatious system of internal customs-barriers. It is well known that the French Revolution, like all others we know of, was hastened and, in part, rendered inevitable by financial muddle and disorder. The change-over from what we call a "feudal" economy to that which still prevails (or until recently prevailed) in most of Europe was effected, in different countries, in various ways and at differing rhythms. In early medieval times the business of government was carried on by the sovereign's resources, augmented by a number of special taxes, "fines," etc. In France, until the end of the *old régime*, a considerable portion of the population—and of the richest part of the population, the "nobles" and the ecclesiastics—paid, proportionately, less in taxes than the rest of the people, and it was therefore found impossible to abrogate such vexatious and old-fashioned dues as those of the internal customs. In fact, the tradition of indirect taxation lingered on in France. Income-tax was levied only from the eve of the 1914 war.

But, under the *old régime*, the internal customs-barriers were a real impediment to the development of trade and commerce. Of course, as happens always when we have the combination of an ineffective administration and a thoroughly unpopular law, circumventing the internal customs-barriers became a popular and profitable occupation.

In 1759, in the reign of King Louis XV, the "Well-Beloved," as his courtiers sycophantically described him (though it must be recorded to the honour of the King's good sense that he would remark "I can't think what I have done to make people love me so much"), was born at Le Pin-en-Mauges, in the old province of Anjou, one Jacques Cathelineau, son of a mason. Jacques, early in life, distinguished himself by his great personal strength, courage and piety. Indeed, so striking was his piety, that the peasants dubbed him the "Saint of Anjou." Jacques was, by trade, a pedlar, and principally a pedlar of goods smuggled through the internal customs-barriers. Probably, he himself took a hand in the smuggling from time to time. Cathelineau was one of the first to join the uprising of the peasants of western France, an uprising fomented by priests and landowners. Doubtless it was his piety that persuaded him to a course that was directly opposed to his own social and economic interests. Cathelineau soon became one of the principal leaders of the movement. He and his men captured Chemillé, Cholet, Vihiers and Chalonnes. His troops, a rabble of ill-armed peasants, committed many atrocities which, in their turn, provoked violent reprisals from the Republicans who had been taken by surprise. The uprising spread. Stofflet and Gigot d'Elbée seized Beaupréau. Cathelineau became the leader of the whole insurrectionary forces, but he had little command of his men except when they were actually attacking. When they occupied Nantes, their leader was mortally wounded.

Le Pin-en-Mauges church is now a shrine to the memory of the Vendean leader. His tomb of variegated marble is surmounted with a statue by Biron of Cathelineau in white Carrera marble. But the monument contains only part of the leader's remains brought hither from Saïnt-Florent-le-Vieil. The stained glass in the church windows depicts episodes in Cathelineau's life.

## "*The Wizard's Box*"

LE PLESSIS-BOURRÉ. Jean Bourré, the famed finance minister of King Louis XI, struck the imagination of his contemporaries as vividly as do financial "wizards" astound and confound, until their final collapse, the wiseacres of our time. Juggling with figures, "book-keeping operations," creation of "new money" are nothing new, but the Frenchmen of Jean Bourré's time were convinced that he drew the immense sums needed for his buildings, not from his fellow-countrymen's pockets, but from *la boëte à l'enchanteur*—the wizard's box. Anyway, Bourré did spend a great deal of money, and in 1462 he bought the old Castle of Le Plessis, and six years later set about refashioning the place into an unrecognisably sumptuous residence. The window-glass for the new castle was ordered on 14th January, 1472, so, we may conclude that, by this date, the house was finished and stood much as we see it to-day, a living-wing raised above the other three, a broad moat and walls and towers devised to stand up against the new warfare of artillery, of flanking-fire and of attack from a distance.

Bourré enlarged the old moat, so that his new castle seemed to be floating on the face of a broad lake. To this day his *château* has survived as one of the sights of the Loire country. The rectangular mass is regular and imposing, mirrored with walls and towers in the waters. The masonry of Le Plessis-Bourré is especially fine, well-worked and smooth-jointed.

The great place must be viewed from all sides.

The 15th century castles, of which this is a splendid example, were still, in appearance at least, fortresses. The general plan is still the simple, old one—four wings around a central courtyard, at each corner a stout tower, one of which, stronger than the rest, served as a keep. The moats are still part of a real system of defence that comprised, in addition, machicolations, crenellations, a drawbridge, a portcullis and ramparts.

But, although these fortresses scowled so grimly from the

outside, within, and around the central court, the façades of the living apartments were conceived in a style of lightness and grace unknown before. Once you have passed through the barbican you are transported into a new world of country-houses made primarily to be lived in comfortably and not constructed as fortresses.

Let us walk slowly round it, and then, with the image of its pale-grey outline, for all the world reminding us of the fresh and living castles the miniaturists painted in the splendid Books of Hours, with this image of a living Middle Ages in our minds, let us cross the long, low bridge over the moat, and reach the great fortified barbican pierced with a square, massive doorway scored at the sides by the deep cuts which once held the drawbridge chains. Opposite, across the court, rises the façade of the principal lodging. It is high, irregular in style, but bright, almost gay. The two storeys are topped by a steep attic lighted by gabled dormers. To the right is the usual staircase turret, whose entrance is framed in pillars, and surmounted by a gable adorned with the royal arms of France supported by two angels. There is not much ornamentation, and what there is is sober and confined to the frames of the windows carved with a design of thistles and vine-leaves. The windows, moreover, in the Touraine tradition of the 15th century, are not all of the same width, some being only half as broad as their neighbours. The general effect is noble and impressive.

Near the entrance, and adjoining the northern wing, is the chapel. Here are no innovations. The whole little building is conceived and executed in the purest style of later Gothic.

Next to the chapel is the entrance into a vast guard-room, whose ceiling is most curious. It is divided into six compartments of wood painted with the images of strange beasts and scenes illustrating proverbs whose rhyming legends are spread along the rafters. For instance:

> "*Sur barbe de foul*
> *Il apprend à rère*"
>
> ("*On the fool's beard*
> *He learns how to shave*")

an apt reference to the cunning Bourré, who gained his business experience fleecing fools. Bourré was a man after the heart of the avaricious, miserly, able and far-seeing man who was his royal

Lord and Master. Louis XI would have no aristocratic fools about him, and his plebeian tools had to be exceptionally bright fellows. We know something of Bourré's appearance. He was a little, long-nosed, cross-eyed customer, capable enough, but with nothing impressive about him. His wife was a 'lady' by birth and, as so often happens, her children by her cunning husband had their mother's brains and their father's looks. The later Bourrés were an undistinguished lot.

Le Plessis-Bourré boasts no fewer than thirteen staircases, with magnificent newels fanning out like palm trees at their summits. Most of the great house is now empty, but is, perhaps, none the worse for that. The interior is certainly more imposing than that of, say, Langeais, not only because Le Plessis is a place of spacious apartments, saloons and halls, but also because it is not stuffed with masses of furniture which, however interesting, detract from the effect of the rooms containing them. These medieval places were not full of furniture.

The *grand' salle,* or great saloon, of Le Plessis is an astounding apartment—grey, luminous, smooth of wall. The magnificent vaulted ceiling is supported on pillars, and for sole adornment there is a noble, square and sculptured chimney-piece. In some of the apartments are 18th century furnishings and panelling.

Le Plessis-Bourré was sold by its old owners as long ago as 1730. Early in the 19th century it was bought by an attorney of Angers. Luckily, nothing much was done to the great house until it became the property of M. Waisse, whose restoration has been very tactful. Le Plessis-Bourré is a magnificent and melancholy place.

## *"The Universal Spider"*

PLESSIS-LÈS-TOURS. Plessis-lès-Tours lies not a league from Touraine's capital, and is an insignificant village with the remains of what was not only for years the real capital of France, but also of a house whose importance in the history of architecture is considerable.

Tours sprawls out over a plain treeless and cultivated, dotted, here and there, with the graceless cement, brick and tile shacks which to-day deface so much of the French countryside. We must imagine the surroundings of Plessis-lès-Tours as much more sylvan five hundred years ago, when King Louis XI, whom his contemporaries often called the "Universal Spider," sat at the centre of his web.

But if the immediate scene is a little disappointing, the landscape is still framed by pale-blue hills, and the wide valley of the Loire is as lovely as ever.

You reach a clump of trees, and nearby is one wing of what was once a manor of rose-red brick and white stone. It is true that what we see to-day seems sawn-off and truncated. There are no gardens. There is little shade. Still, in the soft Touraine sunlight which bathes a northern scene with a southern suavity, Plessis-lès-Tours seems more attractive than it does in a photograph. Too often, the images offered to us of this little house remind us of the suburban villas of some eastern European city where you pass, in one street, from a stucco "*Château de Blois*" to a lath-and-plaster "*Petit Trianon*" through a miniature "*Louvre*" of painted boards. Plessis-lès-Tours, to-day, *is* sawn off and truncated —though it escaped all hurt during the last war—the other wings, the stables, the servants' quarters, the outbuildings have all disappeared. Their stones and bricks have gone into the cottages of the hamlet now straggling over what was once the park of King Louis XI.

There is nothing sinister about Plessis-lès-Tours, although the old chroniclers picture the place as a gloomy fortress or a bleak prison. It was just the harsh, cunning, relentless and powerful personality of the King which made men see his residence as a place of terror and doom. Houses, they say, make the men who live in them. But men also make the houses they live in.

Plessis-lès-Tours was built slowly—the King hated spending money—and well, during eighteen years from 1453 to 1471. On the 30th August, 1483, Louis XI died here. For years he had been ailing and had not travelled much. He lived meanly, and only took some pains with his appearance when he received foreign envoys. Then he would deck himself in costly stuffs and paint his face and lips. Philippe de Commynes, his faithful servant and his chronicler, has left a vivid account of the King's last hours after he had been struck down with apoplexy.

None of Louis' successors resided at Plessis, but here was held the States-General meeting in 1506, when the servile assembly

voted to accord King Louis XII the title of "Father of the People."
In 1589 King Henri III of France and King Henry of Navarre
(afterward Henry IV of France) met at Plessis, and there made an
agreement by which both the royal forces and those of the French
Huguenots should serve under the same flag against the "Leaguers"
members of the insurrectionary movement designed to depose
Henri III and put the Duke of Guise on the throne.

In 1773 Plessis was turned into a prison. It was sold at the
Revolution as national property, and after many ups and downs
of fortune came into the possession of a doctor, who fitted up
part of the building as a medical museum. The ground-floor has,
however, been restored to something of its early appearance. In
1947 the Touraine Silk Museum was housed at Plessis, which also
sheltered the magnificent collection of MSS. and incunabula formerly in the Tours municipal library which was destroyed in
June 1940.

The exterior of Plessis is interesting, because when the
manor was constructed its style was quite novel. It was a style
arising, as it were, spontaneously from the soil of Touraine. The
middle years of the 15th century were a time when sumptuous
private houses were beginning to be built in different parts of
France. But no architect, not even he of Jacques Coeur's house
in Bourges, had imagined that subtle combination of brick and
white stone which harmonises so well with the changing skies of
the Loire valley.

We do not know who was the architect who imagined the
charming and impressive novelty of Plessis. But the style he
created—simple façade, regular rows of mullioned windows, the
gabled dormers, the subtle combination of brick and stone—prevailed for nearly three generations, and then, after a period of
eclipse, in a new form, but with the essential combination of
brick and stone, flourished and spread. The style of Louis XIII
in France, the William and Mary and Georgian houses of Britain
and the colonial houses of the New World all owe something to
anonymous artists who designed a new house for the "universal
spider." Never was there spun so elegant a web.

From 1472 to 1490 one Jean Regnard was "master of the King's
building" in Touraine. It may be that he was the man who set up
Plessis and perhaps some of the older parts of Amboise. The

wing of Blois castle (erected by Charles d'Orléans and pulled down by Gaston d'Orléans in the 17th century) was, it appears, much in the same style as Plessis. And this part of Blois was the work of one Jean de Reims *masson*—architects in the 15th century bore no more pretentious name.

Plessis was formerly surrounded with a walled moat. What remains of the manor is the King's lodging. There were two other wings and a chapel, and the court, enclosed by the three wings, was surrounded by an arcaded gallery, richly sculptured, and rather like that still existing in the Louis XIII wing at Blois, for which gallery, indeed, that of Plessis served as a model.

The little chapel near the house is built, it is said, upon the site of the lodging where Saint Vincent de Paul lived during his stay at Plessis.

## Barber and King's Counsellor

BARBERS have, even to this day, the reputation of being men of counsel. At least, they seem to talk a good deal. Olivier le Daim, barber to King Louis XI, was also the confidant of his royal master. The barber-counsellor certainly exercised considerable influence, and rumour made him more powerful probably than he really was. In any case, Olivier was hanged after the King's death.

Between Plessis and Tours are some lodgings, more or less of the same type as the sovereign's house. These places served, no doubt, to shelter members of the small and very queerly composed Court of Louis XI. La Rabaterie is said to have been the property of Olivier le Daim. Then there is the *Hôtel* Sanglier, and, also, a charming little manor formerly known as *la petite Bourdaisière*. It lies in a bosk of greenery, through which you can see peeping the façade of brick and stone, the octagonal staircase tower, the wide windows and the gabled dormers.

## The Man Who Would Not Shake Hands

LE PLESSIS-MACE. Gédéon Tallemant, generally called "Tallemant des Réaux," was an entertaining gossip-writer of the 17th century whose caustic, often malevolent and highly amusing *Historiettes,* or "Little Histories," form a collection of pen-portraits invaluable for an understanding of the persons and events of his time.

His 385th *historiette* he devotes to one Charles du Bellay, a most degenerate descendant of the famous Anjou family that we meet so often in and about the Loire valley. This Charles du Bellay was not only highly effeminate, but he was also a sort of dwarf, with a figure like that of "Punch"; indeed, Tallemant calls him *bossu devant et derrière*—humped back and front—and moreover he had a morbid dislike to shaking hands. He would, in fact, go to almost any lengths to avoid such greetings, and was known to take to his bed for days in order to escape handshakes. Perhaps he feared sorcery or witchcraft—what we, to-day, might call contagion. Perhaps he just did not like showing his hands. In our days a Central European financier was notorious for always wearing kid gloves to avoid catching skin complaints, but, then, he also refused to allow anyone in the same room with him. Charles du Bellay, on the other hand, liked society—of his own choosing.

Bellay, in 1648, sold the *château* of Le Plessis-Macé to Guillaume Bautru of Serrant, who made a present of the place to his daughter, the *marquise* de Vaubrun. An elder son having died, the younger, known as the *abbé* de Vaubrun, inherited the estate.

## *"An Ugly and Dangerous Snail"*

THIS ecclesiastic was of a manner of life which was no credit to his cloth. In fact, the *duc* de Saint-Simon, the famous memoir-writer, calls him *un vilain et dangereux escargot*—an ugly and dangerous snail—and, despite a most unprepossessing appearance, he made himself so obnoxious to the ladies by his pressing and indiscreet advances that his conduct shocked even the Court of Louis XIV. The unworthy *abbé*, after a particularly scandalous attempt to force his attentions upon some young girls, was bundled off into the Bastille, and then, in virtue of a *lettre de cachet*, exiled to his Anjou estates. But he soon tired of a country life, and on the death of his only sister, the *duchesse* d'Estrées, he got rid of all his properties for the sum of 824,000 *livres*, of which only 125,000 represented the purchase-price of Le Plessis-Macé. He then made off, to continue his amorous career in more favourable surroundings.

The new owner of Le Plessis-Macé was Messire Antoine Walsh

of Serrant, but neither he, nor his immediate successors, either lived in or repaired the house. It was, indeed, let to farmers, one of whom more than half ruined the place. From 1860 to 1872 the widow of *comte* Théobald Walsh spent a good deal of money in repairing and in restoring Le Plessis-Macé, which in 1878 she gave to her daughter, who had married a *baron* d'Hérisson.

## A New Old House

TWO miles out from Angers by the Segré road you pass the *Champ des Martyrs,* where lie buried more than two thousand men and women who were slaughtered in 1794 during one of the last campaigns of repression ordered by the Government of the First Republic.

The *château* of Le Plessis-Macé is about eight miles farther on. It takes its name from the Macé family, who were lords of the fief in the 11th century, and part of the fortified walls they constructed may still be seen. The oldest parts of the present house date from the fourteen hundreds, and there is a chapel built by the du Bellay family in the first bloom of the French Renaissance.

Not so long ago Le Plessis-Macé was a fine fortress in ruins. An imposing battlemented enclosure set with towers rose behind a wide moat. And the place is still striking, from its mere size and bulk, but it has been too thoroughly restored. When you get near, the façade on the court bears a hybrid, half-ashamed air, with its too-white, too-new gables and rather harsh lines. Fortunately, the walls are more than half-covered with creeper and ivy, and the masses of roses and flowers near the dwelling lend it a "lived-in" and friendly aspect.

## The Old Loire Bridge

PONTS-DE-CÉ. Leaving Angers by the southern road, you are soon in Ponts-de-Cé, which the old Counts and Dukes of Anjou made into a strong fortress. The town is a straggling sort of place, stringing along one road for more than two miles, and crossing, by seven bridges, the Authion canal, three broad arms of the Loire and the Louet. The old houses and dwellings of Ponts-de-Cé give the town a very picturesque appearance.

Ponts-de-Cé was, throughout French history until the Revolution, an important junction, since here was the only bridge over

Château-du-Loir — The Little Manor of Riassey

Richelieu — The Gardens of the *Château*

**Richelieu**    South Gate of the Town

**Preuilly** Romanesque Basilica

**Rochecorbon**    The Loire

**Rochefort-sur-Loire**
*Château de Saint-Symphorien*

**Rochecorbon**    The Church

The "Lantern"

the Loire between Saumur and Nantes. All the traffic of Anjou
had to pass this way. So the history of Ponts-de-Cé has been one
of siege and storming, of efforts to hold and efforts to take.

For Frenchmen the name is well enough known, since hereabouts took place an engagement between the partisans of Marie
de' Medici, the Queen-Mother, and those of her son Louis XIII,
by which the latter gained so easy a victory that the engagement
was known as the *drôlerie des Ponts-de-Cé* or the "phony" battle
of Ponts-de-Cé. The French call *la drôle de guerre* that phase of
the last world war from September 1939 to April 1940 in the west.

The Church of Saint-Aubin is worth a visit, and the fine old
keep of Ponts-de-Cé castle was often lived in by "good King
René." The statue on the bridge is of Dumnacus, the Gaulish
chieftain from the Lower Loire, who kept up the struggle against
the Roman invaders after the defeat of Vercingetorix. At Ponts-
de-Cé in 1793 Captain Bourgeois, his young wife and his six
hundred *bleus,* or raw recruits, were cut to pieces by 10,000 Vendeans commanded by d'Autichamp. Bourgeois, his wife and a
handful of survivors from the massacre, plunged to death from the
heights overlooking the river rather than surrender.

**P**OUANCÉ. South-west from Craon, the road runs through the
Forest of Lourzais, and so down to Pouancé on the Verzée.
Above Pouancé, the river widens out into the broad mere known
as the *étang de Pouancé*, in whose waters are reflected the walls
of old Pouancé castle, where in 1443 Jean de Pouancé held out
against a siege by the English. Eleven ivy-clad towers lend the
place a romantic air, but within the battlements is nothing but
cottages and little gardens. The 15th century Clock Gate, or
*Porte de l'Horloge,* is an interesting relic of the town-walls.
Downstream from the town, the Verzée swells out into another
lake called the *étang de Tressé*. A few miles farther on you are
out of Anjou and into Brittany.

### The Finest Romanesque Building in all Touraine

**P**REUILLY-SUR-CLAISE. The Church of Saint-Pierre, at
Preuilly-sur-Claise, is one of the principal sights of all
Touraine, and must be held to be the finest Romanesque edifice
in the province. It has, unfortunately, been over-restored, but as
it is, the church is most noteworthy.

It was, originally, part of a monastery founded about the year 1000 by a certain Effroy. However, the existing building is not, in its oldest parts, more ancient than the beginning of the eleven hundreds. The belfry is modern.

Inside, the church appears of noble proportions. It is about 180 feet long and, as is usual in Romanesque buildings, not very lofty for the length, being only some fifty-five feet high, but the general effect is one of archaic impressiveness. The nave consists of five bays rising to a barrel-vaulted roof. The side-aisles are very narrow. The capitals of the columns are sculptured, in many cases, with representations of historical events. The sanctuary is encircled by an ambulatory, and there is a lady chapel at the east end. Huysmans, the French writer who loved Preuilly, used to say that if its choir is not in exactly the same axis as the nave that was because the building represented Christ dying on the Cross and because Preuilly symbolised also the ever-suffering Church.

The Church of Saint-Pierre is not only interesting in itself, as a fine monument, but also as showing a transition between the Romanesque styles of Touraine to the north and of Poitou to the south.

Adjoining the presbytery is a 15th century chapter-house, which has not been too much "reconstructed." Behind the church is the hospice that was, formerly, the city-manor of La Rallière, dating, as it now stands, to the sixteen and seventeen hundreds.

The abundance of what may be called "town-manors (which are often fully-fledged *châteaux*) in the cities and even villages of France is often puzzling to the modern observer, but, in most cases, the towns of France grew up as an amalgamation of more than one fief. Each manor collected around it its own dependants, whose houses linked up with those of another fief, and gave, thus, an appearance of unity to a settlement really made up of different "holdings." In this way, and until the Revolution swept away the traces of old property-tenure, the towns of France grew, not as units, but as a conglomeration of fiefs and manors each ruled by its own lord and governed by its own usages (see p. 2).

Preuilly is rather a picturesque little place, of under two thousand inhabitants, whose dwellings cover a natural amphitheatre stepped back from the right bank of the river Claise. Up on the crest of the hills are the ruins of the feudal fortress of the old barons of Preuilly. Lower down the slope, the town hall is an interesting late 16th or early 17th century building. The Romanesque collegiate Church of Saint-Melaine is in ruins, but one is inclined to think none the worse for that, since the edifice is untouched, unrestored and still impressive in its typically Angevin style of Romanesque, which it is interesting to compare with the transition architecture of Saint-Pierre.

Not far from Preuilly lies Bossay on the Claise, with still another Romanesque church. The nearby Castle of Ris has walls which in part are of 13th century workmanship. The fine white wines of Bossay are little known outside Touraine, but they are delicious.

## Prime Minister for Three Days

NEAR Preuilly was born Louis Charles Auguste Le Tonnelier, *baron* de Breteuil, who occupied various diplomatic posts, until in 1783 he was appointed by Louis XVI Minister of the King's Household, and in 1789—fateful year of the Revolution—chief Minister in succession to the Swiss financier Necker (father of Madame de Staël). This was on the 11th July, 1789. On the 14th July the Bastille fell and Breteuil with it. He had been Prime Minister of France for three days.

Breteuil was one of the first to emigrate, and until the Queen's execution he was active in the diplomacy of the exiled princes of the Royal House. After the death of Marie-Antoinette, Breteuil took no further part in politics. He returned to France in 1802, and died in Paris five years later.

## The Virgin's Girdle

LE PUY-NOTRE-DAME. The Girdle of the Virgin is a piece of Oriental stuff, mixed linen and silk, over four and a half feet long, and only very slightly over an inch and a half wide. The relic is enclosed in a triple sheath with two locks of gold engraved with the Annunciation and shields of the blazon of France. Two circular openings, set with crystal, afford a peep at part of the precious girdle. The relic is said to have been brought from the Holy Land during the Crusades, and to have the property of assuaging the pangs of child-birth. When she was expecting to be delivered of the infant who, afterwards, was known as Louis XIV, Anne of Austria had the Holy Girdle brought in great state to the Castle of Saint-Germain-en-Laye where she lay.

In 1482, Louis XI founded at Le Puy-Notre-Dame, and in honour of the Girdle, a chapter of canons. To this day, on the Sunday following the 8th September, the Girdle is displayed to the veneration of the faithful who flock to Le Puy in pilgrimage.

Le Puy-Notre-Dame lies about six miles from Doué-la-Fontaine, on the Montreuil-Bellay road, and the *puy* (that is, hill) overlooks a fertile upland, on which are grown excellent vines, making a renowned vintage and adding not a little to the edification of pilgrimage.

The town was formerly known as Le Puy-en-Anjou, and was a fortress until 1784. The church is one of the finest examples in existence of the style known as Angevin. The west front, decorated with three rows of arcades, is flanked by two rectangular turrets ending in stone steeples, while a larger tower, rebuilt in the 15th century, and terminating in an octagonal spire, adjoins the south transept.

The side-aisles' vaults are as high as those of the nave (as is usual in the Angevin style), and from the south side of the church give four chambers. The one under the tower is 13th century, the three others about a hundred years younger. The sacristy, opening from the end of the south transept, has a Renaissance door of splendid carvings. The largest of the chambers, at the angle of the nave and south transept, shows a very fine vaulted ceiling of a type characteristic of the 13th century architecture in Anjou.

Near the church are some remains of the former priory.

## The Road to Richelieu

RICHELIEU. As you go farther south in France from the line of the Loire valley, you will think that each dale marks a transition to a climate more clement and to a countryside more kind. On the southern side of the Vienne river the country is less hilly than back beyond Chinon. As you run along the Île-Bouchard road you will see on the right the most intriguing "Sleeping Beauty" *château* imaginable. From the road bites back into the ploughed fields a great square of high trees enclosed within tall walls. Through the wood is a fairly broad avenue, revealing, at its end, a bold, dark-grey keep of small slits and inconspicuous windows. The contrast between the archaic grimness of the dwelling and the gracious greenery of the trees is almost startling.

Soon we touch the Veude stream, barred at one point by an immense and antique mill lying diagonally across the water.

The vale of the Veude seems very southern, not only because it is soft, but principally because there is apparently no great contrast between the southern softness of the valley and that of the enclosing hills you glimpse through tall poplars. The heights glow even in quite late autumn, and the verdure has a bluish tinge, reminding you of the hill-country of Tuscany. From time to time slips by an elegant image of a pink-brick and white-stone house in the true tradition of Touraine.

After Champigny-sur-Veude you are in the Richelieu country. The land is all chalk. It was not the sort of region to have attracted our remote ancestors when they needed caves, but there are plenty of megalithic monuments hereabouts, showing that in New Stone Age times this was already a fairly thickly populated area. The Normans did not get as far south as this except upon marauding raids, and the country, from having originally been dependent on the Counts of Poitou and then on those of Touraine, passed under the control of the Counts of Anjou and from them to their descendants, our Plantagenet Kings of England.

## Mr. "Wakedog" and Miss "Wildboar"

TOWARDS the end of the fifteenth century one François Duplessis married a lady with an odd name. She was called Regnée Eveillechien, or "Wakedog," and her mother's maiden name was Marie Sanglier, or "Wildboar." We have not yet reached the point when all the landed gentry of France disguised themselves under high-sounding territorial surnames. Now this Marie Sanglier, after her husband's death, married Louis de Clérembault, the descendant of a squire who in 1436 had received royal permission to fortify his little house of Richeloc, or Richelieu, which his family had purchased a generation or two before.

About 1486 Louis de Clérembault, who had no children of his own, left his estate of Richeloc to the husband of his wife's daughter by her first marriage. Thus did the family of Duplessis become possessed of the Richelieu that they were to render world-famous. There are, in Touraine alone, about fifty places called "Plessis," that is, the "Enclosure," but the village from which the Duplessis de Richelieu took their name is situated near Néon (or Néans), on the right bank of the river Creuse, some forty miles to the south-east of Richelieu.

The Duplessis de Richelieu were not a very distinguished lot. One of them, Antoine, acquired some notoriety in leading the Tours mob in a massacre of Protestants. Another, François, the Cardinal's father, was captain of King Henri III's bodyguard.

## Duplessis de Richelieu

THIS François got some fortune with his wife Suzanne de La Porte, the daughter of a Paris lawyer—a person not at all of the "landed gentry" class, and the Cardinal was always very sensitive about the "nobility" of his stock, since the cruel pasquinades of his day never let him forget the humble associations of his mother's kinsfolk. One contemporary exclaimed, on seeing the great man pass in to some ceremony just after the King, "I never thought to see the grandson of old scrivener La Porte walk ahead of the Emperor Charles V's grandson."

François Duplessis died young. His children were left in the charge of their capable mother, whose principal financial resources (apart from her own dowry and the petty revenues of the Richelieu estates) came from the Bishopric of Luçon (the poorest see in France), nominations to which had been accorded to the Duplessis by the King as a reward for services rendered.

## A Crazy Family

HENRY, the eldest son, was killed in a duel, and his will was set aside on the grounds of the testator's madness. Alphonse, the second, who rose to be Cardinal-Archbishop of Lyons, a man of a morose temperament, was persuaded, from time to time, that he was God the Father. At other moments he would give balls, masques and routes, at which he would appear disguised as a sprightly shepherd, while the pious ladies of Lyons society danced around him.

Françoise, the most normal member of the family, made an obscure marriage with one Vignerod, Vignerot or Wignerod, by whom she was the ancestress of the later *ducs* de Richelieu. Françoise, a woman of strong character, was the Cardinal's favourite. It was the younger daughter Nicolle who married Urbain de Maillé and died raving mad in Saumur castle (see p. 56).

## The Great Lord Cardinal

THE great Cardinal himself was not only one of the most remarkable statesmen France has ever known, but he was also an unpleasant sort of man, highly suspicious, touchy, testy and cantankerous. It is almost certain that he was tuberculous, and he also possessed a most unecclesiastically ardent temperament.

Like most men of melancholy stamp, he enjoyed the diversions of clowns, masks, buffoons, jesters and the like, in whose antics he sought some alleviation from his migraines, rheumatism, abscesses and the hundred other ills which plagued him. And he was not above the superstitions of his day. He observed dates and seasons as clement or inclement. He did not disdain magic and charms. Dressed up in green velvet, and clacking castanets, he had, in his youth, danced sarabands to amuse the famous Florentine adventuress, Galigaï, the favourite of Marie de' Medici. And Richelieu found it quite natural that the Italian should poultice her head with the bleeding bodies of pigeons and cocks as a remedy against the evil eye.

And the great Cardinal kept strange hours. He would retire to bed about eleven o'clock, and sink into a fitful, feverish sleep until two or three in the morning. Then he would have papers brought to him, and set to work until about six, when he would doze off into a dream-haunted slumber for an hour or two.

The regular treatment inflicted upon him by his physicians included bleeding once or twice a week and purging every day. There is little wonder that he died of tuberculosis at the age of fifty-seven. There is no wonder also that he did not suffer fools gladly or even that he was quite mad on one or two occasions and for a short time imagined that he was a horse.

But we may remember that, all-powerful minister as he was, Richelieu depended for his position upon the whim of a monarch who might, had he felt so inclined, have discarded him at any moment.

Richelieu's was an all-important influence on the history of France. He made France the First Power in the world. He stabilised the monarchy, and set the French upon the road they were to tread until 1789 and even later. His figure is hardly one of charm, but it is one without an appreciation of which all of the story of France from his time onwards is a little incomprehensible.

## *Le Magnifique Chasteau de Richelieu*

THE Great Lord Cardinal, whose revenues for years exceeded three millions of *livres*—a colossal sum for the time—was set upon the magnification of his family, and the history of the great palace he built and of the town he created is instructive.

By 1612 the fortunes of the Duplessis family had sunk so low that Richelieu was seized by creditors and put up for sale. Alphonse (the ecclesiastic who imagined that he was God Almighty) bought the family property for seventy-nine thousand *livres*. No great sum—perhaps three thousand pounds gold.

By 1625 Richelieu was already thinking of great buildings, and had ordered Jacques Le Mercier, the architect, to submit designs for a palace and a town.

The palace, graced with the work of the leading painters, sculptors and decorators of the day, was stuffed with precious things.

Although the man who had commanded the marvels never beheld his palace or his town, *le magnifique chasteau de Richelieu* ("the magnificent Castle of Richelieu") soon became one of the leading sights of all France.

## *The Fall of the House of Richelieu*

THE later history of Richelieu is a melancholy one. The *duc* de Richelieu at the time of the Revolution "emigrated." His lands were duly confiscated. This *duc* had a varied career. He was Governor-General of New Russia and founder of Odessa for the Emperor of Russia. At the Restoration he was twice Prime Minister of France.

In 1792 the furniture of Richelieu *château* was valued at 28,015 *livres* 6 *sols*. Most of the contents of the mansion had already been stolen or sold. In 1793 the furniture was revalued at 14,411 *livres*. The pillaging of the "great house" is of course a regular local sport whenever occasion arises. As the *duc's* two sisters had remained in France, they were able to plead that they had an interest in the property, and eventually the First Republic awarded them one-third of Richelieu revenues. In 1805 the estate was carved up and sold in lots for a total of about twenty thousand pounds gold. The house became the property of one Boutron and was dismantled. A certain F. R. de Quinson, who had bought Champigny as *bien national* or national property, acquired Richelieu park.

Napoleon thought, at one time, of giving Richelieu to one of his marshals, but the experts sent down to examine the place reported it was in such bad repair that the cost of repairing it would be prohibitive. So the pillage and destruction went on, and by 1835 Richelieu was in ruins. Boutron died in 1843, and then the palace was razed to the ground. So nothing but the entrance and an odd outbuilding or two survive to remind the visitor of Richelieu's glories.

The title of *duc* de Richelieu was confirmed to M. Chapelle de Jumilhac, son of the last *duc's* sister, and from him the later Richelieus are descended.

## A Place Vendôme in Touraine

THE borough of Richelieu, unlike the palace, remains untouched and unique. It is, indeed, one of the most curious monuments in France. It is a section, a slice, or a quarter of 17th century Paris cut out, as it were, enclosed by a wall, and dumped on to the Poitou countryside.

Until the time of the Cardinal, the village that had given him his name was nothing but a hamlet, but in 1631 it was made the centre and seat of his *duché-pairie*.

## Dukes and Peers

WE often have occasion to refer to *duché-pairies* or "duchy-peerages," and the old French peerage was a thing so different from the English peerage that a word or two about the former may be useful.

Titles under the *old régime* were attached to properties. The old saying was, "No nobility without a title and no title without land." Anyone technically a "noble" (the clearest proof of which status was exemption from paying the tax known as the *taille*), who acquired an estate carrying with it a marquisate or a barony, might assume the title of such lands. On the other hand, men were not created counts, barons or marquises, but their lands were "raised" to the status of *comté, baronnie* or *marquisat,* and strictly such men or their descendants could only enjoy these titles while they were still in possession of the fief giving them their titles.

The French peerage of the *old régime* (not to be confounded with the Restoration peerage that was modelled on that of England and membership of which gave a seat in the Upper House of Parliament) was mostly confined to dukes, and yet not all dukes were peers. The peers were held to represent the leaders of the nobility, and moreover, they became associated in a vague and constantly disputed fashion with the *parlement* of Paris (a quasi-legislative or law-enregistering and directly judicial body) while remaining a sort of standing committee of the whole (and most numerous) body of "nobles." It was the great ambition of the famous memorialist, the *duc* de Saint-Simon, to secure for the peers recognition as a sort of Grand Council of the nation. Of course, he did not succeed. The old absolutist monarchy had no use for grand councils of any sort or kind. So, as a matter of fact, the dignity of a French peer remained honorific without even carrying with it as much privilege as did that of Spanish grandees.

The common French proverb, *comme un pair de France,* referring to someone very prosperous and sumptuously housed or equipped, may date back to the time of the old pre-revolutionary "peers," but is probably a relic from the days of the legislative "peers" of the Restoration and of Louis Philippe's time.

## Richelieu Town

THE little town of Richelieu does not hold more than seventeen hundred inhabitants, and it is shrunken within its high walls. The place is a rectangle, measuring about two thousand two hundred feet long by some sixteen hundred feet wide, and the moat is fed by the little river Mable which has been twisted to flow round the walls. Permission was granted by Letters Patent to the Cardinal in 1631 to build a *bourg clos de murailles et fosses*—a town enclosed by walls and moat—and six monumental entrances gave access to the borough. The *grand' rue* or main street (that is, a section of the *route nationale* or national highway No. 749) cuts through Richelieu from north to south. You cross a bridge, pass under the high gateway, and find yourself in a street of lofty private houses of a size and appearance that would grace the *faubourg Saint-Germain* in Paris.

Le Mercier was the architect of the town, as he has been of the *château*, and the Cardinal forced his hangers-on and toadies to pay for the twenty-eight great *hôtels* of the main street. The men of the Cardinal's Court were most unwilling to sink their gains in a God-forsaken provincial hole like Richelieu, but they had to obey orders. No. 17, the house known as that of the *sénéchal* (i.e. the steward or major-domo of the Richelieu duchy estates), is particularly fine and can be visited.

The main street cuts through two small squares, each of which is bisected by a transversal street. The houses in the side-streets are rather smaller than those of the main street, but everywhere in the town the buildings are fine, and there are no cottages or mean dwellings to be seen.

In the northern square are the buildings of the former Academy or Royal College founded by the Cardinal in 1640. He did everything he could think of to enhance the importance of his town and to attract population thereto. The neighbouring place of Loudun was deposed from being *chef-lieu d'élection* (this democratic-sounding title merely covered the local tax-gatherer's organisation), and the *grenier à sel*, or Government salt-monopoly store, was removed from Mirabeau to Richelieu.

But even in the days of its glory Richelieu never held more than six thousand inhabitants.

The southern square, or *place du marché*, contains a fine 17th century covered market-place, the town hall and the classical, urban and sober church that Le Mercier conceived in what is sometimes called the "Jesuit" style.

Nothing seems to have changed at Richelieu. There have been no repairs, no ameliorations, no restorations. Richelieu has remained intact, because it served no purpose at all except that of glorifying the memory of the great Cardinal and that of providing visitors to Touraine with one of their most satisfying impressions.

But the Richelieu countryside is rich, and if you come here on market-days you will see the fat poultry, the luscious beans and the fine apples for which this corner of Touraine is noted. And the horse-fairs are famous.

The old *hôtel du Faisan*, in the *place du marché*, is not only a pleasing place, but you can eat there the excellent fare of Touraine, just merging into Poitou, and drink the wines of Brézé.

You leave by the south gate on the Châtellerault road. Across a semicircular space, set with a statue of the Cardinal, are the wrought-iron gates of the "*chasteau*" park. It is large for France —about twelve hundred acres—but of the magnificent castle nothing remains but one small pavilion, two hot-houses and the moat. Of the place's splendours we can get some idea from the famous marble table that, with Michelangelo's group of the two chained slaves, is now in the Louvre.

Perhaps the best comment upon Richelieu town was that made by the fabulist La Fontaine, who gave his impressions of the great Cardinal's fief in a series of epistles in verse addressed to Madame La Fontaine:

> "*Enfin, elle est à mon avis,*
> *Mal située et bien bâtie.*
> *On en a fait tous les logis*
> *D'une pareille symétrie.*"

> ("*So, in my opinion, the place*
> *Is well built in a bad site,*
> *And all the houses have been*
> *Made exactly alike.*")

## A Mysterious Manor

LA ROCHE-EN-MÉZANGERS. The Maine Hills that mark the border between the departments of the Sarthe and the Mayenne merge into a great plain, limited and bordered to the south and the west by the Forests of Charnie and Hermet. Then you come to the imposing little fortress-town of Sainte-Suzanne.

Here and there on this plain you catch a glimpse of old grey walls through the thickets, or see sharp-pointed roofs rise above the trees. The sight of the country, however, is La Roche-en-Mézangers, about a thousand yards west of the village of Mézangers and two miles from the town of Evron. The *château* du Rocher or La Roche-en-Mézangers is a mysterious place. You make your way through dark woods, and you see nothing of the house until you come upon a mere whose broad waters mirror majestic towers and walls.

The oldest part may date back to the 15th century, when the property was in the possession of the Bouillé family. The southern face and the chapel are apparently of the late fourteen hundreds. The rich Renaissance façade—comparable with those of Chenonceau or the *Hôtel* d'Escoville at Caen—and the charming ground-floor gallery are 16th century work.

You can let fancy play in this secret retreat which evokes some of the most exciting periods of France's history.

Whether we look at the massive, yet somehow graceful façade dropping sheer into the lake, and its splay-footed towers reflected in the placid waters, or whether we stand on the court terrace admiring the harmonious jumble of Gothic, feudal, Renaissance and wholly French styles, we shall not soon wish to move away from La Roche-en-Mézangers. It is one of the places where you want to walk, perhaps alone, with a book that stimulates rather than absorbs, and close the book often and let your imagination roam up and down the years.

## *The Green Lady*

ELÉONORE-RENÉE DE BOUILLÉ, the heiress of La Roche-en-Mézangers, wife of Henry de Daillon, *marquis* d'Illiers, sold the place to her sister's husband. This Eléonore-Renée, generally known as the *duchesse* du Lude, figures once or twice in Madame de Sévigné's letters. The *duchesse* was a masculine sort of woman, of a kind, perhaps, rarer at all times in France than in Spain or with us. It is not that the French have ever lacked virile women, but, generally speaking, the French women manage rather cunningly to hide their forcefulness. Eléonore-Renée was a hard rider to hounds, and a harsh, hard and obstinate creature. She is reported to have followed on horseback her hounds into the Benedictine Church at Estival, and to have proffered no excuses nor to have expressed any regrets for so unlady-like and, indeed, so sacrilegious an act. She also thrashed a peasant to death who had inadvertently caused her horse to stumble. In fact, a great Lady of the Old School.

There is a portrait of her in the castle, and it shows an uninviting face. She must have been rather unattractive and perhaps, therefore, malevolent. As the "Green Lady" she is said to haunt La Roche-en-Mézangers. Perhaps as the light fails we may see her, as Madame de Sévigné describes her, a bony woman "with a grey hat jammed down over her ears, and striding along switching a riding-whip."

## The Wines of Southern Anjou

ROCHEFORT-SUR-LOIRE. Rochefort is an agreeable little place, standing in more broken country than Savennières across the Loire on the north bank. Again, here the countryside is set with *châteaux* and manors, but the end all and be all of Rochefort is wine. The southern-bank Anjou vintages that are most sought after are: *Quart de Chaumes* [which, when real, is excellent, but the name often means as little as "Beaujolais" on a bottle], the *Bellerive* of Rochefort, and the wines of Rablay. A *Château-de-Bellerive 1921* is one of the most noble of all vintages. There is a whole string of secondary growths—Saint-Aubin-de-Luigné, Martigné-Briand, Faye and others. In fine years—"good" years—they are all splendid, but it is wise to take expert advice before embarking upon unknown *crus* or vintages.

Rochefort, by the wooded banks of the Louet stream, has an excellent inn, where you will be served with the traditional Angevin suavity and grace. The Angevins are a little slow, perhaps, much given to the drinking of their own wines (one reason why there is so little good Anjou wine out of Anjou is that the Angevins drink most of their products themselves!), but they are a charming people. Anjou is, in fact, one of those rather surprising places where the mass of the people is thoroughly civilised and just a little old-fashioned, for which we may be thankful. You will come across girls with the faces and figures of 13th century statues and men of pre-Revolutionary nobility of feature and bearing.

Between Rochefort and Chalonnes runs the so-called *corniche angevine* or cliff-drive. It is a pretty highway half-way up the hill-side and overlooking the boundless Loire valley.

Chalonnes-sur-Loire has a much-restored 12th and 15th century church. At Chalonnes the Loire breaks up into four arms, embracing an archipelago of little islets joined to each other and to the main banks by bridges. It is a suitable place to stop and have luncheon on the way to Lower Brittany or the Vendée.

## A Curious Woman

LA ROCHE-PICHEMÈRE. Catherine de Cervon, wife of the Lord of La Roche-Pichemère, was a woman of an inquiring, though somewhat callous, turn of mind. She was interested in what was in those days known as "natural history" and, on one occasion, had a peasant and a bullock tied together and kept without food or water so that she might observe which would die first. She also indulged in other peculiarities of conduct, gaining a reputation for cruelty and debauchery. Popular legend, ever ready to wreak poetic justice, has it that, as the "Red Lady," the ghost of Catherine de Cervon haunts the corridors and chambers of La Roche-Pichemère. But the "Red Lady" is rather a modern ghost, since Catherine died only in 1724—at a ripe old age.

Catherine's daughter-in-law, when left a widow, married morganatically Louis Philippe d'Orléans, the father (by his first wife) of the famous "Philippe Egalité."

La Roche-Pichemère still retains some feudal features, but the house was remodelled about 1560 by Louis du Plessis. His grandson, known as the *marquis* de Jarzé, was a great ladies' man, and he cut something of a figure at the Court of Louis XIII. When, however, he started to make love to the Queen, Anne of Austria, the Regent, Mazarin, who considered the Queen's affections were his special care, swiftly cut in and exiled Jarzé (ruined in any case by his gay Court life) to his crumbling manor of La Roche-Pichemère. The place was sold in 1645 to the Jean-Baptiste de Montesson, who was the husband of the "Red Lady."

The interior of La Roche is attractive enough. The ceilings have bold rafters in the Louis XIII style, and there is fine early 16th century panelling, with motifs of flowers and fruit. The chimney in the library is magnificent, with cabochon inlays of rose and black marble in white stone.

In one of the saloons the wood panelling is painted with coats-of-arms in a manner common enough in English Inns of Court or university colleges, but rare in France—the result at La Roche-Pichemère is not wholly a happy one.

## Montsurs

WHEN on the Évron–Laval highway you have passed Brée, you reach Montsurs, that was in the Middle Ages a barony of the

Counts of Laval. On an isolated hill nearly four hundred feet high lie the crumbling ruins of the old castle, burned by the English in 1430. Twenty years before, within its walls was born André de Laval, *maréchal* and *connétable* of France, and one of the most valiant companions-in-arms of Joan of Arc. To-day, in the cellars and ruined lower chambers of the old fortress, live a few poor outcasts. . . .

La Roche-Pichemère is two miles away to the north.

## A Pastoral Poet

LA ROCHE-RACAN. Racan's figure is an attractive, if rather pathetic one, and his poetry is of some importance, not only for its intrinsic merits, but also as marking a phase of French literary development.

Honnorat de Bueil, *marquis* de Racan, was born at Aubigné-Racan in 1589, and when only sixteen years of age was left an orphan with a very embarrassed estate; indeed, Henry IV granted him letters-patent protecting him from his creditors for two years. Luckily one of his cousins had married the *duc* de Bellegarde, Master of the Horse, and young Bueil was introduced to Court and then received a commission in the army. In Paris Bueil got to know Malherbe, one of whose most devoted disciples he became. He had had, like so many of the lesser gentry of his day, a wretched education, and took Malherbe's advice on a career. This advice was presented in the form of the famous poem known as *Le Meunier, son fils et l'âne.*

Tallemant des Réaux, always spiteful, pilloried Bueil in the *Historiettes.* According to Tallemant, apart from his poetic gifts, Bueil (or Racan as he is generally called) had no sense at all. He looked like a farmer, stuttered, and could not pronounce his own name, since "*r*'s" and "*c*'s" were the letters he had the most trouble with. Tallemant's *Histoire des Trois Racan* is a masterpiece of rather cruel satire.

In later life Racan married an Anjou woman, on the advice of his cousin Madame de Bellegarde, who left him some money. In fact, Racan's later years were comparatively prosperous, but, as so often happens, when things went well for his pocket they did not go so well for his pen. In fact, Racan dried up. When he was poor, amorous and often, because poor, unhappy in love, Racan

**Le Plessis-Bourré**                    **The Drawbridge**

The Castle

*Notre-Dame de Nantilly*

Cattle Market

The Town Hall

Military Tournament

The Town Hall

**SAUMUR**

wrote charming poetry. As a squire in Touraine he sought to immortalise himself by building.

La Roche-Racan, quite near Semblançay (La Roche was formerly called La Roche-au-Majeur—Racan gave it its present name), was rebuilt. He pulled down neither the towers nor the sturdy walls of the old fortress, but on the old foundations he put up a new residence composed of a central wing (with a gallery below and one storey with attics) and two lateral wings. Only one wing now remains. Racan wrote, "I wished in my buildings to leave a proof that I had existed." Poor Racan's *château*, or what remains of it, makes a brave show, its white walls and octagonal tower backing on a wooded hill and looking over an elegantly balustraded terrace on to the right bank of the Escotais stream.

No one remembers his castle now, though his memory is still alive as that of one of France's charming minor poets. Although Racan wrote (or at least published) nothing for twenty years after Malherbe's death, the Lord of La Roche-Racan was elected one of the founder members of the French Academy. But the old man was bewildered and baffled by the new Paris he saw. His friends were dead. Manners had changed. Customs were different. The very spoken language was strange, and Racan hurried back to his Touraine.

Racan's verse, at its best, is delightful, suave in manner and full of sentiment. He sang of his countryside, of his own invincible melancholy, of his long meditations, of his solitary walks in the lovely land of Touraine.

> ". . . au long de ses fontaines,
> De qui les petits flots font luire dans les plaines
> L'argent de leurs ruisseaux parmi l'or des moissons."

> ("Beside the springs
> Whose wavelets twinkle in the plains
> The silver of their streams among the harvest gold. . . .")

## One of the Most Powerful Baronies of Maine

SABLÉ-SUR-SARTHE. As you approach Sablé, the scene is very picturesque—the broad road narrows to the bridge, and before you, on a spacious terrace backed by wooded heights, stands the great square mass of Sablé *château*, a splendid early 18th century building, surrounded by a fine park, and overlooking the Sarthe at a point where the Erve and the Vaige fall into the larger stream. Sablé house was built by Colbert "de Torcy," nephew of the famous minister of Louis XIV. The place now belongs to Monsieur Williot, who has transformed part of it into a chicory factory. It is best to admire the *château* from a distance.

Sablé town huddles under the terrace of its great house, and offers little to the visitor but a very fine 16th century stained-glass window representing the Passion. This light was brought from the old church and set up in the modern building.

Sablé was, from the 11th century, the seat of one of the most powerful baronies in the province of Maine. On the 20th April, 1488, was sealed at Sablé the treaty between Charles VIII of France and François II, Duke of Brittany, whereby the latter engaged himself not to marry off his daughters and heiresses without the permission of the French king, who then gave the permission to himself and wedded Anne of Brittany, thus gaining the duchy.

Sablé was formerly the centre of a certain amount of anthracite mining which was carried on by Benedictine monks for many years in the Middle Ages. Although the mines have been, of late, neglected, their coal was extensively worked until the end of the last century and in order to feed the local lime-kilns. But the marble quarries are still active. Between Juigné and Sablé the Sarthe flows at the foot of the glossy black marble rocks of Port-Etroit.

## The Sin of Witchcraft

AT Rovère, near Sablé, was born in 1590 a man whose name recalls the most curious case of "witchcraft" and "possession" known in 17th century France. Spanish history, and that of some other lands, is checkered, here and there, with strange stories of hysterical nuns, enchantments and sorcery, but in France wizardry has been rather rare though now and again the newspapers tell a strange tale of witchcraft from some remote province.

Urbain Grandier was the son of a royal notary, and he was educated by the Jesuits at Bordeaux. Soon after he had been ordained he was appointed vicar of the Church of St. Pierre at Loudun, a town, though in Poitou, not far from Richelieu. And

the position of Loudun as a neighbouring town to Richelieu had
a good deal of bearing on the sad tale of poor Urbain Grandier's
misfortunes.

After a few years as vicar of his parish, Urbain was preferred
to a canonry in the collegiate Church of Sainte-Croix, also at
Loudun. Urbain, as the saying is, had everything in his favour.
He was an excellent preacher, he was good-looking and of fine
presence, he was popular with his congregation—and especially
with the ladies—he was an amusing conversationalist and he was
endowed with a pleasant wit. But though he was clever and intelligent, he was never clever nor intelligent enough to hide his
cleverness and intelligence. In fact, he made a good many
enemies among the duller inhabitants of Loudun and especially
among the Carmelite monks, whose privileges and pretensions he
did not hesitate to attack and to make fun of in his sermons.
Moreover, he was of a somewhat haughty demeanour, and did not
suffer fools gladly. That is to say, he was riding for a fall in a
stuffy, humdrum little borough. Soon it was rumoured that he had
leanings towards Protestantism, that he was too fond of feminine
society, that he maintained a young lady called Madeleine de Brou
in his house, and that he was a truculent and dangerous man. He
does, indeed, seem to have been indiscreet, for he fell foul of his
Bishop, My Lord of Poitiers, and in 1630 he was condemned by
the ecclesiastical courts to suspension for five years, to the loss
of his benefice, to perpetual banishment from Loudun, and to eat
and drink nothing but bread and water every Friday for three
years.

Urbain appealed against the sentence and successfully. His
metropolitan, the Archbishop of Bordeaux, reinstated him in his
canonry at Sainte-Croix. Urbain should have learned his lesson,
but he belonged to the not small class of men who become more and
not less headstrong when, by good luck or good management, they
have "got away with it."

In 1626 a Ursuline convent had been established at Loudun,
and the nuns were what is known as "young ladies of good
family," and this fact, that the Loudun Ursulines were drawn
from the more privileged social groups, is of importance. We may
take it that most of these nuns were young women induced, for
family reasons, to take the veil. Putting surplus, undowered or

otherwise troublesome daughters into nunneries was a regular practice in pre-Revolutionary France—as in other lands. Such girls were, as a rule, far from feeling any vocation, and they were also often less amenable to discipline than poor peasant wenches or older and more subdued persons.

Anyway, when the Ursulines set up their establishment at Loudun, Urbain put in for the job as their spiritual director. He did not get it. In fact, a fellow-canon, one Mignon, was appointed, and Mignon was a personal enemy of the handsome Urbain. Later chroniclers of the Grandier story have, of course, attributed to him the basest motives for wanting the job at the convent, but there is no reason to suppose that he was aiming at anything else but a piece of professional preferment.

Now we come to the heart of the matter. In October 1632 the strangest rumours began to get about in Loudun. Ghosts had been seen in the convent. The nuns become very agitated, and some of them were showing clear signs of demoniacal "possession." The regular exorcisms seemed to do no good. It was whispered that they had been bewitched, and indeed that they had been the victims of Urbain Grandier's sorceries. The only sorcery the poor man ever exercised seems to have been that of his considerable charm that women found very fascinating.

Things got to such a pitch that Urbain very ill-advisedly brought a suit for defamation before the ecclesiastical court of the Bishop of Poitiers.

While the suit was pending, there turned up at Loudun one Laubardement, Councillor of State and creature of Richelieu. Laubardement's job at Loudun was to superintend the destruction and dismantlement of the old castle in accordance with the royal edict of Louis XIII, whereby all castles and fortresses except those on the coast were to be "slighted." Urbain Grandier's enemies at once seized upon Richelieu's envoy as a person to get them out of possible trouble. Urbain was accused of having written a scandalous lampoon on Richelieu and his family. The "*Cordonnière de Loudun*," as the piece was called, was a poor production, violently defamatory and wretchedly written. Now, Richelieu was sensitive to the numerous anonymous libels that assailed him during nearly all his career, and he was especially touchy when his family was attacked. The Cardinal did not like being reminded of his own idiosyncrasies nor of the fact that one of his sisters and both his brothers were crazy. When Laubardement went back to Paris, it was with a full report on Urbain's case, and when he returned to Loudun, in December 1633, it was with orders to arrest the canon pending investigation of his case.

The list of Urbain's misdeeds was long. He was accused of immorality and even of scandalously unbecoming conduct in his own church; but the real damning accusation was that he had thrown a bewitched sprig of a rose-bush over the convent wall, a sprig endowed with such diabolical properties that any nun touching it would immediately become possessed of a devil and do Urbain's bidding.

It would not appear, however, that the hysterical nuns displayed all or any of the canonical sure signs of "possession," that are divination, comprehension and command of languages not learned in the normal, mundane way, and monstrous or extraordinary strength of body.

The Mother-Superior had, indeed, it would seem, mumbled some Latin, but it was dog-Latin. The "instruction," or hearing of the evidence before the case was sent for trial, took months and aroused great excitement. Two bold spirits, Mark Duncan, a Scottish physician in practice at Saumur, and one, Claude Quillet, ventured to protest against the whole proceedings. Duncan was dressed down by Richelieu himself and Quillet found it prudent to leave France.

The devils who tortured the Loudun nuns had made known their names through the mouths of their victims, and the evidence of the devils was solemnly taken by the court. There was "Astaroth of the Order of the Seraphim, Chief of the Loudun region," and "Asmodée, Leviathan, Béhémoth, Elimi, Aman, Edzas, Grésil, Zabulon, Uriel, Nephthalin, Céon" . . . and others. The diabolical host had descended on Loudun in force.

Meanwhile, Laubardement had again been to court, and had been entrusted by Richelieu in 1634 with letters-patent constituting to try Urbain Grandier, an extraordinary tribunal of twelve judges drawn from the law courts of different towns in Anjou and Tourain.

Nothing had been found at his lodging in Loudun that might incriminate him except the MS. of a book against the celibacy of the clergy, and not much could be made of this effusion, since clerical celibacy is a discipline of the Church and not a doctrine. But Urbain was charged with magic, witchcraft and sorcery, and condemned to be burned alive. Even under torture, applied to force a confession of "confederates," Urbain would only admit some backslidings due to "human frailty."

In the 17th century it had become the custom to strangle prisoners condemned to burning, and that before the fire was lit, but Urbain's enemies pursued him to the end. It was found that there was a knot in the rope, so that it could not be drawn tight, and the unfortunate Urbain was slowly burned in agony.

The demons did not, however, flee when Urbain was sacrificed. Several eminent exorcists had to try their hands before the devils would release their prey. "Leviathan," the demon who had taken up his abode in the Mother-Superior's head, was only expelled on the 5th November, 1635. "Béhémoth," the most persistent of all, lingered until towards the end of 1637.

The Good Old Times.

## The Lily in the Valley

SACHÉ. After you leave Azay-le-Rideau and move up the valley of the Indre, the countryside is one of freshness and sweetness. This is the enchanted landscape of Balzac's most poignant tale, *Le Lys dans la Vallée*. You can hardly pass this way without being haunted by the image of Madame de Mortsauf. And at no time is this lovely dale more enthralling than during those mauve twilights that last so long in the Touraine summer and autumn.

Opposite the *château* de Saché, where Balzac stayed often from 1829 to 1837, is the *château* de Chevrière, that is, the "Cloche-gourde" of the book. We know that its mistress, Madame de Berny, was, in a measure, the model of Madame de Mortsauf.

The "Lily in the Valley" is, of all Balzac's works, the one which time has dealt most kindly with. When we reflect that Balzac was a man of thirty-six years of age when he made this masterpiece, and that in it he wrote pages breathing the very spirit of first love with its violences, its reticences, its timidities, its self-deception, its immense sincerity, its selfishness and its self-sacrifice, we can see clearly enough, when we reflect on these things, that Balzac must be accounted one of the greatest of writers. The man who could write, without seeming silly, cynical or hypocritical, that even hopeless love may be happiness, and can make us believe what he writes, is marked with genius.

We must read again and again some pages of *Le Lys dans la Vallée* if we would understand Balzac, appreciate his knowledge of the human heart and admire his interpretation of mankind as represented in his fellow-countrymen.

Saché, in Balzac's day, belonged to a Monsieur Margonne, who was supposed to be the real father of Henri Balzac, the author's brother.

Now, alas! this charming country-house, where not only *Le Lys dans la Vallée*, but *Le Père Goriot*, *Louis Lambert* and *Recherche de l'Absolu* were written, is abandoned and dilapidated. Balzac's room, which formerly was preserved as a sort of little literary museum, is unkempt and mouldering. There used to be a "Society of Friends of Balzac" that not only looked after the writer's house (still open to the public) in the *rue Raynouard* in Paris, but also did something towards keeping up Saché.

## Balzac's Secret

"*I HAVE often been astonished*," wrote Baudelaire, not only a great poet, but one of the most perspicacious literary critics of the 19th century, "*that Balzac's fame is that of an observer. It has always seemed to me that his outstanding merit was that he was a visionary and a passionate visionary.*"

Baudelaire's acute remark applies to the whole of the novelist's work. Even those parts of the *Human Comedy* which are generally regarded as having been inspired by the most middle-class realism were written by a man who was an inveterate dreamer. And this dreamer created a world of his own, a world so plausible that nearly all readers of Balzac's books have taken this imaginary world to be the faithful reflection of the real world of the writer's time.

Balzac's universe is an image of his own will and his own prodigious imagination. Perhaps the best of all introductions to Balzac's wonder-world is *Les Illusions Perdues*, where we may discover his main themes, a little hidden, at first glance, under an apparently normal or even commonplace story. And Balzac, like all decisive writers, forged his own language, which carping critics have often characterised as a "jargon." As a matter of fact, Balzac is one of the greatest of stylists. But his style is his own, just as his plan and his presentation and his arrangement of his material are his own. Hardly any great writers have escaped the accusation of not knowing how to write their own language, of being slovenly, disorderly and careless. Yet their productions live, while the carefully planned, conventional and reassuring stuff generally withers away, leaving no traces.

## The Layon Valley

SAINT-AUBIN-DE-LIGNÉ. The Layon Valley is the only part of the old Mauges country where the vine is cultivated, but these vines yield some of the choicest wine in all northern France. Nearly every village and hamlet in this fertile dale bears a name famed for its vintages. Saint-Aubin-de-Ligné has an interesting old presbytery, and not far off, amid the grapes, is a spring which gushed forth, they say, from the ground at the feet of St. Lézin, the evangelist of this countryside. Opposite Saint-Aubin is Chaudefonds amid vines and limekilns. Farther upstream is Beaulieu, then comes Saint-Lambert-du-Lattay which preserves the name of an ancient forest whose thickets resisted men's axe for 400 years, since the great woods did not finally disappear until the 15th century. After Rablay, Faye-d'Anjou and their excellent vineyards you see the Romanesque belfry of Thouarcé and then, farther off, Notre-Dame-d'Alençon on its bold hill. An enchanted valley.

## French Cunninghams

SAINT-AVERTIN. One of the numerous Scots who for many generations past have found a lasting home in France, a Jean de Coningham or Cunningham from Ayrshire, in the time of King Louis XI of France—and readers of *Quentin Durward* will remember that Scots soldiers and adventurers flocked to France as much in the mid and later years of the 15th century as at any other time —built on to the old Romanesque nave of Saint-Avertin church a Gothic choir.

Saint-Avertin is a pleasing place and is only a short drive out from Tours. You go down the *avenue de Grammont*, and after passing the fine wrought-iron gate of the Grammont *château* (on the site of the old Abbey of Grandmont), the road bifurcates. You leave on your right the highway leading through the magnificent Forest of Chinon to Chinon and the Vienne's banks, and you turn left on the Saint-Avertin road, bordered, on the right, by delightful woods.

## *Fouqueux*

THE slopes behind Saint-Avertin yield a noted wine which, with the vintages of Montlouis, Saché, Candes and a score of others such as Chenonceau and Genillé near Loches, make up what may be called the lesser-known wines of Touraine. This little village, on the southern bank of the Cher, is, perhaps, most famed to-day for its excellent restaurant. Curiously enough, in this Touraine land of plenty, really good restaurants are rather rare. The men and women of Touraine eat, very wisely, at home. They also have a tendency to think that visitors to their privileged countryside should put up with what they find. Of course, we do not mean that the food in Touraine is poor. It is not, although at some places one will be a little disappointed. What we do mean is that the general run of eating-places hardly seem worthy of the "Garden of France."

Fouqueux, at Saint-Avertin, is different. When the weather is fine—and it nearly always is in Touraine at those times of the year when you will be tempted to visit the Loire valley—you can eat out-of-doors in rustic arbours and leafy bowers. Too often, at home and abroad, the "picturesque" setting seems to afford an excuse for rather indifferent meals served in charming surroundings. But *chez* Fouqueux, at Saint-Avertin, you will get fine fare whether in or out-of-doors. The famous French *gourmet* Curnonsky says, however, that the fried river fish, the *friture,* at Pont-de-Cisse on the Loire, is much better than the *friture* of the Cher at Saint-Avertin. It's all a matter of sand and water, it seems.

The great specialities of Touraine and Anjou are, besides the pike and shad with "white butter" and the *rillettes*: the *boudin blanc* (a glorified edition of the old, familiar black pudding) in which, instead of breadcrumbs, white chicken meat is added to the pork; filets of veal cooked in cream and then the excellent vegetables, asparagus (that of Candes is famous) and stuffed mushrooms; the Sainte-Maure and Saint-Benoît goat's milk cheeses; and the plum duffs, the jams and the pastry of Tours. All very wholesome and rather filling.

## For a Few Days the Capital of France

THE village of Saint-Avertin is built upon the site of an ancient Gallo-Roman settlement called VENTIACUM. St. Avertin was a canon of Canterbury Cathedral, who, after the murder of Thomas à Becket, decided that further residence in our island might expose him to the same sort of fate that overtook his archbishop, so the canon, whose experience of life had convinced him of the excellence of the hermit's existence, betook himself to the leafy banks of the Cher, where he built a cell and lived in the odour of sanctity until his death in 1180. His relics are still preserved in the Romanesque church erected over his tomb. It was not until the beginning of the twelve hundreds that the village took the name of its sainted anchorite.

In June 1940, the tragic June that witnessed the German seizure of France, the nearby *château* of Cangé was prepared to receive the President of the Republic, M. Albert Lebrun, and here, at Saint-Avertin, was, for a few days, the capital of France. In the house were held those anxious and pathetic cabinet councils, when a handful of bewildered and helpless men talked and talked and decided to decide nothing.

Cangé *château* is a charming place, as our picture shows. It has changed a good deal since Jean de Coningham reared it nearly five hundred years ago, but it has maintained throughout its transformations a friendly and gracious air, and it ranks to-day among the most comfortable and pleasing of the innumerable manors, country-houses and *châteaux* that adorn the Touraine countryside. Writers especially flock to Touraine. M. Farigoule, better known by his pseudonym of "Jules Romains," the author of the *Hommes de Bonne Volonté*, has his house and vineyard at Saint-Avertin. Francis Poulenc lives at Noizay.

## A Dynasty of Master-Printers

FOR generations books bearing the imprint ANTVERPIAE, EX OFFICINA PLANTINIANA—"At Antwerp, from the Plantin Workshop"—have been sought after by readers and bibliophiles. Indeed, the presses set up by Plantin rivalled those of any printer's in Europe. In the 16th century, and for years afterwards, book-selling, bookbinding and printing were trades all exercised together by the same men.

In 1518 was born, at Saint-Avertin, the celebrated Christophe Plantin. In 1549 he decided to settle at Antwerp. The Low Countries were, in those days, the centre of the European printing-trade, and even in the Spanish Netherlands there was more free-dom of speech and writing than in France, and the United Provinces, that later became the Netherlands as we know them, developed into a real home of human freedom. We should never forget the deep debt that all of us owe to the (compara-tively) liberal régime of the Dutch. As we saw at La Haye, great Descartes himself felt freer and happier living and working in Holland, and the Dutch, in our times, have not belied their ancient traditions. There has always existed a close bond of intellectual intercourse between the Netherlands and France. In our day, the famous French physicists of the Becquerel family have lived and worked more in Holland than in their own country.

In 1555, Plantin, having been wounded in the arm, turned his attention to fine typography, and the volumes issued from his press, thenceforth, rival the best of the period. In 1563, Plantin floated a private company in order to extend the field of his operations. The books he gave to the world, in Hebrew, in Latin, in Greek and in Dutch, are renowned for their beauty and accuracy. Plantin carried through the production of the famous *Biblia Polyglotta,* and, despite a reputation for secret heretical opinions (his independence of character and his freedom of thought were determining factors in his decision to emigrate from France), Plantin was appointed "First Royal Typographer" to His Catholic Majesty of Spain, Philip II. Plantin suffered much from the de-predations wrought by the Spanish troops during the sack of Antwerp in 1576, and for a time he removed to Leyden, the old university town of Holland, but two years later he was back in the great and bustling seaport, where he died in 1589.

After his death his son-in-law John Moretus—the later books from the Plantin presses bear the added imprint APUD JOHANNEM MORETUM—and his descendants continued to print in the "Plantin Workshop" until 1876, when the City of Antwerp bought the Plantin buildings and their contents for forty-eight thousand pounds gold. Today a museum, that is one of the sights of Holland, occupies the workshops of the Plantins, for over three hundred years master-printers to the civilised world.

## The Man who Built the Bank at Monte Carlo

SAINT-CALAIS. It is rather the fashion to decry Charles Garnier and his works, yet the man who built the Paris Opera House and the Casino at Monte Carlo was a man who certainly had a style of his own which, for want of a better name, might be called "19th century rococo." Certainly, each of these two buildings, in its different way, sums up and expresses the attitude of an epoch, and now, as both the Opera and the Gambling Den have become almost ancient monuments, we could ill afford to part with either.

Garnier was born at Saint-Calais in 1825, the son of a wheelwright, and was brought up in the hard-working tradition of old-fashioned French artisans. His mother, as so many mothers, had grandiose ideas, and saw a splendid future for her son. She thought that if he worked hard, and was lucky, he might get a nice, steady job as a land surveyor, and eventually earn as much as six francs a day—for her times and class an income which seemed princely—almost ninety pounds a year. But young Garnier, with a little help from friends and much scraping on the part of his parents, managed to get to Paris, where in 1848 he won the *Grand Prix de Rome,* the famous prize whose winner spends three years at the French school of the Villa Medici in Rome. Garnier was an excellent draughtsman and his drawings are beautiful. One of his finest is now in the Royal Collection at Windsor. It represents the old *Hôtel de ville* or Town Hall of Paris (burned down during the *Commune* in 1871), and it was included in an album presented to Queen Victoria during her visit to Napoleon III and Paris in 1855.

In 1860 Garnier won the prize offered for the best design for an "Imperial Opera House." The Empress Eugénie seems to have been puzzled by Garnier's design and she asked him what was its style. He replied, "The Napoleon III style, M'am." The building was begun in 1861 and finished, under the Third Republic, in 1875. It is such a familiar object to all visitors to and residents of Paris that few take the trouble to examine it as a work of art, but it is a building, magnificent in conception, whose interior, however much we may feel to-day that the decoration is overcharged and too elaborate, remains one of the most imposing as well as the most sumptuous put up in the 19th century. A relic of the original "Imperial Opera-House" plan may still be observed. To the left of the building, as you observe it from the *place de l'Opéra*, is the inclined ramp and special entrance that was to be reserved for the Imperial family.

Garnier died a rich man, and loaded with honours, decorations and medals. He had "got on" even more than his poor old mother could have imagined possible in her wildest dreams.

## The City of the Holy Hermit

GARNIER was not the only celebrity to see the light in the little town of Saint-Calais, in the Anille valley. Here also was born a now almost-forgotten worthy, Poitevin, the inventor of carbon prints for photographs.

The Gallo-Roman settlement of ANISOLA appears to have occupied the site of the town, which derives its modern name from that of Carilef, or Calais, a holy hermit from the Auvergne, who here established a monastery in the time of Clotaire I (*d.* 561), one of the four sons of Clovis, founder of the Frankish monarchy. The Church of Notre-Dame is noteworthy. The west front has a large gable richly decorated in the Renaissance taste. At the base of the tower is the shrine of Saint-Calais.

There are a few picturesque houses and the ruins of the old feudal castle. The town hall, the municipal library, the post office, the theatre *and* the museum are all housed, and amply housed, in the uninteresting buildings of the abbey, rebuilt during the 16th century by Jean Ronsard, the uncle of the poet. The abbey was sacked and partially burned during the Revolution, and only the town hall façade on the main square is of note.

## The Borders of Normandy

SAINT-DENIS-SUR-SARTHON. On the Alençon-Mayenne road you run through Condé-sur-Sarthe, and then, about seventeen miles from Alençon, you reach Saint-Denis-sur-Sarthon. The place is in the modern department of the Orne, but, historically, Saint-Denis is not a Norman town. It lies on the southern side of the Norman divide, and is overshadowed, to the north, by the *Butte Chaumont* (whose name suggests most readily the hilly little park in the north-eastern part of Paris), a peak nearly twelve hundred feet high, from whose summit you can see far and wide over Normandy, Perche and Maine. Saint-Denis church is in the Transition style, and within is some excellent Renaissance stained glass.

After Saint-Denis, you leave the valley of the Sarthon, and pull up steeply to a plateau. To your left stretches the dark Forest of Multonne, whose mantle is thrown over the summits of the Avaloirs and Souprat mounts. The former mountain is the loftiest in western France, but the way up is easy, and the summit is a wild table of broom and gorse and scraggy firs.

At the feet of the *Mont des Avaloirs* is the *Font-du-Maine* or spring, whence gush forth the waters of the Mayenne stream about a mile and a half from La Lacelle, that is, the last place in the Orne department, since neighbouring Pré-en-Pail is in the Mayenne.

## A Notable Church

SAINT-ÉPAIN. Saint Spanus, a disciple of Saint Martin of Tours, was martyred, so runs the legend, on a spot now covered by the village of Theillé. The town of Saint-Épain, named after him, lies some way out of Sainte-Maure, and on a site where the Montgauger rivulet flows into the Manse. Saint-Épain church is a notable building with a double nave. The southern half, built in the 12th century and vaulted with enormous and primitive ogees, was widened in the sixteen and seventeen hundreds. At the intersection of the transepts and the nave is a dome supporting a fine square Romanesque lantern-tower. The choir is mostly of Romanesque workmanship.

About a mile and a half from Saint-Épain is Montgauger house in a large park. The mansion, originally put up in the fourteen hundreds, was rebuilt in the 18th century and extensively restored about eighty years ago. Montgauger lands were in 1762 raised to the status of a duchy, which afterwards was inherited by the Praslin branch of the Choiseul family, a branch that was distinguished in the early years of the last century by a ducal murderer.

Farther on the Cravant road lies Crissay, with a fine Flamboyant church and some picturesque old houses, while near Avon are the ruins of the old collegiate Church of Les Roches-Tranchelion, which was consecrated in 1527.

## Spare the Prisoners

SAINT-FLORENT-LE-VIEIL. Near Saint-Florent-le-Vieil was La Baronnière, the *château* of Charles-Melchior-Arthus de Bonchamps, but what we now see is a modern house. It was at La Baronnière that the Vendeans came and induced him to put himself at the head of their anti-Republican and Royalist rising. As has been acutely pointed out, what was very remarkable in the French Revolution was not that the King and Queen and a host of other men and women (both "privileged" and not) lost their lives, but that the oppressed, miserable and half-starved peasants of the Vendée, at the prompting of their priests and leaders, should have taken up arms and courted death in an attempt to restore the old order of things.

Bonchamps was mortally wounded at the Cholet combat, but his men had taken five thousand Republican prisoners whom they intended to kill. Bonchamps' last words were a command to spare the prisoners, and the order rang through the camp:

"GRÂCE AUX PRISONNIERS, BONCHAMPS LE VEUT, BONCHAMPS L'ORDONNE"

*("Spare the prisoners, Bonchamps wills it, Bonchamps orders it.")*

The prisoners' lives were saved.

Bonchamps' tomb is in Saint-Florent parish church, and it is a splendid monument by David d'Angers, who detested Bonchamps' opinions, but who so much admired his character that he insisted on making the monument as a perpetual tribute to the Vendean leader's memory.

## The Imperial Christ

BOUZILLÉ is nearby. The name has rather a comic sound in French ears since it is slang for "all shot up," but this Bouzillé is leafy and sylvan and moreover nearby is the chapel of La Bourgonnière. This house is mostly modern and a rather uninteresting place but it contains the marvellous oratory begun in

1508 and finished in 1523 by Charles du Plessis and Louise de Montfaucon his wife. The nave has four bays and the vaults are adorned with 35 painted bosses. The altar is half-hidden by a rood-screen upon which are three large polychrome statues. The Virgin is in the centre and she is robed as a Princess of the Renaissance. In one hand the Child holds a golden orb while with the other hand He plucks at the Virgin's veil with a charming gesture. On the left-hand side of the nave is the celebrated Crucifixion. Above a Renaissance altar and framed in a splendid pagan and Italianate border is the Christ crucified, but robed and living in majesty. The hands are not pierced, the visage is royal and serene, the gilden robe is imperial. The background is frescoed with angels and Charlemagne and St. Louis, faded, faint, archaic.

If you are coming down the Loire stream, after Chalonnes you see Montjean, on the cliffs of the river's left bank. Nine miles farther on is Saint-Florent-le-Vieil, which can best be reached by following the Loire levée from Montjean and by crossing the Ingrandes suspension bridge.

## Victory March

SAINT-LÉONARD-DES-BOIS. On the 13th August, 1944, the American Combat Command Hickey Force moved north-wards to close the escape-gap still open to those elements of von Klück's Seventh Germany Army which were squeezed in the Falaise-Argentan pocket. The axis of advance of the American forces was along the Pré-en-Pail, Carrouges, Rânes, Fromental highway.

The really heavy fighting leading to the smash-through and the complete discomfiture of the enemy began just beyond Pré-en-Pail.

Pré-en-Pail was formerly the capital of a small "independent" province known as the *Pail* (pronounced Pell), but there is not much to see to remind one of its past. We shall want to move on south-east to the delightful country around Saint-Léonard-des-Bois.

## The Capital of the Maine Alps

SAINT-LÉONARD-DES-BOIS is most charmingly situated on a bend of the Sarthe river and within a circle of cliffs and hills, grey, rocky, wild, making up the most "Alpine" scenery in all the so-called *Alpes Mancelles*. On the left bank of the river is the

Looking down the Loire

To the left the Castle, centre the Church of Saint-Pierre, to the right the River

**SAUMUR**

**Sablé**

**Sainte-Suzanne**     The Castle

**Sablé**     *Château* above the Sarthe     **Saint-Calais**     The Church

**Saint-Léonard-des-Bois**     Banks of the Sarthe     **Saint Cénéri-le-Gérei**

great curved wall of the *Grande-Fourche,* while on the right are the *Deluge, Narbonne* and *Chemasson* ridges, rising some four hundred feet above the valley.

Downstream from Saint-Léonard is the lonely and savage *Misère* gorge, whose craggy cliffs are tufted with broom and gorse.

Saint-Léonard church is a Romanesque and Gothic building. On the south side of the choir is an unrestored 12th century chapel, with curious sculptures.

Saint-Léonard-des-Bois is perhaps the best centre for excursions in the regions known sometimes as the *Alpes Mancelles,* while Fresnay-sur-Sarthe (that has good hotels) is the best place for exploring the beautiful Sarthe valley, the deep, savage and sometimes strangled valley from Saint-Céneri-le-Gérei through the fine amphitheatre surrounded by high hills—almost mountains —where is Saint-Léonard down to Fresnay-sur-Sarthe.

The so-called "Alps of Le Mans" extend from the immediate environs of Alençon on the north-east to Sillé-le-Guillaume, Évron and Sainte-Suzanne to the south-west. This region of hills and great forests split into ravines, sometimes gloomy and wild and cut through with deep and twisting valleys, is surprising in the flat north of France where, except for this region (and a very few others), no land is over six hundred feet.

The region of the *Alpes Mancelles* is really part of the Armorican spine of ancient rocks, here and there burst through with eruptive masses. The country is, indeed, the southern side of the Norman *bocage.* The backbone of the formation is the line of the Coëvrons, which are hills of Armorican sandstone with rounded summits, whose highest point is Mont Rochard (357 metres), five miles north-east of Évron.

The Coëvrons are rich in minerals of various sorts, very hard porphyries, "petrosilex," taking a high polish, fine-grained blue granite, and refractory stones like feldspar. On the western fringe of Sillé forest is the wildest part of the Coëvrons, the so-called *landes* or heaths of the Coëvrons, rocky and barren, with here and there a cottage half-hidden in clumps of age-old holly-bushes. This was for long the classic country of the *Roubille* or band of gipsies, whose depredations and exactions have left a vivid and indeed almost legendary memory on the countryside.

To the south, the Coëvrons are prolonged as the *Charnie,* a rocky region covered with great heaths, pools, meres and woods, and cut through by the charming valley of the Erve that flows down from the Coëvrons towards the Sarthe and curls round the foot of Sainte-Suzanne's craggy prow and passes the Saulges grottoes.

Northwards, the *Alpes Mancelles* merge into the great forest-clad masses of Pail (south of Pré-en-Pail), of Perseigne (south-east of Alençon), of Écouves (to the north of Alençon), to hump up, in these latter south Norman forests, to the highest peaks in northern France.

## Ancient Sanctuaries

SAINT-MACAIRE. Saint-Macaire on a crest dividing the Moine from the Evre was built in a clearing of the great Gaulish Forest and near six dolmens. Now only one megalithic monument survives, a menhir about twenty feet high at La Petite-Bretellière. Not so far off is Bellefontaine Abbey, a 11th century foundation that was all rebuilt in the 19th century and is now occupied by Trappist monks. In the church is preserved St. Bernard of Clairvaux's crook which has a delicately carved and curved finial ending in an archaic monster's head.

Near Bellefontaine, at Bégrolles, for long stood in the middle of a heath a great oak in which was set and fixed an image of the Virgin in glazed pottery. In 1792 the Republicans cut down the tree and carried off the statue to Cholet but, in March 1793, the Vendeans returned the image to Bellefontaine.

## *The First Benedictine Abbey of France*

SAINT-MAUR. We should linger a little at Gennes, after having had our fill of its good fare and its splendid views. Down in the dale is the church of Saint-Vétérin. It is mainly Romanesque, but the exterior walls of the nave and the transepts are pre-Romanesque.

The Gennes region was evidently thickly populated in Roman times. There is a fairly well-preserved *nymphaeum* (or shrine sacred to the nymphs, deities of fountains and springs), and traces of a large amphitheatre.

The highway drops a little after Gennes. You pass the great Romanesque keep of Richebourg and the village of Le Thoureil, where, in the 12th century church, are two splendid reliquaries from Saint-Maur.

Up on the plateau to the west are several megalithic monuments, the most important of which is the gallery-grave of *La Bazouillière* or *La Pierre-Couverte*. It is over twenty feet long.

Of the ancient Abbey of Saint-Maur, the first to be founded in France by the disciples of St. Benedict, little remains but a 17th century conventual lodging. The monastery buildings were restored by the Benedictines in 1890, but in 1903, at the time of the suppression of the religious orders, the monks had to leave.

Above the abbey and half-way up the hill is a small 12th century chapel built, it is said, on the spot where Saint-Maur, founder of the abbey, died and was buried. A crystal shrine encloses the fragments of his sarcophagus. Nearby are the stumps of a circular Roman temple, which, it is reputed, was transformed by the saint into a Christian sanctuary.

All the way down to Ponts-de-Cé the road is bordered with villages, manors and the ruins of old castles. There is Saint-Rémy-la-Varenne, with a very ancient church dating from the ten hundreds. Then comes the imposing feudal Castle of Monsabert, and so to Ponts-de-Cé and the bridge leading to Black Angers.

## La Clarté-Dieu

SAINT-PATERNE. About a mile and a half farther along the road from La Roche-Racan and in the direction of Château-du-Loir, you come upon the hamlet of Saint-Paterne, whose modest little Flamboyant-style parish church houses some remarkable works of art—most of them brought hither from the (now ruined) Abbey of *La Clarté-Dieu*, a Cistercian monastery founded in 1239 by a Bishop of Winchester.

The show-piece at Saint-Paterne is a 16th century "Adoration of the Magi." The seated figure of the Virgin has been attributed to Leonardo da Vinci (without much justification, although that universal genius was, on occasion, sculptor as well as painter, engineer, inventor, poet and architect and musician and natural philosopher)—in any case, the image is very beautiful.

And there are statues of Saints, of Doctors of the Church—most of these sculptures are rather late in date (17th and 18th centuries), but of fine execution and artistry.

In the sacristy is preserved a set of Mass vestments worked in *petit-point* embroidery by Mme de Racan, the wife of the pastoral poet, whose manor of La Roche-Racan is nearby (see p. 272).

A little over a mile to the west of Saint-Paterne you may see the remains of *La Clarté-Dieu*. The abbey buildings now serve for a farm, but the refectory (built in 1239), the Gothic chapel and an elegant lodging (dating from 1713) are in quite good repair and worthy of a visit.

## The "Scourge of the English"

LESS than two miles down the valley of the Escotais you come to Saint-Christophe, spreading up the hill to the blurred rump of a 10th century fortress. The parish church contains some interesting statues and notably a 13th century Virgin over the sacristy door.

Bueil, about three miles from Saint-Christophe, is a more notable place. It was the cradle of the once-famous Bueil family, for generations one of the most prominent in Anjou. The great man of this stock was Jean de Bueil, nicknamed the "Scourge of the English." He was one of the companions-in-arms of Joan of Arc, but he lived to see the freeing of his country, and died at a good old age in 1478, when the whirligig of time had brought about such a change in relative positions of the French and English realms that old Bueil must have found the new world unrecognisable from that of his youth. For when he was a young man, the English held down most of France. The French kingdom was split and almost extinguished. When Bueil was a boy he had seen our Henry V proclaimed heir to the throne of France, and then had heard of the coronation in Paris of our Henry VI as King of France and England. Before old Bueil died, France was a united kingdom, strong, wealthy and dominant. The envoy of the French king was paying out tips, largess and pensions to our Edward IV and his Court. England had sunk into the slough from which it was to be rescued by the Tudors. France was set upon the high road, from which it was only to be temporarily deflected by the civil wars of the 16th century.

Another, later and very different Bueil was the humanist and man of letters who was Belon's friend (see p. 154).

Bueil parish church is a little Romanesque structure, which was rebuilt, or at least refashioned, in the Gothic taste at the end of the 15th century. There is a particularly fine font (with a carved wood cover dated 1521) and one or two good statues. Opening out of the nave is the chantry, put up in 1470, and containing four tombs of the Bueil family, which are most interesting and in comparatively good repair. Such family chapels with monuments intact are far rarer in France than with us. The fury of the revolutionaries was, from the first, directed against all obvious monuments of "feudal times."

## The Sword of Victory

SAINTE-CATHERINE-DE-FIERBOIS. On the road from Montbazon to Sainte-Maure, about five hundred yards off the highway to the left, lies Sainte-Catherine-de-Fierbois. The hamlet grew up around a chapel where, it is said, Charles-Martel, the grandfather of Charlemagne and the conqueror of the Moors at "Sinones" somewhere between Tours and Poitiers (the great battle that routed Abd-er-Rahman and kept Europe safe in Christian tradition), laid up his sword as an offering. On the 23rd April —St. George's day—on precise instructions, given, it is said, by Joan of Arc, the precious blade was found, and, so the tale goes, the sword which had beaten back the Moors was used by the Maid against the English invader.

The chapel is a charming Flamboyant building. Within is an altar-frontal of the 15th century, and in the village is an old building dated about 1515 called the "Dauphin's house." In the middle of the little square is one of the innumerable statues of Joan of Arc that are scattered throughout France. This one, and quite a good one of its sort, is by Charpentier.

## Julie's Garland

SAINTE-MAURE. For her fête-day (i.e. the festival day of her patron saint, still, in France, more observed as an anniversary than one's birthday) in 1641, when she had attained the mature age of thirty-four, Mademoiselle Julie d'Angennes received a present which has remained famous in French literary history. It was a collection of madrigals, copied by a famed calligraphist, and bearing on each page the painting of a flower. The contributors were men famous in their day—Jean Chapelain, possibly

Pierre Corneille, Guillaume Colletet, Georges de Scudéry, Simon Arnault de Pomponne, Jean Desmarets de Saint-Sorlin and others, and, especially, Charles de Sainte-Maure, *marquis* de Montausier. The "incomparable Julie," as her friends named her, was the daughter of the "incomparable Arthenice," otherwise Catherine de Vivonne, *marquise* de Rambouillet, the mistress of the renowned literary *salon* and, in some measure, the inspirer of Molière's famous satire, *Les Précieuses Ridicules*.

Catherine was the daughter of Jean de Vivonne, by Giulia, of the distinguished Roman family of Savelli. As a matter of fact, Mme de Rambouillet's *salon* was the first and most famous and most influential of the French literary "circles," and here conversation as a fine art was practised with incalculable consequences for the development of the French language. The standards of clear and adequate expression evolved by the greatest wits, writers and men of fashion of the day, at the *hôtel* de Rambouillet became the standards of 17th century French writing. The *hôtel* de Rambouillet and the French Jesuits between them may be said to have forged, tempered and sharpened the French language, until it became the incomparable instrument it has since remained.

The "incomparable Julie" was, perhaps, a little more "precious" than her mother, and, indeed, much of the ridicule poured by the groundlings upon the *précieuses* was aroused by Julie's posing. She was, however, a woman of very real culture, and the *marquis* de Montausier was her faithful swain. He had been wooing her for a biblical period of seven years when he conceived the *Garland* as a final assault upon her indecision. However, she kept him waiting for a further four years, until in 1645, when she had reached the mature age of thirty-eight, she consented to marry him.

Charles de Sainte-Maure was born at Sainte-Maure in 1610 (he was thus three years younger than his incomparable Julie) and was bred a Huguenot and a soldier. He retained to his death, in his roughness of manner and, also, in his austerity, the double trace of his military and Protestant upbringing. He distinguished himself in the wars, abjured his Protestantism to please his Julie, and became, after his marriage, a favourite with his king, who created him a *duc*. The gossips of the day attributed not a little of his royal favour to the intrigues of his Julie, who is said to have favoured the liaison between Louis XIV and Mlle de La Vallière, and, later, to have pushed the career of Mme de Montespan who, when she left her husband, found a refuge with the *duchesse* de Montausier.

In 1668 the *duc* was appointed tutor to the *Grand Dauphin*, eldest son of Louis XIV (and grandfather of Louis XV). The *Grand Dauphin* (of whom Saint-Simon paints an unflattering portrait) was a dull, gross, uninteresting personage, whose natural mediocrity was intensified by the severe rule of his tutor, who had prepared for him (by Huet) the famous bowdlerised editions of the classics sub-titled *ad usum Delphini,* for the special use of the Dauphin—a phrase that has lasted in French to designate a clumsy and ridiculous expurgation of books. Montausier's régime resulted, as may be supposed, in the *Grand Dauphin* conceiving for learning, science, books and literature the stupid man's aversion, strengthened by the dull man's resentment at the discipline to which he had been subjected.

Montausier lived to a ripe old age. Luckily, his former pupil died before his father.

## *Arciacum*

SAINTE-MAURE. There ought to be a good deal to say about Sainte-Maure, a place you must pass through on your way south from Touraine to Poitou, but, despite historical memories, the chief title to fame of this straggling, rather dull place is its excellent goats'-milk cheese. It is a fair-sized town, and spreads over the slopes of a hill overlooking the river Manse and a lateral valley. As ARCIACUM, Sainte-Maure was known in Gallo-Roman times. Here, according to legend, were discovered, in the 5th century, the bodies of Saints Maure and Brigitte (no connection with our Irish Saint Bridget or Saint Bride or with the Swedish saint), and around the shrine erected to the honour of Sainte Maure's bones arose a settlement that took her name. Later the place was a southern outpost of the Counts of Touraine until, about 1020, fierce Fulk Nerra seized it and erected here a fortress to protect his dominions from the east. In the Middle Ages one Benedict or Benoît of Sainte-Maure had a great reputation as a *trouvère* (the northern equivalent of the provençal *troubadour*), or poet and ballad-singer. In later times, Sainte-Maure passed into the possession of several different families, including those of La Rochefoucauld, d'Estouteville and

Rohan-Montbazon. During the Revolution the men of the town, who had for long been feudal dependants, renamed their home "Sainte-Maure-Libre." For the rest, Sainte-Maure has a 15th century *château*, a 17th century covered market and a 12th century church that has, except in the crypt, been very much restored.

The surrounding country, generally known as the "plateau of Sainte-Maure," but more properly that of Bossée and Dolus, is pitted with *falunières*, or pockets of sand studded with marine and freshwater shells. The formations date from Miocene times, and were formerly used to improve the soil of other regions.

The road towards Chatellerault slopes down to the Vienne valley, and about the last village before you cross the Creuse (here forming the boundary between the departments of the Indre-et-Loire and the Vienne) is La Celle-Saint-Avant, with a rather notable Romanesque church.

## A Miniature Carcassonne

SAINTE-SUZANNE. Sainte-Suzanne is one of the most curious places in northern France. It is a walled town, which in its way is as worthy of note as the renowned city-fortresses of Carcassonne, in south-western France, or as Rothenburg-ob-der-Tauber, in Germany. Both of these latter places have been very much restored and wear a rather self-conscious air of "museum-pieces." Sainte-Suzanne is guiltless of reconstruction. There it stands on a rocky spur overhanging the right bank of the Erve. Nearly all the old battlements have been preserved, and they enclose the little city within a triangle, whose apex rises up to the imposing outline of the ancient castle.

The town has spilt over a little towards the west, but you still enter the place by the *Porche du Guichet*, and can then follow the ramparts overlooking the river winding away below among rich pastures and green meadows. When you get to the *Porte de Fer*, there is a splendid view from the cliff's height. Right across the Erve is the *Tertre Ganne*, an ancient artificial mound, and it is worth while going over to the left bank and climbing this hillock so as to get a general impression of a medieval fortified city.

You can walk right round the city walls under the shadow of the castle, and then turn right and enter the fortress by an antique nail-studded door. On the one hand you have the old feudal keep a hundred and thirty feet high, with walls twelve feet thick, and pierced with loopholes. On the other side is the "New Castle," built in the Renaissance style, but in the reign of Louis XIV. Sainte-Suzanne is a place to wander about in.

As early as the 11th century Hubert II, Viscount of Beaumont, used Sainte-Suzanne as a lair, whence he issued to sweep the countryside with his raids. In the 15th century, Thomas de Montacute, 4th Earl of Salisbury, who had distinguished himself in the French campaigns, was created *comte* du Perche by Henry V. Against this formidable warrior, Sainte-Suzanne, under the command of Ambroise de Loré, Joan of Arc's companion-in-arms, held out for several months, but we stormed the town at last and held it for fifteen years. Then it was lost in the general decline that preceded our final retreat from France. One Jean de Bueil carried this stronghold, and to him a grateful king, Charles VII, granted in 1439 the governorship of the town.

The surroundings of Sainte-Suzanne are charming. A thousand yards or so away, on the Assé-le-Béranger road, is the "English Camp"—an earthwork thrown up by William the Conqueror. Less than a mile farther on is the megalithic gallery-grave known as *Erves*.

Hidden in the Charnie forest, not far off, are the romantic ruins of old Bouillé castle.

## Stalactites and Stalagmites

SAULGES. As far as we know, there are in the Loire region, none of the painted or engraved caverns which are the peculiar glory of the south-west of France, but the famed Saulges grottoes are curious enough. From Saulges village a shaded road leads down to the grotto and well of Saint-Sérené, at the foot of the cliffs. You can then follow the banks of the Erve through the Suzon woods as far as the caves.

The Rochefort grotto is perhaps the most interesting of the lot. A corridor, some eighty feet long, leads to the "Great Hall," from which you can pass through passages lined with stalagmites and stalactites down to a subterranean lake and to other halls and caverns and chambers. This is just the sort of place that, had it been during the times of Upper Paleolithic Man in a region of more clement climate (and had its entrance been lost), might have been adorned with the paintings and engravings which preserve for us the beginnings of pictorial art and evidence for the hunting-magic and religious cults of our far-off ancestors. The *grotte à Margot* is also curious. The *Chèvre* and *Bigotte* caves are very small.

Saulges village is on a plateau over the right bank of the Erve, and you reach the place by the road from Sainte-Suzanne to Sablé. If you are coming up from Sablé you drive through the Forest of Moncor and then drop down into the rather wild but altogether delightful valley of the Erve. At Saint-Pierre-sur-Erve there is a Romanesque belfry and an ancient stone bridge over the river. In Saulges church is a "Pilgrims of Emmaus" painting, which is optimistically attributed to Titian. There is also a particularly fine 15th century painted and gilded bas-relief of the Trinity. Under the Chapel of Saint-Sérené, opposite Saulges church, is a Romanesque crypt, in which is preserved a highly venerated image of the Virgin.

## Madame de Montespan's Penitence

SAUMUR. From Montsoreau, downstream, on the left bank of the Loire, the highway runs between the green, gently shelving fringes of the great river on the one side and, on the other, a line of hills, often breaking into white cliffs, here and there, cut and hollowed into habitations and huge caves and cellars, where are grown mushrooms, and where also are stored the wines of the countryside. Hereabout, some of the naturally sparkling—"*pétillant*"—vintages of the Loire are treated so as to give them some of the characteristics of champagne. The *mousseux* wines of the Saumer country can be very good, and need not be looked upon just as fake champagne or as an inexpensive (or relatively inexpensive) substitute for the bubbling *crus* from the east of France.

You run past Parnay, or rather below Parnay—for the village is up on the crest of the hills, and commands views over the far-reaching valleys of the Loire and its tributaries. Parnay church is late Romanesque, with 15th century Gothic additions. The wines of Parnay are excellent, and will be the first of the *Saumurois* that you will taste in Anjou.

Souzay, a mile or so farther on than Parnay, has some picturesque old houses.

Miles before you reach Saumur the sharp, imposing outline of its castle stands out upon the hill. To your left you used to see a rather astonishing church—*Notre-Dame des Ardilliers*—with a huge central dome in the style of the Italian *seicento*, but the cupola collapsed under the bombardments of June 1940.

In 1454 was found in the clay soil of a field nearby an antique image of the Virgin. The nave of the present church was begun in the fifteen hundreds, but the place was finished in the middle of the following century, while the rotunda or dome was only completed in 1695 at the expense of the famous Mme de Montespan, who, when she had fallen from royal favour and had adopted the attitude of a penitent, frequently visited her sister, the Abbess of Fontevrault, and in going to or coming from that illustrious abbey, would stay in a small house near *Notre-Dame des-Ardilliers* in order to receive spiritual comfort from her director of conscience, Father de La Tour, the General of the Oratorians.

The spacious interior of the church was full of rich carving, and afforded a bold and impressive scene of neo-classical and Italianate splendour.

## The Capital of Eastern Anjou

AT first sight Saumur may seem rather empty and lifeless. It is, with the exception of the old quarters of huddled houses and winding alleys, a town of wide streets, and it sprawls over the two banks of the Loire and the twin islands in midstream. A wide highway drives right through the city from the station—far away on the right bank—over the islands and out to the bridge over the river Thouet to the south. Saumur suffered in the war. The station on the right bank of the Loire was destroyed in 1944. The Croix-Verte suburb is very knocked about, as are also the islands and the quays.

The men and women of Saumur, without displaying the reserved and slightly reticent manner of the *Tourangeaux*, are different from the typical Angevins of farther west. You feel that you are in a city that has old Huguenot traditions, a city which, by its famed cavalry school, has for generations attracted a military *élite* from all over the world.

Moreover, the sights of Saumur are not to be missed. The castle is one of the most interesting feudal edifices in France. Two, at least, of the old churches are not only fine, historic buildings, but they house tapestries of great beauty and worth.

The gastronomical specialities of Saumur are famed. There is the *pâté de sarcelles,* or teal pasty. In the liberal interpretation given in France to Church laws as to food lawful on Fridays and other fasts, teal is, by a pious fiction, counted as a fish. The *pâté de lamproie,* or lamprey pasty, is excellent. Nowhere in Anjou are the *rillettes* (or potted pork) more luscious. Both of the more esteemed Loire fish, the *alose* (shad) and the pike, may be eaten at Saumur and with great satisfaction.

The *Saumurois* countryside is beautiful and full of interesting monuments. We can do worse than spend a few days in the town, and make it our centre for visiting Fontevrault, Montreuil-Bellay, and all the fascinating region of eastern Anjou.

## Old Saumur

IN 848 the ruler of Brittany, having burned about its monks' heads the monastery of Saint-Florent-le-Vieil, Charles the Bald, King of the Franks and Roman Emperor, gave the dispossessed religious a domain known as *villa johannis,* which was situated somewhere on the site of Saumur town. Not so many years after their settlement in their new home, the monks were again burnt out, this time by the Norman pirates, whose incursions were becoming a scourge to all the northern and western parts of the Frankish kingdom. The survivors from *villa johannis* fled to Burgundy and did not return to Anjou until about 950, when Thibault "the Trickster," Count of Touraine and Blois, built for them a fine, new, fortified monastery surrounded by strong ramparts—a *salvus murus*—which gave, it is said, the name of "Saumur" to the settlement that grew up under the sheltering walls of the fortress-abbey. In the 13th century Saumur was occupied by the forces of the French kings and ever remained loyal to them. We never occupied the town, even during the Hundred Years' War.

Nowhere in western France did the Reformation make more converts than here and, in the time of Henry IV, the city, governed by the renowned "Duplessis-Mornay" (Philippe de Mornay, Lord of Le Plessis-Marly), counsellor of the King, and nicknamed the "Huguenot Pope," became the metropolis of French Protestantism, but it was ruined by the Revocation of the Edict of Nantes.

Thousands of its inhabitants emigrated—many of them to Britain.

Saumur existed obscurely for generations until, in 1768, was founded the "School of Horsemanship" (*école d'équitation*), which was the forerunner of the world-famous cavalry school of to-day.

The *Place de la Bilange* opens on to the quays just south of the Loire bridge. On one side is the theatre, a large but characterless edifice. Beyond it (upstream) is the town hall, a charming Gothic building, outwardly a little city-fortress, but inwardly a gracious Renaissance lodging given on to a central courtyard. The library, on the second floor, is largely composed of volumes formerly belonging to the Abbeys of Fontevrault and of Saint-Florent-le-Vieil. It contains about thirty MSS., ranging in date from the 12th to the 15th centuries. Some of them are very fine, and can be examined.

The nearby Chapel of St. John is a small place in the 13th century Angevin style. The vaulting of the choir is impressive.

The Church of Saint-Pierre, still farther eastwards, is the most interesting one of the town, and should not be missed, even if you are pressed for time. The 17th century west front screens a 12th century Romanesque shrine, whose single nave is bordered with chapels added during the fourteen and fifteen hundreds. At the intersection of the nave and the transepts, a dome supports a lantern-tower, whose spire is modern.

The interior was restored in 1862, but it does not look too much "reconstructed." The fine choir-stalls date from about 1480, and there is to be seen in the choir a curious carved panel of Saint George and the Dragon. In the sacristy are preserved two collections of tapestries. One (about 1524) depicts the "Legend of Saint-Florent," and the other (about 1542) the "Life of St. Peter." Of the two, perhaps the former is the finer. It would seem that the Saint-Florent series consisted originally of nine hangings. Six are at Saumur. One is in the Angers Tapestry Museum, and the two others "disappeared" during the 19th century.

The tapestries were given to the Abbey of Saint-Florent-le-Vieil by Abbot Jacques Le Roy in 1542. The stuffs were most probably woven at Saumur itself by one of the travelling workshops which used to move about from town to town in the 15th and 16th centuries. We know the price paid by Le Roy for the lot. It was

2,066 *livres*. It is difficult to say exactly what this sum represents in modern money—perhaps about a hundred pounds gold a tapestry. The "Legend of Saint-Florent" is in treatment, design and workmanship very like the "Life of St. Stephen," now in the Cluny Museum of Paris.

The hangings remained at Saint-Florent until the Revolution, when they were transferred to the Church of St. Peter at Saumur. During the last century the tapestries were, for a time, "mislaid," but in 1888 all, except two, were brought to light again.

## *Saumur Castle*

ON the way up to the castle from St. Peter's you pass several old houses.

The castle, which is such a prominent landmark up and down the Loire valley for miles, is an imposing feudal fortress of exceptionally fine masonry and workmanship. The existing building was put up in the 14th century on 10th century foundations, and although the castle was often refashioned in later times (for it was the residence of the *Saumurois* governors), it is still, essentially, a medieval fortress with Renaissance features. But, imposing as it is, Saumur Castle is but a shadow of its elaborate self as we see it depicted in the miniature paintings of the Très Riches Heures of the *duc* de Berry, in the Chantilly Museum. There Saumur seems all pale grey and delicate, spiky, pinnacled, carved and adorned with finials and weathercocks, and outlined against the pale azure Anjou sky. From 1789 to 1815 the castle was used as a State prison and then as a barracks. In 1906 it was bought by the Saumur Town Council, restored and fitted out as a museum.

Of the three original curtains only three remain. To the north-west the court is open. The northern end of the north-east wing has a turret sheltering a richly decorated staircase.

The castle contains two museums. The Municipal Museum houses some fine furniture, porcelain, faience and pottery. The latter is of great importance, and consists of over thirteen hundred pieces (from the collection of the *comte* Lair) mostly of French kilns—Nevers, Marseilles, Rouen, Sèvres, Moustier, Strasbourg pottery—and porcelains of Rouen, Sèyres, Vincennes and Arras, with a few pieces attributed to the master-potter Bernard Palissy. There are also enamels, ivories, illuminated MSS., fine

17th and 18th century bindings, and some 17th century Gobelins tapestries. Saumur is one of the more noteworthy of the French lesser provincial museums usually little known to visitors and even to the French themselves. Now (1947) that all the museums of France have been regrouped under a new central administration in Paris, it is to be expected that their treasures will become better known.

*The Musée du Cheval*, founded in 1911–12 by Jolly, a *vétérninaire-major* of the Army, is unique. It is particularly rich in harness of all countries and ages, and in documents, prints, pictures, etc., relating to horses.

In the south-west of the town is the Church of Notre-Dame-de-Nantilly, a very fine example of early 12th century Romanesque.

In the church is preserved the richest collection of tapestries contained in any church in France. The hangings are frequently exposed in the choir and nave. Among the most remarkable of these tapestries are the 15th century "Capture of Jerusalem" and the "Savages' Ball.' In the former you see the horsemen, cannoneers and infantry of Titus's army (furnished with the weapons of the 15th century) moving to the assault of the Jewish soldiers. The portion preserved at Saumur is only part of the whole. Other morsels are in the Lyons and Vienna museums and in several private collections.

The "*bal des sauvages*" was certainly never meant to be exposed in a church, and how the hanging got to Notre-Dame-de-Nantilly is unknown. Below a balcony where musicians are playing you see men and women dancing or chatting. Some are dressed in a rich Court costume, while others are naked under a beast's fell, disclosed by a mantle lightly draped on the shoulders. The floor is dark blue dotted with flowers. The strange subject of this tapestry recalls the famous *bal des ardents* held in 1393 at the Royal *Hôtel Saint-Pol* in Paris. A ball was held in the presence of the imbecile King Charles VI and his sprightly Queen Isabeau of Bavaria, when the candles set light to some of the fancy-dresses of the dancers and the whole Court barely escaped being burned alive.

There are also several panels from the "Life of the Virgin" (1520), from the "Life of Christ" (1619), of "St. Peter" (15th century), a "Tree of Jesse" (1528), a 16th century "Adoration of the Shepherds," 15th century hunting scenes, and others. A most notable treasure.

It is probable that some, at least, of these tapestries have been at Saumur ever since they were woven. From the so-called "Workshops of the Loire valley" came the "Concert" in the Angers museum, the "Lives of SS. Gervase and Protasius" at Le Mans, and the "Legend of Saint-Florent" in St. Peter's church at Saumur. These "Loire workshops" were flourishing all through the 16th century, but particularly in its earlier years. However, the *Bal des sauvages* is certainly not of local weave. Perhaps the panel was stored in the church at the time of the Revolution.

Notre-Dame was begun during the 12th century in the purest Romanesque style. Louis XI doubled the width of the nave by the addition of a Flamboyant side-aisle. The transept is also of the 15th century.

On one of the nave's columns is a Renaissance bas-relief of John the Baptist preaching in the desert. On another column is an epitaph composed by "Good King René" for his nurse *dame Tiephaine*, who was buried here. This little tribute from one of the most attractive of the Valois princes strikes a pleasing note from the Middle Ages.

Also in the nave is a 13th century crozier, enamelled and damascened with gold. The baptistry is the former oratory of Lousi XI, and in the south-eastern chapel is the image of Our Lady of Nantilly, which is possibly of 12th and certainly not later than of 13th century date.

Behind the church is the botanical garden containing a viticultural school, where is taught everything connected with the culture of the vine and the making of wine.

## The Stand on the Loire

WESTWARDS, on the broad *place du Chardonnet,* is the Cavalry School put up in 1768. The famous displays of horsemanship known as the *carrousels* take place during July and August on the Carrière fields behind the school. If you are in this part of the world during the summer months when the *carrousels* are on, you should not fail to attend one of these great shows. In June 1940 the officers and cadets of the Cavalry School put up a brave stand

**Tours**                                   House near the Cathedral

**Saumur** The Portal of *Saint-Pierre*

**Saumur** The Town Hall

**Saumur** North African Spahis

**Serrant** The *Château*

**Saumur** Cavalry Cadet

**Saumur** "House of the Queen of Sicily"

on the Loire against the enemy. For three days, from 18th to 20th of June, the Saumur men managed to hold up the Germans on a front of fifteen miles from Gennes to Montsoreau. It was during this fighting that Saumur sustained great damage.

## The Wines of Anjou

SAVENNIÈRES. Angers is but five miles or so from the Loire at Bouchemaine, where the Maine empties into the broader stream of the Loire. The road downstream towards Nantes and the sea is delightful. The great wide river stretches away, free of boat or skiff or barge, but most often smiling and spacious, grey-green and pale, set with buff sand-banks, and bordered here and there with white houses roofed with that *ardoise fine*—delicate slate—that Du Bellay prized above the haughty Italian marbles.

There is a Romanesque church at Bouchemaine, and the right-bank road runs between the gently shelving margins of the Loire and rising ground that often closes in on you as white cliffs. Here and there are shacks with wooden terraces on piles and overlooking the river broad as a lake. Here you can eat a *friture de la Loire*—fried river-fish—or a *matelotte d'anguilles*—eels with a red wine sauce—for the eels and lampreys are fat and luscious hereabouts. The scene is often softly clear and mildly exhilarating, with some hint of sea-air in the breeze that blows inland from the estuary not really so very far off.

But the eels and the lampreys and the gudgeons and perch, pike or bream are but the pretext for drinking the white wines of Anjou, cool, capitous and sparkling. We are, in fact, on our way to the heart of the Anjou vineyards. You can, of course, get excellent bottles at the Angers restaurants and cafés—those with the red or green sealing-wax on the corks are the best, but, somehow, these delicious wines drunk in the country are doubly delightful.

For the wines of Anjou, in our opinion at least, are the most interesting and satisfying of all the Loire wines. Do not judge Anjou wine by the sour, sullen stuff they serve you with oysters, crab and other shell-fish at the smart fish-restaurants of Paris. Anjou wines must be drunk in Anjou. Either they do not travel well, or during their travels they attract the attention of unscrupulous merchants. It is true, of course, that these northern vineyards of Anjou do not always get enough sun, and that in some years sugar has to be added to the wine . . . but here we are getting into trade secrets . . . but the famous years, such as 1921 (now almost unobtainable, but the finest since 1893 or even 1874) and 1928, and the fine seasons of the '30's are incomparable.

The great years before 1921 were 1893, 1900, 1906, 1911 and 1919, and it cannot be too often insisted on that the Anjou wines are very capricious and a vintage that one year is nectar may the next year be rather indifferent stuff. The wines of the Savennières region extend for some distance along the Loire's course; there is the La Roche-aux-Moines, the Saint-Barthélemy and the Posson-nière. This latter place is the next village downstream from Savennières and the pike with *beurre blanc* sauce is especially famed at La Possonnière, which is, indeed, in the vulgar speech of the land generally called La Poissonnière.

And these north bank vintages are rather clearly distinct from those of the south bank, just across the river. The Bellerive, the Beaulieu, the Faye, the Rablay, the Thouarcé and, of course, Rochefort's famed *Quart de Chaume*, are richer, sweeter, perhaps, than the north bank's wines which many will find, however, incomparable in their freshness and perfume. And in the less distinguished years when the *pineau blanc* grapes do not achieve their *pourriture noble*, their "noble rot," the north-bank wines show up rather better than those of the south. For the trouble with these northern vineyards is, of course, the early autumn frosts which kill the grapes before they have been fully transformed into globules of golden sugar.

Farther west the south-side wines of Murs, Soulaines and Mont-jean partake more of the quality of the Saumur vintages which, however, are something apart. They are delicate, graceful, light beyond belief and yet strong. The Brézé, the Saint-Cyr-en-Bourg, the Dampierre, the Souzay, the Montsoreau and the Parnay wines are worthy of a special visit to the south-east of Anjou and a carefully planned wine-tasting or potological tour. Even when the wines of Saumur are mussed up into "champagne" they are still honourable.

The *muscadets* of the Lower Loire come hardly into our survey, for most of them are grown on either bank of the Loire but in Brittany, though there are some *muscadet* vineyards in the extreme west of Anjou on the left bank of the river. The *muscadets* are cool, greenish, capitous and thirst-quenching. They are the only wines of Brittany but they are delightful.

The Loir vineyards are much less extensive than those of the Loire, but try a good Cheffes or Briollay and above all a Huillé and a Lézigné-sur-Loir when you are in the Baugé country.

The red wines of Anjou are hardly known outside the province, but in addition to the La Roche-aux-Moines (which also yields a fine white wine) there is the rare and splendid Champigny that grows between Parnay and Saint-Cyr to the east of Saumur.

The country opens out a little before you get to Savennières. On the right is the Rock of the Monks—*La Roche-aux-Moines*— near which was fought the battle between the troops of our John Lackland and those of the French king that gave the French the Plantagenets' domains in northern France. Varenne house on the hill-side is a 17th century place disfigured by an absurd addition in the "Scottish baronial style."

Savennières church is not only one of the oldest Romanesque buildings in Anjou, but also one of the least restored.

Here the Loire is wide, enclosing a curious island called the *île Béhuard,* part of which is often drowned in the Loire's floods. On Béhuard is raised fine hemp in quality rivalling that of the *varennes* of higher upstream near Tours and Ussé. There is quite a good restaurant where you may eat Loire fish and drink Savennières wines. Béhuard church is a 15th century structure consisting of two naves one above the other. The pilgrimage to Our Lady of Béhuard is still celebrated, and in the shrine is a panel-portrait of King Louis XI who was devoted to the cult of *Notre-Dame de Béhuard* and was privately anointed King, it is said, at Béhuard before his coronation at Rheims.

Savennières itself is a bright, clean, rather straggling place, with some spacious houses. The village has a prosperous air, and the nearby countryside is dotted with manors, *châteaux* and castles.

The best-known of the Savennières vintages is the *coulée de Serrant* (the fief of Savennières depended, in pre-revolutionary times, on the lordship of Serrant, not far off), but it seems that in recent years this wine has fallen off in quality.

Just beyond Savennières the Loire is crossed by a suspension-bridge leading to an avenue that takes you right into the left-bank town of Rochefort, the capital of the southern Anjou wines.

## *FitzJames*

SEGRÉ. As you go up the valley of the Oudon stream and before you get to Segré, you see the *château* de La Lorie, a magnificent country-house, built in the 18th century and for long the seat of the *ducs* de Saint-James. The Segré race-course is just outside the park gates.

The fortunes of the two branches of the family founded by the famous *maréchal* de Berwick (illegitimate son of our King James II by Arabella, sister of the first Duke of Marlborough) have been contrasting. The *duque* de Alba, representative of the elder branch, may be said to stand at the head of the Spanish aristocracy, while the younger, or French branch of the family, which received from Louis XIV the title of *duc* de FitzJames, still exists but its members are neither wealthy nor prominent.

## *Madame Swetchine's Spiritual Salon*

WHERE the Oudon and Verzée streams meet, the rivers run between dark cliffs of schist, and here is Segré, dominated by the dome of the Madeleine church built at the time of the French Restoration. The older parts of the town spread up the hill between the two rivers and the houses stare at each other over the streams and from one height to the other. There is iron-ore scattered about the countryside, and an iron-mine has been opened up within the town's boundaries. The summit of the rock forms a terrace circled by the old containing walls of the castle, and contains a modern Gothic chapel and the Swetchine Hospital founded by the *comte* de Falloux, who thus perpetuated the memory of one of the most curious figures of the neo-Catholic renaissance of the 19th century's first half.

Madame Swetchine was a Russian of good family, who at sixteen years of age became a maid of honour to the Empress Marie and, the following year, married a General Swetchine twenty-five years older than herself. These were the times when French *émigrés* were still spread over Europe. Russia had its share, and St. Petersburg society counted a number of Frenchmen and women. Probably the most distinguished of these foreigners was Joseph de Maistre, who was in 1803 Sardinian minister at the Russian capital. Whether Joseph de Maistre played as large a part in her conversion as is generally reported is not quite clear, but in 1815

Madame Swetchine became a convert from Orthodoxy to Roman Catholicism. In 1816 she settled in Paris, and remained in France until her death in 1857.

Madame Swetchine, whom Sainte-Beuve called "the eldest daughter of Monsieur de Maistre and the youngest daughter of St. Augustine," maintained for some forty years a *salon* where writers, artists, men and women of society, priests and prelates met and mingled. The tone of the gatherings was highly serious, intellectual and strongly religious. Lacordaire was the brightest ornament of the circle and the influence Madame Swetchine exercised upon him was considerable. The *comte* de Falloux, one of the political leaders of the Catholic renaissance, was the devoted friend of Madame Swetchine and founded the Segré hospital in her memory. This Russian lady, so different from other religiously-minded fellow-countrywomen such as Madame de Krüdener, is a significant figure in the French religious life of a century ago.

## An Enchanted Glen

A FEW miles to the north-west of the town are the ruins of the Benedictine Abbey of Nyoiseau, that is *niosellum,* or "little nest," in Low Latin. The Oudon almost encircles the site, while the Araise, the Pantière and the Misengrain—fairy-book names—twist and twine and sparkle among trees and hedges. Of the conventual buildings you may see eight Romanesque arches with alternate voussoirs of red and white stone; some short columns; cube-shaped capitals and a great door. There is a grange with an elaborate open-work roof and there is the almoner's lodging bearing the date 1647.

Between Segré and Château-Gontier to the north are as many manors and castles as you can see in a day's outing—Mortier-crolles, now a farm, Chemazé and Montguillon where, also, are three high stones, all that now remain out of 14 formerly standing of the Forges cromlech.

At Bourg d'Iré, about five miles west of Segré, a picturesque bridge spans the river, on one side of which you see the *château* de la Douve, belonging to the d'Armaillés, and on the other the *château* de La Maboulière that was Falloux's house. It is a modern building in the Louis XIII style. In the chapel is a fine late 15th century altar in wood, ornamented with seven bas-reliefs of the Passion. There is a monument to Falloux.

On the Candé road, about a mile and a half from Segré, lies Sainte-Gemmes-d'Andigné, at the junction of the Verzée and the Argos; here are six menhirs. Two miles to the south-west is the *château* de La Blanchaie, rebuilt in 18th century style. The chapel was consecrated in 1536. There is, for France, a very large park, and the property extends to over two thousand acres.

### Fine Touraine Fare

SEMBLANÇAY. Semblançay is a place of historic memories and of more immediate and material interest as being one of the few villages in Touraine where you may taste of a cooking worthy of the fine products of the Loire Valley's soil. Go *chez Hamard,* and you will not be disappointed.

To the east of the village are the fine but crumbling ruins of an old fortress rising from the waters of a small lake. The stout square keep still makes a brave show.

The Romanesque church has four splendid lights of 16th century glass. There is also a statue of a *Vierge des douleurs* or Virgin of the Sorrows, about four hundred years old, and an ancient bell engraved with the arms of the Beaune-Semblançay family, for Semblançay was a barony owned by that Jacques de Beaune, baron de Semblançay (whom we meet at Tours), finance minister to François I. Poor Jacques was accused of malversion of public funds, and hanged in 1527 from the gibbet of Montfaucon. Later, Beaune's condemnation was "revised" and his memory cleared of crime. The reason for these not infrequent posthumous "rehabilitations," as the French call them, was, of course, that they allowed of the condemned man's property (or some of it) being returned to his family.

Of the lodging put up at Semblançay by Jacques de Beaune, no trace now remains.

### *"An Irreproachable Veteran of the Revolution"*

IN 1824 Louis Jérome Gohier published an apology for his life under the modest title of *An Irreproachable Veteran of the Revolution.* He was born at Semblançay in 1746, the son of the local notary, and was himself bred to the law. He had quite a brilliant revolutionary career and was Minister of Justice from 1793 to 1794. When Bonaparte returned from Egypt in 1799, Gohier was President of the Directory, but he withstood valiantly the blandishments of the "Man of Destiny." After Napoleon's *coup d'état* of 18th Brumaire (the 9th November), 1799, Gohier refused to resign, and bearded Bonaparte in the Tuileries. The "irreproachable republican" was imprisoned for some time and then banished to the country. Time brought about for him one of those half-ludicrous, half-pathetic transformations which were common enough in the fabulous days of the Napoleonic epic. The ragged little subaltern had become the most powerful sovereign in the world, the President of the Directory was on the outside looking in, and glad enough to accept the humble job of consul at Amsterdam! But Gohier lived through the Restoration, and died just before Louis-Philippe became "King of the French."

## *Irish Counts*

SERRANT. About ten miles from Angers, along the right bank of the Loire, you pass the high railings and wrought-iron gates of Serrant park, leading to the imposing mass of a great Renaissance mansion, brown and buff, flanked by great round towers capped with slate-covered bell-shaped cupolas.

Serrant was built by one Charles de Brie about 1546, and it may well be that the plans were drawn by the celebrated Philibert Delorme, the architect of the *château* of Anet, the great country-house of Diane de Poitiers, of part of Chenonceau, and also of the Tuileries in Paris, burned down in 1871. However, Serrant was rebuilt in 1636, and also much changed and added to in 1705. The additions and alterations have not destroyed all the character of this country palace, but its general aspect to-day is that of a Louis XIII *château*. It is true that Serrant is a little heavy and perhaps pretentious, but it by no means lacks grandeur.

Serrant was sold in 1602 to an Italian financial adventurer, one Scipione Sardini, but the heirs of the Brie family were able to buy it back and then to sell it for more than they paid for it.

In 1636 one Guillaume de Bautru became possessed of Serrant, which rounded off his considerable estates in this part of Anjou, for he was lord of Savennières, of La Roche-aux-Moines and of Le Plessis-Macé. His daughter and heiress married the *marquis* de

Vaubrun, and her son, the scrubby little *abbé* we meet at Le Plessis-Macé, sold the place to one Walsh. When Walsh became the owner of Serrant the estates were reputed to bring in an income of fifty thousand *livres*. In 1790, when the place was valued under the National Assembly, the rent-roll was up to 77,730 *livres*, whose purchasing power was almost certainly less than the fifty thousand *livres* of two generations before, so considerable had been the fall in the value of the French currency during the 18th century.

This Walsh, who already had acquired the lordships of Ingrandes, Champtocé, Savennières, La Roche-Serrant and the delightfully named Petit-Paris, was an opulent southern Irish merchant, who had not only followed James II in exile to France, but had lent him considerable sums of money. Whether he was ever repaid is not clear, but Walsh retained enough fortune to set up as a French country magnate. In 1755 the Walsh family were gratified with the title of *comte*. In the 19th century one of the Walsh girls married, as his third wife, the eighth *duc* of the historic La Trémoïlle family. After her death in 1887, Serrant became the property of the La Trémoïlles, and this Anjou estate was, indeed, until the extinction of the family in the male line, the only landed property in France belonging to the once wealthy and powerful house. The La Trémoïlles lost all their lands at the Revolution. The last *duc* de La Trémoïlle was burned to death at the age of twenty-two in 1933, during a country-house fire in the south of England.

## A Luxurious Mansion

SERRANT consists of three wings forming three sides of a square; the fourth side is closed by railings and a monumental gateway, and the whole house is surrounded by a broad moat. The old buildings of Charles de Brie comprise the northern tower, half the main wing and part of the wing near the northern tower. In the middle of the main façade is an entrance surmounted by a pediment bearing the arms of La Trémoïlle, quartered with those of Aragon and the Two Sicilies, Jerusalem and other historic coats, and surrounded by the four "T's," initials of the four titles of the family—La Trémoïlle, Talmont, Tarento and Thouars.

Local architects, knowing nothing of what the foreign master-masons were doing in the Île-de-France, went on imitating the old styles in the provinces. Serrant is a place in rather a bastard style, though it is finer in conception than the colossal and much-over-rated *château* of Valençay (Indre) which is of the same date, that is about 1547. But there is something mechanical about Serrant and cold, and truth to tell rather tiresome.

## A Magnificent Tomb

DESPITE the fine things in the apartments, the greatest sight at Serrant is the chapel, a lofty and majestic shrine, comparable for its "grand manner" with that of Blenheim. Moreover, the chapel is to all intents and purposes a mausoleum, since the tomb of the *marquis* de Vaubrun dominates the sanctuary. Madame de Vaubrun was a model of conjugal piety. Madame de Sévigné describes her as spending long hours lost in contemplation of her husband's portrait. After his death at the battle of Altenheim in 1675 she erected to his memory a notable monument. The carving was executed by Coysevox, the artist who created the tombs of Colbert and Mazarin and the group of "Mercury and Fame" in the Tuileries Gardens in Paris.

Vaubrun is represented mortally wounded, but still clenching his commander's baton, while at his side his *marquise* weeps. Hovering above is a Victory bearing a trophy and a crown. Although it is all a little formal and courtly, the monument is somehow strangely moving.

In the house itself room after room is hung with Tours tapestries, woven at a time when the Touraine looms were among the most famous in Europe. There are rooms of Chinese silks and rooms of 18th century elegance. . . . It is a bright, light house, with no mystery. There are innumerable saloons filled with priceless furniture and hangings, and all the main bedrooms have their bathrooms in the thickness of the wall. Enormous sums were spent on Serrant during the time of the late *duc* and his *duchesse,* and it is one of the best kept-up of country houses in France. In one of the towers is preserved the rich library and the ancient archives of the House of La Trémoïlle.

Serrant has housed many illustrious visitors. Louis XIV, Napoleon and the Duchess of Berry all slept at Serrant. Napoleon III (in 1849 when he was Prince-President) spent some days here.

## The English Achilles versus Bluebeard

SILLÉ-LE-GUILLAUME. William the Conqueror took Sillé-le-Guillaume towards the end of his reign, and in the early 15th century the place was besieged by John FitzAlan, Earl of Arundel [and even Duke of Touraine], known as the "English Achilles," who died from his wounds when only twenty-seven years of age at Beauvais in 1435. Sillé was delivered by Gilles de Laval, Lord of Retz or Rais and Marshal of France, the original of "Bluebeard," whose debaucheries and numerous erotic murders procured for him a sinister reputation long before he was strangled and his body burned at Nantes in 1440 (see p. 73).

The castle that was the stronghold of the town and defied so many attacks is imposing in its ruin. The splendid keep is a huge mass of masonry about 125 feet high and over 44 feet in diameter. This grand tower is surmounted by a crenellated and machicolated platform that is capped with a conical tower.

From the keep's top the view is very fine. To the north, about a mile and a half from the town, on the slopes of the Coëvrons Hills, is the dark mantle of Sillé Forest.

The Church of Notre-Dame was founded by the first Barons of Sillé. The belfry is Romanesque, but has been restored. At the base of this tower is a delightful 13th century Gothic doorway, surmounted with carvings of the Virgin and Child, the Last Judgment and the Twelve Apostles. On the southern façade of the church are Romanesque windows with carved masks and faces.

An early Gothic crypt is below the choir and the transepts. The choir-stalls are of rather fine 16th century work.

Just behind the church is the *place* des Minimes, with the town hospital in the old Louis XIII convent.

On the Sillé–Conlie road there are one or two interesting places —Tennie, with a 11th century church by the side of the Vègre stream, and Verniette, with some 13th century Romanesque wall-paintings depicting the Life of Saint-Eutropius. The pictures are not in very good state, and have been restored, but they are rather far north for Romanesque mural paintings.

Nearer Conlie is the Romanesque Church of Neuvy-en-Champagne, with one of the rather rare French recumbent effigies—in this case of Antoine de Girois, who died in 1624.

## Benedictine Splendour

SOLESMES. If you come to Solesmes on some great festival of the Church, such as the Feast of the Assumption, which has always been so splendidly observed within the bounds of the archdiocese of Tours, you will not only enjoy the magnificent Gregorian music for which the Benedictine monks are famous, but you may also see the moving medieval ritual of the Black Friars' consecration to their life of work and song. The impression is still strong with us of such a ceremony with the hot murmur of summer dying at the open doors of the long, lofty and narrow church that widens towards the east into a spacious and rectangular choir of the most sober and splendid style of 15th century Gothic.

The only touch of colour was lent by the dull gold of the high altar and by the Lord Archbishop of Tours sitting before it clad in his pontificals. Before him, evocatory of our ancient Black Friars, was a number of cowled, sombre figures, each holding to its breast the document of Profession, and then, with its fellows, prostrating itself before the altar. And the gravely gorgeous cadence of the plain-song abolished all thought of time. You were back in the Middle Ages.

The Benedictines are so famed for their literary and artistic labours that we are inclined to forget that the principal duty of St. Benedict's sons is to sing the praises of God. As the French writer, J. K. Huysmans, put it:

*"The peace that is spread by this divine office is a peace of joy . . . men who taste of it are transfigured, they are consoled and stripped of their terrestrial trappings. . . ."*

## Dom Guéranger

THE maker of modern Solesmes was the famous Dom Guéranger, who in 1833 took possession of the ruined Priory of Solesmes with the intention of transforming it into a great Benedictine abbey.

In 1010 a lord of the neighbouring fief of Sablé founded a priory for a handful of monks. The lower courses of the chapel's walls are still those laid in the 11th century, whereas the roof of high vaulting was added in 1470, when the priory was restored after the devastation wrought during the Hundred Years' War. About 1494, in order to create a shrine worthy of a relic from the Crown of Thorns, Prior Guillaume Cheminart added to the south transept the noble chapel known as that of Our Lady of Pity. In this sanctuary is the Holy Sepulchre, carved about 1496 and attributed (in part at least) to Michel Colombe, the great Touraine sculptor. Prior Jean Bougler, some years later, placed in the north transept a number of statues and sculptures, of which the Entombment of the Virgin is the most moving. Some authorities consider that Italian and Flemish influence is visible in the works of Prior Bougler's shrine, whereas it is clear that the Chapel of Our Lady of Pity illustrates "the most significant tendencies of French sculpture at the end of the 15th century," and is to be situated "both by its date and its geographical position at the very heart of French national art."

A description of the "Saints of Solesmes," as these precious statues are called, would demand a volume, but in addition to the superb Entombment, the Assumption and the Last Communion of the Virgin are of the first rank. Some of the other pieces, interesting as they are, do not reach the same level of execution. The latest in date would not seem to have been carved after 1550.

The Flamboyant windows in the nave and the graceful and airy lierne vaulting belong to the additions made from 1470 onwards.

This nave of the old priory church now seems like a corridor leading to the spacious sanctuary added by Dom Guéranger in 1865, when he doubled the area of his abbey chapel. Nine modern chapels were added to the nave.

From 1556 to 1664 Solesmes was administered by a series of commendatory priors. Then came the occupation of the place by the reformed Benedictines of the congregation of Saint-Maur. It was these "Maurists," so famous for their editions of patristic literature and for their historical researches, who rebuilt the priory in 1722. To this day, Solesmes consists of two distinct parts —on the one hand, the 18th century conventual buildings of the Maurists, and, on the other, the great new monastery put up to the plans of Dom Mellet in 1896.

Two wings are still standing of the 18th century priory—one facing towards the town of Sablé, and the other, a sober and classical Louis XV monument rising above the sluggish, iridescent waters of the Sarthe.

The Revolution ruined Solesmes. The monks were scattered, the bells were melted down, the contents of the treasury were sold and the priory buildings and lands put up for auction. The priory itself was, luckily enough, bought by a man who admired and valued the priceless statues and preserved them from harm. But they had become private property, though a meddling prefect ordered the statuary to be removed from Solesmes and put up in Le Mans Cathedral. The prefect's order was clearly abusive, and the owner of Solesmes appealed to Napoleon himself, who in a decree signed at his headquarters of Vilna in 1812 gave instructions that the statues should remain at Solesmes.

The conventual buildings had been bought by other speculators, and were stripped of their furnishings and allowed to fall into ruin. Such was the position when the *abbé* Prosper Guéranger bought all the remaining parts of Solesmes in 1832.

In July 1833 the new monastery was opened, and Guéranger went to Rome, where he was recognised by the Benedictine abbot of Saint Paul beyond the Walls. Pope Gregory XVI raised Solesmes to the rank of abbey, and appointed Dom Guéranger its first Abbot and superior of the Benedictine Order in France.

Guéranger, who was an administrator and organiser of the first class and a man of exceptional energy and strength of character, also founded the Benedictine nunnery of Saint Cecilia, at the other end of the village from his abbey. He died in 1875, and is buried in a vault under the third bay of his church's nave. He had made his foundation into a world-famous centre of Benedictine learning and Benedictine song.

## The New Abbey

THE overwhelming sight of Solesmes is the new abbey rising sheer from the river-side next to the gracious priory of the old Maurist monks. The formidable fortress-like monastery towers up ten storeys and more, into the sky, a citadel of rose-coloured granite, strengthened by great buttresses, and pierced with numberless arched windows. This imposing, severe and powerful monument is only fifty years old, but it is ageless, as befits an abode of peace. Here at Solesmes, life goes on under the Benedictine motto of "PAX."

The monks had to leave Solesmes in 1901, under the provisions of the Law on the "Congregations," but the Benedictines returned in 1922.

## Le Clerc de Juigné

SOLESMES village is just a hamlet, with, however, a decent inn or two. Those who want to spend a few days near the abbey and enjoy its peace and magnificent song can easily find lodgings.

Solesmes lies about two miles to the north-east of Sablé, and you follow the right bank of the Sarthe, until you see the huge mass of the abbey from afar. It is a sight for miles, since the new abbey buildings are nearly three hundred feet long and over a hundred and fifty feet high.

The highway leads on between the river's banks, and under picturesque cliffs pitted with marble quarries, until you reach Juigné-sur-Sarthe, stepped up the sides of the deep valley. The 18th century *château* de Juigné belongs to the *marquis* de Juigné, head of the ancient Leclerc family that played such a part in the history of Anjou. The Leclercs moved back here to their original fief from Verdelles, when they had built their fine new house in Louis XV's time. Among the supporters and subscribers to Dom Guéranger's work, the members of the Juigné family were foremost.

If you climb to the top of the hill behind Juigné, you have a most evocatory view over hill and dale, and over Solesmes set in its circlet of woods.

## A Valetudinarian Magnate

SOURCHES. Sourches is an immense and imposing Louis XV palace in a great park that was designed and laid out by Mansard. Nothing could show more clearly the architectural character of the classical French garden or the rôle that such gardens were held to play in the general plan of a country-house than this "building" of a garden by the most famous architect of his day.

Sourches is splendidly situated. Down the broad alleys and through the tall avenues of the grounds you are faced with a succession of rich scenery: the dark beauty of Perseigne forest, the line of the Coëvrons hills and the heights of the "*Alpes Mancelles*" the shady slopes of the *Grande Charnie*, the twisted peaks of Voutre, the "camp" of the *Vache Noire*, and the broad, green plains of the *mancelle* Champagne.

Sourches had known many masters before it came into the possession of the du Bouchet family. These du Bouchets were great people in their day, though their name is better known to us as that of a brand of cognac or, more esoterically, as that of the mother of Lord Chesterfield's son! The du Bouchets held, for several generations, the dignified office of "Grand Provost of France," and it was Louis-François du Bouchet, *marquis* de Sourches, who had his old house surrounded by Mansart's sumptuous gardens. The *marquis* himself superintended the laying out of his grounds, although this work did necessitate a disagreeable, and even dangerous, exposure to the open air. However, a careful dosing with decoctions of Peruvian bark, with nettle tea and gin, as well as the protective chewing of marsh-mallow pastilles, warded off the worst effects of the outdoor life, and the *marquis* lived to admire his men's handiwork.

Monsieur de Sourches had married the heiress of the Chambes family, Lords of Montsoreau, whose ancestor in the 16th century was such a treacherous host. When Madame de Sourches died, the *marquis* found that the gay life at Versailles had nearly ruined him. He sold off all his father's furniture from Sourches, and removed his own either to his house in the Vaugirard suburb of Paris or to Montsoreau. He declared that he would rather make a bonfire on the terrace at Sourches of every stick he possessed than sell any of his own furniture. He seems to have been an agreeable man, and when he died in 1716 he was much regretted. He also left behind him four hundred thousand *livres* in debts—as well as the MS. of his *Mémoires* covering the years from 1681 to 1712.

His grandson and successor, the fourth Grand Provost of his family, lived all his career at Court, until his wife's death so upset him that he decided to tour the country and visit, for the first time, his lands at Sourches, Montsoreau, Bellay and other places.

In 1765 he began the construction of the new *château* de Sourches, and soon found, as do most builders, that the cost of the building was running up much higher than had been estimated. The lands of Bellay-en-Anjou had to be sold, and brought in 240,000 *livres* that were swallowed up at Sourches. And the Grand Provost also had ten children to look after.

## "*The Governess of the Children of France*"

ONE of the sons, the *marquis* de Tourzel, died in 1786, leaving a widow. Marie-Antoinette chose her to look after the royal children—to whom her devotion was great. Later, leaving Paris, she lived at her *château* d'Abondant until her death in 1832. Her son, created *duc* de Tourzel at the Restoration, left Sourches to the *duc* des Cars.

The designer of Sourches was Pradel—architect to the *comte* de Provence—and he put up a classical Louis XV monument. There is a noble façade, two slightly projecting wings at either end, a central cupola (such as we can see in the *École Militaire* in Paris), and the whole stands back from a fine sweeping balustraded double drive, meeting in front of the palace, and leading down over a bridge through the formal grounds set regularly with conical yew-bushes. It is all very magnificent and courtly.

The house has some 229 doors and windows, and contains some good 18th century furniture and a few fine pictures, including a large and stately painting of Louis XVI given to the *marquis* de Tourzel by the King.

There used to hang in the Sourches gallery a splendid conversation piece by François-Hubert Drouais (the father of the better-known J.-G. Drouais), representing the builder of Sourches with his second wife and their family. The picture had a curious and unusual history. After being sold from Sourches and taken to the United States, it was bought back by the *marquis* de La Ferronays, a descendant of the du Bouchet family, and is now in his house in Paris.

L A SUZE-SUR-SARTHE. Beyond Le Mans lies La Suze-sur-Sarthe, a place of some 2,400 inhabitants on the left bank of the river. There are large flour-mills. Of the old castle, rebuilt in the 15th century, there remains only one wing, now occupied by a school. The parish church is the former chapel of the castle, and is built over a Romanesque crypt. Above the entrance door is a fine 15th century statue of the Virgin and Child.

The nine-arched bridge over the Sarthe was built in the time of Henry IV. To the west of the town are the remains of the *château* de la Roche-Patras, that is now a farm.

The Village Street

The Romanesque Apse

**SAVENNIÈRES**

Sillé-le-Guillaume      The Castle

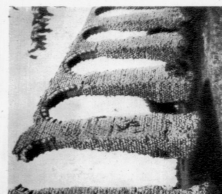

Tours      The old Loire Aqueduct

The painted Crypt

Tavant

Tours      Tomb of Sons of Charles VIII

The Monastery

Solesmes

Sautré      The Storeyed Manor

## The Painted Crypt

TAVANT. On the way from Chinon to Richelieu you turn off, about four miles from the former place, cross the Veude stream, and, passing Brétignolles, with its 15th century castle, you must stop at the hamlet of Tavant, just a few miles before L'Île-Bouchard. The church is late 11th century, and is small, massive and but little touched. The crypt is, however, the sight. It is narrow and low, a real subterranean sanctuary, and divided into three aisles by two rows of round, stumpy pillars, from which spring rough rib-vaultings.

The crypt was originally entirely painted. On the pillars you can see traces of pink background splashed here and there with white. Only the vaulting now retains its pictures. The ribs are picked out in carmine, bordered with yellow. The roof is painted with figures, one of which, in most cases, occupied a whole segment of the vaulting. There are "Virtues," and "Adam and Eve" and "David playing his Harp," "Lust" figured as a woman piercing her ravaged self with a lance, Adam digging and Eve spinning, a "Descent from the Cross," "Christ in Hades," the "Crucifixion of St. Peter." And near the entrance figures of doves very like those in the early Roman catacombs. The paintings are apparently of the same date as the building, that is undoubtedly 12th century. The figures have vigour, movement and life. Dull red is the dominant tone, and some of the faces lined in carmine look fierce enough. The whole thing is very archaic, and makes us think of the painted caverns of south-western France and the sacred places of later Old Stone Age men's mysteries and magic.

## Altionos

TOURS. Altionos, the Gallo-Roman town, lay upon the heights of Saint-Symphorien, on the north bank of the Loire, and opposite the modern city of Tours. The Roman emperors moved the settlement across the river, named the place CÆSARODUNUM and raised it in 374 to the rank of capital of the province known as the Third *Lugdunensis*. By the 4th century the town had become known as URBS TURONUM—the City of the Turones—of a Gaulish people who lived in what is now Touraine.

Christianity seems to have been introduced, in a discreet way, by Saint-Gatien as early as the 3rd century, but it was great Saint

Martin, the Apostle of the Gauls and third "bishop" of Tours, who really evangelised the countryside, though what a "bishop" really was in Roman Gaul of seventeen hundred years ago, it would be difficult to say.

## An English University

FROM their strongholds in the south of Gaul, the Visigoths advanced to the occupation of Tours in 473, but by 507, Clovis had made the town and its province a part of his Frankish dominions. Thirty-eight years later St. Clotilda, his wife and the daughter of the Burgundian king, died at Tours, in the odour of sanctity, for she it was who induced her pagan husband to adopt the Christian religion.

At the end of the 8th century, our Alcuin of York, the most eminent humanist of his day in western Europe, opened at Tours, under the patronage of Charlemagne, the first school of theology ever to be established on Gaulish soil and the first school of philosophy to be set up in Gaul since the fall of the Roman Empire.

When we reflect upon the dominant position enjoyed throughout our western world by the University of Paris right up to the devastation of the Hundred Years' War, we may also remember that the first university in France was founded by an Englishman, and that one of our fellow-countrymen was the first to teach the Franks Latin and the learning of the classics.

Indeed, from the 6th to the 9th centuries, western Europe was penetrated with English influences carried by the Anglo-Saxon missionaries. Boniface and his English disciple, Bishop Burchard of Würzburg, were the men who, thanks to their influence in Rome, were able to persuade the Pope that it would be prudent to connive at the revolution brought about by Charlemagne. In gratitude for services rendered, the Carolingians became firm supporters of the Anglo-Saxon missionaries, the greatest of whom our Boniface, or Wynfryth (from Crediton in Devon), organised Church and State administration in newly-converted Germany. The impetus given to learning and scholarship by the Anglo-Saxons in the gloom of Carolingian Europe was considerable. The script we write and the type we read were shaped by Alcuin (or Alchvin) of York, whose prestige and influence dominated the spiritual life of western Europe for several generations.

### Martinopolis

DURING the great part of the Middle Ages Tours was a distinct city from the neighbouring town of Martinopolis, which grew up around Saint Martin's shrine and basilica.

From the first the twin cities had different administrations. Tours was governed by the Bishop, while Martinopolis, or *Châteauneuf* as it was later called, was controlled by the Chapter of the Basilica. Later, both places were enfeoffed to Counts, and our Henry II, as heir of the Counts, annexed Tours and Touraine to his Anglo-French empire.

In addition to the towns of Tours and Martinopolis, another settlement around the Abbey of Saint-Julien sprang up between them, while the feudal town, with its castle of the count, formed a fourth city. And, indeed, without stepping out of built-up streets, the traveller in the early Middle Ages could walk into a fifth, a sixth, a seventh and an eighth town.

As late as the 16th century, united Tours, the royal borough of Touraine, was still split up into no less than thirty-one separate fiefs and thirty-one different feudal lords divided between them administrative and judicial authority over the city. And each fief had its little urban castle or manor, its special subjects, its own code of laws, its own customs and its own privileges.

### A Capital of France

UNTIL the end of the 17th century Tours was one of the most prosperous and wealthy towns in France. The shrine of Saint Martin brought prestige and riches. Industries were flourishing. Nearly all the Kings of France, from Saint Louis to François I, resided at Tours. Louis XI made the place the capital of France, since, from his nearby manor of Plessis-lès-Tours, he ruled all his realm. If this wily monarch abolished the "liberties" of the commune and forced upon the town magistrates appointed by the sovereign, he did much for the material welfare of the place, encouraging the establishment of silk and gold- and silver-stuff weavers. The privileges and protection afforded to workmen and artisans attracted ever new inhabitants.

During the reigns of Henri III and IV a fortified wall was erected, including within its circuit the houses of both of the twin towns.

Although the Court removed from the Loire valley at the end of the Valois dynasty, the real blow to Tours' prosperity was struck by the revocation of the Edict of Nantes. Since the end of the 17th century, Tours has been nothing but a provincial capital, albeit one bearing many traces of a glorious past.

## A Princely Murderer

IN 1870, Tours was chosen as the site of the High Court appointed to try Prince Pierre Bonaparte for the murder of Victor Noir.

This sensational case, which did so much to discredit the already battered imperial régime, was a nine days' wonder.

Pierre Napoleon was one of the sons of Lucien Bonaparte, the next younger brother of Napoleon, but a brother who, from the time of his own second marriage, was estranged from the Emperor and who lived the latter part of his life, and ended his days, as a Roman prince entitled *principe di Canino*. Most of his revenues had been derived from the sale of Etruscan antiquities excavated on his estate in the *Maremma* to the north of Rome.

On the establishment of the Second Empire, Pierre Bonaparte, his son (who had led an adventurous life in Italy and England), became reconciled to Napoleon III, and received from him the title of imperial prince (which the uncle, the great Napoleon, had always refused to Lucien). Pierre, though far from stupid, displayed a marked preference for a debauched life, and maintained a gay existence throughout the Second Empire. Towards its end, in January 1870, he was called out by a journalist named Pascal Grousset. Lucien got into a violent altercation with the two seconds sent to present him with the challenge and, drawing his revolver, shot one of them dead, a certain Victor Noir. Under official pressure Bonaparte was acquitted, but the verdict was hailed as a scandal by the opposition Press. His later life was obscure, and he died at Versailles in 1881.

Pierre had had, by the daughter of a Paris plumber named Ruffin, a son, christened Roland, who was legitimatised by the subsequent marriage of his parents. This Roland Bonaparte (who assumed, apparently without right, the appellation of "Imperial Highness" as well as the additional Christian name of Napoleon) lived to be a patron of the sciences and an anthropologist of note.

He married one of the daughters of the famous Monsieur Blanc, the ex-waiter who gained a huge fortune as the organiser and chief profiteer of the Monte Carlo gambling casino. Roland's only child, Marie, who inherited her father's anthropological interests, married Prince George of Greece.

## Tours again the Capital of France

A FEW months after the acquittal of Pierre Bonaparte, the Second Empire had tumbled to ruins on the field of Sedan, and the Government of National Defence left Paris to reside at Tours from the 13th September to the 9th December, 1870, on which latter date they left for Bordeaux. The Germans bombarded Tours on the 21st December, but occupied the city only from the 18th January until the 8th March.

During the doleful days preceding the Battle of the Marne, in September 1914, the French Government passed through Tours on its way to Bordeaux. From 1917 the town was the headquarters of the American Army administration. It was not until the fateful June of 1940 that Tours, for a few days, again sheltered a fugitive French Government.

## A Battered City

ON the 14th June, before the German advance, the French Government left Tours for Bordeaux and for the night of humiliation which was to last over fifty months. On the 18th June, French sappers blew up the Pont Wilson, the stone bridge crossing the Loire in the main axis of the town. At the same time Germany artillery and German dive-bombers attacked the French forces defending the passage of the river. A huge fire swept Tours and ravaged all that part of the city on either side of the *rue Nationale* between the Loire and the *rue Emile-Zola*. The fine vista of the main street, the view that struck all visitors to Tours, is no more. The church of Saint-Julien is very gravely damaged and much of the "Old Tours" is lost for ever. In 1944 Tours was again bombarded in order to hamper the enemy's troop movements. Tours railway station and the houses near it were very much knocked about and the suburb of Saint-Pierre-des-Corps (the railway junction on the main Paris-Bordeaux line) was severely mauled. But it was the bombardments of 1940 which smashed Tours, and not the lightning advance in 1944. However, very much of interest still remains in Tours, where the main historical monuments have emerged unscathed from the torment of war.

## Old Tours

A FEW crumbling fragments of Cæsarodunum's walls still stand, but the existing monuments are all of the Middle Ages.

Several of the old churches of Tours and of its suburbs hide, under their Gothic finery, traces of their Romanesque selves. Of such are Saint-Symphorien, Saint-Pierre-des-Corps, Saint-Julien, Notre-Dame-la-Riche and the magnificent cathedral, in which we can trace, from the commencement of the 12th century until the end of the 16th, the evolution of the typically French architecture of the Loire valley.

Of the ancient Palace of the Counts of Touraine, little remains for us but the descriptions of the old chroniclers. The place was erected about 1160 by our Henry II, and on the Loire's banks to the west of the city's ramparts. There exist of it a few bits of wall now built into other edifices, and a rugged, medieval tower known as *La Tour de Guise*, since in it was incarcerated the *prince* de Joinville, son of the Guise, murdered at Blois by the orders of King Henri III.

## Saint Martin

TOURS was, in the early Middle Ages, the home of two men most illustrious throughout the Europe of their time. There was Saint Martin, from distant Pannonia (i.e. Croatia with some adjoining lands). His name is still remembered for his Summer, his Mass, and his Cloak which he divided with the beggar.

And there was the old chronicler, Gregory of Tours, the man from whom the trouble of his time wrang forth the cry MUNDUS SENESCIT—"the world grows old"—but all writers have been inclined to deem their own age more scourged with calamities than any other known.

Saint Martin was Bishop of Tours in the 4th century, and the legend of his virtues spread throughout Gaul. After he had died at Candes his disciples brought his body to Tours, but it was not until 472 that a church was erected worthy of his memory and of the miracles wrought by his remains.

This first basilica of Saint Martin was the most spacious ecclesiastical building to be put up in western Europe from the fall of the Roman Empire until the reign of Charlemagne. Gregory of Tours tells us that the church was 160 feet long, 60 feet wide and 45 feet high inside. This was, indeed, a notable edifice for the Dark Ages.

The Merovingian Frankish kings (i.e. Clovis and his successors) were devoted to the cult of Saint Martin. A saint's popularity and prestige were nicely proportioned to what was held to be the efficacy of his relics. Those of Saint Martin were exceptionally wonder-working. The Merovingian sovereigns were, indeed, accustomed to carry about with them on their campaigns the celebrated cope (or cloak) of the saint, together with some of his bones. Such objects acted as a sure palladium and guarantee of victory. The Carolingian sovereigns and their successors, the first Capetian monarchs, continued the salutary tradition of travelling with Saint Martin's relics.

The shrine of Saint Martin became one of the most favoured in all western Christendom. For fourteen centuries pious gifts poured into the basilica and the abbey, adorning the shrine and enriching the happy monks, canons and abbots. The pilgrimage to Martinopolis or Châteauneuf rivalled in efficacy those to the tombs of Saint Peter, Saint James, or Saint Thomas of Canterbury.

The original basilica was burned down in 997. By the 12th century its successor was in ruins. A third church was put up from 1175 onwards. The splendid place was 360 feet long, 220 feet wide at the transepts, and nearly 90 feet high to the roof inside.

The old basilica of Saint Martin disappeared in 1802, during the régime of the Consulate, as did so many of the ancient monuments of France. The *rue des Halles* runs right through the site of the third Church of Saint Martin. Nothing now survives but two towers, known respectively as *La Tour de l'Horloge* and *La Tour Charlemagne*, together with a precious fragment of the cloister.

To-day, a magnificent, new, shiny sanctuary perpetuates the memory of Saint Martin. The building is more or less in the style of the 4th century Mediterranean basilicas, but it is a style, as one writer puts it rather grimly, *corrigé et amélioré*—"corrected and bettered." This remark recalls the German salesman in Berlin who assured that the furniture he was offering was *verbesserter Louis XV*—"improved Louis XV."

## La Psalette

ON the south side of the basilica was put up, from 1508 to 1518, a charming Renaissance cloister. The name of the architect is known. He was Bastien François, nephew of the great sculptor Michel Colombe (see p. 337). In this Cloister of Saint Martin, François transformed the style of French Gothic construction. The arches of the gallery are not ogival (or pointed), but rounded. The vaulting is supported on brackets, and the ribbing is arranged so as to form rectangular compartments. The general effect is one of great spaciousness.

The decoration, on the other hand, is quite Italian—spirals, palmettos, medallions, floral motifs and antique heads. But the over-emphasis, the awkwardness even, is proof that this "new-style" sculpture was executed by French workmen, and is not the product of Lombard or Genoese sculptors' easy mastery. Only the east gallery of the cloister has survived.

## "The World Grows Old"

GREGORY OF TOURS is the earliest of French historians and the precursor of Joinville, of Villehardouin, of Froissart and of Commynes. For our knowledge of the fierce and bloodthirsty and luxurious times of the Merovingian Kings of the Franks, Gregory of Tours is an indispensable guide. Gregory sat and watched and wrote in his solitary monk's cell. Everything went into his book— the wildest legends, the most miraculous fables and the most improbable tales; yet his chronicle lives and impresses the reader by its honesty. Of course, there is much concerning the life and wonders of great Saint Martin himself, but from Gregory's unfaltering pen came also a stream of words calling into life and movement the horrors committed by the men of war, the misery of the masses and the abominations of his time—but then Gregory, unlike so many of our present-day prophets of doom, lived in the hope, in the expectation, in the certitude, even, of better things.

## Golden Age

THE golden age of the Touraine lands was the 15th century— the century of the Renaissance in France. Tours was a royal town, while Paris was more a city housing a university than the capital of the realm of France.

The poets, the writers and the artists followed the Court to Touraine. It was at Tours that lived and worked Jean Bourdichon, Jean Fouquet, the Clouets, Michel Colombe the Justes and, later, Ronsard and Rabelais—and others.

There are still standing several houses dating from the second half of the 15th century. No doubt at Tours was developed that happy combination of warm-toned brick and cool white stone, delicately yet soberly carved, a combination which offers an architectural style at once essentially French and adapted to exportation all over northern Europe.

In the Loire valley this mode is an admirably unpretentious one, even when exemplified in the houses of wealthy and eminent men. Measure, proportion and grace are the key-notes of the tradition. Not until the time of Louis XVI did French secular architecture again achieve such harmony and such perfection as it did in the 15th and 16th century brick and stone buildings of Touraine and Anjou.

It is the little Manor of Plessis-lès-Tours (see p. 251)—now so forlorn-looking in its shorn and truncated remnant—which was the first masterpiece of the new "Touraine manner."

## *"Gable on the Street"*

IN Tours itself there are several old houses in the Touraine style. Two of them are very notable.

The first is the so-called *Hôtel Tristan.* There is no reason for thinking that the house ever had any connection with Tristan L'Hermite, Provost of the Marshals of France, under Kings Louis XI and Charles VIII, and the man who carried out many of the savage but salutary sentences of the former sovereign.

As a matter of fact, the *Hôtel Tristan* was built about 1490 by one Pierre du Puy.

The street front is pierced by a door with a curved lintel and by windows framed in carved stone. The whole place is crowned with a high gable—the famous *pignon sur rue* that still, in popular French phrase, is used to describe a man of substance and importance in his community.

The courtyard is now a little built-in, but it is most worthy of admiration. Everywhere is the cunning juxtaposition of brick and stone; in the gallery, in the well with its sculptured rim, in the staircase door (it is a little low and mysterious as though discouraging importunate visitors), and over the windows, where you may read ASSEZ AURONS, PEU VIVRONS, PRIE DIEU POUR, which are anagrams hiding the name of the founder, PIERRE DU PUY.

Another house, roughly contemporary with that of *Tristan*, is that of the Binet family, and it is also almost intact.

The dwelling surrounds a court, and it is knit together by a charming arcade or gallery rising to the height of the first storey and supported on delicate wooden pillars. Two spiral staircases (also of wood) give access to the upper floors.

The whole place is peaceful and prosperous-looking, and breathes the spirit of the solid but prudently unassuming burgesses of late medieval Tours.

## Old Houses

HERE and there in the city are—or were—other houses or parts of houses dating back to the 15th century or the beginning of the 16th, but most of these dwellings have been rebuilt or in some way mutilated. But it is rather fun to poke about in the narrow streets and to discover, every now and again, some fine door or window ennobled by delicate and admirable sculpture.

On the *Grand-Marché* square there is a curious entrance giving access to a little cluster of houses, which were formerly the property of the Treasurer of Saint Martin's basilica.

Nearby lived Jean Fouquet (1416–1480), a Tours man born and bred, painter and miniaturist, and one of the creators of French painting. All these houses were in a purely French style and were untouched by Italian influence. But the new Italianate mode, imported from Lombardy into the Loire valley after the Italian campaigns of King Charles VIII, is exemplified in a number of Tours buildings which Francesco Florio [an Italian traveller, and, therefore, in matters of Italian-inspired architecture a rather captious critic] calls "magnificent" in the curious notes he left on his trip through 16th century Touraine.

## Italian Magnificence

FIRST of Tours "Italian" houses came the *Hôtel Gouin*, a Gothic mansion which was refashioned and transformed (between 1510 and 1520) by one René Gardette, who had just bought it and wanted an up-to-date and smart town house. The name *Hôtel Gouin* is comparatively modern, and commemorates a family which acquired the place in 1738.

The northern façade was little touched by Gardette, but the south front was completely remade. A central porch forming a sort of Italian loggia was added, and the small lodging on the west side was built. You could still trace the remains of the old Gothic decoration, but everywhere had been added pilasters, friezes, cartouches adorned with Italian motifs, ribbons, foliage and "candelabra." Now, alas, the *Hôtel Gouin* is no more. It was destroyed in the fighting during the last war, though the façade is still standing.

## Galland Treasures

ANOTHER large and fine old house in the Italian taste is the *Hôtel Galland*. Jean Galland was goldsmith to Kings Louis XI and Charles VIII. The mansion, however, improperly bears his name, since the building is not older than the first part of the reign of François I (i.e. about 1515–25).

Although the mansion was "repaired" and "restored" in the 17th century, it is still a very interesting place as offering the image of a rich man's town-dwelling of four hundred years, and more, ago.

On the ground floor of the west wing, on either side of the low arcade—which must once have been an open gallery—are two medallions, one representing the Emperor Galba and the other Cicero. These works are of an exceptionally fine and cunning workmanship.

Unfortunately, the winter climate of Touraine, with its abundant rainfall and comparatively cool weather (cool compared with that of Tuscany, but not with that of the Thames valley!), induced many of the owners of places which had been set up with open galleries, in the Italian mode, to brick them up or glaze them in. Of course, one of the great difficulties of successfully transplanting an architectural style from one region to another is that if there is a marked difference of climate, then the style, which has been largely dictated by the exigencies of convenience, must be modified, and, in effecting the modification, men often find that they change the whole character of the architecture. The great merit of the French has been that they have never [save for short periods after the first introduction of a new style] been slavish imitators, but skilful adapters, knowing how to create out of imported elements something new and peculiarly French. Not all other peoples have been as cunning in borrowing.

Since the year 1919 the *Hôtel Galland* has housed the Museum of Touraine Antiquities. There is a fine show of prehistoric stone implements (mostly from the region of Le Grand Pressigny and offering us typical specimens of the famed honey-coloured flint from which was chipped the prized stone tools, exported far and wide in New Stone Age times), the collection of Gallo-Roman antiquities is large, there are some Merovingian relics and curious objects of late medieval and Renaissance date.

One of the most interesting exhibits is the reconstruction of Rousseau's "physics laboratory" as he had it at Chenonceau during the time that he was tutor and bear-leader to young Dupin (see p. 98).

## *Beaune's House*

UNDOUBTEDLY the finest private house whose remains have come down to us was the Hôtel of Jacques de Beaune-Semblançay, Treasurer of the Finances, who fell from royal favour in 1525 and was later on executed.

Jacques de Beaune was, in the heyday of his prosperity, one of the most considerable personages of the town. His name is still known, not only for the dramatic story of his fall—that sort of tale can be told of not a few financiers in modern as well as in ancient times—but also because he was a lover and a patron of the Fine Arts.

At La Carte, near Semblançay, he set up a superb country-house, of which no traces remain. He presented to the Church of Saint-Saturnin several splendid pieces of tapestry, and he it was who set up at Tours the fountain bearing his name.

This Renaissance fountain is situated in the heart of old Tours, and its general form is that of a "candelabrum" carved out of Genoa marble, while the basin is of Volvic stone from Auvergne. The pyramidal structure was, formerly, surmounted by a gilded bronze crucifix. It disappeared in 1562. Pierre de Valence, *maître fontainier*, had charge of the engineering, while Bastien and Martin François sculptured the decorations with superb artistry.

Pierre de Beaune's house—or what remains of it—is half-hidden by modern and characterless buildings, and you risk passing by the splendid place without guessing what you are missing. You have to search at the corner of the *rue Colbert* and the *rue nationale* to find the entrance through the priggish 18th century façades which were put up less than two hundred years ago to prolong the *rue Royale* (now *rue Nationale*).

Beaune began his house in 1507. His architect was a local man, one Guillaume Besnouard. So great a part does the splendid decoration play in the design of this dwelling, that the whole thing, one is tempted to say, must be a good deal later than the accepted date for the building. But there is little or no doubt that what we see *does* date from the early years of the 16th century. There are always architects who are ahead of their times. Every now and again we come across Louis XIV houses affording a foretaste of Louis XV style.

However, the gallery on the first floor, and its windows, framed with flat pilasters ornamented with chimeras, do seem to be not earlier than 1530 or 1540, but the windows and the fine Louis XV balcony were destroyed during the war of 1939–45.

Practically nothing remains of the sumptuous town house put up by Thomas Bohier (see p. 95), a building described by an old chronicler as "magnificent above all those to be found in the city."

Then, finally (although we have not exhausted all the old houses in Tours), there is the *Hôtel Cottereau,* a small place with an arcaded ground floor and a very carefully planned and proportioned façade. It is true that we have here no traces of a great artist's handiwork. The frieze over the windows, the pilasters, the little medallions (framing busts or bas-reliefs of heads) may, perhaps, be the product of some master-mason's chisel. But their very awkwardness is interesting. Have we here the legacy of some local innovator "going all modern" without quite understanding what he was trying to do?

## The Capital of Touraine

DURING much of the 19th century there used to be settled in and around Tours a colony of British people attracted to the middle reaches of the Loire by the climate, the cheapness of living, and the supposed advantages to be derived from residing "where the best French was spoken." Of course, the climate is pleasing (at least compared with any in our islands), but there are other regions of France where the atmosphere is less enervating, the winter shorter and the sunlight more lasting. The legend of the "cheap living" died hard. Of course, what most of the expatriates meant when they said that it cost less to get by in Touraine than in Tunbridge Wells, was that in Touraine they felt they could do things which, in Victorian England, they could only have done at the cost of losing a good deal of "prestige." As for the "best French" fable, well, the *Tourangeaux* do talk quite good French, but no better than that of many other countrymen north of the Loire. It is a peasant's speech retaining many words no longer "classical" French since the rigid pruning by the pedants in the 16th and 17th centuries.

But, for some years now, Tours and Touraine have not known many English settlers. Our compatriots have moved off farther south, and you will probably find more in and around, say, Saint-Raphael on the Mediterranean coast, than you will in all Touraine.

Still, Touraine (and to a lesser extent Anjou) once had English clubs, tea-rooms and churches. Some of the expatriates were not as conventional as one might expect. All readers of his biographies will remember something of young Richard Burton's adventures in and around Tours when he was staying with his father and mother. It is a long cry from Marmoutier to Mecca or from Balzac's country to those of the "Arabian Nights," but even in his old age the traveller never ceased to keep a warm place in his heart for the Touraine of his early youth.

Tours is altogether a very pleasing town. First and foremost among its attractions we may reckon one of the best hostelries in provincial France, the famed *Hôtel de l'Univers,* where, not only may you taste of Touraine fare at its best, but also meditate upon the mutability of human affairs—if you are inclined to moralising. For here, several times in the last few generations, have men thronged and met when their country's fortunes were at their ebb. In 1870, in 1914, and again in 1940, the halls and corridors of the *Hôtel de l'Univers* were filled with a jostling crowd of politicians, journalists, women of fashion, soldiers and fugitives who had fled before the enemy and who were wondering whether the knell had sounded for the doom of France. It never had. The recuperative power of the French is one of the most remarkable things about them. But you will hardly find in Paris the reasons for this resurgence. Perhaps a few weeks in Touraine and Anjou will teach us more about the essence of France than years in Paris.

There are things in Tours which we may just mention, leaving the visitor to appreciate them for himself. There were some fine, if uninspired, modern buildings—the law courts, the theatre and the town hall. They were worthy of an important provincial capital, or were thought worthy of it when they were erected. There are plenty of gardens—that known as *le jardin des Prébendes d'Oé*, and the *parc de Grammont,* for instance.

The stone bridge over the Loire (thrown across from 1765 to 1779) was, of its type, one of the most elegant and satisfying buildings to be erected in the 18th century.

There are museums and libraries.

## *Precious MSS.*

THE main library was housed in the old town hall, a rather imposing 18th century edifice which was entirely destroyed in the war.

Within was a collection, begun in 1791, of 2,030 MSS. drawn from the libraries of the cathedral, of Saint-Martin's basilica and of Marmoutier abbey. Ever since the end of the 18th century the store of MSS. and printed volumes has been enriched. Here also are deposited the municipal archives beginning with those of 1358.

The treasure of MSS. is one of the most precious in provincial France. Here is the 8th century *Evangelium* (or collection of gospels) of Charlemagne. This superb book, written entirely in golden majuscules, was the volume upon which the Kings of France took oath as abbots and honorary canons of Saint-Martin's basilica. Then there is the 11th century *Evangelium* of Charles the Bald, the 10th century *Sacramentary of Pope Gregory the Great,* an 11th century *Life of Saint Martin,* with pen-drawings, missals from Saint-Martin's, Saint-Gatien's and from Marmoutier. There are two *Books of Hours* (known as those of Anne of Brittany and of Charles V), formerly in the Carthusian monastery of Le Liget (see p. 180), and many, many more rare and beautiful books. The MSS. were still in 1948 housed temporarily in the *château* of Plessis-lès-Tours.

## A Notable Museum

THE old archiepiscopal palace (parts of which were 14th century work) had housed, since 1910, the Museum of Fine Arts. As so often is the case of these local French museums, the building itself was worthy of almost as much attention as its contents, but it was destroyed in the war.

The noteworthy collection of pictures was removed to a place of safety. The show-pieces are two Mantegnas—the "Resurrection" and "Christ in the Garden of Gethsemane." These paintings, together with a third, "Christ between the two Thieves" (now in the Louvre), formed part of the retable of the high altar in the Church of St. Zeno at Verona. And there are Bouchers, Rembrandt's "Portrait of Saskia" and many fine paintings of the French school. It is a splendid collection.

The enamels, porcelains, faiences, silk-stuffs, ivories and wood carvings are also important.

## The Cathedral

ALTHOUGH Saint-Gatien's cannot be called one of the foremost cathedrals of France (i.e. to be placed in the same class as the wonders of Chartres, Rouen, Bourges or Amiens), still, it is a noble and impressive edifice.

The north tower of Saint-Gatien's was finished in 1547, when the Gothic spire was replaced by an octagonal lantern covered with a cupola. Pierre de Valence began the work (but, probably, with the assistance of the brothers Bastien and Martin François, since the latter is entitled, in deeds dated 1505 and 1515, "master of the masonry work of the city of Tours"), and here we have what was, for Touraine, quite a novel sort of decoration all coming straight from Lombardy. But if the inspiration of this lantern is quite Italian, its execution is wholly French.

The south tower was not finished until a good deal later than the northern. The style is more compact, more classical perhaps.

In one of the cathedral's transepts is a most charming and pathetic monument. It is the tomb of the two infant children of King Charles VIII. It was carved in 1506.

The sarcophagus is adorned with *motifs* drawn both from pagan legend and Biblical story and the carving is from a master's chisel. There can be no doubt that this tomb is of Italian workmanship,

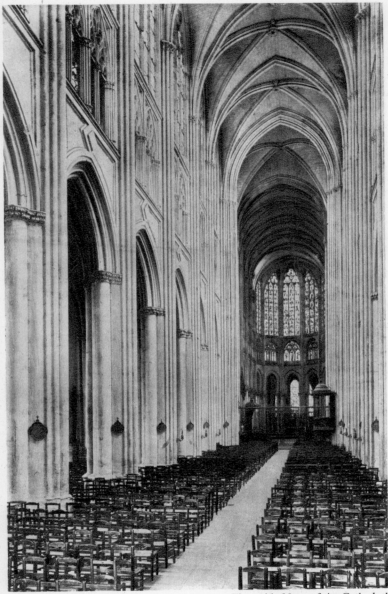

**Tours**                    The noble Nave of the Cathedral

The *Tour Charlemagne*

The *Fontaine de Beaune*

The *Croix Blanche*

The *Hôtel Gouin*

**TOURS**

and one of the artists was, probably, that Girolamo da Fiesole who carved the magnificent altarpiece (from Gaillon) representing St. George and the Dragon and now in the Louvre.

But if the sarcophagus is Italian, the ingenuous and wholly charming little recumbent figures of the infant princes are certainly French, and may have been, if not carved by the great Michel Colombe himself, at least fashioned by one of his close followers and pupils.

Of the original Romanesque cathedral nothing remains but the lower parts of the towers. Saint-Gatien, as we see it, is a Gothic shrine, enriched and decorated with Renaissance additions. The interior is one of stately slimness.

The choir was put up first, and then the nave was constructed on rather a less spacious plan, but, despite this disadvantage, and also despite a sinking of the foundations which has produced some distortion of the walls, Tours Cathedral, though, in its dimensions a moderate-sized church, is, by the beauty of its architecture and its splendid west front and its magnificent lights, worthy of a high rank among the numerous great cathedrals of France.

The west front, although cleared of most of its statuary in Renaissance times, is a masterpiece of the Flamboyant style.

After Chartres and Bourges, Tours ranks with Le Mans and Troyes as that cathedral of France where precious stained-glass windows may be enjoyed in profusion. The colours and the luminosity of the lights are marvellous, and in the rich Touraine sun, the noble interior of the delicately tinted, pale-buff church is enriched with a thousand shimmering visions.

## The "Curé de Tours"

ROUND about the *rue de la Psalette*, the east end of the cathedral and the curious *place Grégoire-de-Tours*, you can get a good view of the old archiepiscopal chapel, and also trace out the circuit of old Roman Tours, since here was the imperial town of CÆSARODUNUM.

You can look up to the rich, embroidered towers of the great church and fill your mind with memories of Balzac's *Curé de Tours*. The sinister old maid Mlle Gamard (who, with the assistance of the wicked *abbé* Troubert, procured the downfall of the *abbé* Birotteau) had her house on the north side of the cathedral.

Some of Balzac's books—especially those in which he deals with his native province—should be slipped in our pockets when we set forth to explore the "Garden of France." Even if Balzac's world is his own, his men and women do obey the eternal motives that move us and dictate our actions.

Although Honoré de Balzac was born in Tours in 1799, his forbears were not men of the north, but came from Canezac, in the far-off Tarn department. They were all people of humble condition, and their patronymic was Balssa. It was Honoré's father who "ameliorated" his name, as have done so many men after leaving their homes and setting up far afield and prospering. It is more than probable that Honoré himself never knew that his rightful name was not Balzac, though he it was who added the *particule* "de" about 1830.

Balzac's first schooling was had at Vendôme, although he returned to his native city to attend its *collège* or secondary school. But after his move to Paris in 1814, as a boy of fifteen, Balzac was never again in Touraine except as a visitor (see p. 278).

## Tours Worthies

THE list of Tours worthies is a long one. There was that Berengarius in the 11th century, who (despite two retractations) remained to the end of his life such an opponent of the doctrine of transubstantiation. Jehan le Maingre, called "Boucicault" *maréchal* de France (whose traces we often cross in Touraine and Anjou), was born in Tours, and died in captivity in England in 1421.

In addition to Michel Colombe, and Fouquet, among the artists, Robert Pinaigrier, the greatest painter of stained glass in the 16th century, was also a man of Tours.

The famous dynasty of the Clouets (Flemings by origin) were also men of Tours by adoption. The original Jean or Janet Clouet lived at Tours, but was never naturalised as a Frenchman. He is thought to have been the author of the marvellous portrait drawings now mostly preserved in the Chantilly and *Bibliothèque Nationale* collections. Jean Clouet had a brother known as *Clouet de Navarre*, also a painter, and Jean's son François Clouet (born at Tours) carried on the family tradition after his father's death.

Later on, Tours was the birthplace, not only of world-famous figures such as Mlle de La Vallière and Balzac, but of at least two writers of merit and of very different styles.

Philippe Néricault (who wrote under the name of Destouches) was born at Tours in 1680. During the time that he was attached as a secretary of the French Embassy in London, he married one of our fellow-countrywomen, by name Dorothea Johnston, and of her and of his marital adventures he drew a picture in a rather diverting work entitled *Le Philosophe Marié*.

Lastly, Georges Moinaux, or "Georges Courteline" (the French writers have ever been more addicted than ourselves to the use of pseudonyms), was a Tours man. Courteline, who died about twenty years ago, was one of the foremost comic authors of his time, but his bustling clowning and his brilliant fun do not hide acute observation and sometimes bitter satire.

## Our Lady the Rich

THE quarter called *La Riche* had any number of old houses abutting on quaint, narrow and twisting streets, but the most interesting sight in this part of Tours is still the Church of *Notre-Dame-la-Riche*. On its site has been a church since the beginning of the 4th century, for hereabouts was the earliest Christian cemetery of the town, and the faithful of those remote days called their little chapel *la pauvre,* afterwards (when the cult of the Virgin became established) *Notre-Dame-la-Pauvre*. The shrine was quite rebuilt in the 15th century, and then, in the fashion of the time, re-called *Notre-Dame-la-Riche*. The place was sacked by the Huguenots in 1562, but it has been, in recent times, repaired and even "embellished." Within may be seen some fine 16th century lights attributed to Robert Pinaigrier of Tours, one of the most famous of the master-glaziers of his time.

The Church of Saint-Julien was formerly attached to a Benedictine abbey, founded, it is said, by Clovis. Of a Romanesque building, only the west front porch and the chapter-house survive. The Saint-Julien we saw was a Gothic shrine in the purest style of the 13th century. Within, the vast and splendid nave and the shallow transepts glowed with gorgeous glass. All is now but a memory.

Saint-Saturnin, once the chapel of a Carmelite monastery, was begun in 1473 at the command and at the expense of King

Louis XI. There is some imposing Flamboyant carving and sculpture.

## Novelist and Philosopher

SO full of interesting things is the countryside of Tours, that, in a short walk, you may be sure of coming across some house, or monument or even only a name that will awake a crowd of memories. Stroll out into the country, past the vines, through the fields, the woods and between the high hedges, then, cutting into the bright blue sky you will see a weather-vane—a dolphin. You are at La Béchellerie where Anatole France spent his last years. There is an avenue of walnuts and chestnuts and then a great gateway; the garden is admirably kept and the long white house, so typical of Touraine and the Loire country, will be warm and perfumed with the odours of summer. The open windows give on the valley of the Choisille and towards the slopes of the Frondettes Hills. Inside the dwelling is the desk where France wrote some of his later works, *Le Petit Pierre* and *La Vie en Fleur*. And he who looks after the place is Lucien Psichari, grandson of Anatole France and great-grandson of Ernest Renan. A literary heritage, indeed.

You can visit all the simple, comfortable, unpretentious house, the attic room where France died, his bibelots, his Tanagra figurines and all the miscellaneous stuff, some in rather poor taste, which he collected in his house of the *Villa Saïd* in Paris. Then there is the writer's bust by Bourdelle. Whatever may be the eventual verdict on France's works it seems more than probable that they will emerge from the neglect which now obscures them.

On the other side of the country road from La Béchellerie is a house evoking very different memories. It is called La Gaudinière. The garden is weed-grown and shabby. The place is now a holiday-camp for poor children. But here at La Gaudinière for several summers lived Henri Bergson, the philosopher. He was the man whose daring and subtle speculation anticipated in many ways the conclusions of modern quanta physics. Bergson, paralysed and sick, was, because of his partly Jewish origin, harassed during the German occupation of France and he died before learning of the atomic bomb. But in his acute analysis of many of the anxieties which afflict us, Bergson wrote the weighty phrase, *notre corps agrandi réclame un supplément d'âme,* or, perhaps, "*our body got so powerful calls out for more soul.*"

# TOURAINE

## *The Tragic June*

TOURS was from the time of the Franco-Prussian war conceived as the centre of a region to which, in case of dire menace, the French Government could retire.

When, in March 1918, it looked as though the Germans had broken through and that Paris might fall, orders were given (and countermanded only at the eleventh hour) for the evacuation to the Tours region of the ministries, the military command and the foreign missions. The British Military Mission was to have been moved to the Port-Boulet area.

In the tragic year of 1940 arrangements had been made to settle the ministries into various *châteaux* of the Tours neighbourhood. The evacuation started soon after the break-through in the middle of May, and when the French Government, with the unfortunate M. Paul Reynaud at its head, left Paris on the 10th June, the *châteaux* of Langeais, Azay-le-Rideau and Ligeuil were already filled with clerks and civil servants, while the President of the Republic (M. Albert Lebrun) was installed at the *château* de Cangé. The *château* de Chissay had been prepared for M. Reynaud and his staff.

M. Reynaud, on his way to Tours, stopped at Briare, south of Montargis, and there met Messrs. Churchill and Eden and General Dill. Things were already desperately bad, and it does not seem that the British representatives knew quite as much of their seriousness as did the French—not unnaturally. After the interview with Reynaud, it would appear that General Georges, commanding the northern group of French armies, told Mr. Churchill privately the whole truth on the collapse of the French resistance.

The French Prime Minister reached Chissay late in the evening of the 11th June. On the morning of the 12th a Cabinet Council was held at Cangé under the chairmanship of the President of the Republic. Here it was decided to ask Mr. Churchill to fly at once to Tours. The majority of the French cabinet was already then, if not in favour of imploring an immediate armistice from the victorious Germans, at least very desirous that the British Government, in the person of Mr. Churchill, should relieve the French of the obligation they had assumed earlier in 1940, not in any circumstances to make a separate peace or conclude a separate armistice with the enemy.

341

On the morning of the 13th June, Reynaud received two telegrams from America in one of which Roosevelt suggested that Reynaud should publish in the French Press the telegram in which he had declared that he would continue the struggle in North Africa or, if necessary, in the French colonies of America.

Mr. Churchill arrived about two o'clock in the afternoon of the 13th June, accompanied by Lords Halifax and Beaverbrook, Sir A. Cadogan and General Hastings Ismay. It will be remembered that the Germans had marched into Paris early that same morning.

Reynaud had already addressed a desperate appeal to President Roosevelt asking for an immediate intervention of the United States. No one, of course, imagined that President Roosevelt, even had he thought it expedient, could have committed his country to war. Everyone knew that the answer must be negative; still, on the French side, the President's answer would, it was felt, in some way absolve the French from blame in breaking their promise, and on the British side it was felt that anything was better than taking a decision in a moment when everything was crashing about our ears.

The interview between Reynaud and Churchill took place inside the Prefecture of Tours. At no time did the British Prime Minister agree (as the Vichy propagandists state) that the French should demand an armistice. Later, the two men continued their talk in the gardens. It was decided that Churchill and Reynaud should meet again shortly at a place on the Brittany coast, south of Brest. There was still cherished the fantastic idea that Brittany might be fortified and could hold out against the Germans.

Reynaud and Mandel returned to Cangé, where the cabinet was sitting, about 5 o'clock. Reynaud announced to the Ministers that in agreement with the British the struggle would go on. Bouthillier, the Minister of Finance and Chautemps, the Minister of State, objected. Whereupon, Weygand, the Commander-in-Chief, stated that Maurice Thorez, the Communist leader, had taken up his quarters in the Palace of the Elysée, the official residence of the French President in Paris. Weygand added that the telephone lines to Paris had been cut. Neither of these statements was true, but Weygand refused to leave France and retire to North Africa and Pétain backed him up. In the evening of the 13th June orders were given that the ministers should take the road for Quimper, on the western coast of Brittany. However, late in the night orders came from Reynaud that the whole Government was to go to Bordeaux. He himself took off early in the morning of the 14th June, and arrived that evening. Two days later he resigned.

## Fine Slate

TRÉLAZÉ. From Saumur to Angers the Loire flows broad and slow, a stately, sober stream.

As you approach Angers, along the north bank's *levée,* you reach Trélazé, that is really a suburb of the Anjou capital and itself a capital of all the slate of France. Like some North Wales town, Trélazé is a place living by slate. There is no castle, manor, *château* or great church, but from Trélazé comes the fine, sharp, pigeon-coloured slate that du Bellay sang of when he lived in sumptuous, stuffy Rome:

*Plus que le marbre dur me plaist l'ardoise fine. . . .*
*("More than harsh marble melikes the delicate slate")*

and, then, the *marbre dur* of beyond the Alps is too often cunningly daubed stucco.

And this slate of Trélazé not only serves for roofs, but, surely and cleverly cut, it adorns, for instance, the pilasters and chimneys of Chambord's great Renaissance palace. And, alternating with squares of white, the slate of Trélazé gives us one of the most splendid floorings imaginable.

The slate of Trélazé, with the white *tuffeau* building-stone of Touraine and Anjou, mingle with the verdant countryside under a sky of silvery grey or radiant blue, to make up the paradise that is the Garden of France.

## How the Treasure was Saved

USSÉ. At the beginning of the last war, in 1939, the more precious objects from the Paris museums and private collections were removed and stored in castles and country-houses all over western France.

The priceless MSS. of the National Library in Paris were packed away in the cellars of Ussé, and there remained untouched until 1945. The librarians of the *Nationale,* like their colleagues, the keepers and guardians of the museums, had, at times, not a little difficulty with the forces of occupation. The Germans always wanted to see and to examine, but not (of course!) to seize or carry off—so they said—numberless objects from among the treasures of France. With German thoroughness, the different "experts," dressed up as Lieutenant-Colonels and so forth, had lists of what they wanted to "examine," and the French needed all the resources of their not inconsiderable guile to "string the enemy along." It must be said that either the Germans were not very determined or the dilatory tactics of the French were superb, since nothing of any importance disappeared from the national collections. Indeed, the most deplorable loss to the museums of France during the war was the "exchange" with Franco's "neutral" Government of the priceless "Lady of Elche" bust and other objects desired by the Spaniards.

Anyway, the *Bibliothèque Nationale* collection of illuminated MSS.—the largest and most valuable in the world—lay safely at Ussé until the days of 1944, when war fanned out over the Loire valley, with the Germans retreating before the American advance. The Loire formed, in places, the line of demarcation between the Allies and the enemy. Only a short time before the complete evacuation by the Germans of the area to the west of the Seine, the enemy artillery began lobbing shells if not on to, at least very near to, Ussé *château*. Staying there was a most venturesome young lady, the American-born wife of the *duc* de Talleyrand. The *duchesse* decided to put a stop to the menace, and made her way in her small car to the nearby German head-quarters, saw the commander, made him feel thoroughly ashamed of himself, got a promise that the bombardment would cease, and calmly drove back to Ussé, having saved a priceless treasure.

## The Road to Ussé

IF you cross the Loire by the Langeais suspension bridge and keep to the embankment road skirting the left shore, you run past the rich *varennes*, where is raised the finest hemp in France. At Rupuanne you go over the old bed of the Cher—that river is now diverted by a barrage so that its waters fall into the Loire opposite Cinq-Mars—that is, upstream from Langeais.

Just after Rupuanne you turn off to the right, and find yourself in an avenue of tall trees stretching for over a thousand yards across the two arms of the Indre River and leading right up to Ussé castle. It backs against the wooded heights that are the last fringes of the great Chinon forest. The house is surrounded by a walled park of some six hundred acres.

## A Great Engineer

USSÉ was not, as were so many of the Loire *châteaux,* the creation of some upstart royal favourite. Jean de Bueil, the man who set about rebuilding and enlarging the old manor about 1475, was a member of one of the oldest Touraine families. He was, moreover, a celebrated captain and his son Antoine married the daughter of King Charles VII and Agnes Sorel.

The lordship of Ussé was, indeed, an ancient one. Here by Loire and Cher had stood a stronghold for centuries. In the 11th century the place was held by a Danish chieftain—Scandinavian adventurers and robber-barons were still carving out for themselves fortunes in northern France. This notable Dane was one Geldwin, Lord of Saumur, and the implacable enemy of Fulk Nerra, Count of Anjou. Geldwin seems, indeed, to have been a foeman worthy of Fulk, for the wretched serfs and burgesses of the day surnamed the fierce Norseman the "Devil of Saumur."

The Bueils did not keep their new castle for long. Anyway, by 1485 they had sold Ussé to Jacques d'Espinay, a royal chamberlain. He and his son carried on Bueil's programme, and by 1535 Ussé must have looked recognisably the same place we see to-day. Ussé bears clear affinities to Langeais, of which it may have been in part a copy. The property has often changed hands. One of the owners, Louis de Bernin de Valentinay, married the daughter of the illustrious Vauban, and that famous engineer, soldier and architect enlarged the castle for his son-in-law.

Vauban's career was a startling one for old France. Sébastien Le Prestre de Vauban, the most famous of all military engineers and *maréchal* of France, was left a penniless orphan at the age of ten; he was lucky enough to attract the attention of the Carmelite prior at Semur, and the worthy monk gave the boy a thorough grounding in the sciences of the day. At the age of seventeen young Le Prestre enlisted as a foot-soldier in Condé's regiment, and fought all through the uprising of the *Fronde.* He was recommended for a commission, but had to refuse it, since he was so poor. In 1655, however, when he was twenty-three, he was gazetted. His fighting career was brilliant, and indeed, his superb mastery of siege-tactics and his success in reducing strongholds should be remembered even more than his engineering works. But he may be said to have fortified the whole empire of Louis XIV. He took part in more than three hundred engagements, he conducted forty sieges, and he constructed or rebuilt more than a hundred and sixty fortresses.

His fortunes waned towards the end of the *grand monarque's* reign, and the great soldier's reputation suffered in high places from his interest in social matters. In his study, *"The Project for a Royal Tithe,"* he foreshadowed some of the principles of the French Revolution. And, most suspect of all, he was deeply touched by the French peasants' wretched lot, and realised that the foundations of French strength and power were being steadily sapped by inept administration, by far-reaching abuses and by the ever-increasing misery of the mass of the people. Such a man, whatever may have been his services to the monarchy, was hardly likely to be popular at the Court of Louis XIV.

Vauban died in 1707 a disappointed man and one full of misgiving. At the Revolution his tomb was profaned, his ashes scattered to the winds, but his heart was recovered, and was placed, by Napoleon's orders, in the Church of Saint-Louis of the Invalides in Paris.

For some time past Ussé has belonged to a younger branch of the notable Provençal family of Soleilhas de Blacas, whose head bears the title of *duc* de Blacas.

## A Masterpiece of the French Renaissance

THE imposing mass of Ussé gives on to storeyed terraces that were laid out and constructed in the 17th century by Vauban. At their feet flow the waters of the Indre.

In the park, and only a few paces from the house, is the chapel. It is a masterpiece of the French Renaissance. Jacques d'Espinay on his death-bed ordered his son to found a collegiate church at Ussé, and his son piously carried out his father's wishes.

Ussé chapel must rank with the collegiate Church of Montrésor, with the *sainte chapelle* at Champigny-sur-Veude, in Touraine, and with that of Oiron, the famous palace of the Gouffier family in

Poitou, as one of the gems of French religious architecture of the 16th century.

Although Ussé chapel was built when the tradition of the Renaissance was already prevalent, it is, like all its contemporaries, of Gothic design. Religious architecture always tends to be a little old-fashioned and archaic. Builders of churches rather build backwards than forwards in time. The chapel is composed of a nave and a polygonal apse. The nave has four bays, and is roofed with sexpartite vaulting. The choir and apse have star vaulting, from which hangs a superb pendant of carved stone worthy to be compared with those at Tillières in Normandy or in our Henry VII's chapel at Westminster. Side chapels give on to the nave and the sacristy entrance is splendid.

The choir-stalls are carved and sculptured with floral motifs interspersed with a multitude of graceful little figures. These splendid seats—that are a little later in date than the chapel itself —repay very careful examination.

The west front displays a most happy mingling of Italianate and Gothic decoration. The doorway is flanked by two elegantly grooved pillars, and is surmounted by a huge, but delicate, seashell. Above the entrance is a tall, two-light window topped by a Flamboyant gable. The windows are decorated with medallions enclosing exquisitely carved scenes. Everywhere, with delightful ingenuity, "antick," rather than pagan, motifs are mingled with traditional religious emblems.

This lovely chapel is, alone, worth the pilgrimage to Ussé, and it may always be visited, even when we can only view the outside and not the inside of the *château* itself.

## A Lordly Residence

USSÉ is a fine and lordly residence, but it is externally a fortress with stout, machicolated towers, corbelling and a keep. It may be regarded, indeed, as a more amiable and friendly Langeais. For it is both majestic and charming.

The varied tones of the old stone harmonise with the greenery of the vegetation, quickened by the slowly-rolling waters of the Indre.

Three wings surround the Court of Honour that is open to the north. The north wing was cut down in the 17th century when all the remaining "feudal" castles were slighted by Richelieu's order. The outside façades, machicolated and set with towers, either date from the 15th century or have been built in the style of that age. The keep in the southern angle is possibly older than the 15th century constructions, and may be a relic of the original manor pulled down by Jean de Bueil.

Seen from some distance, the place shows an astonishing variety of roofs and levels. There are little conical roofs, little pyramidal roofs, long ridges of roof, dormers and chimneys great and small. Ussé really looks like those castles we used to trace and smudge and ink over in our childhood's fairy-books.

The living-wings face each other, and are joined by a gallery. The south wing is the oldest. The east wing dates from the 15th century, but it has been much restored without, however, losing its archaic appearance. Another façade shows Renaissance influence, and here and there are traces of alterations, made probably by Vauban in the 17th century. The face of the west wing is frankly "classical." Beyond a certain amount of quite discreet restoration, no change has been made in Ussé's appearance since Vauban's time.

Within are magnificent apartments. In the west wing a 17th century staircase leads to the King's Chamber, hung with antique silk, but never occupied by a King.

From Ussé village you can drive through Huismes to the 16th century *château* of Uzaze. Thence the main Tours-Chinon road is only three miles away.

## *The Roman Castellum*

VÉRETZ. If you go from Tours through Saint-Avertin and along the shady banks of the Cher, you soon come on to Larçay, where there is a Gallo-Roman *castellum* that, though far from rivalling Jublains, is well worth a visit. The south front is the best preserved, and it has kept four towers. The enclosure is an oblong, about two hundred and fifty feet in length. There were originally towers at the four corners as well as one in the middle of each of the two longer sides. The walls, that are nowhere more than eighteen feet high, are about twelve feet thick at the base, and are, in part, composed of sections of columns mixed with smaller cubes. The place is of fairly late date, and was obviously constructed, in some measure, with materials from other buildings that had either been ruined or were sacrificed to the needs of the troublous times towards the end of the Gallo-Roman régime.

Nearby, you can see the stumps of an aqueduct that formerly brought water from Bléré to Tours.

About a mile and a half along the valley from Larçay is Véretz, on the left bank of the Cher. The Renaissance church has some 16th century (and restored) wall-paintings and a few noteworthy 18th century statues. The fief of Véretz was part of the patrimony of Armand de Rancé, the founder of the Trappist Order. The modern *château* is on the site of one put up in 1519 by Jean de La Barre, chamberlain of Charles VIII. Only a tower remains of this manor, which in the 18th century was lived in by the *duc* d'Aiguillon, of the Richelieu family, and nephew of the famous *maréchal* de Richelieu. D'Aiguillon was a particularly unsuccessful and oppressive governor of Brittany; he was one of the instruments in the downfall of the *duc* de Choiseul, and he was a singularly inept Minister of Foreign Affairs—a post he owed to Mme Dubarry—until, at the instance of the new Queen Marie-Antoinette, he was finally sacked and retired into obscurity at Véretz, where he died in 1782.

## Paul-Louis Courier

TWO miles south-east of Véretz village is the country-house of La Chavonnière. Here lived Paul-Louis Courier, a striking figure in his time, and remarkable also for the mysterious circumstances of his death.

One Sunday afternoon, the 8th August, 1825, Paul-Louis' body was found in his Larçay woods. Courier had been shot dead, and for years, despite his widow's accusations, no one was brought to justice for the deed.

But in the fifty-two years before his death Courier had lived a full life. Paul-Louis was born illegitimate, but was legitimatised when he was five years old by the marriage of his father and mother. The elder Courier was a merchant of some substance and also a man of adventurous temperament, for he was nearly beaten to death by the servants of some "noble" with whose wife Courier the elder was suspected of being too intimate. After this misfortune Courier took his young son to live in the country at

Méré in Touraine, where the boy was brought up. The elder
Courier was not exempt from a little *bourgeois* snobbery, and
used to style himself "Courier de Méré"—an appellation Paul-
Louis never used. The lad's remarkable independence of character,
his courage, his slightly irregular birth, the rancour he felt at the
ill-treatment meted out to his father all tended to make young
Paul-Louis an exceptional youth. All his life Paul-Louis was
moody, difficult to get on with, and he refused to be driven or
ordered about.

He was, moreover, a man of exceptional ability, who became,
despite a life, or rather a youth, of travel and campaigning, a
distinguished Greek scholar. Paul-Louis fought throughout the
Revolutionary wars, but left the army after the battle of Wagram.
He discovered in Florence the complete MS. of Longus' *Daphnis
and Chloe* that he edited. The story is well known of his having
upset an inkpot over the precious MS.

After the second restoration of the Bourbons he began his
career as a political pamphleteer and champion of the lower middle
class and the peasantry. His profession of faith began, "Gentlemen, I am from Touraine, and I live at Luynes." Paul-Louis soon
developed into one of the most dreaded opponents of the reactionary régimes of Louis XVIII and Charles X. He was put
into prison for his *Simple discours de Paul-Louis, vigneron de la
Chavonnière*. He violently opposed the use of public money to
purchase that white elephant, the *château* de Chambord, for the
*duc de* Bordeaux (son of the *duc* de Berry and grandson of King
Charles X), afterwards the Pretender "Henry V," who is said to have
ruined his chances of mounting the French throne because he refused to accept the tricolour flag.

Armand Carrel, the fiery journalist whose career was, in a way,
not unlike that of Paul-Louis', wrote his biography. Courier was
undoubtedly a sincere liberal and a cogent and effective pamphleteer. Sainte-Beuve, however, while admitting Courier's ability,
regarded his writings as containing "little matter but much art."

When Paul-Louis' body had been found his widow had at once
accused Frémont the gamekeeper, who was tried and acquitted.
Five years later Frémont was denounced by a girl named Guirault,
who was, apparently, a chance witness of the slaying. For some
reason or another, the wench kept her mouth shut for years.

Anyway, although he had been once acquitted, Frémont was rearrested on the same charge—a proceeding strange to our ideas of legal procedure—and while awaiting his second trial died in prison of "apoplexy" in 1830.

It has never been certainly established who had the best reasons for wishing Paul-Louis out of the way, but he had hosts of enemies in high circles, and it is obvious that his murderer was suborned.

## An Enchanted Manor

VERDELLE. Verdelle is the most romantic-looking place you can imagine, and recalls some of those Scottish castles which are so high for their width that they look, at first glance, like the simple peel towers of the North country, until you realise that they are really quite large houses of fine proportions.

Verdelle is an old manor of the famous Lecler or Leclerc de Juigné family, one of whom, Jean Leclerc, Cupbearer to King Charles VII, married Anne de Meslay, heiress of Verdelle. Their son, Colas or Nicolas, made the Verdelle we see now. The date is about 1490.

This Colas was a rather headstrong man, for he went to work building his little castle without getting the permission of his feudal lord, the mighty Hardouin de Maillé, Lord of Champagne—a magnificent title. Hardouin, informed that Colas had dared to put up a *chastel et forteresse*—"a castle and fortress"—unduly and improperly, cited the presumptuous fellow before the feudal Assize Court of Champagne. The trouble was not, of course, that Hardouin cared a fig for Leclerc's building—the days of private wars and robber barons were over—but Hardouin did care that he had not been paid his fees for granting permission to embattle. So Colas came to heel and was "granted" (the usual historical euphemism for "bought") his licence. Evidently his lord bore him no ill-will, for in 1522 Leclerc married Hardouin's daughter.

In Henry IV's time royal approval was obtained further to "fortify" Verdelle, i.e. to add on to the building in the same style. No longer could local lords grant such permission. Licensing had become a royal prerogative and perquisite and a source of royal revenue. The history of "royal," i.e. what we should call "public" or "national," financing is one of increasing difficulties in making both ends meet, as the expenses of the central government became ever greater.

The Leclercs de Juigné went on living at Verdelle until the 18th century, when the old manor seemed perhaps cramped to them, and they moved for good to their original fief of Juigné, where they had a larger house. And then, by the 18th century the family had acquired more than local importance. They had a noted Archbishop of Paris to help on their fortunes.

Verdelle is, moreover, not far from Juigné, that is itself only three miles from Sablé.

After you leave Brûlon, on the Sablé road, you dip down rather steeply to Avessé, where there is a small but well-preserved Romanesque church. A little farther on lies Poillé, on the right bank of the Vègre, and near the village are the ruins of the old priory, in which is a fine Gothic chimney-piece. You turn off at Poillé, on the Asnières road, towards Verdelle. After skirting a hill you discover the manor quite suddenly.

There it rises from the ground, with no sort of transition between the building and the fields. Hayricks and farm carts and clumps of trees nearly touch it, but it stands intact and undefiled. At first sight it seems a jumble of towers, some square, some polygonal, some higher than others, one machicolated and the others not. The towers are four and five storeys high, and fairly slender for their height, but clustering together as they do, the whole place gives an impression both of strength and of friendliness. Here and there are Renaissance windows. The whole has a delightful patina of age, not the harsh patina of northern damp and cold, not the scorched blush of the south, but a delicate, rather melancholy weathering that sets you dreaming, musing or imagining all sorts of things leading far from the lives of the local magnates and on to a larger stage. Within, it is a fascinating sort of dwelling, all ups and downs and unexpected corners and queer-shaped chambers.

## Country-house Life in the 15th Century

LE VERGER. One of the most striking and charming of all the great tapestries in Angers museum is that known as the "Concert." Against a background of dark blue, strewn with flowers and beasts, is seated a lady, richly robed. She lets her

**Tours**  The Cathedral's Towers beyond the Archiepiscopal Palace

**Ussé**  The Castle from the Air

**Tours** ———— House of Tristan L'Ermite ———— Psalette Cloister

**Tours** *Place Plumereau* **Trélazé** Slate Quarries

**Trèves** The Tower **Ussé** The Pastures

hands stray over the keys of a portable organ while a page works the bellows. Standing up before the lady is a man singing and holding a musical score in his hand. To the left of this main group are two children. One is pulling a cat up by its tail and the other is teasing a dog.

Tradition has it that the principal figures represent Pierre de Rohan, Lord of Gié and *maréchal* of France, with his wife, Marguerite d'Armagnac. But it is not certain that this fine hanging came from Rohan's Castle of Le Verger, although the Rohan arms figure on the lower border of the tapestry, for this band of stuff is not an original part of the "Concert."

However, there is, in the Gobelins Tapestry Museum in Paris, another hanging which is, like the first, a product of the Loire valley looms, and this Paris tapestry may well have been made for Rohan and have adorned the walls of Le Verger castle.

This second panel is a little more spirited than the first. The general design is the same, but the details are different. A lady is drawing water from a well with one hand while, with another, she is tugging on the cloak of a knight who, apparently, wants to walk away. On the rim of the well is poised a portable organ played by a young woman, who is accompanied on the mandoline by a youth. In the background a bald-headed man is leaning over the well, and next to him is a huntsman with a falcon on his wrist. In the foreground is a girl playing a viol, while another young woman is toying with a wooden horse and a rattle.

This charming vision of 15th century country-house life was hanging, at the beginning of the last century, in Saverne castle (Alsace), the former residence of the Bishops of Strasbourg, and four members of the Rohan family (including the famous Cardinal of the "Diamond Necklace" scandal) held the see of Strasbourg in the 18th century. It is therefore, at least, possible that this tapestry came from Le Verger.

## Vanished Splendours

OF Le Verger castle, built at the end of the 15th century by Pierre de Rohan, only ruins remain—crumbling towers, the guard-room, the stables and a tangled park. The Cardinal de Rohan had Le Verger pulled down. Indeed, from the middle of the 18th century, the vast and magnificent dwellings erected by the proud men of the 15th, 16th and 17th centuries were found to be too big and too costly. The Kings set the example in house-breaking. Louis XV had Clagny destroyed. Louis XVI ripped down Choisy and the *Château de Madrid* in the Bois de Boulogne. And this holocaust seems strange to us if we reflect how many hospitals, schools, or even barracks and prisons, could have been fitted into the buildings which were swept away. Sometimes the great private houses were sold with the express stipulation that the buyers should pull them down. The Revolution, therefore, only speeded up a movement already existing. The first French Republicans squandered the immense riches represented by the confiscated buildings. Such places as Bellevue, Le Raincy and Sceaux (all near Paris) fell into decay. Other palaces and pleasure-houses such as Saint-Maur-les-Fossés, Marly and Choisy were demolished and their grounds cut up between 1796 and 1820. While, in Touraine, Richelieu and Chante-loup fell victims to land-speculators no less avid of gain than those of to-day.

But Le Verger was, in its heyday, one of the most magnificent houses of Old France, and its vanished splendours may be imagined from the drawings of Israël Silvestre. Le Verger was an elongated quadrilateral set with six stout towers, one at each corner and one in the middle of each of the longer sides. The two median towers were joined by a wing which was the regular residence of Le Verger's lords and ladies. The entrance to this splendid lodging was surmounted by an equestrian statue of Pierre de Rohan in his armour and accoutrements as *maréchal* of France. The apartments of this central wing were numerous and richly decorated. The walls were hung with rich tapestries, such as those at Angers and in the Gobelins Museum.

Surrounded by its flowing moat, Le Verger was finished by 1499, and, in its glory, rivalled Blois as a fortress-palace. In February of 1499 Rohan and his wife here entertained King Louis XII and his bride Anne of Brittany, who were on their way from Nantes, where they had been married, to Amboise.

But the splendid hospitality shown by Rohan to his royal master and mistress did nothing to assuage the hatred the Breton Queen bore to her fellow-Breton for the presumptuous way in which his father had pushed his son's suit for the Brittany heiress's hand.

## The Prince of Poets

THE charming valley of the Loire does not hold, perhaps, such imposing residences and castles as does the greater valley of the Loire and its tributaries, but few regions of northern France are more attractive than this dale of greenery dotted with little, half-hidden, modest villages set by the sparkling, swift-flowing waters of the river. This is the smiling, soft countryside that was the land of Ronsard, the poet whose superb technical mastery and splendid language set him at the head of the 16th century bards known as the Pléïade, and gave him an influence which was lasting on French literature. Ronsard was born, it is true, outside Touraine and in the province of Vendôme at a place called Couture, but he is the poet of the Loire valley.

When King James V of Scotland (father, by his second wife, of Mary, Queen of Scots) married Madeleine of France, Ronsard went in the young Queen's suite to Scotland. After the premature death of Madeleine, he spent most of his time in England, on no very definite mission, but just learning about our ancestors "on the spot." Altogether he passed some three years in these islands. Towards the end of his life he divided his time between his house in Vendôme town, his abbey (for although not in orders he was a commendatory abbot) of Croix-Val nearby, in Paris, or at his Priory (for he was also a commendatory prior!) of Saint-Côme, near Tours. There he died and there he was buried.

## "Pray for him who never let his friends' prayers go unheeded."

VERNANTES. All the eastern land of Anjou—the old *Baugeois* and subsidiary fiefs and lordships—is a land of old castles and delightful manors. Near Vernantes the *château* de Jalesnes seems a living picture of the Middle Ages. Avenues of old trees, moat, broad terraces, a lofty edifice, dappled with light and shade as you see it in its woods, a fine house of the old Maillé family. In the church is the tomb of a *marquis* de Jalesnes and his wife. The long inscription in letters of gold asks us to pray "for him who never let his friends' prayers go unheeded."

And on the way to Mouliherne, there is, at every turn, a manor or a castle; of such are La Lande-Chasles on its gorse-flecked heath, the *château* du Theil crumbling into the Chadelais Forest. And then you have Vendangé, a village almost untouched for four hundred years. Between Mouliherne and Vernantes there are the ruins of Loroux Abbey which the English burned in 1370.

## Sully's Elms

VERNOU-SOUS-BRENNE. On the north bank of the Loire you cross into the Indre-et-Loire department, and into Touraine, just before Limeray. About nine miles farther on lies Noizay, whose castle was rebuilt in the 16th century. Here it was that the *duc* de Nemours surprised one of the leaders of the Amboise conspiracy (see p. 3).

You cross the valley of the Brenne and arrive at Vernou-sous-Brenne, the ancient VERNADUM, now a prosperous little town with a Romanesque and Gothic church. Near the church is one of "Sully's elms." Sully, the restorer of French economy after the ravages of the civil wars, used to say, "Tilth and tendance are the two teats feeding France, the veritable mines and treasures of Peru." And his words are learned by every French boy and girl at school, when they are are taught the aphorism attributed to Sully's master, King Henry IV, "I should like every family in France to be able to eat a dish of boiled chicken every Sunday." *La poule au pot* sounded good in the ears of peasants of the 16th century as it did to their descendants right up to our times. Not until the 19th century was well advanced did the peasants of France see much meat on their tables, and until after the 1914-18 war most of the French countrymen and women were very frugal. Perhaps the most striking change that has come over the habits of the French people in our times is the adoption of a new style of living by the peasantry. Since the Liberation in 1944-5, not only have the peasants been revealed as much enriched and as the principal owners of their countryside but, to-day (1948), the countrymen spend money as they never have done and eat a more nutritious and palatable diet. It is the town-dwellers who have suffered, not the men of "tilth and tendance."

Sully's elms that you may see here and there scattered about the villages of France are evidence of the wise statesman's care for agriculture and afforestation.

At Vernou also are some crumbled remains of a building that

may be Gallo-Roman, but is more probably Merovingian (i.e. dating from the first Frankish dynasty of France); the ruins are known as "Pepin the Short's Palace," though it is not clear what justification exists for linking wtih them the name of Charlemagne's father. The charming little *château* de la Côte (16th century) lies to the right of Vernou in the valley of the Brenne where are also the country-houses of Madères and Jallanges. You can follow the valley of the Cisse as far as Vouvray.

## Umbrella Handles

VIBRAYE. Just after the highway from Montmirail crosses the valley of the Braye on the way to Le Mans lies Vibraye, a much larger, though less interesting, town than Montmirail. To your north stretches the mantle of the great Vibraye forest.

The men and women of Vibraye have a peculiar and almost a sole industry—it is the making of umbrella-handles. And the Vibraye people have kept quite up to date. Many a smart umbrella, parasol, *en-tout-cas* or what you will, adorned with a Vibraye handle, knob or top, is displayed by *Parisiennes* without the owners ever realising, or caring, that such tricky little gadgets were fashioned by men and women working in an out-of-the-way village, and most of whom had never been nearer to the French capital than, say, Le Mans—and that is farther off from Paris than Vibraye itself.

A few miles to the south-west of Vibraye is Le Luart, whose church has a fine 13th century belfry. Nearby is an earthwork, known, of course, as "Cæsar's Camp."

## A Red and Black Castle

VIHIERS. The *château* of Coudray-Monbault, near the village of Le Bourneau, and some two miles to the south-west of Vihiers town, is a splendid place. The moat and parts of the towers are very ancient—possibly they date from the eleven hundreds—but the major part of the castle is of 15th and 16th century workmanship. The building is adorned with elegant sculptures, and the walls are gay with lozenges of red and black enamelled bricks.

Nearby are the overgrown ruins of a priory, of whose Romanesque church little remains but a sort of courtyard enclosed by walls of masonry, against which are set columns with splendid capitals, statues of kings, saints and prophets, the fragments of what must have been a splendid Holy Sepulchre, a tomb with a battered recumbent effigy and patches of mural paintings. It is a rather pathetic jumble.

Vihiers itself is a sizable place for this southern part of Anjou, where large townships are rare. The houses of the seventeen hundred-odd inhabitants fan out up a natural amphitheatre of hills above the course of the Lys, a little tributary of the Layon.

Of the fortress, built at Vihiers about 1015 by great Fulk Nerra, nothing remains but the *motte*, or mound, and the town was burned two or three times in the course of its history.

### Roman Baths on a Hill

VILLAINES-LA-JUHEL. From Pré-en-Pail to Evron the highway runs along a hog's back, with the great, dark forest of Pail stretching away to your left. Then the road dips down to Villaines-la-Juhel, a place of over two thousand inhabitants, quite large for this sparsely populated countryside. Then the road rises and falls over the undulating country of the Mayenne hills. When you pull up to the top of the steep climb out of Bais you see, to your left, Mont-Rochard, about eleven hundred feet high.

At a place called Le Rubricaire, half-way up the mountain's flanks, have been found the substructure and the ruined walls of Roman baths. The Romans built baths and centrally heated houses wherever they went. We may remember that, until the beginning of the 5th century, the climate of north-western Europe was a good deal damper and cooler than it became later on (and even damper and cooler than it turned after the climate-change in the 13th century). The Romans, at any rate abroad (and probably at home), were a people accustomed to harsher weather than the Italians of to-day. In which things we may perhaps see some explanation for the failure of the modern Italians to emulate their ancestors' exploits.

Farther on, the road dips down to Saint-Gemmes-le-Robert, in the chapel of whose Romanesque church are early wall-paintings. They have unfortunately been much "restored," since in these damp regions the frescoes fade and flake all too readily. Near Saint-Gemmes are "Druidical stones," i.e. megalithic monuments.

The Castle and its formal Gardens

The great House

**VILLANDRY**

**Verdelle** ———————— The Castle ———————— Flamboyant Gothic Doorway

**Véretz**            The Village by the Cher

**Vernou-sous-Brenne**            A Touraine Farm

## "*The Greatest Refreshment to the Spirits of Man*"

VILLANDRY. It is difficult to say whether Villandry is a magnificent house set in magnificent gardens or whether it is a splendid garden adorned with a splendid house. But, in any case, it is safe to say that of all the great mansions of Touraine, Villandry is one kept up as might have been a French magnate's country-seat in the 17th century.

If you leave Tours by the Chinon road, in some ten miles you reach the village of Villandry, where, in 1189, our Richard Coeur de Lion signed a treaty of peace with Philip Augustus, the French king. Beyond this historical memory, the hamlet does not hold much to attract attention. All the interest of the place centres in its famous *château*.

We may say that, for us, Villandry's history begins early in the fifteen hundreds, when one Jean Le Breton bought up cheap one of the many dilapidated feudal castles which the ruin of the old nobility had left strewn about the Garden of France. This Le Breton was a "new man," and Secretary of State to King François I. In 1532 the lucky minister set out to build a fine house for his residence and for the glorification of his family.

Le Breton retained—as was the custom—the old feudal keep, symbol of "nobility" and privilege, and this massive tower still rises at the corner of the south-west wing. But on three sides of a rectangle—the fourth side lies open northwards looking on to the valley—Le Breton put up his great house.

The whole place is surrounded by a moat.

The architecture is simple, imposing and sober. The base of the *château* is bathed in the waters of the moat that is crossed by a bridge leading into the *cour d'honneur*, or great courtyard. You are faced with an imposing mansion crowned with graceful Renaissance balconies. The three wings display faces of great architectural variety. On the ground-floor of the lateral wings is a porticoed gallery, whose arches and columns are carved with a surprising number of designs. The main façade shows three rows of mullioned windows framed by pilasters with most delicately sculptured capitals. The dormer windows are modern, but have been conceived and executed in the spirit of 16th century work. The projecting wings are almost as long as the main block.

In the 18th century Villandry was the property of the noted

Castellane family, and a *marquis* de Castellane of that time "did
the place up" in what he considered modern taste. He greatly
modified the appearance of the façades on the courtyard. He
walled up the porticoed galleries, removed the mullions from the
windows, took off the decorated gables over the dormers and had
false windows painted between the real ones.

What alterations he made did not, however, change the essential structure of the house, and luckily little or nothing was done
to it during the 19th century. But, when the late Dr. Carvalho
bought Villandry some forty years ago, it was in a sorry state.
He devoted the rest of his life to the task of restoring this splendid
mansion to its earlier self. Carvalho brought to his labours, not
only a considerable fortune, but an informed and cultivated taste.
The incongruous additions and ornaments stuck on in the 18th
century were removed. Luckily, Carvalho had to go on an
abundance of old plans, views and engravings of Villandry. We
can look and compare, and it must be admitted that rarely has
any "restoration" been so happily and tactfully accomplished,
though we cannot say that what we see now is the old Villandry
of the 16th century.

## *"La Demeure Historique"*

DR. CARVALHO not only recreated Villandry, but he did
much to arouse interest in and protection for the historic houses
of France. Subdivision of property, encouraged, if not indeed
imposed, by the Napoleonic Code of Laws, the impoverishment
of the squire class in France and heavy taxation had already, in
the years between the two World Wars, brought about a sad
decay of those fine country-houses in which France—until the
Revolution the most populous as well as the richest country in
Europe—is so rich. Carvalho founded a society known as the
*Demeure Historique*, or the "Historic Dwelling," whose avowed
object was to secure preferential treatment for historic houses,
both by the alleviation of taxation burdens and by modification of
the inheritance laws. Of course, in this direction he had little
success; but much was done to make the French public realise
how fast they were losing their priceless possessions.
It must be admitted that, with some outstanding exceptions,
the country-houses are falling into decay. In a very short time

many of them will be only shadows of their former selves. Very few will even come to rest in rather fossilised security as museums. The plight of the *châteaux* of France is a sad one. A number of houses were thrown open, for the price of an entrance fee, to the public. To secure that French landowners should allow members of the public to view their residences and gardens was extremely difficult. It is not in the French tradition to admit strangers into one's house on any pretext, and no Frenchman would think of letting his country-house (unless, possibly, it were empty of furniture) if by any means he could avoid it.

To-day it is possible to visit quite a number of *châteaux,* and, if "the family" is away, it is often relatively easy to gain admittance to others that are not visible in the ordinary way.

Luckily, many of the great places of Touraine are either public property or are kept up as show-places. For this reason Touraine, more than any other province of France, should attract the visitor, who would enjoy some of the incomparable castles and *châteaux* of the French countryside.

## *Of Gardens*

BUT the crowning glory of Villandry is its gardens, laid out according to the designs left by Silvestre and du Cerceau, who portrayed them as they were in their heyday. The grounds of Villandry are set on three terraces. The lowest holds the kitchen gardens, arranged for all kinds of vegetables, herbs and simples, in a neat, geometrical 16th century mosaic. The middle terrace is laid out with parterres, a boxwood labyrinth, yews and topiary work, perspectives and fountains with great stone basins and masses of flowers—of flowers known and cultivated in the Garden of France four hundred years ago. There are alleys "spacious and faire," and there are beds with "little low Hedges, Rounds like Welts, with some pretty Pyramides." All very symmetrical and sober, gay and friendly under the mellow, diffuse light of the Loire valley.

The uppermost terrace is the water garden, measuring over three hundred by about two hundred and thirty feet. Here are cascades and pleached alleys, pergolas and pools.

No description can do full justice to the splendour and dignity of Villandry's "policies." At one moment you will be admiring the cunning of the old French architects in wedding the design of house and garden. Then, again, you will be remembering the passages of Bacon's *Essays*, where he lets his fancy roam among the gardens of his imagination. Villandry's grounds are indeed "Prince-like" and almost unique in their presentation of 16th century magnificence that was, later, to be swallowed up by the rather chilly splendours of the "classical" style that we associated with the name of Le Notre.

## A Spanish Picture Gallery

ALTHOUGH much was done to restore Villandry within, the interior holds rather less for us than does the exterior. Still, a visit to the saloons of the *château* should not be missed. There is some very good 15th and 16th century furniture, and in one of the apartments the hispano-moresque polychrome and gilt coffered (*artesonado*) ceiling is indeed sumptuous.

In the left wing is a picture-gallery, with a collection of paintings mostly of the Spanish school—Velasquez, Ribera, El Greco, Zurbaran, Morales and Goya. There is a Titian.

You glance from the magnificence of 17th century Spain and gaze through the lofty mullioned windows over the gardens to the broad countryside of Touraine—delicate, vivid and essentially French.

The village has fewer than eight hundred inhabitants. It bore, originally, the name of Coulombières or Coulombiers, and the fief was made into a marquisate in 1619 for Balthazar Le Breton, Lord of Villandry. By letters-patent dated 1639, the name of Coulombières was changed to that of Villandry.

Villandry church is for the most part Romanesque. The stained-glass window of the Last Judgment was dated 1543, and showed, not only Renaissance motifs similar to those decorating the *château*, but also a portrait of the donor, Anne Gedouin.

Four miles on from Villandry by the Tours road is Savonnières, with a Romanesque church. Nearby are stalactite caves.

## A Virgin in Parian Marble

VIVOIN. In the north transept of Saint-Hippolyte's church at Vivoin is what appears to be a 14th century statue of the Virgin executed in Parian marble. Marble statues of as early a date as this are rare, and those fashioned from Grecian marble are rarer still. It is a notable treasure.

This little Church of Vivoin—only about a mile and a half to the north-east of Beaumont-sur-Sarthe—is remarkable. The lower courses of the north transept are of 11th century workmanship, and although the whole place has been much restored, it is still a beautiful 13th century building with 14th century additions. There are rich azure and crimson fragments of early Gothic stained glass in the choir windows, and some portions of the 13th century glazed tile flooring is still in place. The appearance of Romanesque and early Gothic churches has been much modified by the disappearance of the glazed tiles that in shining, sober and subdued colour paved the shrines with a carpet of designs—heraldic, floral, geometrical and faunal.

In the Lady Chapel, besides the floor-tiles, you may see traces of mural paintings; they are faded and patchy, but they have not been repainted; and they are, apparently, of the 14th century.

At the entrance of the 15th century choir are some striking terra-cotta statues of the Virgin and Saint John, modelled probably about two hundred and fifty years ago. Against the left wall of the sanctuary is the fine altar-tomb of Prior Hughes Belon, who died in the 14th century.

Saint-Hippolyte was the church of a Benedictine priory whose buildings are now used as a farm. There are vaulted chambers in early Gothic style—the court-room and the prison—for the Prior was a feudal lord who administered his own justice.

In Vivoin village is an ancient hospice, whose Romanesque doorway must be over eight hundred years old.

Some eight hundred yards to the east of Vivoin and on the Meurcé highroad are the crumbled remains of Malitourne castle, but the tower, the small oratory and the 16th century pigeon-loft are fairly well preserved.

## The White Wines

VOUVRAY. As you move up the banks of the Loire stream from Marmoutier you see, from afar, on the crest of the cliffs, a singular watchtower, straight, square and slender, and you will think "how familiar it seems." Indeed, this 14th century look-out may well be familiar, for its picture adorns the labels of the most renowned of Touraine wines—the delicate and delicious white wines of Rochecorbon. From hereabouts are grown some of the most highly prized vines of northern France, vines that yield the vintages of Vouvray. The real Vouvray taste, strong yet delicate, rich but not cloying, is easily recognisable, although the name "Vouvray" on a bottle is not always a guarantee that the contents come from the banks of the Loire. The famous appellation often means as little as, let us say, "St. Emilion." What the men of Touraine consider as their finest growths are the "Pineaux" of the Vouvray and Montlouis slopes. More ordinary strains are the "Gris meunier" and the "Gascon," but wines made from these grapes are always artificially coloured.

It is said that in the time of great Saint Martin himself the monks of Marmoutier learned in an odd, and indeed quasi-miraculous way, how to trim their vines. One day the monastery's asses got loose and feasted on the vine-shoots. The monks gave up their plants for lost, and great was the holy men's astonishment to find that, in the succeeding year, their vines grew stronger and better than ever before and yielded magnificent grapes. Whatever truth there may be in the story there is no doubt that wine-making owes much to the religious orders.

To-day we may class the Vouvray vintages right at the top of the Touraine list though the heady Montlouis wines tasting, as they say, of *pierre à fusil*, or fire-flints, run the Vouvray very close. The fruity red wines of Chinon and Bourgueil fall into quite another class, while the tingling wines of Saumur and the splendid vintages of western Anjou are of another quality from those of Touraine. The great years for Touraine and Anjou wines are (since the First World War) 1921, 1928, 1933, 1934, 1937, 1942, 1943, 1945 and, greatest of all it seems, 1947.

If it is possible you should sample these Loire wines in the dry, dark caves and cellars which riddle the cliffs of the valley. These cellars are generally disused quarries whence has been hewn out the malleable micaceous chalky stone, or *tuffeaux*, which is the common building material of Touraine and Anjou. In these underground treasure-houses are often held feasts and banquets. When you go to taste the wine the glasses they give you have no stems or feet, you cannot put down your goblet until it is empty. First of all you will get the new wine "of the year." Then the vintner will pull out